Essays in Persuasion

Essays in Persuasion

John Maynard Keynes

with a new Introduction
by Donald Moggridge

palgrave
macmillan

For the Royal Economic Society

First edition published 1931
Second edition published 1972
This edition published 2010 by
PALGRAVE MACMILLAN

Palgrave Macmillan in the UK is an imprint of Macmillan Publishers Limited,
registered in England, company number 785998, of Houndmills, Basingstoke,
Hampshire RG21 6XS.

Palgrave Macmillan in the US is a division of St Martin's Press LLC,
175 Fifth Avenue, New York, NY 10010.

Palgrave Macmillan is the global academic imprint of the above companies
and has companies and representatives throughout the world.

Palgrave® and Macmillan® are registered trademarks in the United States,
the United Kingdom, Europe and other countries.

ISBN 978–0–230–24957–8   paperback

This book is printed on paper suitable for recycling and made from fully
managed and sustained forest sources. Logging, pulping and manufacturing
processes are expected to conform to the environmental regulations of the
country of origin.

A catalogue record for this book is available from the British Library.

A catalog record for this book is available from the Library of Congress.

10   9   8   7   6   5   4   3   2
19   18   17   16   15   14   13   12   11

Printed and bound in the United States of America

Contents

I   THE TREATY OF PEACE

II   INFLATION AND DEFLATION

VI LATER ESSAYS

GENERAL INTRODUCTION

This new standard edition of *The Collected Writings of John Maynard Keynes* forms the memorial to him of the Royal Economic Society. He devoted a very large share of his busy life to the Society. In 1911, at the age of twenty-eight, he became editor of the *Economic Journal* in succession to Edgeworth; two years later he was made secretary as well. He held these offices without intermittence until almost the end of his life. Edgeworth, it is true, returned to help him with the editorship from 1919 to 1925; MacGregor took Edgeworth's place until 1934, when Austin Robinson succeeded him and continued to assist Keynes down to 1945. But through all these years Keynes himself carried the major responsibility and made the principal decisions about the articles that were to appear in the *Economic Journal*, without any break save for one or two issues when he was seriously ill in 1937. It was only a few months before his death at Easter 1946 that he was elected president and handed over his editorship to Roy Harrod and the secretaryship to Austin Robinson.

In his dual capacity of editor and secretary Keynes played a major part in framing the policies of the Royal Economic Society. It was very largely due to him that some of the major publishing activities of the Society—Sraffa's edition of Ricardo, Stark's edition of the economic writings of Bentham, and Guillebaud's edition of Marshall, as well as a number of earlier publications in the 1930s—were initiated.

When Keynes died in 1946 it was natural that the Royal Economic Society should wish to commemorate him. It was perhaps equally natural that the Society chose to commemorate him by producing an edition of his collected works. Keynes himself had always taken a joy in fine printing, and the Society, with the help of Messrs Macmillan as publishers and the Cambridge University Press as printers, has been anxious to give Keynes's writings a permanent form that is wholly worthy of him.

The present edition will publish as much as is possible of his work in the field of economics. It will not include any private and personal correspondence or publish letters in the possession of his family. The edition is concerned, that is to say, with Keynes as an economist.

Keynes's writings fall into five broad categories. First there are the books which he wrote and published as books. Second there are collections of articles and pamphlets which he himself made during his lifetime (*Essays in Persuasion* and *Essays in Biography*). Third, there is a very considerable volume of published but uncollected writings—articles written for newspapers, letters to newspapers, articles in journals that have not been included in his two volumes of collections, and various pamphlets. Fourth, there are a few hitherto unpublished writings. Fifth, there is correspondence with economists and concerned with economics or public affairs.

This series will attempt to publish a complete record of Keynes's serious writing as an economist. It is the intention to publish almost completely the whole of the first four categories listed above. The only exceptions are a few syndicated articles where Keynes wrote almost the same material for publication in different newspapers or in different countries, with minor and unimportant variations. In these cases, this series will publish one only of the variations, choosing the most interesting.

The publication of Keynes's economic correspondence must inevitably be selective. In the day of the typewriter and the filing cabinet and particularly in the case of so active and busy a man, to publish every scrap of paper that he may have dictated about some unimportant or ephemeral matter is impossible. We are aiming to collect and publish as much as possible, however, of the correspondence in which Keynes developed his own ideas in argument with his fellow economists, as well as the more significant correspondence at times when Keynes was in the middle of public affairs.

Apart from his published books, the main sources available to those preparing this series have been two. First, Keynes in his will made Richard Kahn his executor and responsible for his economic papers. They have been placed in the Marshall Library of the University of Cambridge and have been available for this edition. Until 1914 Keynes did not have a secretary and his earliest papers are in the main limited to drafts of important letters that he made in his own handwriting and retained. At that stage most of the correspondence that we possess is represented by what he received rather than by what he wrote. During the war years of 1914–18 Keynes was serving in the Treasury. With the recent opening of the records under the thirty-year rule, many of the papers that he wrote then and later have become available. From 1919 onwards, throughout the rest of his life, Keynes had the help of a secretary—for many years Mrs Stevens. Thus for the last twenty-five years of his working life we have in most cases the carbon copies of his own letters as well as the originals of the letters that he received.

There were, of course, occasions during this period on which Keynes wrote himself in his own handwriting. In some of these cases, with the help of his correspondents, we have been able to collect the whole of both sides of some important interchange and we have been anxious, in justice to both correspondents, to see that both sides of the correspondence are published in full.

The second main source of information has been a group of scrapbooks kept over a very long period of years by Keynes's mother, Florence Keynes, wife of Neville Keynes. From 1919 onwards these scrapbooks contain almost the whole of Maynard Keynes's more ephemeral writing, his letters to newspapers and a great deal of material which enables one to see not only what he wrote, but the reaction of others to his writing. Without these very carefully kept scrapbooks the task of any editor or biographer of Keynes would have been immensely more difficult.

The plan of the edition, as at present intended, is this. It will total twenty-five volumes. Of these, the first eight will be Keynes's published books from *Indian Currency and Finance*, in

1913, to the *General Theory* in 1936, with the addition of his *Treatise on Probability*. There will next follow, as vols. IX and X, *Essays in Persuasion* and *Essays in Biography*, representing Keynes's own collections of articles. *Essays in Persuasion* will differ from the original printing in two respects; it will contain the full texts of the articles or pamphlets included in it and not (as in the original printing) abbreviated versions of these articles, and it will have added one or two later articles which are of exactly the same character as those included by Keynes in his original collection. In the case of *Essays in Biography*, we shall add one or two other biographical studies that Keynes wrote later than 1933.

There will follow four volumes, XI to XIV, of economic articles and correspondence, and one volume of social, political, and literary writings. We shall include in these volumes such part of Keynes's economic correspondence as is closely associated with the articles that are printed in them.

The further nine volumes, as we estimate at present, will deal with Keynes's *Activities* during the years from the beginning of his public life in 1905 until his death. In each of the periods into which we propose to divide this material, the volume concerned will publish his more ephemeral writings, all of it hitherto uncollected, his correspondence relating to these activities, and such other material and correspondence as is necessary to the understanding of Keynes's activities. These volumes are being edited by Elizabeth Johnson and Donald Moggridge, and it is their task to trace and interpret Keynes's activities sufficiently to make the material fully intelligible to a later generation. Until this work has progressed further, it is not possible to say with exactitude whether this material will be distributed, as we now think, over nine volumes, or whether it will need to be spread over a further volume or volumes. There will be a final volume of bibliography and index.

Those responsible for this edition have been: Lord Kahn, both as Lord Keynes's executor and as a long and intimate friend of

Lord Keynes, able to help in the interpreting of much that would otherwise be misunderstood; Sir Roy Harrod as the author of his biography; Austin Robinson as Keynes's co-editor on the *Economic Journal* and successor as secretary of the Royal Economic Society. The initial editorial tasks were carried by Elizabeth Johnson. More recently she has been joined in this responsibility by Donald Moggridge. They have been assisted at different times by Jane Thistlethwaite, Mrs McDonald, who was originally responsible for the systematic ordering of the files of the Keynes papers; Judith Masterman, who for many years worked with Mrs Johnson on the papers, and more recently by Susan Wilsher, Margaret Butler and Barbara Lowe. Since 1977 Judith Allen has been responsible for much of the day-to-day management of the edition, as well as seeing the volumes through the press.

EDITORIAL FOREWORD

Throughout his working life from 1919 onwards Keynes contributed to the stimulation of economic thought and argument not only in articles in the learned journals and in letters to the newspapers but also, and perhaps most effectively, in pamphlets. His contemporaries and pupils remember some of these—and notably *The Economic Consequences of Mr Churchill*, *The End of Laissez-Faire*, *The Means to Prosperity*, and *How to Pay for the War*—more vividly than almost anything else that he wrote.

Their republication has presented something of a dilemma. He himself collected his earliest writings of this character in 1931 in a volume which he called *Essays in Persuasion*, which has sold through many printings in subsequent years and has acquired a fame and identity of its own. For this small volume, intended for a popular audience, he took extracts from some of his books and abbreviated most of the pamphlets that he included. His method, as he described it in his Preface, was 'to omit freely (without special indications in the text) anything which appeared to be redundant or unnecessary to the main line of the argument or to have lost interest with the passage of events'. In any complete collection of his writings, however, it is obviously desirable that the pamphlets shall somewhere be available in full and as originally written.

Both to reprint *Essays in Persuasion* and also to duplicate a large part of it in a reprinting of the full text of the pamphlets was an obviously unsatisfactory solution. At the same time it was desirable to preserve, so far as might be possible, something of the flavour and design of *Essays in Persuasion*. It has been decided to compromise by retaining both the name and the general structure and ordering of that book, while printing the pamphlets concerned in full. In all cases an indication is given of the excisions made by Keynes in shortening them for inclusion.

An exception to the policy of avoiding duplication has been made in the case of the short extracts from *The Economic Consequences of the Peace*, *A Revision of the Treaty*, *A Tract on Monetary Reform* and *A Treatise on Money* which Keynes included in *Essays in Persuasion*. To have eliminated them completely would have involved too great a departure from Keynes's original design of the book.

Essays in Persuasion was published, as has been said, in 1931. Keynes continued to write pamphlets in subsequent years. *The Means to Prosperity* (1933) and *How to Pay for the War* (1940) represent later writings of essentially the same character as those included in the 1931 volume. It has been decided to include in this volume such later writings as seem most appropriately to belong here.

In this volume when a pamphlet or article included in *Essays in Persuasion* is reproduced in its original and fuller form, the parts deleted by Keynes for purposes of that book (which range from sentences to whole chapters) have been indicated by the symbol § placed at the beginning and end of the words omitted (see, for example, pp. 44 and 84). When a passage taken from another of his published books is given here in its abridged, *Essays in Persuasion* form, it is left to the interested reader to make his own comparison.

The essays are presented here in the same order as they occupied in the 1931 table of contents. Keynes's list of sources at the back of the original volume is replaced by a brief editorial note preceding each essay. Further details of the circumstances surrounding the original publication and any correspondence relating to it are given in volumes XVI and following of this series. Keynes's own footnotes introduced specially into *Essays in Persuasion* remain in the square brackets in which he put them. Where possible we have printed examples of cartoons stimulated by the essays and pamphlets.

PREFACE

Here are collected the croakings of twelve years—the croakings of a Cassandra who could never influence the course of events in time. The volume might have been entitled 'Essays in Prophecy and Persuasion', for the *Prophecy*, unfortunately, has been more successful than the *Persuasion*. But it was in a spirit of persuasion that most of these essays were written, in an attempt to influence opinion. They were regarded at the time, many of them, as extreme and reckless utterances. But I think that the reader, looking through them today, will admit that this was because they often ran directly counter to the overwhelming weight of contemporary sentiment and opinion, and not because of their character in themselves. On the contrary, I feel—reading them again, though I am a prejudiced witness—that they contain more understatement than overstatement, as judged by after-events. That this should be their tendency is a natural consequence of the circumstances in which they were written. For I wrote many of these essays painfully conscious that a cloud of witnesses would rise up against me and very few in my support, and that I must, therefore, be at great pains to say nothing which I could not substantiate. I was constantly on my guard—as I well remember, looking back—to be as moderate as my convictions and the argument would permit.

All this applies to the first three of the five books into which these essays naturally group themselves, rather than to the last two; that is to say, to the three great controversies of the past decade, into which I plunged myself without reserve—the Treaty of Peace and the war debts, the policy of deflation, and the return to the gold standard,[1] of which the last two, and indeed

---

[1] I still stand—substantially—by the *Positive Suggestions for the Future Regulation of Money*, which I wrote in 1923 before our return to the gold standard and which are here reprinted (p. 183) as the third essay of Book III. Whilst we were on the gold standard, these proposals were necessarily in abeyance. But anyone who wishes to know the general outline of how the author would settle our currency problem, as it presents itself today, will find it in this essay.

in some respects all three, were closely interconnected. In these essays the author was *in a hurry*, desperately anxious to convince his audience in time. But in the last two books time's chariots make a less disturbing noise. The author is looking into the more distant future, and is ruminating matters which need a slow course of evolution to determine them. He is more free to be leisurely and philosophical. And here emerges more clearly what is in truth his central thesis throughout—the profound conviction that the economic problem, as one may call it for short, the problem of want and poverty and the economic struggle between classes and nations, is nothing but a frightful muddle, a transitory and an *unnecessary* muddle. For the western world already has the resources and the technique, if we could create the organisation to use them, capable of reducing the economic problem, which now absorbs our moral and material energies, to a position of secondary importance.

Thus the author of these essays, for all his croakings, still hopes and believes that the the day is not far off when the economic problem will take the back seat where it belongs, and that the arena of the heart and head will be occupied, or reoccupied, by our real problems—the problems of life and of human relations, of creation and behaviour and religion. And it happens that there is a subtle reason drawn from economic analysis why, in this case, faith may work. For if we consistently act on the optimistic hypothesis, this hypothesis will tend to be realised; whilst by acting on the pessimistic hypothesis we can keep ourselves for ever in the pit of want.

The essays have been taken out of the author's printed writings, whether books or pamphlets or newspaper and magazine articles, indiscriminately. The method has been to omit freely (without special indications in the text) anything which appeared to be redundant or unnecessary to the main line of the argument or to have lost interest with the passage of events; but to alter nothing in the text which has been retained. New explanatory footnotes, which have been added in this volume, have been placed between square brackets. The author has endeavoured to secure that the omissions shall not be such as to make the balance of argument appear in any way different from what it was in the original context. But for the curious inquirer, if there be any, there is provided on the last page of the book a table of references showing the source from which each essay has been taken, and where it can be found in its complete contemporary setting.

I have thought it convenient to choose this date of publication, because we are standing at a point of transition. It is called a national crisis. But that is not correct—for Great Britain the main crisis is over. There is a lull in our affairs. We are, in the autumn of 1931, resting ourselves in a quiet pool between two waterfalls. The main point is that we have regained our freedom of choice. Scarcely any one in England now believes in the Treaty of Versailles or in the pre-war gold standard or in the policy of deflation. These battles have been won—mainly by the irresistible pressure of events and only secondarily by the slow undermining of old prejudices. But most of us have, as yet, only a vague idea of what we are going to do next, of how we are going to use our regained freedom of choice. So I should like to clinch the past, as it were, by reminding the reader of what we have been through, and how it appeared at the time, and the nature of the mistakes we made.

J. M. KEYNES

8 November 1931

Introduction to New Edition

By Donald Moggridge

On 21 September 1931 Britain was driven off the gold standard amidst an international financial crisis. The events leading up to this dramatic outcome led Keynes to reflect on his writings relating to the events of the previous 12 years.

A fortnight later, Keynes proposed to his publisher, Daniel Macmillan, that he prepare for the Christmas market a selection of his writings. Macmillan accepted the proposal two days later and told Keynes that if they could have copy by the end of the following week the firm would try to publish on 27 November. Keynes met Macmillan's deadline with a collection provisionally entitled *Essays in Prophecy and Persuasion*. He passed the last of his paged proofs for what became *Essays in Persuasion* to the printer on 9 November, the day after he finished his preface which began.

> Here are collected the croakings of a Cassandra who could never influence the course of events on time. The volume might have been called 'Essays in Prophecy and Persuasion', for the *Prophecy*, unfortunately, has been more successful than the *Persuasion*. ...

> [W]e are standing at a point of transition. ... There is a lull in our affairs. We are, in the autumn of 1931, resting ourselves in a quiet pool between two waterfalls. The main point is that we have regained our freedom of choice. Scarcely any one in England now believes in the Treaty of Versailles, or in the gold standard, or in the policy of deflation. These battles have been won – mainly by the inevitable pressure of events and only secondarily by the slow undermining of old prejudices. (below, xvii–xix)

The book was published, as promised, on 27 November.

In its original form *Essays in Persuasion* had 25 chapters. They contained material from his pamphlets *The Economic Consequences of Mr. Churchill* (1925), *A Short View of Russia* (1925), *The End of Laissez-Faire* (1926) and *Can Lloyd George Do It?* (1929); his books *The Economic Consequences of the Peace* (1919), *A Revision of the Treaty* (1922), *A Tract on Monetary Reform* (1923) and *A Treatise on Money* (1930); one previously unpublished article; and broadcasts, speeches and journalism, most frequently from the *Nation and Athenaeum* and its successor the *New Statesman and Nation* of which Keynes was chairman from 1923. Keynes abbreviated the pamphlets and book extracts, and occasionally, an article. For this edition we have used the version printed in *The Collected Writings of John Maynard Keynes*. There the editors left the extracts from the books as Keynes had intended, but, to avoid having to put complete versions elsewhere in the edition, printed the pamphlets and articles in full, providing an indication of the excisions Keynes had made in 1931. That edition also included two later pamphlets, *The Means to Prosperity* (1933) and *How to Pay for the War* (1940), which are of the same character as those included in the 1931 volume.

Keynes organised *Persuasion* around five themes: I The Treaty of Peace, II Inflation and Deflation, III The Return to the Gold Standard, IV Politics and V The Future. This introduction attempts to provide background for each theme, as well as for the post-1931 pamphlets and an indication of how Keynes's views changed after 1931.

I

At the end of the First World War, Keynes was the senior Treasury civil servant concerned with Britain's external finances. This meant that he was the senior Treasury civil servant for the peace treaty negotiations which opened in Paris on 18 January 1919. Keynes, then aged 35, was the only Treasury official in Paris with significant experience of financial diplomacy with both Britain's European and America allies. At first he had little to do with the terms of the treaty itself, but he was responsible for inter-allied finance and bodies concerned with finance, food, blockade controls, shipping and raw materials. The reparations issue was not part of his brief, but he saw most of the relevant papers and he and his Treasury colleagues in Paris provided services and expert advice for committees. From the middle of March he became involved in the intricacies of the negotiations and related treaty drafting.

By early May the treaty was nearing its final form. The experts who had been working in relative isolation saw their contributions falling into place in a larger scheme. Given the Treasury's coordinating role in Paris, Keynes had seen or heard of more fragments than many others and had unsuccessfully tried through various devices, including a scheme for European financial rehabilitation, to minimise its adverse consequences. But Keynes reconsidered his position. Nine days after the treaty was presented to the Germans, he decided to resign and, gradually, to disengage himself from the conference. Just over three weeks later, on 7 June, he left Paris. The treaty was signed on 28 June.

On 24 June Keynes started writing *The Economic Consequences of the Peace*. The book was finished in just over three months. It was published in England on 12 December 1919. It was several books in one: a political pamphlet attacking the morality of the treaty in the light of the understandings at the time of the Armistice; an illuminating, if elegiac, discussion of the relations between nations and classes before 1914; a technical discussion of the economic provisions of the treaty and their effects; and a series of proposals for dealing with European problems as they existed in 1919. Added to these were vivid, mordant and arresting portraits of those involved which attempted to explain why such a disastrous document had emerged from the hands of seemingly intelligent men.

The Economic Consequences of the Peace became an international best-seller. By the early summer of 1920, it had sold 100,000 copies in Britain and the United States; by the end of the year translations had appeared in Belgium, Bulgaria, China, Denmark, France, Germany, Hungary, Italy, the Netherlands, Spain and Sweden. The book aroused widespread controversy. The book made possible Keynes's lucrative career as a commentator and journalist. Initially, his journalistic forays concerned the successive stages of the reparations saga, but readers developed an appetite for views on other issues from this lively mind with a controversialist's pen. The impact of Keynes's writing, first as a prophet and later as an effective advocate, also reflected his own skills as an author.

Keynes reprinted parts of four chapters from *Economic Consequences* in *Essays in Persuasion*. He opened Part I with his atmospheric introduction to the book, before turning to his 1919 estimate of Germany's capacity to make reparation payments to the Allies over a period of years. He was re-working figures from his own Treasury memorandum of December 1918 to take account of subsequent events. He estimated that over a period of 30 years, Germany might be able to manage payments with a present value of £1,700 million. To this he added an estimate of £300 million for immediately transferable wealth and ceded property to get total reparations of £2,000 million – a far cry from the £8,000 million implied by the terms of the treaty. He concluded with his proposed remedies: a revision of the treaty; the settlement of inter-allied war debts through mutual forgiveness and the organisation of an international loan for European reconstruction. The remaining chapters of Part I carried the reparations and war debt sagas down to the middle of 1928. They included two extracts from *A Revision of the Treaty*, a sequel to *Economic Consequences* that Keynes hurriedly put together at the end of 1921.

The first extract was a clear statement of Keynes's view of the role of public opinion in politics. He saw reform and change as the products of discussion through which public opinion was formed and guided. The political elite of senior politicians, civil servants and 'higher' journalists was open to two influences: rational persuasion and public opinion. It was privy to its own 'inner opinion' expressed 'upstairs, backstairs and behind-stairs' as to what was feasible or desirable (35). In public speeches and magazine and newspaper articles, the political leadership and 'higher' journalists formed an important part of what was taken as 'outer' or public opinion. Although in a democracy, the elite was ultimately subject to public opinion, through its own links with that opinion it could significantly shape it. To Keynes one of the duties of the elite was to prevent too wide a gap developing between inner and outer opinion on any issue – if the gap became too wide, as it had over the treatment of Germany in 1918–19, the process of returning to sensible or feasible proposals could be lengthy and costly.

There was another complication. Outside opinion was never as definite as it appeared in the press. For ordinary people there was always an element of doubt which left their views vulnerable to changing events. It also left them open to persuasion. With this view of human behaviour, Keynes saw persuasion as encouraging the articulation of outside opinion as well as altering the views of the political elite. Thus his own exercises were intended to play a dual role: to undermine and remove old habits of thought and prejudice; and to highlight likely trends to prepare the ground among the public at large. The elite once persuaded could successfully lead rather than follow.

In Keynes's scheme of things meetings with ministers, officials and MPs, public speeches, articles in the quality and popular press and, later, broadcasts each had their place. In the early 1920s Keynes was only beginning to learn to use them to maximum advantage – although no one could deny that over the peace treaty he had influenced opinion. By the outbreak of the Second World War, he would be even more skilled and, with *How to Pay for the War*, more successful in shaping events.

By then, he had added another layer to the discussion: expert or professional opinion such as that for which he wrote *The General Theory of Employment, Interest and Money* (VII, xxi).[1] As he summarised it in November 1934

> Dora Russell asks, 'Why cannot we adopt a new economic policy by Mr. Keynes tomorrow, if nobody is exerting power to prevent it?' Because I have not yet succeeded in convincing either the expert or the ordinary man that I am right. If I am wrong, this will prove to have been fortunate. If, however, I am right, it is, I feel certain, only a matter of time before I convince both; and when both are convinced, economic policy will, with the usual time lag, follow suit. (XXVIII, 35)

The second extract from *A Revision of the Treaty* was an amalgamation of his proposals in chapters 6 and 7 for a revision of the reparations fixed by the Reparations Commission in 1921 and the cancellation of inter-allied war debts. The rest of the chapter comments further on the issue of war debts in the light of the settlements made with the United States by Britain, France and Italy.

II

Part II of *Persuasion* opens with a Keynes-manufactured statement:[2] 'Lenin is said to have declared that the best way to destroy the capitalist system is to debauch the currency' (57). Keynes's basic argument was that inflation undermined the capitalist system by arbitrarily redistributing wealth. Such redistributions produced disorder in the relations between debtors and creditors and reduced the process of wealth creation in whole or in part to a lottery. Moreover, the almost completely unanticipated inflations of the First World War, when the previous century had been one of long-term price stability, created in the public estimation a class of 'profiteers' against whom governments sought to direct public indignation.

> These profiteers are, broadly speaking, the entrepreneur class of capitalists, that is to say, the active and constructive element in the whole capitalist society, who in a period of rising prices cannot but get rich whether they deserve it or not. ... By directing hatred against this class, therefore, the European governments are carrying a step further the fatal process which the subtle mind of Lenin had consciously conceived. ... By combining a popular hatred of the class of entrepreneurs with the blow already given to social security by the violent and arbitrary disturbance of contract and of the established equilibrium of wealth ... these governments are fast rendering impossible a continuance of the social and economic order of the nineteenth century. (58)

Keynes extended the argument by reprinting as his second chapter a shortened version of the opening chapter of *A Tract on Monetary Reform*, 'The Social Consequences of Changes in the Value of Money'. There he dealt with the effects of changes in the value of money on the distribution of wealth among the investing class, the business class, and the wage-earner, and on the production of wealth. The crux was that 'The individualistic capitalism of today, precisely because it entrusts saving to the individual investor and production to the individual employer, presumes a stable measuring rod of value, and cannot be efficient – perhaps cannot survive – without one.' (75)

After two pieces on the post-war inflation in France. Keynes turned to deflation. The first piece, *Can Lloyd George Do It?*, was a pamphlet Keynes wrote with Hubert Henderson supporting Lloyd George's 1929 election pledge to reduce unemployment to normal proportions within a year through a programme of public investment that would not add to the burden of taxation. They attempted to prove that the increased public investment would not, as the Treasury argued, crowd out an equivalent amount of private domestic investment. Moreover, the consequential savings in other directions, such as unemployment insurance, and the increased buoyancy of government revenues attributable to the investment would maintain budgetary equilibrium – though they allowed that some reduction in expenditure on armaments might be necessary.

Can Lloyd George Do It? reflected Keynes's efforts to refine his monetary theory in *A Treatise on Money* published in September 1930. According to the general case of the *Treatise*, the authorities could make savings equal to investment and achieve price stability through a monetary policy directed at the long-term rate of interest. However, in the special case of the UK which had returned to the gold standard at an overvalued exchange rate in 1925 and had not fully adjusted her level of costs to the new régime, a decline in the British rate of interest to encourage increased investment would lead to a capital outflow, a loss of gold reserves and a need to increase interest rates. More public investment at the existing rate of interest would make investment equal to savings and reduce deflationary pressure. It was this 'special case' for public works (VI, 337–8) that lay at the centre of Keynes's recommendations for Britain through 1929 and 1930.

The final three chapters of Part II reflect Keynes's reactions to the emerging Great Depression of 1929–33. In 'The Great Slump of 1930' he reported presciently that 'we are living in the shadow of one of the greatest economic catastrophes of modern history' (126). The explanation and remedies for the major industrialised countries were, as he explicitly admitted, pure *Treatise on Money*. In the essay on 'Economy' he dealt with British problems associated with the 1931 financial crisis which was to drive her from the gold standard. Here his advice was not always helpful because he refused to make public what he was prepared to admit in private – that Britain should leave the gold standard to let the pound depreciate. The final essay highlighted the effects on bank balance sheets of the deteriorating quality of the assets that served as collateral for their loans.

III

The essays in Part III reflect another pre-occupation of Keynes's *Persuasion* – British currency policy. Britain remained legally on the gold standard throughout the First World War. Gold convertibility was only suspended in 1919 after the Americans ceased providing loans to their former allies. Thereafter the exchange rate fluctuated freely. The stated policy of the authorities following the acceptance of the Report of the Cunliffe Committee on Currency and Foreign Exchanges after the war was to return to gold at the pre-war par which implied a dollar exchange rate of $4.8656, but there were issues of timing and method. When it came to replacing the gold export embargo under wartime regulations, the Gold and Silver (Export Control) Act of 1920, which initially had no expiry date, got one of 31 December 1925 as a result of back-bench pressure.

In January 1919 Keynes had proposed the pound be pegged at 10 per cent below pre-war par through a tax on gold exports, which could be reduced on the advice of the Governor of the Bank of England and the Chancellor of the Exchequer to work sterling back to pre-war par (XVII, 168–71). In April 1922 at the time of the international financial conference at Genoa he advocated pegging sterling to gold at the existing rate of $4.20 and left the possibility of appreciation to pre-war parity open (XVII, 355–69). In a December 1922 lecture to the Institute of Bankers he recommended a peg of $4.00 to $4.50, but he was already less enthusiastic about taking sterling back to pre-war par (XIX, 50–76).

Keynes gave more thought to the issue in the course of 1923 as he prepared *A Tract on Monetary Reform* published in December. There he made, as we have seen, a strong case for domestic price stability on the grounds that capitalism worked best in such circumstances. He argued that the Bank of England through its discount rate policy and open market operations had the tools to achieve a modicum of price stability. But if the authorities had a goal of price stability, exchange-rate policy needed rethinking: a gold standard régime would oblige Britain to inflate and deflate at the same rate as the rest of the world. One possible way to avoid this might be to attempt to stabilise the international value of gold in terms of commodities. Such a proposal, the work of Ralph Hawtrey, had been part of the resolutions on currency agreed at the 1922 Genoa Conference. Keynes thought Hawtrey's scheme was defective: with the existing distribution of gold among central banks, it would put responsibility for the British price level and the handling of credit cycles in the hands of the US Federal Reserve Board. He did not believe that the Fed was sufficiently insulated from American sectional interests to manage the price level in the international interest. There was also a further risk of gold falling in value as national monetary authorities restricted its use as hand-to-hand currency or commercial bank reserves and concentrated it in cental reserves.

Domestic price stability thus entailed flexibility in sterling's exchange rate with gold standard countries. Given recent experience with freely floating exchange rates, Keynes suggested what economists later called a 'crawling peg'. The Bank of England would announce every Thursday, when it posted the Bank rate, its buying and selling prices for gold and it would only change those prices to prevent externally generated price disturbances from affecting Britain.

This was the package of the Tract set out in Chapters 2 and 3 of Part III. Keynes kept to these recommendations in his journalism and in evidence to official committees. His efforts at persuasion had some effect. The Committee on the Currency and Bank of England Note Issues, for example, although accepting the ultimate goal of a return to gold at pre-war par and accepting that a deflationary monetary policy could achieve that goal, rejected such a policy in two draft reports in 1924 on the grounds that it expected American inflation to do the job instead. It recommended that the authorities wait for up to 12 months for American prices to rise. Politics then intervened: in October Ramsay MacDonald's first minority Labour Government was defeated in the House of Commons; in the ensuing election the Conservative Party won a substantial majority. Sterling rose sharply on the exchanges and the Treasury and Bank of England began preparations for a return to gold. Keynes continued to advocate price stabilisation as the preferred goal and to stress the risks of inflation and instability in joining a standard effectively managed by the Federal Reserve.

His journalism found one attentive reader. Winston Churchill, the new, Conservative Chancellor of the Exchequer, was testing his advisers' assumptions about returning to gold in what became known as 'Mr Churchill's Exercise'. After the first round of discussions, he read Keynes's annual survey of the speeches of the chairmen of the London clearing banks to their shareholders. Keynes had taken particular care with the 1925 survey which appeared in the *Nation* on 21 February under the title 'The Return Towards Gold' (192–200). On this article, with its reference to 'the paradox of unemployment amidst dearth' (200), and a commentary by his Controller of Finance, Sir Otto Niemeyer, Churchill penned a powerful critique of British financial policy. Niemeyer replied that the proposed return to gold was, given its effects on world economic stability and the expansion of world trade, an employment policy. Churchill arranged for one more discussion of the issues on the evening of 17 March 1925. Present were P.J. Grigg, his private secretary; Sir John Bradbury, the chairman of the Committee on the Currency and Bank of England Note Issues; Reginald McKenna, chairman of the Midland Bank and a critic of government financial policy; Niemeyer and Keynes.

Keynes and McKenna argued until midnight that at the pre-war parity sterling would be overvalued by at least 10 per cent and that adjustment would lead to more unemployment and industrial unrest over wage cuts, while Bradbury argued for the long-term advantages of a return to gold. After hearing both sides, Churchill asked McKenna, himself a former Chancellor, what decision he would take. McKenna is said to have replied 'There is no escape; you have to go back; but it will be hell.'[3] Two days later, Churchill and the Governor of the Bank met over lunch and agreed that a return to gold would be announced in the forthcoming Budget. The next day a meeting of the Chancellor, Prime Minister, Foreign Secretary, Bradbury and Niemeyer confirmed the decision.

The discussion of 17 March warned Keynes of the likely course of events. As a result his opposition to the return to gold changed its basis – away from advocating a managed currency, or even from delaying pegging sterling to gold, to the straightforward argument that a return to gold in the present circumstances would leave sterling overvalued, not only against the dollar but also against Continental currencies thereby necessitating a fall in British prices and wages.

When Churchill announced the return to gold on 28 April, Keynes rushed into print in the *Nation* with a comment that the authorities had returned to gold 'along the most prudent and far-sighted lines that were open to them' (XIX, 358). Unfortunately he had misread the legislation. But his words of praise were used to the Chancellor's advantage in the House of Commons and it took some time for Keynes to get back on track on the overvaluation of sterling on gold at pre-war par and its consequences. The culmination of his criticism came in a series of articles in the *Evening Standard*, which Keynes turned into a pamphlet on *The Economic Consequences of Mr. Churchill*, published by Leonard and Virginia Woolf's Hogarth Press, at the end of July.

The pamphlet was concerned with three issues: the effects of the return to gold at an overvalued exchange rate, the reasons behind the Chancellor's decision and possible remedies. On these Keynes was at his polemical best, but with the last Keynes pulled his punches. Although he suggested that the only 'truly satisfactory' course of action was to abandon the gold standard, he did not devote much attention to that alternative in 1925 – and even less afterwards. His other possible measures – a voluntary all-round reduction in money wages supplemented by a tax on non-wage incomes, or an expansive monetary policy that would produce gold losses to the United States and lead to inflation there – were either non-starters or far-fetched. The only other expedient, other than public works to reduce unemployment, came in 1930–1 when Keynes came to favour a revenue tariff for Britain. The change came slowly and tentatively before he admitted on 21 July 1930 that 'I have

... become reluctantly convinced that some protectionist measures should be introduced' (XX, 378). That concession came in a memorandum for a government committee. Keynes did not go public with his scheme until his 'Proposals for a Revenue Tariff' appeared in the New Statesman and Nation on 7 March 1931 (231–8). He continued to push the tariff through the summer of 1931. Once sterling left gold it became irrelevant and he withdrew it in a letter to The Times on 28 September (243–4).

Over the return to gold, Keynes's attempts at persuasion were perversely successful. By convincing many of the possibility that American inflation might actually allow Britain to reach pre-war par without domestic deflation, he made the policy seem less dangerous. By cleaving to that line of argument until March 1925, he found it more difficult to swing the argument around to the risks of deflation resulting from the return to gold, or, after the event, of proposing sensible remedies.

IV

Keynes was more politically involved in the 1920s than he had been before 1914. His politics were still Liberal, but now he became part of an attempt to devise for the party, then still in contention with Labour to be the main anti-Conservative party in the state, a modern and progressive platform.

One of the new institutions for Liberal reformers was the Summer School. The idea originated in Manchester in a group including Ernest Simon, a successful businessman who became Lord Mayor in 1921, and Ramsay Muir, Professor of Modern History at Manchester. An experimental School was held at Grasmere in September 1921. The model for the School was the British Association for the Advancement of Science which emphasised education and discussion: it would decide on the issues to be discussed and get the best possible liberally inclined speakers to address them. After the success of the Grasmere trial, annual Summer Schools alternating between Oxford and Cambridge occurred for the rest of the inter-war period. Initially, Walter Layton, Keynes's former Cambridge colleague who was now editor of *The Economist* and Muir were joint directors.

Keynes attended his first Summer School at Oxford in August 1922 and spoke on reparations and war debts (XVIII, 12–17). In the autumn he joined the steering committee organising future Schools. In December he learned from Layton of the Summer School group's plans to take over the *Nation and Athenaeum*, a distinguished liberal weekly. The next month he took part in the discussions. Together with Simon, Arnold Rowntree and Lawrence Cadbury, he formed the New Nation Company to buy the Nation. The original idea was that Ramsay Muir would be the new editor, but this close link with the Summer School disappeared as a result of Keynes's influence as a prominent investor and prospective chairman. He opposed Muir's suggested terms of employment; Muir dropped out; and Keynes installed Hubert Henderson, his former pupil and Cambridge colleague, as editor. He also persuaded Leonard Woolf to remain literary editor. The first issue under the new management appeared on 5 May.

Keynes was a substantial contributor to the paper providing over 150 pieces between 1923 and 1930. As chairman he generally did not interfere in the day-to-day affairs of the paper, although it was he, not the editor, who wrote the Editorial Foreword to the first issue (XVIII, 123–6), and he and Henderson had a long talk each week on the significance of current developments. Keynes often took over as editor when Henderson was on holiday with no marked change in the paper.

Keynes became further involved in Liberal projects, particularly the Liberal Industrial Inquiry and the development of the Liberal proposal on unemployment in its manifesto for the 1929 general election, which he defended with Henderson in *Can Lloyd George Do It?*

Keynes's liberalism had stronger links to the older Asquithian style – 'cool, intellectual and judicious, concerned with the establishment of a just and reasonable order of society as it appeared to cultivated and superior minds' – than with the often less rationalist populism of Lloyd George.[4] Keynes always believed that 'a little clear thinking' or 'more lucidity' could provide grounds for reasonable decisions. As he put it to T.S. Eliot, the poet, in 1945 when discussing full employment policy

> It may turn out, I suppose, that vested interests and personal selfishness may stand in the way. But the main task is providing first the intellectual conviction and then intellectually to devise the means. Insufficiency of cleverness, not of goodness, is the main trouble. And even resistance to change *may* have many motives besides selfishness. (XXVII, 384)

Keynes was also an elitist, as he made clear in his discussion of the formation and changing of public opinion in *A Revision of the Treaty* (34–6) and in part of his 'Am I a Liberal?' (295–6), delivered to the 1925 Summer School in Cambridge. One of his main objections to the Labour Party was that the 'intellectual elements' would never 'exercise adequate control' (297).

Until 1930 Keynes remained a firm adherent of free trade. He was similarly at one with most of the old and new sections of the Liberal Party in his view that in the circumstances there were few resources readily available for expensive schemes of social improvement. The scope for economies in expenditure was limited to defence and overseas military commitments and the level of taxation was such that no large new sources of revenue were available, especially given the need for capital accumulation to employ a rapidly growing labour force (XVIII, 126; XIX 2–3, 3–4, 677). This did not rule out reform in the future. It was not out of character in 1939–40, when there was even less room for fiscal manoeuvre, for Keynes to propose a major scheme of socially improving redistribution.

Keynes accepted the capitalist system – even though he thought that it was morally objectionable, particularly in its over-emphasis on the love of money. As he put it in *A Short View of Russia*:

> [T]he moral problem of our age is concerned with the love of money, with the habitual appeal to the money motive in nine-tenths of the activities of life, with the universal striving after individual economic security as the prime object of endeavour, with the social approbation of money as the measure of constructive success, and with the social appeal to the hoarding instinct as the foundation for the family and the future. (268–9)

Capitalism was probably more efficient for the attainment of economic ends than any alternative. He saw no advantage in revolution (267). The problem was to make capitalism 'as efficient as possible without offending our notions of a satisfactory way of life' (294). He was not explicit as to what end this 'efficiency' was to be directed, although he hinted that the objective was capital accumulation to reach a level of affluence where economic questions could take second place to moral ones (268).[5] I shall return to his goal – the solution of the economic problem.

The means was a *managed* capitalism. This involved *The End of Laissez Faire*: 'the conclusion that individuals acting independently for their own advantage will produce the greatest aggregation of wealth' (284). He rejected this on several grounds ranging from the logical complications posed by formal economic theory which limit the applicability of the economist's competitive model to the real world, to the moral and philosophical. As a result, one had to settle in detail on a case-by-case basis what, borrowing from Bentham, he called the Agenda and Non-Agenda of government – and to do so with no presuppositions (291). In his contributions to the discussions Keynes made a number of suggestions.

First, he made the distinction between matters that are technically social from those which are technically *individual*. The former, if they are not decided on or performed by the state, would not be performed by anyone.

His examples included the control of currency and credit, the level and distribution of saving, and the provision of accurate information about general economic conditions.

Second, he concerned himself with broader issues of industrial organisation: for instance, with the appropriate organisation of public and semi-public corporations – their relations with ministers, parliament and local authorities. He did not advocate nationalisation: he was concerned with efficient operation of what was already in the public sector and with ensuring that within appropriate guidelines such institutions were autonomous and professional. In almost all cases Keynes came down in favour of autonomy in day-to-day operations, and of the encouragement of professionalism even at the cost of some centralisation to provide varied, wide-ranging careers for employees.

There was also the related problem of the organisation of the private sector where he observed a tendency towards large units, the separation of ownership and control, cartels, trade agreements and monopolies. Here Keynes put his faith in greater publicity in general and in regulation where it was necessary to protect investors and the general public. He regarded bigness as inevitable but he leaned towards solutions that allowed the efficiency of decentralised decision-making compatible with the public interest.

Finally he touched on general questions of social reform. His major concerns were with what he provocatively called sex and drug questions. The former included birth control, marriage laws, the treatment of sexual offences, and the economic position of women and the family where 'the existing state of the law and of orthodoxy is still medieval' (300). He realised that these questions had economic implications: the position of women and the family, for example, raised the issue of how wages should be determined. Under drug questions he put drink and gambling.

In politics, there was also the question of Marxism and its manifestation in the Soviet Union. Keynes was 'notoriously tone deaf' to Marx.[6] He described *Das Kapital* as 'an obsolete economic textbook which I know to be not only scientifically erroneous but without interest or application to the modern world' (258). Nor was he impressed with the conditions of day-to-day existence in the USSR of 1925 (the date of his first visit)

> I am not ready for a creed which does not care how much it destroys the liberty and sanctity of daily life, which uses deliberately the weapons of persecution, destruction and international strife ... which finds a characteristic expression in spending millions to suborn spies in every family or group (258).

'The significance of communism to Keynes lay in its ascetic religious appeal to intellectuals.'[7]

> Communism ... is a protest against the emptiness of economic welfare, an appeal to the ascetic in us all to other values. ... The idealistic youth play with Communism because it is the only spiritual appeal which feels to them contemporary, ... When Cambridge undergraduates take their inevitable trip to Bolshiedom, are they disillusioned when they find it all dreadfully uncomfortable? Of course not. That is what they are looking for. (XXVIII, 35).

> There is no one in politics today worth sixpence outside the ranks of liberals except the post-war generation of intellectual Communists under thirty five. Them too, I like and respect. Perhaps in their feelings and instincts they are the nearest thing we now have to the typical nervous non-conformist English gentleman who went to the Crusades, made the Reformation, fought the Great Rebellion, won us our civil and religious liberties and humanised the working classes last century. (XXI, 495)

V

The final section of the original Essays in Persuasion was concerned with 'The Future'.It contained two chapters: a review of H.G. *Wells's The World of William Clissold* and a speculative essay, 'Economic Possibilities for Our Grandchildren', originally written in 1928 for the Essay Society of Winchester College. In May 1930 he revised it for a June lecture in Madrid. In the essay, he suggested that human needs fell into two classes:

> those needs which are absolute in the sense that we feel them whatever the situation of our fellow human beings may be, and those which are relative in the sense that we feel them only if their satisfaction lifts us above, makes us feel superior to our fellows. (327)

This distinction between absolute needs and what economists have come to call positional needs is effectively between needs capable of satiation and those which are not. Keynes believed that capitalism, wisely managed, could, if there were no major wars and no important increases in population, satisfy absolute needs in Western Europe and the countries of recent settlement in less than a century, leaving those societies free to channel their energies in other directions.

> [T}*he economic problem* may be solved, or be at least in sight of solution, within a hundred years. This means that the economic problem is not – if we look into the future *the permanent problem of the human race.* (326)

If this were the case,

> for the first time since creation man will be faced with his real, his permanent problem – how to use his freedom from pressing economic cares, how to occupy the leisure, which science and compound interest will have won for him, to live wisely and agreeably and well. ...
>
> I see us free, therefore, to return to some of the most sure and certain principles of religion and traditional virtue – that avarice is a vice, that the exaction of usury is a misdemeanour, and the love of money is detestable, that those who walk in the paths of virtue and sane wisdom will take least thought for the morrow. We shall once more value ends above means and prefer the good to the useful. (328, 330–1)

How Keynes would have handled the problem of the endless, largely futile striving after positional goods, he did not say. It would certainly require enormous powers of persuasion. Nonetheless, his vision of capitalism saw the centring of social arrangements around fostering further capital accumulation as unnecessary in the long run.

Keynes's was not the first such vision in the history of economics: one might also think of John Stuart Mill's vision of the stationary state or Karl Marx. There was also an important link between economic growth and moral improvement in Marshall.

Such was Keynes's end – the solution of the economic problem.

> But beware! The time for all this is not yet. For at least another hundred years we must pretend to ourselves and to everyone that fair is foul and foul is fair; for foul is useful and fair is not. Avarice and usury must be our gods for a little longer still. For only they can lead us out of the tunnel of economic necessity into daylight. ...
>
> Meanwhile, there will be no harm in making mild preparations for our destiny, in encouraging and experimenting in, the arts of life as well as the activities of purpose.
>
> But ... do not let us overestimate the importance of the economic problem, or sacrifice to its supposed necessities other matters of greater and more permanent significance. (331–2)

The defining concern of economics at the time Keynes wrote was the causes of material welfare.[8] This concern looks odd to the modern economist brought up on Lionel Robbins: 'Economics is the science which studies human behaviour as a relationship between ends and scarce resources which have alternative uses.'[9] With Robbins's definition, the economic problem can never be 'solved'.

Keynes also assumed that increased incomes would lead to a substitution of leisure for work. This substitution had been the historical experience during industrialisation. However, the effect could go the other way as leisure becomes more expensive: there are suggestions that this may have been the case more recently in Britain and the United States, though not in Western Europe. To complicate matters further, technical change has produced new consumer goods that motivate individuals to have enough earnings to afford them. Furthermore, consumption itself is more complex than Keynes posited. As Marshall noted:

> Speaking broadly ... although it is man's wants in the earlier stages of his development that give rise to his activities, yet afterwards each new step upwards is to be regarded as the development of new activities giving rise to new wants, rather than new wants giving rise to new activities.[10]

There is also the observation of Frank Knight that a basic human characteristic is a continuing desire to improve and educate one's tastes.[11]

VI

What happened to Keynes's ideas on the subjects covered by *Persuasion* after 1931? Reparation and war debt payments ended with the Lausanne Conference of July 1932. As far as organised politics were concerned, after the 1929 general election he withdrew from Liberal affairs. He declined re-election as a Vice-President of the National League of Young Liberals in 1931 (XX, 527–8). By 1935 he was refusing to contribute to party funds at election time, not only because he could not see the point of throwing money away but also because he was no longer convinced of the desirability of maintaining the separate identity of the party (XXI, 373). After 1939 he moved back a little towards the Liberals: when he was raised to the peerage he told Viscount Samuel, the Liberal leader in the House of Lords he was 'in truth ... still a Liberal, and, I should like to indicate that by sitting on your benches'.[12] In 1945 he was inclined to refer to Liberal candidates such as Roy Harrod, his future official biographer, as 'funnies' but he gave the party some financial support – a minimal £25.

But he did not eschew politics. He remained chairman of the *New Statesman and Nation* until his death, although his correspondence with Kingsley Martin, its editor after 1931, shows that he disagreed with much that appeared in the paper (XXVIII, ch. 1). In the 1930s he commented on Labour proposals, often sympathetically. But his appointment diaries for the 1930s were singularly free of entries suggesting meetings with the emerging generation of senior Labour politicians. Yet it is notable that many of the important figures in the groups that provided the basis for much of the pro-grammes that emerged over the decade had links to Keynes.

He disliked Soviet Communism in the 1930s even more that in the 1920s. The economic experiment exhibited 'the worst example which the world, perhaps, has ever seen of administrative incompetence and the sacrifice of almost everything that makes life worth living for wooden heads' (XXI, 243–4). 'Stalin has eliminated every independent critical mind, even when it is sympathetic in general outlook. He has produced an environment in which the processes of the mind have atrophied' (XXI, 246). Keynes watched Stalin's purges and show trials with horrified fascination (XXVIII, 17–19, 57–8, 72–3). When Kingsley Martin asked him to comment on Beatrice Webb's 80th birthday in 1938, he replied, 'The only sentence which came spontaneously to my mind was "Mrs. Webb, not being a Soviet politician, has managed to survive to the age of eighty"' (XXVIII, 93).

In the early 1930s, he was more pessimistic about capitalism as an alternative than he had been in *A Short View of Russia*.

> The decadent international but individualistic capitalism ... is not a success. It is not intelligent, it is not beautiful, it is not just, it is not virtuous – it does not deliver the goods. (XXI, 239)

But he was developing his solution to that problem – his *General Theory*.

The ideas of 'Economic Possibilities for Our Grandchildren' continued to feature in his discourse. In December 1931, when he addressed the Society for Socialist Inquiry and Propaganda on 'The Dilemma of Modern Socialism', he said:

> I should like to define the socialist programme as aiming at political power with a view to doing in the first instance what is economically sound in order that, later on, the community may become rich enough to *afford* what is economically unsound.
>
> My goal is the ideal; my object is to put economic considerations into a back seat; but my method at this moment of economic and social evolution would be to advance toward the goal by concentrating on what is economically sound. ... For it will have to be on the basis of increased resources, not on the basis of poverty, that the grand experiment of the ideal republic will be made. (XXI, 34)

Just over a year later, another strand of thought entered the discussion when he lectured in Dublin in April 1933 on 'National Self-Sufficiency'.

The nineteenth century carried to extravagant lengths the criterion of what one can call, for short, the financial results, as a test of the advisability of any course of action sponsored by private or collective bodies. The whole conduct of life was made into a parody of an accountant's nightmare. Instead of using their vastly increased material and technical resources to build a wonder-city, they built slums; and they thought it right and advisable to build slums because slums on the test of private enterprise 'paid'; whereas the wonder-city would, they thought, have been an act of foolish extravagance, which would, in the imbecile idiom of the financial fashion have 'mortgaged the future'; though how the construction today of great and glorious works can impoverish the future no man can see until his mind is beset by false analogies from an irrelevant accountancy. ...

But once we allow ourselves to be disobedient to the test of an account-ant's profit, we have begun to change our civilisation. And we need to do so very warily, cautiously and self-consciously. For there is a wide field of human activity where we shall be wise to retain the usual pecuniary tests. It is the state, rather than the individual, which needs to change its criterion. It is the conception of the Chancellor of the Exchequer as the chairman of a sort of joint-stock company which has to be discarded. (XXI, 242–3)

In his argument leading up to this conclusion, Keynes remarked that if he were in power he would 'set out to endow our capital cities with all the appur-tenances of art and civilisation on the highest standards of which the citizens of each were individually capable' (XXI, 243).

A more general argument relating this line of thought to the arts came in 1936. First of all, in *The General Theory*, as well as echoing 'National Self-Sufficiency' at an earlier point (VII, 131), in the course of discussing his pre-cursors he extended the argument to the arts more generally.

Petty's 'entertainments, magnificent shews, triumphal arches, etc.' gave place to the penny-wisdom of Gladstonian finance and to a state system which 'could not afford' hospitals, open spaces, noble buildings, even the preservation of ancient monuments, far less than the splendours of music and drama, all of which were consigned to the private charity or the mag-nanimity of improvident individuals. (VII, 362)

Then in May 1936, J. R. Ackerly, literary editor of *The Listener*, invited Keynes to write the lead article for a late-summer series on 'Art and the State'. Ackerly told Keynes that he meant by art 'painting, sculpture, architec-ture, and such new forms of art as the pageantry of ceremony and festivity'

(XXVIII, 335), but on Keynes's urging he was prepared to expand his definition to include opera, ballet and drama (XVIII, 336–7). When Keynes's article appeared, it echoed 'National Self-Sufficiency' in referring to

> the utilitarian and economic – one might almost say financial ideal, as the sole respectable purpose of the community as a whole – also called 'the Treasury view' – as the most dreadful heresy, perhaps, which has ever gained the ear of a civilised people,

and to Britain as being 'hag-ridden by a perverted theory of the state' with the 'grandest exercises today in the arts of construction ... [being] arterial roads' (XXVIII, 342–4).

In the article, Keynes was somewhat uncertain as to the role the state could best play in the arts, but less than a decade later, with more experience, he would broadcast on the formation of the Arts Council of Great Britain, of which he was the principal architect and first chairman, that 'At last the public exchequer has recognised the support and encouragement of the civilising arts of life as part of their duty' (XXVIII, 368).

VII

The Means to Prosperity documents an important stage in Keynes's intellectual development – the appearance in print of the output-equilibrating mechanism central to the *General Theory* of effective demand. It also represents the only occasion where Keynes published a proposal for international monetary reform that was not his own: it had been originated by Hubert Henderson and had been developed as a British proposal for the forthcoming World Economic Conference by the government's Economic Advisory Council of which Keynes was a member.

Between 1929 and 1931, the logic behind *Can Lloyd George Do It?* and proposals for public investment lay in the 'special case' of the *Treatise on Money* where interest-rate policy was unavailable to stimulate investment in a country with an overvalued exchange rate. This meant that when Britain left the gold standard and sterling depreciated, public works became theoretically irrelevant, for the use of interest-rate policy to stimulate domestic investment (the 'general case' of the *Treatise*) came into its own. As a result it was some time after September 1931 before Keynes returned to advocating substantial loan-financed public works as a cure for unemployment. Instead his attention shifted to the need to reduce the long-term rate of interest.

Before the 1931 financial crisis, the Treasury had started planning to convert a substantial part of the national debt to a lower rate of interest as it had done in 1888. It had even taken the necessary powers to do so in the April 1931 Budget. The crisis put these plans on hold. Keynes worried that the Treasury would be impatient and try to convert as soon as interest rates started to fall. As he put it in his 'Notes on the Currency Question' of 16 November 1931:

> The iron rule of the Treasury should be to issue no new loan, whether as a conversion issue or as a new loan, unless it is repayable at the issue price, at their option, within ten years, until it can be done on a three per cent basis. (XXI, 25n)

Events moved more quickly than Keynes expected as Bank rate fell from 6 per cent at the time sterling left gold to 2 per cent on 30 June 1932 (the first time it had been at that level since 1897). That evening, the Chancellor of the Exchequer announced a conversion scheme for a 5 per cent War Loan 1929/47 (which accounted for over a quarter of the national debt) to a 3½ per cent basis.

By then, Keynes had started to doubt whether cheap money would be enough to stimulate recovery.[13] As he put it in a February 1932 lecture.

> I am not confident ... that on this occasion the cheap money will be sufficient by itself to bring about an adequate recovery of new investment. Cheap money means that the riskless, or supposedly riskless rate, of interest will be low. But actual enterprise always involves some degree of risk. It may still be the case that the lender, with his confidence shattered by his experiences, will continue to ask for new enterprise rates of interest which the borrower cannot expect to earn. ...
>
> If this proves to be so, there will be no means of escape from prolonged and perhaps interminable depression except by direct state intervention to promote and subsidise new investment. ... I predict with an assured confidence that the only way out is for us to discover *some* object which is admitted even by the dead-heads to be a legitimate excuse for largely increasing the expenditure of someone on something! (XXI, 60)

He began, cautiously and tentatively, to advocate pump-priming investment to raise the level of activity to the point where lenders' and borrowers' expectations improved sufficiently for cheap money to play its conventional role in promoting recovery. For much of the rest of 1932 Keynes used this sort of argument for the encouragement of 'wise spending', in particular the reversal of the 1931 crisis cuts in local authority investment. But his advocacy took the weak form of signing joint letters to the press drafted by others.[14]

Keynes's arguments favouring increased loan-financed public works soon became stronger and more focused. *The Means to Prosperity*, published in *The Times* between 13 and 16 March 1933 before being issued as pamphlet, and a 1 April article, 'The Multiplier', published in the *New Statesman* (XXI, 171–8) which was incorporated into the American version of the pamphlet (341–6), demonstrate this most clearly. They reflect a crucial step in the development of Keynes's ideas as he moved from *A Treatise on Money*, published at the end of October 1930, and *The General Theory of Employment, Interest and Money*, published at the beginning of February 1936.

The development of Keynes's ideas between the fall of 1930 and the spring of 1933 is relatively straightforward in its outlines. The Treatise was subject to substantial discussion during 1930–31. Much of that discussion was critical – so critical that Keynes decided to re-work his analysis. As he told Nicholas Kaldor on 9 December, 1931. 'I am now endeavouring to express the whole thing over again more clearly and from a different angle; and in two years time I may feel able to publish a revised and completer version' (XIII, 243).

After publishing the *General Theory*, Keynes set out the stages of his quest (XIV, 84; XXIX, 215). His account of the stepping stones to the book had four stages: (i) the enunciation of 'the psychological law' relating consumption to income; (ii) the theory of effective demand; (iii) 'the notion of interest being the measure of liquidity preference'; and (iv) the marginal efficiency of capital.

Scholarly accounts of the making of the *General Theory* normally start from this list and add or subtract items. All lists contain the first two items which emphasise the equilibrating role of changes in output implicit in the multiplier. Agreement on the inclusion of particular items does not mean agreement on the dating of Keynes's development of the ideas, which can range from 'indications of developments in ... [Keynes's] thinking which represented initial insights, even if they were disjointed flashes of illumination' to the exposition of the doctrine in a form intended for a professional readership – the criterion suitable for crediting a person with a scientific discovery.[15] The latter criterion will produce a later set of dates than the former, which also runs another risk, as Keynes recollected after the publication of the *General Theory*.[16]

> The extent to which one sees one's destination before one discovers the route is the most obscure problem of all in the psychology of original work. In a sense it is the destination which one sees first. But then a good many of the destinations so seen turn out to be mirages. Only a small proportion of one's original intuitions survive the struggle of trying to find a route to them.

If we use the available drafts, correspondence, lecture notes and publications, we can date Keynes's adoption of his output equilibration theory of effective demand to late 1932 or early 1933.

One of the two crucial pieces of evidence is the preparation of Keynes's essay on T. R. Malthus for his *Essays in Biography*. This was a revision of a talk he had used for years in the light of reading Malthus's correspondence with David Ricardo on gluts, acquired by Piero Sraffa for his edition of Ricardo's works. Keynes was still re-working the essay in late November 1932 and he returned the galley proofs for paging early in January. Among the many revisions to his paper were references to the theory of effective demand. Keynes saw Malthus as a precursor for his new ideas.

The second is *The Means to Prosperity*, completed on 6 March 1933. After publication he began thinking of expanding the argument, one being 'the train of reasoning by which I arrive at the multiplier relating secondary employment to primary employment' which he published on 1 April. In 'The Multiplier' he argued that in an open economy with no repercussions, allowing for changes in the marginal propensity to consume resulting from changes in the distribution of income, the multiplier would probably be 2. He also set out the symmetrical mechanism for a reduction in expenditure. It was on this basis that he discussed proposals for an expansionary budget containing loan-financed capital expenditure of £60 million and tax cuts of £50 million.

The other concern of *The Means to Prosperity* was a proposal for an international gold currency – a re-working of the Henderson Plan mentioned above. The Plan, 'A Monetary Proposal for Lausanne' was prepared in May 1932. Henderson's Plan was revised in various forms in Whitehall before a less ambitious Treasury version was developed as a recommended British proposal for the forthcoming World Economic Conference.

Keynes's variation on Henderson also saw the Bank of International Settlements issuing gold-equivalent notes but he distributed them on a formula depending on the amount of gold a country held at the end of 1928 provided that no individual quota exceeded £90 million. To receive such notes countries would have to adopt fixed exchange rates and remove exchange restrictions. The countries involved could use their notes to repay debts and/ or finance balance-of-payments deficits resulting from programmes of domestic expansion. The supply of notes or the rate of interest on the gold bonds each country gave in exchange for the notes would be managed 'solely with a view to avoiding ... a rise in the gold price-level of primary products entering into international trade above some agreed norm between the present level and that of 1928 – perhaps the level of 1930' (358).

The existence of the gold notes and gold bonds meant a qualified return to the gold standard by the participating countries – but a gold standard with an allowable range of fluctuation for exchange rates of 5 per cent and with a provision that echoed *A Tract on Monetary Reform* that 'the de facto parity should be alterable, if necessary, from time to time if circumstances were to require, just like bank rate' (362). Such safeguards Keynes believed would make the scheme flexible enough to be acceptable.[17]

As an essay in persuasion, the impact of *The Means to Prosperity* was mixed. The international monetary proposal had already received considerable official discussion before Keynes's articles. The less ambitious Treasury variant had even been shown to the Americans, but American reaction to it, and to Keynes's published version was unsympathetic. But the variant remained available if there was an appropriate moment at the conference. There wasn't: the conference collapsed with President Roosevelt's 'bombshell' message rejecting an exchange stabilisation agreement on 3 July.

The domestic proposals had very little immediate impact. Keynes met Neville Chamberlain on 16 March at the latter's request. He reported that the Chancellor 'seemed pretty virgin soil and to hear everything with an open mind and an apparently sympathetic spirit, but quite for the first time' (XXI, 168). But the Budget itself marked time, as Keynes put it (XXI, 191 6). Later in the year there was some assistance for the construction of the *RMS Queen Mary*, new telephone exchanges and the extension of the London Underground, but it is not clear that these decisions were related in Chamberlain's mind to Keynes's arguments, even if over time these slowly came to influence his officials.

VIII

How to Pay for the War was published on 27 February 1940. The evolution of its message, the tactics of its presentation and their final results provide the classic example of Keynes the practical economist at work. It also shows how much more sophisticated at persuasion he was than previously.

On 20 October 1939 Keynes gave a talk, entitled 'War Potential and War Finance', to the undergraduate economics club in Cambridge. Four days later he sent a draft of his proposals, now entitled 'The Limitation of Purchasing Power: High Prices, Taxation and Compulsory Saving', to the editor of *The Times*. He also sent the draft to Sir John Simon (the Chancellor of the Exchequer), Clement Attlee (Leader of the Opposition), and Josiah Stamp, Hubert Henderson and Henry Clay of the Government's Survey of Economic and Financial Plans. He discussed them at a dinner meeting of MPs and ministers on 27 October and with Sir Richard Hopkins of the Treasury on 1 November.

With encouraging initial reactions, Keynes revised his draft into two articles, improving the balance and removing details that might divert attention from his main proposals. The articles appeared in *The Times* under the title 'Paying for the War' on 14 and 15 November.

Between the publication of the articles and the appearance of the pamphlet Keynes entered into further discussions – in private and in newspapers (including papers more popular than *The Times*) – to get across the reasoning behind his scheme and to find ways of making it more generally acceptable (XXII, 52–99). He attempted to convince the Labour Party and the trade unions who, to put it mildly, had been unenthusiastic about his proposals, of their underlying soundness while altering the details. On 17 January 1940 he met with Eleanor Rathbone and Eva Hubback, long-standing advocates of family allowances. On 24 January he spent the morning with members of Labour's Front Bench and went on in the afternoon to meet a committee of the General Council of the Trades Union Congress. In the weeks that followed he spoke to meetings of MPs and the Fabian Society while continuing discussions with fellow economists of all political persuasions, City representatives and friends.

At the heart of his proposals was the recognition that a long, large-scale war not fought out of stocks in existence at the beginning of hostilities and/or available from day-to-day orders (such as the Falklands war of 1982) involves large shifts in resources away from their previous uses. The problem was how to divert resources from peacetime uses to the needs of war and, particularly after 1939, how to reduce consumption during a period of rising real and money incomes.

As Keynes saw it, there were four possible ways in which the authorities could gain command over additional resources (as well as declines in investment, living off past stocks or allowing a deterioration of the current account of the balance of payments, all of which occurred):

1. individuals could voluntarily reduce their consumption expenditures and directly or indirectly make their savings available to the government by taking up new loans or increasing their cash balances;
2. comprehensive rationing could reduce consumption by fiat;
3. through inflationary policies, the authorities could initially bid resources away from other uses and eventually place the command of these resources in the hands of those who would pass them to the government through taxation, voluntary savings or higher cash balances;
4. increased taxation could reduce the resources available to the public for consumption and transfer them to the authorities.

Since the sums involved implied very sharp increases in average and marginal propensities to save, especially among groups that had not previously saved much, Keynes believed that voluntary savings would not provide the resources for war without inflation. As for rationing, it would be inevitable for essential items of consumption in short supply, but, unless it was comprehensive, it would divert demand to unrationed goods. Comprehensive rationing would, on the other hand, tie up in the bureaucracy labour better used elsewhere and would be restrictive of consumers' choice and, hence, unpopular.[18] Inflation, the main method of restricting private consumption during the First World War, might reduce consumption up to a point, but it would, with a lag, lead to increased wage claims. Given the lags, and workers' increased index consciousness, prosecution of the war by this means would mean continuous and large price increases which would result in charges of profiteering, not to mention leaving the bulk of the post-war national debt in the hands of the wealthy. This left taxation, which would have to reach much further down the income distribution than at present if it were to do the trick as the preferred alternative. The need for a broader tax base pointed to a general turnover tax which had the disadvantage of needing a new bureaucratic machinery or substantial innovation within the existing machinery.

Keynes opted for innovation in the form of compulsory saving or deferred pay. A progressive percentage of all incomes over a stipulated amount would be paid over to the government. Part of this would be in the form of direct taxes; part would be in the form of compulsory savings credited to the accounts of individuals. These accounts would pay interest, but, except in certain circumstances, they would be blocked until after the war. For those not paying income tax, the scheme would operate though the existing national insurance system.

As a result of his consultations, Keynes's proposals in *How to Pay for the War* contained several alterations. The major changes affected those with lower incomes: he proposed a family allowance of 5 shillings per week per child up to age 15 (the prospective school-leaving age), the allowance to be paid to the mother, and a limited set of necessities or 'iron ration' available at low, fixed prices, even if this necessitated subsidies. These two changes would actually *improve* the lot of the worst off as compared with before the war. But these concessions cost real resources; so Keynes had to make his scheme generate more revenue. He recommended that children's allowances under the income-tax system be reduced to zero. He also increased the progression of the combined rates of income tax and compulsory savings with the top rate rising to 85 rather than 80 per cent. Finally he proposed, at the suggestion of Friedrich Hayek, that the repayment of compulsory savings be financed by a progressive capital levy. Thus he had 'endeavoured to snatch from the exigency of war positive social improvements' including 'advances towards economic equality greater than any which we have made in recent times' (368).

Keynes's campaign continued after publication with a specially arranged debate in the House of Lords the next day, more meetings, letters to the press and on 11 March a BBC broadcast discussion with Donald Tyerman, the Deputy Editor of *The Economist.* Support for the proposals remained mixed. He gained some ground on the left with some trade unionists and Labour Party activists and advisers but made little progress with the Labour Front Bench and none at all with Ernest Bevin. In the City he had some support from the Governor of the Bank of England and several of its directors, but there was opposition from the those associated with the National Savings Movement. Among economists and economist-advisers there was very strong support. He was making progress except with 'the bloody politicians whose bloody minds have not been prepared for anything unfamiliar to their ancestors'.[19] But circumstances changed quickly with the German victories in Western Europe, the resignation of Neville Chamberlin and the formation of a coalition government under Winston Churchill.

On 28 June Keynes was offered a place on the new Chancellor of the Exchequer's Consultative Council which met for the first time on 8 July. On 12 August, he was offered a room in the Treasury and a share of a secretary which he supplemented by bringing his own Mrs Stevens to the office. He had no routine duties and no official hours, but he had membership of certain committees and 'a sort of roving commission' as he told the Provost of King's. His major preoccupation during his early period in the Treasury was a continuation of his campaign associated with *How to Pay for the War.* He gained influence: from 21 October he was a member of the Chancellor's top secret Budget Committee.

Over the months before the Budget was presented in the House on 7 April 1941, Keynes's detailed proposals, like those of others, fell by the wayside – either as the result of administrative complexities or their looking 'too much like a rehash of income tax' (XXII, 253). Yet, the publication with the Budget of a White Paper, *Analysis of the Sources of War Finance and an Estimate of National Income and Expenditure in 1938 and 1940* (Cmd. 6261), the first published official national income estimates in Britain prepared by Richard Stone and James Meade, showed Keynes's enormous success in getting his methods of analysis accepted. The authorities committed themselves to noninflationary war finance and used Keynes's analytical framework in coming to a decision as to how large a gap there existed between output and potential expenditure that had to be bridged by voluntary savings and/or tax increases if it were not to be automatically closed by inflation. As he told his mother, 'the logical structure, and method of a wartime Budget which, together with the new White Paper, is really a revolution in public finance' (XXII, 354).

The method of the Budget was simple. There was some fine tuning of the wartime Excess Profits Tax. The programme of consumers' subsidies which had grown up piecemeal was brought together with the Chancellor's commitment that he would endeavour to prevent any rise in the cost of living index. There were sharp increases in income taxes. Personal allowances fell, along with the earned income allowance, bringing almost 4 million new taxpayers into the income tax net. The standard rate of income tax went to 50 per cent and the top marginal rate to 97.5 per cent. The increases in tax payments caused by the reduction in allowances were to be considered forced savings or deferred pay and would be repaid after the war (they were repaid in 1972). The size of the deferred pay, £125 million in the first year as compared to Keynes's original proposal of £600 million, looked more like an experiment than a centrepiece, but it, plus the commitment to the stabilisation of the cost of living index and the methodological revolution were the result of a successful 'essay in persuasion'.[20] As R. S. Sayers, the official historian of wartime financial policy put it, 'at last Britain's leaders had a financial policy'.[21] That they had a policy and a means of systematically thinking about changes in it was the measure of Keynes's polemical and persuasive achievement.

Notes

1. In the pages that follow all references to *The Collected Writings of John Maynard Keynes*, edited by Elizabeth Johnson and Donald Moggridge other than to *Essays in Persuasion* will take the form of roman numeral volume number and page number. For *Essays in Persuasion* the reference will simply be the page number. Unpublished writings by J. M. Keynes copyright The Provost and Scholars of King's College Cambridge 2010.

2. For the latest piece of the literature on Keynes's fabrication, which has references to the earlier material see N. White and K. Schuler, 'Who Said "Debauch the Currency": Keynes or Lenin?', *Journal of Economic Perspectives*, Spring 2009.

3. P. J. Grigg, *Prejudice and Judgment*, Cape 1948, 182–4.

4. John Campbell, *Lloyd George: The Goat in the Wilderness, 1922–31*, Cape 1977, 54.

5. As he put it in some rough notes in April 1926: 'Our object is to preserve as much of the capitalistic efficiency as is compatible with releasing for other ends the energies now occupied by the money motive and with a due regard for non-economic (i.e. non-monetary goods and to Social Justice).' R. O'Donnell, 'The Unwritten Books and Papers of J. M. Keynes', *History of Political Economy*, Winter 1992, 810.

6. D. Winch, *Economics and Policy: A Historical Study*, Hodder and Stoughton 1969, 346,

7. *Ibid.*, 348

8. See, for example, Alfred Marshall, *Principles of Economics*, 8th edn, Macmillan 1920/61, 1,

9. *An Essay on the Nature and Significance of Economic Science*, Macmillan 1932/35, 16.

10. Marshall, *Principles of Economics*, 8th edn, 89.

11. F. Knight, *The Ethics of Competition*, Allen and Unwin 1935, 19–40.

12. Modern Archive Centre, King's College, Cambridge, Keynes Papers L/42, 24 June 1942.

13. In the *Treatise on Money* he had suggested that this might have been the case during the depression of the early 1890s (VI, 151–2).

14. To *The Times* on 5 July (drafted by Roy Harrod and James Meade signed by forty-one academic economists and to *The Times* on 17 October (drafted by A. C. Pigou, the Professor of Political Economy in Cambridge) and signed by the David Macgregor, the Professor of Political Economy at Oxford, Keynes, Walter Layton, Josiah Stamp and Arthur Salter.

15. The two extremes are from P. Clarke, *The Keynesian Revolution in the Making*, Clarendon Press 1988, 258 and D. Patinkin, *Anticipations of the General Theory? and Other Essays on Keynes*, University of Chicago Press 1982, Part I.

16. British Library, ADD.57923, JMK to O. T. Falk, 19 February 1936.

17. Later in the 1930s Keynes came to believe that such an adjustable peg might lead to large undesirable speculative capital movements and would only work if there were exchange controls (XI, 501), a view he carried over in his wartime proposals for what became the International Monetary Fund.

18. Keynes undoubtedly underestimated the popularity of the notion of 'fair shares' and did not see the possibility of 'points' rationing as a substitute for the market.

19. Modern Archive Centre, King's College, Cambridge, Keynes Papers, HP/3, JMK to R. McKenna, 28 January 1940.

20. Family allowances took longer: the scheme reached the Statute Book in June 1945 and payment began in August 1946.

21. R. S. Sayers, *Financial Policy, 1939–1945*, Longmans Green for Her Majesty's Stationery Office 1956, 62.

Notes on Further Reading

Sixty-four years after his death, the literature on Keynes is vast and flourishing. What follows is only a brief guide relating to the issues raised in this introduction.

The largest archival sources of Keynes materials are his papers in the Modern Archive Centre at King's College, Cambridge, and the National Archives at Kew. The King's material is available on microfilm in several libraries. The standard published source of Keynes's writings is *The Collected Writings of John Maynard Keynes*, edited for the Royal Economic Society by Elizabeth Johnson and Donald Moggridge. The 30 volumes were published by Macmillan and Cambridge University Press between 1971 and 1989.

The official biography of Keynes is Sir Roy Harrod's *The Life of John Maynard Keynes* (Macmillan, 1951). Although it is useful, it suffers from the reticence of its author on personal matters and his being too close to his subject and involved in controversies over policy where his views were not Keynes's. A very good short sketch is Sir Austin Robinson's obituary 'John Maynard Keynes, 1883–1946' (*Economic Journal*, March 1947). Since Harrod's book there have been a number of biographies based on primary sources, most notably Lord Skidelsky's multi-volume study *John Maynard Keynes* (Macmillan, 1983, 1992 and 2000), which is now available in a one-volume abridged version *John Maynard Keynes, 1883–1946: Economist, Philosopher, Statesman* (Macmillan, 2003), and D. E. Moggridge, *Maynard Keynes: An Economist's Biography* (Routledge, 1992). These biographical studies provide fuller discussions of Keynes's attempts at persuasion collected together in this volume.

In addition for the individual Parts of the Introduction the following will be useful.

Part I: B. Kent *The Spoils of War: The Politics, Economics, and Diplomacy of Reparations, 1918–1932* (Clarendon Press, 1989).

Part II: P. Clarke, *The Keynesian Revolution in the Making, 1924–1936* (Clarendon Press, 1988), ch 4.

Part III: D. E. Moggridge, *British Monetary Policy, 1924–31: The Norman Conquest of $4.86* (Cambridge University Press, 1972) and R. S. Sayers, *The Bank of England, 1891–1944*, Vol. I (Cambridge University Press, 1976).

Part IV: D. Winch, *Economics and Policy: A Historical Study* (Hodder and Stoughton, 1969), Appendix; M. Cranston, 'Keynes: His Political Ideas and

Their Influence' in A. P. Thirwall (ed.) *Keynes and Laissez-Faire* (Macmillan, 1978); Michael Freeden, *Liberalism Divided: A Study of British Political Thought, 1914–1939* (Clarendon Press, 1986); and A. Peacock, 'Keynes and the Role of the State' in D. Crabtree and A. P. Thirlwall (eds) Keynes and the Role of the State (Macmillan, 1993).

Part V: L. Pecchi and G. Piga (eds) *Revisiting Keynes' 'Economic Possibilities for Our Grandchildren'* (MIT Press, 2008).

Part VI: E. Durbin, *New Jerusalems: The Labour Party and the Economics of Democratic Socialism* (Routledge 1985); S. Howson, *British Monetary Policy, 1945–51* (Clarendon Press, 1993), ch. 2; D. E. Moggridge, 'Keynes, Art and the State' (*History of Political Economy,* Fall 2005)

VII: D. Patinkin, *Keynes's Monetary Thought: A Study of its Development* (Duke University Press, 1976); D. Patinkin, *Anticipations of the General Theory and other Essays on Keynes* (University of Chicago Press, 1982), Part I; and P. Clarke, *The Keynesian Revolution in the Making, 1924–1936*, Part 3; D. Winch's introduction to Keynes's *Essays in Biography* (Palgrave Macmillan, 2010); and S. Howson and D. Winch, *The Economic Advisory Council: A Study of Economic Advice during Depression and Recovery* (Cambridge University Press, 1977), ch. 5.

Part VII: R. S. Sayers, *Financial Policy, 1939–1945* (Longmans Green for Her Majesty's Stationery Office 1956), chs 2–3.

Corrections to this Edition

Page	Line	
xi	3–4	The Keynes Papers are now held at the Modern Archive Centre of King's College, Cambridge.
xi	36	The completed edition now consists 30 volumes
34	10	For 'the' read 'be'.
47		The sign § should precede the paragraph starting 'Such a settlement'.
68	11	For 'mortgages' read 'mortgagees'.
253	5	For '25' read '24'.
297	35	For 'it' read 'is'.
315	5	For 'autnes' read 'autres'.
438	37	For 'IXII' read 'XXII'.

PART I
THE TREATY OF PEACE

1 PARIS (1919)

From *The Economic Consequences of the Peace* (1919), chapter 1, 'Introductory'.

The power to become habituated to his surroundings is a marked characteristic of mankind. Very few of us realise with conviction the intensely unusual, unstable, complicated, unreliable, temporary nature of the economic organisation by which western Europe has lived for the last half-century. We assume some of the most peculiar and temporary of our late advantages as natural, permanent, and to be depended on, and we lay our plans accordingly. On this sandy and false foundation we scheme for social improvement and dress our political platforms, pursue our animosities and particular ambitions, and feel ourselves with enough margin in hand to foster, not assuage, civil conflict in the European family. Moved by insane delusion and reckless self-regard, the German people overturned the foundations on which we all lived and built. But the spokesmen of the French and British people have run the risk of completing the ruin, which Germany began, by a Peace which, if it is carried into effect, must impair yet further, when it might have restored, the delicate, complicated organisation, already shaken and broken by war, through which alone the European peoples can employ themselves and live.

In England the outward aspect of life does not yet teach us to feel or realise in the least that an age is over. We are busy picking up the threads of our life where we dropped them, with this difference only, that many of us seem a good deal richer than we were before. Where we spent millions before the war, we have now learnt that we can spend hundreds of millions and apparently not suffer for it. Evidently we did not exploit to the utmost the possibilities of our economic life. We look, therefore, not only to a return to the comforts of 1914, but to an immense

3

broadening and intensification of them. All classes alike thus build their plans, the rich to spend more and save less, the poor to spend more and work less.

But perhaps it is only in England (and America) that it is possible to be so unconscious. In continental Europe the earth heaves and no one but is aware of the rumblings. There it is not just a matter of extravagance or 'labour troubles'; but of life and death, of starvation and existence, and of the fearful convulsions of a dying civilisation.

For one who spent in Paris the greater part of the six months which succeeded the Armistice, an occasional visit to London was a strange experience. England still stands outside Europe. Europe's voiceless tremors do not reach her. Europe is apart and England is not of her flesh and body. But Europe is solid with herself. France, Germany, Italy, Austria, and Holland, Russia and Roumania and Poland, throb together, and their structure and civilisation are essentially one. They flourished together, they have rocked together in a war, which we, in spite of our enormous contributions and sacrifices (like though in a less degree than America) economically stood outside, and they may fall together. In this lies the destructive significance of the Peace of Paris. If the European civil war is to end with France and Italy abusing their momentary victorious power to destroy Germany and Austria-Hungary now prostrate, they invite their own destruction also, being so deeply and inextricably intertwined with their victims by hidden psychic and economic bonds. At any rate an Englishman who took part in the Conference of Paris and was during those months a member of the Supreme Economic Council of the Allied Powers, was bound to become, for him a new experience, a European in his cares and outlook. There, at the nerve centre of the European system, his British preoccupations must largely fall away and he must be haunted by other and more dreadful spectres. Paris was a nightmare, and everyone there was morbid. A sense of impending

4

catastrophe overhung the frivolous scene; the futility and small-ness of man before the great events confronting him; the mingled significance and unreality of the decisions; levity, blindness, insolence, confused cries from without—all the elements of ancient tragedy were there. Seated indeed amid the theatrical trappings of the French saloons of state, one could wonder if the extraordinary visages of Wilson and of Clemenceau, with their fixed hue and unchanging characterisation, were really faces at all and not the tragic-comic masks of some strange drama or puppet-show.

The proceedings of Paris all had this air of extraordinary importance and unimportance at the same time. The decisions seemed charged with consequences to the future of human society; yet the air whispered that the word was not flesh, that it was futile, insignificant, of no effect, dissociated from events; and one felt most strongly the impression, described by Tolstoy in *War and Peace* or by Hardy in *The Dynasts*, of events marching on to their fated conclusion uninfluenced and unaffected by the cerebrations of Statesmen in Council:

Spirit of the Years

Observe that all wide sight and self-command
Desert these throngs now driven to demonry
By the Immanent Unrecking. Nought remains
But vindictiveness here amid the strong,
And there amid the weak an impotent rage.

Spirit of the Pities

Why prompts the Will so senseless-shaped a doing?

Spirit of the Years

I have told thee that It works unwittingly,
As one possessed, not judging.

2 THE CAPACITY OF GERMANY TO PAY REPARATIONS (1919)

From *The Economic Consequences of the Peace*, chapter 5, 'Reparation'.

It is evident that Germany's pre-war capacity to pay an annual foreign tribute has not been unaffected by the almost total loss of her colonies, her overseas connections, her mercantile marine, and her foreign properties, by the cession of ten per cent of her territory and population, of one-third of her coal and of three-quarters of her iron ore, by two million casualties amongst men in the prime of life, by the starvation of her people for four years, by the burden of a vast war debt, by the depreciation of her currency to less than one-seventh its former value, by the disruption of her allies and their territories, by revolution at home and Bolshevism on her borders, and by all the unmeasured ruin in strength and hope of four years of all swallowing war and final defeat.

All this, one would have supposed, is evident. Yet most estimates of a great indemnity from Germany depend on the assumption that she is in a position to conduct in the future a vastly greater trade than ever she has had in the past.

For the purpose of arriving at a figure it is of no great consequence whether payment takes the form of cash (or rather of foreign exchange) or is partly effected in kind (coal, dyes, timber, etc.), as contemplated by the Treaty. In any event, it is only by the export of specific commodities that Germany can pay, and the method of turning the value of these exports to account for reparation purposes is, comparatively, a matter of detail.

We shall lose ourselves in mere hypothesis unless we return in some degree to first principles and, whenever we can, to such statistics as there are. It is certain that an annual payment can only be made by Germany over a series of years by diminishing her imports and increasing her exports, thus enlarging the balance in her favour which is available for effecting payments abroad. Germany can pay in the long run in goods, and in goods only, whether these goods are furnished direct to the Allies, or whether they are sold to neutrals and the neutral credits so arising are then made over to the Allies. The most solid basis for estimating the extent to which this process can be carried is to be found, therefore, in an analysis of her trade returns before the war. Only on the basis of such an analysis, supplemented by some general data as to the aggregate wealth-producing capacity of the country, can a rational guess be made as to the maximum degree to which the exports of Germany could be brought to exceed her imports.

In the year 1913 Germany's imports amounted to £538 million and her exports to £505 million exclusive of transit trade and bullion. That is to say, imports exceeded exports by about £33 million. On the average of the five years ending 1913, however, her imports exceeded her exports by a substantially larger amount, namely, £74 million. It follows, therefore, that more than the whole of Germany's pre-war balance for new foreign investment was derived from the interest on her existing foreign securities, and from the profits of her shipping, foreign banking, etc. As her foreign properties and her mercantile marine are now to be taken from her, and as her foreign banking and other miscellaneous sources of revenue from abroad have been largely destroyed, it appears that, on the pre-war basis of exports and imports, Germany, so far from having a surplus wherewith to make a foreign payment, would be not nearly self-supporting. Her first task, therefore, must be to effect a readjustment of consumption and production to cover this deficit. Any further economy she can effect in the use of imported commodities, and any further stimulation of exports will then be available for reparation.

Let us run over the chief items of export: (1) Iron goods. In view of Germany's loss of resources, an increased net export seems impossible and a large decrease probable. (2) Machinery.

Some increase is possible. (3) Coal and coke. The value of Germany's net export before the war was £22 million; the Allies have agreed that for the time being 20 million tons is the maximum possible export with a problematic (and in fact) impossible increase to 40 million tons at some future time; even on the basis of 20 million tons we have virtually no increase of value, measured in pre-war prices; whilst, if this amount is exacted, there must be a decrease of far greater value in the export of manufactured articles requiring coal for their production. (4) Woollen goods. An increase is impossible without the raw wool and, having regard to the other claims on supplies of raw wool, a decrease is likely. (5) Cotton goods. The same considerations apply as to wool. (6) Cereals. There never was and never can be a net export. (7) Leather goods. The same considerations apply as to wool.

We have now covered nearly half of Germany's pre-war exports, and there is no other commodity which formerly represented as much as 3 per cent of her exports. In what commodity is she to pay? Dyes?—their total value in 1913 was £10 million. Toys? Potash?—1913 exports were worth £3 million. And even if the commodities could be specified, in what markets are they to be sold?—remembering that we have in mind goods to the value not of tens of millions annually, but of hundreds of millions.

On the side of imports, rather more is possible. By lowering the standard of life, an appreciable reduction of expenditure on imported commodities may be possible. But, as we have already seen, many large items are incapable of reduction without reacting on the volume of exports.

Let us put our guess as high as we can without being foolish, and suppose that after a time Germany will be able, in spite of the reduction of her resources, her facilities, her markets, and her productive power, to increase her exports and diminish her imports so as to improve her trade balance altogether by £100 million annually, measured in pre-war prices. This adjustment is first required to liquidate the adverse trade balance, which in the five years before the war averaged £74 million; but we will assume that after allowing for this, she is left with a favourable trade balance of £50 million a year. Doubling this to allow for the rise in post-war prices, we have a figure of £100 million. Having regard to the political, social, and human factors, as well as to the purely economic, I doubt if Germany could be made to pay this sum annually over a period of 30 years; but it would not be foolish to assert or to hope that she could.

Such a figure, allowing 5 per cent for interest, and 1 per cent for repayment of capital, represents a capital sum having a present value of about £1,700 million.

I reach, therefore, the final conclusion that, including all methods of payment—immediately transferable wealth, ceded property, and an annual tribute—£2,000 million is a safe maximum figure of Germany's capacity to pay. In all the actual circumstances, I do not believe that she can pay as much.

There is only one head under which I see a possibility of adding to the figure reached on the line of argument adopted above; that is, if German labour is actually transported to the devastated areas and there engaged in the work of reconstruction. I have heard that a limited scheme of this kind is actually in view. The additional contribution thus obtainable depends on the number of labourers which the German government could contrive to maintain in this way and also on the number which, over a period of years, the Belgian and French inhabitants would tolerate in their midst. In any case, it would seem very difficult to employ on the actual work of reconstruction, even over a number of years, imported labour having a net present value exceeding (say) £250 million; and even this would not prove in practice a net addition to the annual contributions obtainable in other ways.

A capacity of £8,000 million or even of £5,000 million is, therefore, not within the limits of reasonable possibility. It is for those who believe that Germany can make an annual payment amounting to hundreds of millions sterling to say *in what specific commodities* they intend this payment to be made, and *in what markets* the goods are to be sold. Until they proceed to some degree of detail, and are able to produce some tangible argument in favour of their conclusions, they do not deserve to be believed.

I make three provisos only, none of which affect the force of my argument for immediate practical purposes.

First: If the Allies were to 'nurse' the trade and industry of Germany for a period of five or ten years, supplying her with large loans, and with ample shipping, food, and raw materials during that period, building up markets for her, and deliberately applying all their resources and goodwill to making her the greatest industrial nation in Europe, if not in the world, a substantially larger sum could probably be extracted thereafter; for Germany is capable of very great productivity.

Second: Whilst I estimate in terms of money, I assume that there is no revolutionary change in the purchasing power of our unit of value. If the value of gold were to sink to a half or a tenth of its present value, the real burden of a payment fixed in terms of gold would be reduced proportionately. If a gold sovereign comes to be worth what a shilling is worth now, then, of course, Germany can pay a larger sum than I have named, measured in gold sovereigns.

Third: I assume that there is no revolutionary change in the yield of nature and material to man's labour. It is not *impossible* that the progress of science should bring within our reach methods and devices by which the whole standard of life would be raised immeasurably, and a given volume of products would represent but a portion of the human effort which it represents now. In this case all standards of 'capacity' would be changed everywhere. But the fact that all things are *possible* is no excuse for talking foolishly.

It is true that in 1870 no man could have predicted Germany's capacity in 1910. We cannot expect to legislate for a generation or more. The secular changes in man's economic condition and the liability of human forecast to error are as likely to lead to mistake in one direction as in another. We cannot as reasonable men do better than base our policy on the evidence we have and adapt it to the five or ten years over which we may suppose ourselves to have some measure of prevision; and we are not at fault if we leave on one side the extreme chances of human existence and of revolutionary changes in the order of Nature or of man's relations to her. The fact that we have no adequate knowledge of Germany's capacity to pay over a long period of years is no justification (as I have heard some people claim that it is) for the statement that she can pay ten thousand million pounds.

Why has the world been so credulous of the unveracities of politicians? If an explanation is needed, I attribute this particular credulity to the following influences in part.

In the first place, the vast expenditures of the war, the inflation of prices, and the depreciation of currency, leading up to a complete instability of the unit of value, have made us lose all sense of number and magnitude in matters of finance. What we believed to be the limits of possibility have been so enormously exceeded, and those who founded their expectations on the past have been so often wrong, that the man in the street is now prepared to believe anything which is told him with some show of authority, and the larger the figure the more readily he swallows it.

But those who look into the matter more deeply are sometimes misled by a fallacy, much more plausible to reasonable persons. Such a one might base his conclusions on Germany's total surplus of annual productivity as distinct from her export surplus. Helfferich's estimate of Germany's annual increment of wealth in 1913 was £400 million to £425 million (exclusive of increased money value of existing land and property). Before the war, Germany spent between £50 million and £100 million on armaments, with which she can now dispense. Why, therefore, should she not pay over to the Allies an annual sum of £500 million? This puts the crude argument in its strongest and most plausible form.

But there are two errors in it. First of all, Germany's annual savings, after what she has suffered in the war and by the Peace, will fall far short of what they were before and, if they are taken from her year by year in future, they cannot again reach their previous level. The loss of Alsace-Lorraine, Poland, and Upper Silesia could not be assessed in terms of surplus productivity at less than £50 million annually. Germany is supposed to have profited about £100 million per annum from her ships, her foreign investments, and her foreign banking and connections, all of which have now been taken from her. Her saving on armaments is far more than balanced by her annual charge for pensions now estimated at £250 million,[1] which represents a real loss of productive capacity. And even if we put on one side the burden of the internal debt, which amounts to 240 milliards of marks, as being a question of internal distribution rather than of productivity, we must still allow for the foreign debt incurred by Germany during the war, the exhaustion of her stock of raw materials, the depletion of her live-stock, the impaired productivity of her soil from lack of manures and of labour, and the diminution in her wealth from the failure to keep up many repairs and renewals over a period of nearly five years. Germany is not as rich as she was before the war, and the diminution in her future savings for these reasons, quite apart from the factors previously allowed for, could hardly be put at less than ten per cent, that is £40 million annually.

These factors have already reduced Germany's annual surplus to less than the £100 million at which we arrived on other grounds as the maximum of her annual payments. But even if

---

[1] The conversion at par of 5,000 million marks overstates by reason of the existing depreciation of the mark, the present money burden of the actual payments, but not, in all probability, the real loss of national productivity as a result of the casualties suffered in the war.

the rejoinder be made, that we have not yet allowed for the lowering of the standard of life and comfort in Germany which may reasonably be imposed on a defeated enemy, there is still a fundamental fallacy in the method of calculation. An annual surplus available for home investment can only be converted into a surplus available for export abroad by a radical change in the kind of work performed. Labour, while it may be available and efficient for domestic services in Germany, may yet be able to find no outlet in foreign trade. We are back on the same question which faced us in our examination of the export trade— in *what* export trade is German labour going to find a greatly increased outlet? Labour can only be diverted into new channels with loss of efficiency, and a large expenditure of capital. The annual surplus which German labour can produce for capital improvements at home is no measure, either theoretically, or practically, of the annual tribute which she can pay abroad.

I cannot leave this subject as though its just treatment wholly depended either on our own pledges or on economic facts. The policy of reducing Germany to servitude for a generation, of degrading the lives of millions of human beings, and of depriving a whole nation of happiness should be abhorrent and detestable —abhorrent and detestable, even if it were possible, even if it enriched ourselves, even if it did not sow the decay of the whole civilised life of Europe. Some preach it in the name of justice. In the great events of man's history, in the unwinding of the complex fates of nations justice is not so simple. And if it were, nations are not authorised, by religion or by natural morals, to visit on the children of their enemies the misdoings of parents or of rulers.

3 PROPOSALS FOR THE
RECONSTRUCTION OF EUROPE (1919)

From *The Economic Consequences of the Peace*, chapter VII, 'Remedies'

I THE REVISION OF THE TREATY

Are any constitutional means open to us for altering the Treaty? President Wilson and General Smuts, who believe that to have secured the Covenant of the League of Nations outweighs much evil in the rest of the Treaty, have indicated that we must look to the League for the gradual evolution of a more tolerable life for Europe. 'There are territorial settlements', General Smuts wrote in his statement on signing the Peace Treaty, 'which will need revision. There are guarantees laid down which we all hope will soon be found out of harmony with the new peaceful temper and unarmed state of our former enemies. There are punishments foreshadowed over most of which a calmer mood may yet prefer to pass the sponge of oblivion. There are indemnities stipulated which cannot be exacted without grave injury to the industrial revival of Europe, and which it will be in the interests of all to render more tolerable and moderate...I am confident that the League of Nations will yet prove the path of escape for Europe out of the ruin brought about by this war.' Without the League, President Wilson informed the Senate when he presented the Treaty to them early in July 1919, '...long-continued supervision of the task of reparation which Germany was to undertake to complete within the next generation might entirely break down; the reconsideration and revision of administrative arrangements and restrictions which the Treaty prescribed, but which it recognised might not provide lasting advantage or be entirely fair if too long enforced, would be impracticable'.

Can we look forward with fair hopes to securing from the

operation of the League those benefits which two of its principal begetters thus encourage us to expect from it? The relevant passage is to be found in Article XIX of the Covenant, which runs as follows:

The Assembly may from time to time advise the reconsideration by Members of the League of treaties which have become inapplicable and the consideration of international conditions whose continuance might endanger the peace of the world.

But alas! Article v provides that 'Except where otherwise expressly provided in this Covenant or by the terms of the present Treaty, decisions at any meeting of the Assembly or of the Council shall require the agreement of all the Members of the League represented at the meeting'. Does not this provision reduce the League, so far as concerns an early reconsideration of any of the terms of the Peace Treaty, into a body merely for wasting time? If all the parties to the Treaty are unanimously of opinion that it requires alteration in a particular sense, it does not need a League and a Covenant to put the business through. Even when the Assembly of the League is unanimous it can only 'advise' reconsideration by the members specially affected.

But the League will operate, say its supporters, by its influence on the public opinion of the world, and the view of the majority will carry decisive weight in practice, even though constitutionally it is of no effect. Let us pray that this be so. Yet the League in the hands of the trained European diplomatist may become an unequalled instrument for obstruction and delay. The revision of treaties is entrusted primarily, not to the Council, which meets frequently, but to the Assembly, which will meet more rarely and must become, as any one with an experience of large inter-ally conferences must know, an unwieldy polyglot debating society in which the greatest resolution and the best management may fail altogether to bring issues to a head against an opposition in favour of the *status quo*. There are indeed two disastrous blots on the Covenant—Article v, which prescribes unanimity, and the much-criticised Article x, by which 'The Members of the

League undertake to respect and preserve as against external aggression the territorial integrity and existing political independence of all Members of the League.' These two articles together go some way to destroy the conception of the League as an instrument of progress, and to equip it from the outset with an almost fatal bias towards the *status quo*. It is these articles which have reconciled to the League some of its original opponents, who now hope to make of it another Holy Alliance for the perpetuation of the economic ruin of their enemies and the balance of power in their own interests which they believe themselves to have established by the Peace.

But while it would be wrong and foolish to conceal from ourselves in the interests of 'idealism' the real difficulties of the position in the special matter of revising treaties, that is no reason for any of us to decry the League, which the wisdom of the world may yet transform into a powerful instrument of peace, and which in Articles XI–XVII[1] has already accomplished a great and beneficent achievement. I agree, therefore, that our first efforts for the revision of the Treaty must be made through the League rather than in any other way, in the hope that the force of general opinion, and if necessary, the use of financial pressure and financial inducements, may be enough to prevent a recalcitrant minority from exercising their right of veto. We must trust the new governments, whose existence I premise in the principal Allied countries, to show a profounder wisdom and a greater magnanimity than their predecessors.

I do not intend to enter here into details, or to attempt a revision of the Treaty clause by clause. I limit myself to three great changes which are necessary for the economic life of Europe, relating to reparation, to coal and iron, and to tariffs.

Reparation. If the sum demanded for reparation is less than what the Allies are entitled to on a strict interpretation of their

---

[1] These articles, which provide safeguards against the outbreak of war between members of the League and also between members and non-members, are the solid achievement of the Covenant. These articles make substantially less probable a war between organised great powers such as that of 1914. This alone should commend the League to all men.

engagements, it is unnecessary to particularise the items it represents or to hear arguments about its compilation. I suggest, therefore, the following settlement:

(1) The amount of the payment to be made by Germany in respect of reparation and the costs of the armies of occupation might be fixed at £2,000 million.

(2) The surrender of merchant ships and submarine cables under the Treaty, of war material under the Armistice, of state property in ceded territory, of claims against such territory in respect of public debt, and of Germany's claims against her former allies, should be reckoned as worth the lump sum of £500 million, without any attempt being made to evaluate them item by item.

(3) The balance of £1,500 million should not carry interest pending its repayment, and should be paid by Germany in thirty annual instalments of £50 million, beginning in 1923.

(4) The Reparation Commission should be dissolved or, if any duties remain for it to perform, it should become an appanage of the League of Nations and should include representatives of Germany and of the neutral states.

(5) Germany would be left to meet the annual instalments in such manner as she might see fit, any complaint against her for non-fulfilment of her obligations being lodged with the League of Nations. That is to say, there would be no further expropriation of German private property abroad, except so far as is required to meet private German obligations out of the proceeds of such property already liquidated or in the hands of Public Trustees and Enemy-Property Custodians in the Allied countries and in the United States; and, in particular, Article 260 (which provides for the expropriation of German interests in public utility enterprises) would be abrogated.

(6) No attempt should be made to extract reparation payments from Austria.

Coal and iron. (1) The Allies' options on coal under Annex v should be abandoned, but Germany's obligation to make good

France's loss of coal through the destruction of her mines should remain. This obligation should lapse, nevertheless, in the event of the coal districts of Upper Silesia being taken from Germany in the final settlement consequent on the plebiscite.

(2) The arrangement as to the Saar should hold good, except that, on the one hand, Germany should receive no credit for the mines, and, on the other should receive back both the mines and the territory without payment and unconditionally after ten years. But this should be conditional on France's entering into an agreement for the same period to supply Germany from Lorraine with at least 50 per cent of the iron ore which was carried from Lorraine into Germany proper before the war, in return for an undertaking from Germany to supply Lorraine with an amount of coal equal to the whole amount formerly sent to Lorraine from Germany proper, after allowing for the output of the Saar.

(3) The arrangement as to Upper Silesia should hold good. That is to say, a plebiscite should be held, and in coming to a final decision 'regard will be paid (by the principal Allied and Associated Powers) to the wishes of the inhabitants as shown by the vote, and to the geographical and economic conditions of the locality'. But the Allies should declare that in their judgement 'economic conditions' require the inclusion of the coal districts in Germany unless the wishes of the inhabitants are decidedly to the contrary.

Tariffs. A Free Trade Union should be established under the auspices of the League of Nations of countries undertaking to impose no protectionist tariffs[1] whatever against the produce of other members of the Union. Germany, Poland, the new states which formerly composed the Austro-Hungarian and Turkish empires, and the mandated states should be compelled

---

[1] It would be expedient so to define a 'protectionist tariff' as to permit (*a*) the total prohibition of certain imports; (*b*) the imposition of sumptuary or revenue customs duties on commodities not produced at home; (*c*) the imposition of customs duties which did not exceed by more than five per cent a countervailing excise on similar commodities produced at home; (*d*) export duties. Further, special exceptions might be permitted by a majority vote of the countries entering the Union. Duties which had existed for five years prior to a country's entering the Union might be allowed to disappear gradually by equal instalments spread over the five years subsequent to joining the Union.

to adhere to this Union for ten years, after which time adherence would be voluntary. The adherence of other states would be voluntary from the outset. But it is to be hoped that the United Kingdom, at any rate, would become an original member.

By fixing the reparation payments well within Germany's capacity to pay, we make possible the renewal of hope and enterprise within her territory, we avoid the perpetual friction and opportunity of improper pressure arising out of Treaty clauses which are impossible of fulfilment, and we render unnecessary the intolerable powers of the Reparation Commission.

By a moderation of the clauses relating directly or indirectly to coal, and by the exchange of iron ore, we permit the continuance of Germany's industrial life, and put limits on the loss of productivity which would be brought about otherwise by the interference of political frontiers with the natural localisation of the iron and steel industry.

By the proposed Free Trade Union some part of the loss of organisation and economic efficiency may be retrieved, which must otherwise result from the innumerable new political frontiers now created between greedy, jealous, immature, and economically incomplete, nationalist States. Economic frontiers were tolerable so long as an immense territory was included in a few great empires; but they will not be tolerable when the empires of Germany, Austria-Hungary, Russia, and Turkey have been partitioned between some twenty independent authorities. A Free Trade Union, comprising the whole of central, eastern, and south-eastern Europe, Siberia, Turkey, and (I should hope) the United Kingdom, Egypt, and India, might do as much for the peace and prosperity of the world as the League of Nations itself. Belgium, Holland, Scandinavia, and Switzerland might be expected to adhere to it shortly. And it would be greatly to be desired by their friends that France and Italy also should see their way to adhesion.

It would be objected, I suppose, by some critics that such an arrangement might go some way in effect towards realising the former German dream of Mittel-Europa. If other countries were so foolish as to remain outside the Union and to leave to Germany all its advantages, there might be some truth in this. But an economic system, to which everyone had the opportunity of belonging and which gave special privilege to none, is surely absolutely free from the objections of a privileged and avowedly imperialistic scheme of exclusion and discrimination. Our attitude to these criticisms must be determined by our whole moral and emotional reaction to the future of international relations and the peace of the world. If we take the view that for at least a generation to come Germany cannot be trusted with even a modicum of prosperity, that while all our recent Allies are angels of light, all our recent enemies, Germans, Austrians, Hungarians, and the rest, are children of the devil, that year by year Germany must be kept impoverished and her children starved and crippled, and that she must be ringed round by enemies; then we shall reject all the proposals of this chapter, and particularly those which may assist Germany to regain a part of her former material prosperity and find a means of livelihood for the industrial population of her towns. But if this view of nations and of their relation to one another is adopted by the democracies of Western Europe, and is financed by the United States, heaven help us all. If we aim deliberately at the impoverishment of Central Europe, vengeance, I dare predict, will not limp. Nothing can then delay for very long that final civil war between the forces of reaction and the despairing convulsions of revolution, before which the horrors of the late German war will fade into nothing, and which will destroy, whoever is victor, the civilisation and the progress of our generation. Even though the result disappoint us, must we not base our actions on better expectations, and believe that the prosperity and happiness of one country promotes that of others, that the solidarity of man is not a fiction, and that nations can still afford to treat other nations as fellow-creatures?

Such changes as I have proposed above might do something appreciable to enable the industrial populations of Europe to continue to earn a livelihood. But they would not be enough by themselves. In particular, France would be a loser on paper (on paper only, for she will never secure the actual fulfilment of her present claims), and an escape from her embarrassments must be shown her in some other direction. I procced, therefore, to proposals, first, for the adjustment of the claims of America and the Allies amongst themselves; and second, for the provision of sufficient credit to enable Europe to re-create her stock of circulating capital.

II THE SETTLEMENT OF INTER-ALLY INDEBTEDNESS

In proposing a modification of the reparation terms, I have considered them so far only in relation to Germany. But fairness requires that so great a reduction in the amount should be accompanied by a readjustment of its apportionment between the Allies themselves. The professions which our statesmen made on every platform during the war, as well as other considerations, surely require that the areas damaged by the enemy's invasion should receive a priority of compensation. While this was one of the ultimate objects for which we said we were fighting, we never included the recovery of separation allowances amongst our war aims. I suggest, therefore, that we should by our acts prove ourselves sincere and trustworthy, and that accordingly Great Britain should waive altogether her claims for cash payment, in favour of Belgium, Serbia, and France. The whole of the payments made by Germany would then be subject to the prior charge of repairing the material injury done to those countries and provinces which suffered actual invasion by the enemy; and I believe that the sum of £1,500 million thus available would be adequate to cover entirely the actual costs of restoration. Further, it is only by a complete subordination of her own claims for cash compensation that Great Britain can ask with clean hands for a revision of the Treaty and clear her honour from the breach of faith for which she bears the main responsibility, as a result of the policy to which the General Election of 1918 pledged her representatives.

With the reparation problem thus cleared up it would be possible to bring forward with a better grace and more hope of success two other financial proposals, each of which involves an appeal to the generosity of the United States.

The first is for the entire cancellation of inter-Ally indebtedness (that is to say, indebtedness between the governments of the Allied and Associated countries) incurred for the purposes of the war. This proposal, which has been put forward already in certain quarters, is one which I believe to be absolutely essential to the future prosperity of the world. It would be an act of far-seeing statesmanship for the United Kingdom and the United States, the two powers chiefly concerned, to adopt it. The sums of money (in millions of pounds) which are involved are shown approximately in the following table.[1]

Loans to	By United States £	By United Kingdom £	By France £	Total £
United Kingdom	842	—	—	842
France	550	508	—	1,058
Italy	325	467	35	827
Russia	38	568	160	766
Belgium	80	98	90	268
Serbia and Jugoslavia	20	20	20	60
Other allies	35	79	50	164
Total	1,900	1,740	355	3,995

Thus the total volume of inter-Ally indebtedness, assuming that loans from one Ally are not set off against loans to another, is nearly £4,000 million. The United States is a lender only. The United Kingdom has lent about twice as much as she has borrowed. France has borrowed about three times as much as she has lent. The other Allies have been borrowers only.

[1] The figures in this table are partly estimated, and are probably not completely accurate in detail.

If all the above inter-Ally indebtedness were mutually forgiven, the net result on paper (i.e. assuming all the loans to be good) would be a surrender by the United States of about £2,000 million and by the United Kingdom of about £900 million. France would gain about £700 million and Italy about £800 million. But these figures overstate the loss to the United Kingdom and understate the gain to France; for a large part of the loans made by both these countries has been to Russia and cannot, by any stretch of imagination, be considered good. If the loans which the United Kingdom has made to her Allies are reckoned to be worth 50 per cent of their full value (an arbitrary but convenient assumption which the Chancellor of the Exchequer has adopted on more than one occasion as being as good as any other for the purposes of an approximate national balance sheet), the operation would involve her neither in loss nor in gain. But in whatever way the net result is calculated on paper, the relief in anxiety which such a liquidation of the position would carry with it would be very great. It is from the United States, therefore, that the proposal asks generosity.

Speaking with a very intimate knowledge of the relations throughout the war between the British, the American, and the other Allied Treasuries, I believe this to be an act of generosity for which Europe can fairly ask, provided Europe is making an honourable attempt in other directions, not to continue war, economic or otherwise, but to achieve the economic reconstitution of the whole continent. The financial sacrifices of the United States have been, in proportion to her wealth, immensely less than those of the European states. This could hardly have been otherwise. It was a European quarrel, in which the United States government could not have justified itself before its citizens in expending the whole national strength, as did the Europeans. After the United States came into the war her financial assistance was lavish and unstinted, and without this assistance the Allies could never have won the war, quite apart from the decisive influence of the arrival of the American troops.

But in speaking thus as we do of American financial assistance, we tacitly assume, and America, I believe, assumed it too when she gave the money, that it was not in the nature of an investment. If Europe is going to repay the £2,000 million worth of financial assistance which she has had from the United States with compound interest at 5 per cent, the matter takes on quite a different complexion. If America's advances are to be regarded in this light, her relative financial sacrifice has been very slight indeed.

Failing such a settlement as is now proposed, the war will have ended with a network of heavy tribute payable from one Ally to another. The total amount of this tribute is even likely to exceed the amount obtainable from the enemy; and the war will have ended with the intolerable result of the Allies paying indemnities to one another instead of receiving them from the enemy.

For this reason the question of inter-Allied indebtedness is closely bound up with the intense popular feeling amongst the European Allies on the question of indemnities—a feeling which is based, not on any reasonable calculation of what Germany can, in fact, pay, but on a well-founded appreciation of the unbearable financial situation in which these countries will find themselves unless she pays. Take Italy as an extreme example. If Italy can reasonably be expected to pay £800 million, surely Germany can and ought to pay an immeasurably higher figure. Or if it is decided (as it must be) that Austria can pay next to nothing, is it not an intolerable conclusion that Italy should be loaded with a crushing tribute, while Austria escapes? Or, to put it slightly differently, how can Italy be expected to submit to payment of this great sum and see Czechoslovakia pay little or nothing? At the other end of the scale there is the United Kingdom. Here the financial position is different, since to ask us to pay £800 million is a very different proposition from asking Italy to pay it. But the sentiment is much the same. If we have to be satisfied without full compensation from Germany, how bitter will be the protests against paying it to the United States. We, it will be said, have to be content with a claim against the bankrupt estates of Germany, France, Italy, and Russia, whereas the United States has secured a first mortgage upon us. The case of France is at least as overwhelming. She can barely secure from Germany the full measure of the destruction of her countryside. Yet victorious France must pay her friends and Allies more than four times the indemnity which in the defeat of 1870 she paid Germany. The hand of Bismark was light compared with that of an Ally or of an Associate. A settlement of inter-Ally indebtedness is, therefore, an indispensable preliminary to the peoples of the Allied countries facing, with other than a maddened and exasperated heart, the inevitable truth about the prospects of an indemnity from the enemy.

It might be an exaggeration to say that it is impossible for the European Allies to pay the capital and interest due from them on these debts, but to make them do so would certainly be to impose a crushing burden. They may be expected, therefore, to make constant attempts to evade or escape payment, and these attempts will be a constant source of international friction and ill-will for many years to come. A debtor nation does not love its creditor, and it is fruitless to expect feelings of goodwill from France, Italy, and Russia towards this country or towards America, if their future development is stifled for many years to come by the annual tribute which they must pay us. There will be a great incentive to them to seek their friends in other directions, and any future rupture of peacable relations will always carry with it the enormous advantage of escaping the payment of external debts. If, on the other hand, these great debts are forgiven, a stimulus will be given to the solidarity and true friendliness of the nations lately associated.

The existence of the great war debts is a menace to financial stability everywhere. There is no European country in which repudiation may not soon become an important political issue.

In the case of internal debt, however, there are interested parties on both sides, and the question is one of the internal distribution of wealth. With external debts this is not so, and the creditor nations may soon find their interest inconveniently bound up with their maintenance of a particular type of government or economic organisation in the debtor countries. Entangling alliances or entangling leagues are nothing to the entanglements of cash owing.

The final consideration influencing the reader's attitude to this proposal must, however, depend on his view as to the future place in the world's progress of the vast paper entanglements which are our legacy from war finance both at home and abroad. The war has ended with everyone owing everyone else immense sums of money. Germany owes a large sum to the Allies; the Allies owe a large sum to Great Britain; and Great Britain owes a large sum to the United States. The holders of war loan in every country are owed a large sum by the State; and the State in its turn is owed a large sum by these and other taxpayers. The whole position is in the highest degree artificial, misleading, and vexatious. We shall never be able to move again, unless we can free our limbs from these paper shackles. A general bonfire is so great a necessity that unless we can make of it an orderly and good-tempered affair in which no serious injustice is done to anyone, it will, when it comes at last, grow into a conflagration that may destroy much else as well. As regards internal debt, I am one of those who believe that a capital levy for the extinction of debt is an absolute prerequisite of sound finance in every one of the European belligerent countries. But the continuance on a huge scale of indebtedness between governments has special dangers of its own.

Before the middle of the nineteenth century no nation owed payments to a foreign nation on any considerable scale, except such tributes as were exacted under the compulsion of actual occupation in force and, at one time, by absentee princes under

26

the sanctions of feudalism. It is true that the need for European capitalism to find an outlet in the New World has led during the past fifty years, though even now on a relatively modest scale, to such countries as Argentina owing an annual sum to such countries as England. But the system is fragile; and it has only survived because its burden on the paying countries has not so far been oppressive, because this burden is represented by real assets and is bound up with the property system generally, and because the sums already lent are not unduly large in relation to those which it is still hoped to borrow. Bankers are used to this system, and believe it to be a necessary part of the permanent order of society. They are disposed to believe, therefore, by analogy with it, that a comparable system between governments, on a far vaster and definitely oppressive scale, represented by no real assets, and less closely associated with the property system, is natural and reasonable and in conformity with human nature.

I doubt this view of the world. Even capitalism at home, which engages many local sympathies, which plays a real part in the daily process of production, and upon the security of which the present organisation of Society largely depends, is not very safe. But however this may be, will the discontented peoples of Europe be willing for a generation to come so to order their lives that an appreciable part of their daily produce may be available to meet a foreign payment, the reason of which, whether as between Europe and America, or as between Germany and the rest of Europe, does not spring compellingly from their sense of justice or duty?

On the one hand, Europe must depend in the long run on her own daily labour and not on the largesse of America; but, on the other hand, she will not pinch herself in order that the fruit of her daily labour may go elsewhere. In short, I do not believe that any of these tributes will continue to be paid, at the best, for more than a very few years. They do not square with human nature or agree with the spirit of the age.

27

If there is any force in this mode of thought, expediency and generosity agree together, and the policy which will best promote immediate friendship between nations will not conflict with the permanent interests of the benefactors.

III AN INTERNATIONAL LOAN

I pass to a second financial proposal. The requirements of Europe are *immediate*. The prospect of being relieved of oppressive interest payments to England and America over the whole life of the next two generations (and of receiving from Germany some assistance year by year to the costs of restoration) would free the future from excessive anxiety. But it would not meet the ills of the immediate present—the excess of Europe's imports over her exports, the adverse exchange, and the disorder of the currency. It will be very difficult for European production to get started again without a temporary measure of external assistance. I am therefore a supporter of an international loan in some shape or form, such as has been advocated in many quarters in France, Germany, and England, and also in the United States. In whatever way the ultimate responsibility for repayment is distributed, the burden of finding the immediate resources must inevitably fall in major part upon the United States.

The chief objections to all the varieties of this species of project are, I suppose, the following. The United States is disinclined to entangle herself further (after recent experiences) in the affairs of Europe and, anyhow, has for the time being no more capital to spare for export on a large scale. There is no guarantee that Europe will put financial assistance to proper use, or that she will not squander it and be in just as bad case two or three years hence as she is in now—M. Klotz will use the money to put off the day of taxation a little longer, Italy and Jugoslavia will fight one another on the proceeds, Poland will devote it to fulfilling towards all her neighbours the military role which France has designed for her, the governing classes

28

of Roumania will divide up the booty amongst themselves. In short, America would have postponed her own capital developments and raised her own cost of living in order that Europe might continue for another year or two the practices, the policy, and the men of the past nine months. And as for assistance to Germany, is it reasonable or at all tolerable that the European allies, having stripped Germany of her last vestige of working capital, in opposition to the arguments and appeals of the American financial representatives at Paris, should then turn to the United States for funds to rehabilitate the victim in sufficient measure to allow the spoliation to recommence in a year or two?

There is no answer to these objections as matters are now. If I had influence at the United States Treasury, I would not lend a penny to a single one of the present governments of Europe. They are not to be trusted with resources which they would devote to the furtherance of policies in repugnance to which, in spite of the President's failure to assert either the might or the ideals of the people of the United States, the Republican and the Democratic parties are probably united. But if, as we must pray they will, the souls of the European peoples turn away this winter from the false idols which have survived the war that created them, and substitute in their hearts for the hatred and the nationalism, which now possess them, thoughts and hopes of the happiness and solidarity of the European family—then should natural piety and filial love impel the American people to put on one side all the smaller objections of private advantage and to complete the work that they began in saving Europe from the tyranny of organised force, by saving her from herself. And even if the conversion is not fully accomplished, and some parties only in each of the European countries have espoused a policy of reconciliation, America can still point the way and hold up the hands of the party of peace by having a plan and a condition on which she will give her aid to the work of renewing life.

The impulse which, we are told, is now strong in the mind of the United States to be quit of the turmoil, the complication, the violence, the expense and, above all, the unintelligibility of the European problems, is easily understood. No one can feel more intensely than the writer how natural it is to retort to the folly and impracticability of the European statesmen—Rot, then, in your own malice, and we will go our way—

> Remote from Europe; from her blasted hopes;
> Her fields of carnage, and polluted air.

But if America recalls for a moment what Europe has meant to her and still means to her, what Europe, the mother of art and of knowledge, in spite of everything, still is and still will be, will she not reject these counsels of indifference and isolation, and interest herself in what may prove decisive issues for the progress and civilisation of all mankind?

Assuming then, if only to keep our hopes up, that America will be prepared to contribute to the process of building up the good forces of Europe, and will not, having completed the destruction of an enemy, leave us to our misfortunes—what form should her aid take?

I do not propose to enter on details. But the main outlines of all schemes for an international loan are much the same. The countries in a position to lend assistance, the neutrals, the United Kingdom and, for the greater portion of the sum required, the United States, must provide foreign purchasing credits for all the belligerent countries of continental Europe, Allied and ex-enemy alike. The aggregate sum required might not be so large as is sometimes supposed. Much might be done, perhaps, with a fund of £200 million in the first instance. This sum, even if a precedent of a different kind had been established by the cancellation of inter-Ally war debt, should be lent and should be borrowed with the unequivocal intention of its being repaid in full. With this object in view, the security for the loan should be the best obtainable, and the arrangements for its ultimate repayment as complete as possible. In particular, it should rank, both for payment of interest and discharge of capital, in front of all reparation claims, all inter-Ally war debt, all internal war loans, and all other government indebtedness of any other kind. Those borrowing countries who will be entitled to reparation payments should be required to pledge all such receipts to repayment of the new loan. And all the borrowing countries should be required to place their customs duties on a gold basis and to pledge such receipts to its service.

Expenditure out of the loan should be subject to general, but not detailed, supervision by the lending countries.

If, in addition to this loan for the purchase of food and materials, a guarantee fund were established up to an equal amount, namely £200 million (of which it would probably prove necessary to find only a part in cash), to which all members of the League of Nations would contribute according to their means, it might be practicable to base upon it a general re-organisation of the currency.

In this manner Europe might be equipped with the minimum amount of liquid resources necessary to revive her hopes, to renew her economic organisation, and to enable her great intrinsic wealth to function for the benefit of her workers. It is useless at the present time to elaborate such schemes in further detail. A great change is necessary in public opinion before the proposals of this chapter can enter the region of political politics, and we must await the progress of events as patiently as we can.

I see few signs of sudden or dramatic developments anywhere. Riots and revolutions there may be, but not such, at present, as to have fundamental significance. Against political tyranny and injustice revolution is a weapon. But what counsels of hope can revolution offer to sufferers from economic privation, which does not arise out of the injustices of distribution but is general? The only safeguard against revolution in central Europe is indeed the fact that, even to the minds of men who are desperate, revolution offers no prospect of improvement whatever. There may, therefore, be ahead of us a long, silent process of semi-starvation and of a gradual, steady lowering of the standards of life and comfort. The bankruptcy and decay of Europe, if we allow it to proceed, will affect every one in the long run, but perhaps not in a way that is striking or immediate.

This has one fortunate side. We may still have time to re-consider our courses and to view the world with new eyes. For the immediate future events are taking charge, and the near destiny of Europe is no longer in the hands of any man. The events of the coming year will not be shaped by the deliberate acts of statesmen, but by the hidden currents, flowing continually beneath the surface of political history, of which no one can predict the outcome. In one way only can we influence these hidden currents—by setting in motion those forces of instruction and imagination which change *opinion*. The assertion of truth, the unveiling of illusion, the dissipation of hate, the enlargement and instruction of men's hearts and minds, must be the means.

4 THE CHANGE OF OPINION (1921)

From *A Revision of the Treaty* (1922), chapter 1, 'The State of Opinion'.

It is the method of modern statesmen to talk as much folly as the public demand and to practise no more of it than is compatible with what they have said, trusting that such folly in action as must wait on folly in word will soon disclose itself as such, and furnish an opportunity for slipping back into wisdom —the Montessori system for the child, the public. He who contradicts this child will soon give place to other tutors. Praise, therefore, the beauty of the flames he wishes to touch, the music of the breaking toy; even urge him forward; yet waiting with vigilant care, the wise and kindly saviour of society, for the right moment to snatch him back, just singed and now attentive.

I can conceive for this terrifying statesmanship a plausible defence. Mr Lloyd George took the responsibility for a Treaty of Peace, which was not wise, which was partly impossible, and which endangered the life of Europe. He may defend himself by saying that he knew that it was not wise and was partly impossible and endangered the life of Europe; but that public passions and public ignorance play a part in the world of which he who aspires to lead a democracy must take account; that the Peace at Versailles was the best momentary settlement which the demands of the mob and the characters of the chief actors conjoined to permit; and for the life of Europe, that he has spent his skill and strength for two years in avoiding or moderating the dangers.

Such claims would be partly true and cannot be brushed away. The private history of the Peace Conference, as it has been disclosed by French and American participators, displays Mr Lloyd George in a partly favourable light, generally striving against the excesses of the Treaty and doing what he could,

33

short of risking a personal defeat. The public history of the two years which have followed it exhibit him as protecting Europe from as many of the evil consequences of his own Treaty, as it lay in his power to prevent, with a craft few could have bettered, preserving the peace, though not the prosperity, of Europe, seldom expressing the truth, yet often acting under its influence. He would claim, therefore, that by devious paths, a faithful servant of the possible, he was serving man.

He may judge rightly that this is the best of which a democracy is capable—to be jockeyed, humbugged, cajoled along the right road. A preference for truth or for sincerity *as a method* may be a prejudice based on some aesthetic or personal standard, inconsistent, in politics, with practical good.

We cannot yet tell. Even the public learns by experience. Will the charm work still, when the stock of statesmen's credibility, accumulated before these times, is getting exhausted?

In any event, private individuals are not under the same obligation as cabinet ministers to sacrifice veracity to the public weal. It is a permitted self-indulgence for a private person to speak and write freely. Perhaps it may even contribute one ingredient to the congeries of things which the wands of statesmen cause to work together, so marvellously, for our ultimate good.

For these reasons I do not admit error in having based *The Economic Consequences of the Peace* on a literal interpretation of the Treaty of Versailles, or in having examined the results of actually carrying it out. I argued that much of it was *impossible*; but I do not agree with many critics, who held that, for this very reason, it was also harmless. Inside opinion accepted from the beginning many of my main conclusions about the Treaty. But it was not therefore unimportant that outside opinion should accept them also.

For there are, in the present times, two opinions; not, as in former ages, the true and the false, but the outside and the inside; the opinion of the public voiced by the politicians and the newspapers, and the opinion of the politicians, the journalists and the civil servants, upstairs and backstairs and behind-stairs, expressed in limited circles.

Those who live in the limited circles and share the inside opinion pay both too much and too little attention to the outside opinion; too much, because, ready in words and promises to concede to it everything, they regard open opposition as absurdly futile; too little, because they believe that these words and promises are so certainly destined to change in due season, that it is pedantic, tiresome, and inappropriate to analyse their literal meaning and exact consequences. They know all this nearly as well as the critic, who wastes, in their view, his time and his emotions in exciting himself too much over what, on his own showing, cannot possibly happen. Nevertheless, what is said before the world is, still, of deeper consequence than the subterranean breathings and well-informed whisperings, knowledge of which allows inside opinion to feel superior to outside opinion, even at the moment of bowing to it.

But there is a further complication. In England (and perhaps elsewhere also) there are *two* outside opinions, that which is expressed in the newspapers and that which the mass of ordinary men privately suspect to be true. These two degrees of the outside opinion are much nearer to one another than they are to the inside, and under some aspects they are identical; yet there is under the surface a real difference between the dogmatism and definiteness of the press and the living, indefinite belief of the individual man. I fancy that even in 1919 the average Englishman never really believed in the indemnity; he took it always with a grain of salt, with a measure of intellectual doubt. But it seemed to him that for the time being there could be little practical harm in going on the indemnity tack, and also that, in relation to his feelings at that time, a belief in the possibility of boundless payments by Germany was in better sentiment, even if less true, than the contrary. Thus the recent modification in British outside opinion is only partly intellectual, and is due

35

rather to changed conditions; for it is seen that perseverance with the indemnity does now involve practical harm, whilst the claims of sentiment are no longer so decisive. He is therefore prepared to attend to arguments, of which he had always been aware out of the corner of his eye.

Foreign observers are apt to heed too little these unspoken sensibilities, which the voice of the press is bound to express ultimately. Inside opinion gradually affects them by percolating to wider and wider circles; and they are susceptible in time to argument, common sense, or self-interest. It is the business of the modern politician to be accurately aware of all three degrees; he must have enough intellect to understand the inside opinion, enough sympathy to detect the inner outside opinion, and enough brass to express the outer outside opinion.

Whether this account is true or fanciful, there can be no doubt as to the immense change in public sentiment over the past two years. The desire for a quiet life, for reduced commitments, for comfortable terms with our neighbours is now paramount. The megalomania of war has passed away, and every one wishes to conform himself with the facts. For these reasons the reparation chapter of the Treaty of Versailles is crumbling. There is little prospect now of the disastrous consequences of its fulfilment.

5 WAR DEBTS AND THE UNITED STATES

CANCELLATION (1921)

From *A Revision of the Treaty*, chapter 6, 'Reparation, Inter-Ally Debt and International Trade', and chapter 7, 'The Revision of the Treaty and the Settlement of Europe'.

Who believes that the Allies will, over a period of one or two generations, exert adequate force over the German government, or that the German government can exert adequate authority over its subjects, to extract continuing fruits on a vast scale from forced labour? No one believes it in his heart; no one at all. There is not the faintest possibility of our persisting with this affair to the end. But if this is so, then, most certainly, it will not be worth our while to disorder our export trades and disturb the equilibrium of our industry for two or three years; much less to endanger the peace of Europe.

The same principles apply with one modification to the United States and to the exaction by her of the debts which the Allied governments owe. The industries of the United States would suffer, not so much from the competition of cheap goods from the Allies in their endeavours to pay their debts, as from the inability of the Allies to purchase from America their usual proportion of her exports. The Allies would have to find the money to pay America, not so much by selling more as by buying less. The farmers of the United States would suffer more than the manufacturers; if only because increased imports can be kept out by a tariff, whilst there is no such easy way of stimulating diminished exports. It is, however, a curious fact that whilst Wall Street and the manufacturing East are prepared to consider a modification of the debts, the Middle West and South is reported (I write ignorantly) to be dead against it. For two years Germany was not required to pay cash to the Allies, and during that period the manufacturers of Great Britain were quite blind to what the consequences would be to themselves when the payments actually began. The Allies have not yet been required to begin to pay cash to the United States, and the farmers of the latter are still as blind as were the British manufacturers to the injuries they will suffer if the Allies ever try seriously to pay in full.

The decisive argument, however, for the United States, as for Great Britain, is not the damage to particular interests (which would diminish with time), but the unlikelihood of permanence in the exaction of the debts, even if they were paid for a short period. I say this, not only because I doubt the ability of the European Allies to pay, but because of the great difficulty of the problem which the United States has before her in any case in balancing her commercial account with the Old World.

American economists have examined somewhat carefully the statistical measure of the change from the pre-war position. According to their estimates, America is now owed more interest on foreign investments than is due from her, quite apart from the interest on the debts of the Allied governments; and her mercantile marine now earns from foreigners more than she owes them for similar services. Her excess of exports of commodities over imports approaches $3,000 million a year; whilst, on the other side of the balance, payments, mainly to Europe, in respect of tourists and of immigrant remittances are estimated at not above $1,000 million a year. Thus, in order to balance the account as it now stands, the United States must lend to the rest of the world, in one shape or another, not less than $2,000 million a year, to which interest and sinking fund on the European governmental war debts would, if they were paid, add about $600 million.

Recently, therefore, the United States must have been lending to the rest of the world, mainly Europe, something like $2,000 million a year. Fortunately for Europe, a fair proportion of this was by way of speculative purchases of depreciated paper currencies. From 1919 to 1921 the losses of American speculators fed Europe; but this source of income can scarcely be reckoned on permanently. For a time the policy of loans can meet the situation; but, as the interest on past loans mounts up, it must in the long run aggravate it.

Mercantile nations have always employed large funds in overseas trade. But the practice of foreign investment, as we know it now, is a very modern contrivance, a very unstable one, and only suited to peculiar circumstances. An old country can in this way develop a new one at a time when the latter could not possibly do so with its own resources alone; the arrangement may be mutually advantageous, and out of abundant profits the lender may hope to be repaid. But the position cannot be reversed. If European bonds are issued in America on the analogy of the American bonds issued in Europe during the nineteenth century, the analogy will be a false one; because, taken in the aggregate, there is no natural increase, no *real* sinking fund, out of which they can be repaid. The interest will be furnished out of new loans, so long as these are obtainable, and the financial structure will mount always higher, until it is not worth while to maintain any longer the illusion that it has foundations. The unwillingness of American investors to buy European bonds is based on common sense.

At the end of 1919 I advocated (in *The Economic Consequences of the Peace*) a reconstruction loan from America to Europe, conditioned, however, on Europe's putting her own house in order. In the past two years America, in spite of European complaints to the contrary, has, in fact, made *very large* loans, much larger than the sum I contemplated, though not mainly in the form of regular, dollar-bond issues. No particular conditions were attached to these loans, and much of the money has been lost. Though wasted in part, they have helped Europe through the critical days of the post-Armistice period. But a continuance of them cannot provide a solution for the existing dis-equilibrium in the balance of indebtedness.

In part the adjustment may be effected by the United States taking the place hitherto held by England, France, and (on a small scale) Germany in providing capital for those new parts of the world less developed than herself—the British Dominions and South America. The Russian Empire, too, in Europe and Asia, is to be regarded as virgin soil, which may at a later date provide a suitable outlet for foreign capital. The American investor will lend more wisely to these countries, on the lines on which British and French investors used to lend to them, than direct to the old countries of Europe. But it is not likely that the whole gap can be bridged thus. Ultimately, and probably soon, there must be a readjustment of the balance of exports and imports. America must buy more and sell less. This is the only alternative to her making to Europe an annual present. Either American prices must rise faster than European (which will be the case if the Federal Reserve Board allows the gold influx to produce its natural consequences), or, failing this, the same result must be brought about by a further depreciation of the European exchanges, until Europe, by inability to buy, has reduced her purchases to articles of necessity. At first the American exporter, unable to scrap all at once the processes of production for export, may meet the situation by lowering his prices; but when these have continued, say for two years, below his cost of production, he will be driven inevitably to curtail or abandon his business.

It is useless for the United States to suppose that an equilibrium position can be reached on the basis of her exporting at least as much as at present, and at the same time restricting her imports by a tariff. Just as the Allies demand vast payments from Germany, and then exercise their ingenuity to prevent her paying them, so the American Administration devises, with one hand, schemes for financing exports and, with the other, tariffs which will make it as difficult as possible for such credits to be repaid. Great nations can often act with a degree of folly which we should not excuse in an individual.

By the shipment to the United States of all the bullion in the world, and the erection there of a sky-scraping golden calf, a short postponement may be gained. But a point may even come when the United States will refuse gold, yet still demand to be paid—a new Midas vainly asking more succulent fare than the barren metal of her own contract.

In any case the readjustment will be severe, and injurious to important interests. If, in addition, the United States exacts payment of the Allied debts, the position will be intolerable. If she persevered to the bitter end, scrapped her export industries and diverted to other uses the capital now employed in them, and if her former European associates decided to meet their obligations at whatever cost to themselves, I do not deny that the final result might be to America's material interest. But the project is utterly chimerical. It will not happen. Nothing is more certain than that America will not pursue such a policy to its conclusion; she will abandon it as soon as she experiences its first consequences. Nor, if she did, would the Allies pay the money. The position is exactly parallel to that of German reparation. America will not carry through to a conclusion the collection of Allied debt, any more than the Allies will carry through the collection of their present reparation demands. Neither, in the long run, is serious politics. Nearly all well-informed persons admit this in private conversation. But we live in a curious age when utterances in the press are deliberately designed to be in conformity with the worst-informed, instead of with the best-informed, opinion, because the former is the wider spread; so that for comparatively long periods there can be discrepancies, laughable or monstrous, between the written and the spoken word.

If this is so, it is not good business for America to embitter her relations with Europe, and to disorder her export industries for two years, in pursuance of a policy which she is certain to abandon before it has profited her.

For the benefit of any reader who enjoys an abstract statement,

I summarise the argument thus. The equilibrium of international trade is based on a complicated balance between the agriculture and the industries of the different countries of the world, and on a specialisation by each in the employment of its labour and its capital. If one country is required to transfer to another without payment great quantities of goods, for which this equilibrium does not allow, the balance is destroyed. Since capital and labour are fixed and organised in certain employments and cannot flow freely into others, the disturbance of the balance is destructive to the utility of the capital and labour thus fixed. The *organisation*, on which the wealth of the modern world so largely depends, suffers injury. In course of time a new organisation and a new equilibrium can be established. But if the origin of the disturbance is of temporary duration, the losses from the injury done to organisation may outweigh the profit of receiving goods without paying for them. Moreover, since the losses will be concentrated on the capital and labour employed in particular industries, they will provoke an outcry out of proportion to the injury inflicted on the community as a whole.

Most Americans with whom I have discussed this question express themselves as personally favourable to the cancellation of the European debts, but add that so great a majority of their countrymen think otherwise that such a proposal is at present outside practical politics. They think, therefore, that it is premature to discuss it; for the present, America must pretend she is going to demand the money and Europe must pretend she is going to pay it. Indeed, the position is much the same as that of German reparation in England in the middle of 1921. Doubtless my informants are right about this public opinion, the mysterious entity which is the same thing perhaps as Rousseau's General Will. Yet, all the same, I do not attach to what they tell me too much importance. Public opinion held that Hans Andersen's Emperor wore a fine suit; and in the United States especially, public opinion changes sometimes, as it were, *en bloc*.

If, indeed, public opinion were an unalterable thing, it would be a waste of time to discuss public affairs. And though it may be the chief business of newsmen and politicians to ascertain its momentary features, a writer ought to be concerned, rather, with what public opinion should be. I record these platitudes because many Americans give their advice, as though it were actually immoral to make suggestions which public opinion does not now approve. In America, I gather, an act of this kind is considered so reckless that some improper motive is at once suspected, and criticism takes the form of an inquiry into the culprit's personal character and antecedents.

Let us inquire, however, a little more deeply into the sentiments and emotions which underlie the American attitude to the European debts. They want to be generous to Europe, both out of good feeling and because many of them now suspect that any other course would upset their own economic equilibrium. But they don't want to be 'done'. They do not want it to be said that once again the old cynics in Europe have been one too many for them. Times, too, have been bad and taxation oppressive; and many parts of America do not feel rich enough at the moment to favour a light abandonment of a possible asset. Moreover, these arrangements, between nations warring together, they liken much more closely than we do to ordinary business transactions between individuals. It is, they say, as though a bank having made an unsecured advance to a client, in whom they believe, at a difficult time when he would have gone under without it, this client were then to cry off paying. To permit such a thing would be to do an injury to the elementary principles of business honour.

The average American, I fancy, would like to see the European nations approaching him with a pathetic light in their eyes and the cash in their hands, saying ,'America, we owe to you our liberty and our life; here we bring what we can in grateful thanks, money not wrung by grievous taxation from the widow and orphan, but saved, the best fruits of victory, out of the abolition of armaments, militarism, Empire, and internal strife, made possible by the help you freely gave us.' And then the average American would reply: 'I honour you for your integrity. It is what I expected. But I did not enter the war for profit or to invest my money well. I have had my reward in the words you have just uttered. The loans are forgiven. Return to your homes and use the resources I release to uplift the poor and the unfortunate.' And it would be an essential part of the little scene that his reply should come as a complete and overwhelming surprise.

Alas for the wickedness of the world! It is not in international affairs that we can secure the sentimental satisfactions which we all love. For only individuals are good, and all nations are dishonourable, cruel, and designing. And whilst the various prime ministers will telegraph something suitable, drafted by their private secretaries, to the effect that America's action makes the moment of writing the most important in the history of the world and proves that Americans are the noblest creatures living, America must not expect adequate or appropriate thanks.

II   THE BALFOUR NOTE (1925)

First published in the *Nation and Athenaeum*, 24 January 1925, as 'The Balfour Note and Inter-Allied Debts'.

§Mr Churchill pronounced a *credo* in the Balfour Note before he went to Paris. He has repeated it on coming back. 'The Balfour Note', he says, 'remains for us a dominating guide of principle set up freely by our own hands.' There is some saving grace in the last seven words. Let me plead with Mr Churchill, if he wants a settlement, that freely by our own hands we should take it down again.§

The Balfour Note insists that our receipts from Germany *plus* our receipts from our Allies must equal our payments to the United States. When the Note was written, its effect was indeterminate. We did not know how much it would require

France to pay, or the proportion that this would bear to what Germany would be paying France. Now we can make limiting estimates of both sums.

We have to pay the United States about £35 million a year, rising to £40 million. The Dawes Scheme will yield, if and when it is in *full* operation, and after allowing for various prior charges, about £100 million a year. France's share of this will be about £54 million, Italy's £10 million (less at first), and ours £24 million. (I neglect the minor Allies because they would complicate the calculation and hardly affect the result.) Thus the Balfour Note demands that France and Italy should pay Great Britain not less than £16 million a year. Since the aggregate debts of these two powers to themselves and to the United States respectively are about equal (our share of Italy's total debt is greater, and of France's less), we must assume that the United States will not settle for a smaller sum than what we receive. If the whole of Italy's share of reparations is devoted to her debts, France is left, on these assumptions, with £22 million to pay. In this case the net result of the debt settlements and the Dawes Scheme would be that the receipts from Germany would be distributed as follows:

United Kingdom	Nil
Italy	Nil
France	£32 million
United States[1]	£58 million

Very improbable things are easier said than done. Who believes that this will ever be done?

But we have not yet reached the gravamen of my criticism of the Balfour Note. The above is what would happen if the Dawes Scheme is perfectly successful. If the Dawes Scheme is only partly successful, then, by the principle of the Balfour Note, *France must make good the difference* to ourselves and the United States. For example, if the Dawes Scheme produces half its maximum, which, in the opinion of many good judges, would

---

[1] Including her own direct share.

be a considerable achievement, France will get less than nothing at all and *more than the whole* of Germany's payments will go to the United States. France would become, in fact, a deferred claimant on a third share of the Dawes Scheme, if the Scheme works very well, and a guarantor of Germany, if it works less well. Is not any one very silly who thinks that this can come to pass?

It is obvious that France will never agree to such a settlement. But suppose *per impossible* that she did. In this case Great Britain and the United States have, theoretically, no further interest whatever in the operation or productivity of the Dawes Scheme. France becomes the only interested party—interested not merely as a creditor but as a guarantor who must make deficiencies good.

This fatal objection is necessarily inherent in the Balfour Note. It is of the essence of the Note that the less Germany pays, the *more* France shall pay; that is to say, the less France is in a position to pay, the more she shall pay. Diplomatically and financially alike, this is topsy-turvy. It would never bring us cash; yet it would destroy our diplomatic authority as a moderator between France and Germany. The Foreign Office would have sold its influence for a mess of pottage which the Treasury would never taste.

The Balfour Note, therefore, is bad in principle. There can be no working settlement except on the exactly opposite principle, namely that the less Germany pays, the *less* France shall pay. The amount of France's payment must vary in the same direction as Germany's, not in the opposite direction. This was the principle of the suggestion, which I offered recently, by which France's payment should be a proportion of her receipts from Germany. According to current report, France herself has put forward just this principle through the mouth of M. Clémentel. I suggested that the proportion be one-third. M. Clémentel's reported offer would amount, on the assumption that the United States got the same terms, to about half my figure. But it does not follow that he would not offer more to obtain a settlement on these lines.

Such a settlement would increase, instead of diminishing, the interest of ourselves and the United States in the Dawes Scheme. We should have, between us, a bigger interest than France. We might, in this way, obtain a moderate contribution towards our American debt, corresponding to that part of it which we contracted, indirectly, on French account. We should certainly place ourselves in a strong moral and diplomatic position to claim a moderating and pacific influence in the Franco-German problems which still lie ahead.

§The Balfour Note would be dangerous, if it were not moonshine. Mr Winston Churchill will waste his time and spoil his reputation for common sense, if he lets himself be deceived by its superficial plausibility. There is nothing to be said in favour of the Balfour Note—except in comparison with the confusions of the present American position. For the American Isolationists, indeed, there is only one logical policy—complete cancellation.§

III CANCELLATION (1928)

Prepared as a radio talk for the British Broadcasting Corporation, which was given 3 May 1928, and published in the *Nation and Athenaeum*, 5 May 1928, under the title of 'The War Debts'. This essay was republished in France as part of a collection entitled *Réflexions sur le franc et sur quelques autres sujets* (1928).

§For the moment there is a lull in the acrid discussion which now for nine years has been waged around this question. But it has not been put to rest for long, and the time for its revival will undoubtedly come when the Dawes Scheme is up for revision—as sooner or later, and sooner better than later, it must be. It is opportune, therefore, to take stock of the situation as the negotiations of several years have left it.§

Let us remember the origin of these debts. Soon after the beginning of the war it was clear that certain of our Allies—

Russia and Belgium in the first instance, but subsequently all of them—would require financial assistance. We might have given this in loans or in subsidies. Loans were preferred to subsidies, in order to preserve a greater sense of responsibility and economy in the spending of them. But though financial assistance took the form of loans, it is scarcely to be supposed that the lending countries regarded them at the time as being in the nature of ordinary investments. Indeed it would have been very illogical to do so. For we often gave assistance in the form of money, precisely because we were less able to assist with men or ships. For example, when we sent guns to Italy to help her after her first serious reverse, she had to pay for them by loans. But when matters got worse still, and we sent not only guns but gunners too to man them and to be killed, then we charged nothing. Yet in the former case Italy's contribution was the greater and in the latter ours. In particular, America's contribution for some time after she came into the war was mainly financial, because she was not yet ready to help in any other way. So long as America was sending materials and munitions to be used by Allied soldiers, she charged us for them, and these charges are the origin of what we now owe her. But when later on she sent men too, to use the munitions themselves, then we were charged nothing. Evidently there is not much logic in a system which causes us to owe money to America, not because she was able to help us so much, but because at first she was able to help us, so far at least as manpower was concerned, so little.

This does not mean that the financial help which America gave us was not of the most extraordinary value to us. By the time that America came into the war our own resources as a lender were literally at an end. We were still at that time just about able to finance ourselves, but we had reached a point when we could no longer finance our Allies as well. America's financial assistance was therefore quite invaluable. From the moment she entered the war she undertook to lend whatever was required for the expenditure of ourselves and our Allies in the United States, including some contribution to support the foreign exchanges. But she was not prepared to make loans for use outside America. Great Britain had therefore to go on making loans to her Allies for such expenditure—with the result that we had to lend our Allies after America came into the war an amount almost equal to what we ourselves borrowed. More precisely, we borrowed from the United States, after she came into the war, £850 million, and lent to our Allies during the same period £750 million; so that in effect it was true—what the Americans have always been concerned to deny—that the loans she made to us were for the purpose of financing our Allies rather than for ourselves.

The result was that by the end of the war we were owed by our Allies about £1,600 million, whilst we, in our turn, owed to the United States £850 million.

Since the war, the question has been constantly debated whether these sums ought to be treated as investments, just like any other business transaction, or whether regard should be paid to their origin and to the circumstances in which they were made. It has been the British view that they were not made as business transactions and should not be treated as such. It has been the American view, on the other hand, that they should be taken at their face value, that is to say, as bonds due and payable, tempered only by considerations as to the capacity of the debtor to pay and, in practice, by a willingness on the part of the United States to accept a low rate of interest.

During the Peace Conference the British government urged that the Allied war debts should be entirely cancelled. Mr Lloyd George raised the matter again with President Wilson in August 1920. Finally, in August 1922, in the famous Note written by Lord Balfour, the considered British view, from which we have never gone back, was set forth. In this Note the British government declared their willingness to cancel the whole of what their allies owed them, and also to forgo their own claims on Germany in favour of the other Allies, if the United States in turn would relieve them of their debt. By such an arrangement Great Britain would have been giving up on paper more than twice what she gained. The offer still holds good.

This policy was not accepted by the United States, and a separate settlement has been made between each pair of countries in turn. The settlement made with Great Britain is equivalent to charging a rate of interest of 3·3 per cent on the whole amount due. The American settlement with France is equivalent to repayment at 1·6 per cent interest, and that with Italy to repayment at 0·4 per cent interest. Thus, the American settlement with Great Britain is twice as onerous as that with France and eight times as onerous as that with Italy. Great Britain, in her turn, has made arrangements with France and Italy, and has in both cases let them off lighter even than has the United States— the British settlement with France being 10 per cent easier and that with Italy 33 per cent easier than the corresponding American settlements. Thus, whilst the other Allies have been largely relieved this country is left with the task of repaying her whole burden, subject only to the mitigation that the rate of interest charged, namely, 3·3 per cent, is moderate.

The effect of this settlement is that Great Britain will have to pay to the United States a sum of about £33 million annually up to 1933, rising to nearly £38 million annually thereafter from that year until 1984, when the debt will have been discharged. The reality of the weight of this burden may be illustrated by certain calculations which I made in the summer of 1923 when the details of Mr Baldwin's settlement with Washington were first made public. We shall be paying to the United States each year for sixty years a sum equivalent to two-thirds of the cost of our Navy, a sum nearly equal to our State expenditure on education, a sum which exceeds the total burden of our pre-war debt. Looked at from another standpoint, it represents more than the total normal profits of our coal mines and our mercantile marine added together. With these sums we could endow and splendidly house *every month* for sixty years one new university, one new hospital, one new institute of research, etc. etc. With an equal sacrifice, over an equal period we could abolish slums and re-house in comfort the half of our population which is now inadequately sheltered.

On the other hand, we are now receiving from our Allies and from Germany an important contribution as an offset to what we ourselves pay to the United States. It will be interesting to establish a rough balance sheet.

In 1928 we shall receive from our Allies £12,800,000 and pay the United States £33,200,000; and by 1933 these figures will have risen to £17,700,000 and £37,800,000. Thus apart from our share of German reparations, we shall be paying annually in respect of war debts about £20 million more than we receive. Now if the Dawes annuities are paid by Germany in full, we shall come out just about 'all-square'. For the normal Dawes annuity when it has reached its full figure (less the service of German loans, etc.) will amount to £117 million, of which our share (excluding the receipts of other parts of the Empire) will be about £22 million. Mr Churchill has estimated that in the current financial year, 1928–9, our payments out will be £32,845,000, and our total receipts nearly £32 million.

It is not probable that these receipts will be realised in full. But it will enable us to summarise the situation if we assume for the moment that they are so realised. In this case, each Ally would be able to pay the United States out of their receipts from Germany. When the Allied debt payments to the United States have reached their maximum amount under the existing settlements, they will total £83 million per annum (the *average* amount payable annually over the whole period works out at a total of £61 million). If we add to this the direct American share in German reparations, the United States will be receiving £78 million annually out of the £117 million receivable by the Allies from Germany, or 67 per cent, *plus* £10 million from Italy not covered by reparations; or if we take the average

51

payments, in lieu of the maximum, the United States will be receiving £66 million out of £117 million or 57 per cent. In either case Great Britain would receive, on balance, nothing.

It follows from the above that if the maximum Dawes annuities were to be reduced by one-third—which, in the opinion of many of us, is highly probable—the United States will, by the time that the Allied payments to her have reached their full figure, be the sole beneficiary. In this event the net result of all war debt settlements would be to leave the United States—on balance and off-setting receipts against payments—receiving from Germany £78 million per annum, and no one else getting anything.

I have put the calculation in this form because it renders it very clear why, in the minds of the Allies, the question of further relief to Germany is intimately bound up with the question of their own obligations to the United States. The official American attitude that there is no connection between the two, is a very hollow pretence. The resettlement of the Dawes Scheme is one to which the United States must be, in one way or another, a party. But—let me add—any concession she may make will go entirely to the relief of Germany and the European Allies, Great Britain adhering to her principle of receiving nothing on balance.

If all, or nearly all, of what Germany pays for reparations has to be used, not to repair the damage done, but to repay the United States for the financial part which she played in the common struggle, many will feel that this is not an outcome tolerable to the sentiments of mankind or in reasonable accord with the spoken professions of Americans when they entered the war or afterwards. Yet it is a delicate matter, however keenly the public may feel, for any Englishman in authority to take the initiative in saying such things in an official way. Obviously, we must pay what we have covenanted to pay, and any proposal, if there is to be one, must come from the United States. It fell to my lot during the war to be the official draftsman in the British

Treasury of all the financial agreements with the Allies and with the United States out of which this situation has arisen. I was intimately familiar, day by day, with the reasons and motives which governed the character of the financial arrangements which were made. In the light of the memories of those days, I continue to hope that in due course, and in her own time, America will tell us that she has not spoken her last word.

PART II
INFLATION AND DEFLATION

1 INFLATION (1919)

From *The Economic Consequences of the Peace*, chapter 6, 'Europe after the Treaty'.

Lenin is said to have declared that the best way to destroy the capitalist system was to debauch the currency. By a continuing process of inflation, governments can confiscate, secretly and unobserved, an important part of the wealth of their citizens. By this method they not only confiscate, but they confiscate *arbitrarily*; and, while the process impoverishes many, it actually enriches some. The sight of this arbitrary rearrangement of riches strikes not only at security, but at confidence in the equity of the existing distribution of wealth. Those to whom the system brings windfalls, beyond their deserts and even beyond their expectations or desires, become 'profiteers', who are the object of the hatred of the bourgeoisie, whom the inflationism has impoverished, not less than of the proletariat. As the inflation proceeds and the real value of the currency fluctuates wildly from month to month, all permanent relations between debtors and creditors, which form the ultimate foundation of capitalism, become so utterly disordered as to be almost meaningless; and the process of wealth-getting degenerates into a gamble and a lottery.

Lenin was certainly right. There is no subtler, no surer means of overturning the existing basis of society than to debauch the currency. The process engages all the hidden forces of economic law on the side of destruction, and does it in a manner which not one man in a million is able to diagnose.

In the latter stages of the war all the belligerent governments practised, from necessity or incompetence, what a Bolshevist might have done from design. Even now, when the war is over, most of them continue out of weakness the same malpractices. But further, the governments of Europe, being many of them

57

at this moment reckless in their methods as well as weak, seek to direct on to a class known as 'profiteers' the popular indignation against the more obvious consequences of their vicious methods. These 'profiteers' are, broadly speaking, the entrepreneur class of capitalists, that is to say, the active and constructive element in the whole capitalist society, who in a period of rapidly rising prices cannot but get rich quick whether they wish it or desire it or not. If prices are continually rising, every trader who has purchased for stock or owns property and plant inevitably makes profits. By directing hatred against this class, therefore, the European governments are carrying a step further the fatal process which the subtle mind of Lenin had consciously conceived. The profiteers are a consequence and not a cause of rising prices. By combining a popular hatred of the class of entrepreneurs with the blow already given to social security by the violent and arbitrary disturbance of contract and of the established equilibrium of wealth which is the inevitable result of inflation, these governments are fast rendering impossible a continuance of the social and economic order of the nineteenth century. But they have no plan for replacing it.

2 SOCIAL CONSEQUENCES OF CHANGES IN THE VALUE OF MONEY (1923)

A shortened version of the first chapter of *A Tract on Monetary Reform* (1923), 'The Consequences to Society of Changes in the Value of Money'. Much of the material of this chapter originally appeared as an article published under the same title in the *Manchester Guardian Commercial Supplement, Reconstruction in Europe*, No. v, 27 July 1922.

Money is only important for what it will procure. Thus a change in the monetary unit, which is uniform in its operation and affects all transactions equally, has no consequences. If, by a change in the established standard of value, a man received and owned twice as much money as he did before in payment for all rights and for all efforts, and if he also paid out twice as much money for all acquisitions and for all satisfactions, he would be wholly unaffected.

It follows, therefore, that a change in the value of money, that is to say in the level of prices, is important to society only in so far as its incidence is unequal. Such changes have produced in the past, and are producing now, the vastest social consequences, because, as we all know, when the value of money changes, it does *not* change equally for all persons or for all purposes. A man's receipts and his outgoings are not all modified in one uniform proportion. Thus a change in prices and rewards, as measured in money, generally affects different classes unequally, transfers wealth from one to another, bestows affluence here and embarrassment there, and redistributes Fortune's favours so as to frustrate design and disappoint expectation.

The fluctuations in the value of money since 1914 have been on a scale so great as to constitute, with all that they involve, one of the most significant events in the economic history of the modern world. The fluctuation of the standard, whether gold, silver, or paper, has not only been of unprecedented violence, but has been visited on a society of which the economic organisation is more dependent than that of any earlier epoch on the assumption that the standard of value would be moderately stable.

During the Napoleonic Wars and the period immediately succeeding them the extreme fluctuation of English prices within a single year was 22 per cent; and the highest price level reached during the first quarter of the nineteenth century, which we used to reckon the most disturbed period of our currency history, was less than double the lowest and with an interval of thirteen years. Compare with this the extraordinary movements of the past nine years. From 1914 to 1920 all countries experienced an expansion in the supply of money to spend relatively to the supply of things to purchase, that is to say *inflation*. Since 1920 those countries which have regained control of their financial situation, not content with bringing the inflation to an end, have contracted their supply of money and have experienced the fruits of *deflation*. Others have followed inflationary courses more riotously than before.

Each process, inflation and deflation alike, has inflicted great injuries. Each has an effect in altering the *distribution* of wealth between different classes, inflation in this respect being the worse of the two. Each has also an effect in overstimulating or retarding the *production* of wealth, though here deflation is the more injurious. The division of our subject thus indicated is the most convenient for us to follow—examining first the effect of changes in the value of money on the distribution of wealth with most of our attention on inflation, and next their effect on the production of wealth with most of our attention on deflation.

A CHANGES IN THE VALUE OF MONEY, AS AFFECTING DISTRIBUTION

I *The Investing Class*

Of the various purposes which money serves, some essentially depend upon the assumption that its real value is nearly constant over a period of time. The chief of these are those connected, in a wide sense, with contracts for the *investment of money*. Such contracts—namely, those which provide for the payment of fixed sums of money over a long period of time—are the characteristic of what it is convenient to call the *investment system*, as distinct from the property system generally.

Under this phase of capitalism, as developed during the nineteenth century, many arrangements were devised for separating the management of property from its ownership. These arrangements were of three leading types: (1) Those in which the proprietor, while parting with the management of his property, retained his ownership of it—i.e. of the actual land, buildings, and machinery, or of whatever else it consisted in, this mode of tenure being typified by a holding of ordinary shares in a joint-stock company; (2) those in which he parted with the property temporarily, receiving a fixed sum of *money* annually in the meantime, but regained his property eventually, as typified by a lease; and (3) those in which he parted with his real property permanently, in return either for a perpetual annuity fixed in terms of money, or for a terminable annuity and the repayment of the principal in money at the end of the term, as typified by mortgages, bonds, debentures, and preference shares. This third type represents the full development of *investment*.

Contracts to receive fixed sums of money at future dates (made without provision for possible changes in the real value of money at those dates) must have existed as long as money has been lent and borrowed. In the form of leases and mortgages, and also of permanent loans to governments and to a few private bodies, such as the East India Company, they were already frequent in the eighteenth century. But during the nineteenth century they developed a new and increased importance, and had, by the beginning of the twentieth, divided the propertied classes into two groups—the 'business men' and the 'investors'—with partly divergent interests. The division was not sharp as between individuals; for business men might be investors also, and investors might hold ordinary shares; but the division was nevertheless real, and not the less important because it was seldom noticed.

By this system the active business class could call to the aid of their enterprises not only their own wealth but the savings of the whole community; and the professional and propertied classes, on the other hand, could find an employment for their resources, which involved them in little trouble, no responsibility, and (it was believed) small risk.

For a hundred years the system worked, throughout Europe, with an extraordinary success and facilitated the growth of wealth on an unprecedented scale. To save and to invest became at once the duty and the delight of a large class. The savings were seldom drawn on and, accumulating at compound interest, made possible the material triumphs which we now all take for granted. The morals, the politics, the literature, and the religion of the age joined in a grand conspiracy for the promotion of saving. God and Mammon were reconciled. Peace on earth to men of good means. A rich man could, after all, enter into the Kingdom of Heaven—if only he saved. A new harmony sounded from the celestial spheres. 'It is curious to observe how, through the wise and beneficent arrangement of Providence, men thus do the greatest service to the public, when they are thinking of nothing but their own gain';[1] so sang the angels.

The atmosphere thus created well harmonised the demands of expanding business and the needs of an expanding population with the growth of a comfortable non-business class. But amidst

[1] *Easy Lessons on Money Matters for the Use of Young People*, published by the Society for Promoting Christian Knowledge. Twelfth Edition, 1850.

the general enjoyment of ease and progress, the extent to which the system depended on the stability of the money to which the investing classes had committed their fortunes, was generally overlooked; and an unquestioning confidence was apparently felt that this matter would look after itself. Investments spread and multiplied, until, for the middle classes of the world, the gilt-edged bonds came to typify all that was most permanent and most secure. So rooted in our day has been the conventional belief in the stability and safety of a money contract that, according to English law, trustees have been encouraged to embark their trust funds exclusively in such transactions, and are indeed forbidden, except in the case of real estate (an exception which is itself a survival of the conditions of an earlier age), to employ them otherwise.[1]

As in other respects, so also in this, the nineteenth century relied on the future permanence of its own happy experiences and disregarded the warning of past misfortunes. It chose to forget that there is no historical warrant for expecting money to be represented even by a constant quantity of a particular metal, far less by a constant purchasing power. Yet money is simply that which the State declares from time to time to be a good legal discharge of money contracts. In 1914 gold had not been the English standard for a century or the sole standard of any other country for half a century. There is no record of a prolonged war or a great social upheaval which has not been accompanied by a change in the legal tender, but an almost unbroken chronicle in every country which has a history, back to the earliest dawn of economic record, of a progressive deterioration in the real value of the successive legal tenders which have represented money.

Moreover, this progressive deterioration in the value of money through history is not an accident, and has had behind it two great driving forces—the impecuniosity of governments and the superior political influence of the debtor class.

[1] German trustees were not released from a similar obligation until 1923, by which date the value of trust funds invested in titles to money had entirely disappeared.

6-2

The power of taxation by currency depreciation is one which has been inherent in the state since Rome discovered it. The creation of legal tender has been and is a government's ultimate reserve; and no state or government is likely to decree its own bankruptcy or its own downfall so long as this instrument still lies at hand unused.

Besides this, as we shall see below, the benefits of a depreciating currency are not restricted to the government. Farmers and debtors and all persons liable to pay fixed money dues share in the advantage. As now in the persons of business men, so also in former ages these classes constituted the active and constructive elements in the economic scheme. Those secular changes, therefore, which in the past have depreciated money, assisted the new men and emancipated them from the dead hand; they benefited new wealth at the expense of old, and armed enterprise against accumulation. The tendency of money to depreciate has been in past times a weighty counterpoise against the cumulative results of compound interest and the inheritance of fortunes. It has been a loosening influence against the rigid distribution of old-won wealth and the separation of ownership from activity. By this means each generation can disinherit in part its predecessors' heirs; and the project of founding a perpetual fortune must be disappointed in this way, unless the community with conscious deliberation provides against it in some other way, more equitable and more expedient.

At any rate, under the influence of these two forces—the financial necessities of governments and the political influence of the debtor class—sometimes the one and sometimes the other, the progress of inflation has been *continuous*, if we consider long periods, ever since money was first devised in the sixth century B.C. Sometimes the standard of value has depreciated of itself; failing this, debasements have done the work.

Nevertheless it is easy at all times, as a result of the way we use money in daily life, to forget all this and to look on money as itself the absolute standard of value; and, when besides, the actual events of a hundred years have not disturbed his illusions, the average man regards what has been normal for three generations as a part of the permanent social fabric.

The course of events during the nineteenth century favoured such ideas. During its first quarter, the very high prices of the Napoleonic Wars were followed by a somewhat rapid improvement in the value of money. For the next seventy years, with some temporary fluctuations, the tendency of prices continued to be downwards, the lowest point being reached in 1896. But while this was the tendency as regards direction, the remarkable feature of this long period was the relative *stability* of the price level. Approximately the *same* level of price ruled in or about the years 1826, 1841, 1855, 1862, 1867, 1871, and 1915. Prices were also level in the years 1844, 1881, and 1914.[1] If we call the index number of these latter years 100, we find that, for the period of close on a century from 1826 to the outbreak of war, the maximum fluctuation in either direction was 30 points, the index number never rising above 130 and never falling below 70. No wonder that we came to believe in the stability of money contracts over a long period. The metal *gold* might not possess all the theoretical advantages of an artificially regulated standard, but it could not be tampered with and had proved reliable in practice.

At the same time, the investor in consols in the early part of the century had done very well in three different ways. The 'security' of his investment had come to be considered as near absolute perfection as was possible. Its capital value had uniformly appreciated, partly for the reason just stated, but chiefly because the steady fall in the rate of interest increased the number of years' purchase of the annual income which represented the capital.[2] And the annual money income had a purchasing power which on the whole was increasing. If, for example, we consider the seventy years from 1826 to 1896 (and ignore the great improvement immediately after Waterloo), we find that the

---

[1] [And again, it is now possible to add, in 1931.]
[2] If, for example, the rate of interest falls from 4½ per cent to 3 per cent, 3 per cent Consols rise in value from 66 to 100.

capital value of consols rose steadily, with only temporary setbacks, from 79 to 109 (in spite of Goschen's conversion from a 3 per cent rate to a 2¾ per cent rate in 1889 and a 2½ per cent rate effective in 1903), while the purchasing power of the annual dividends, even after allowing for the reduced rates of interest, had increased 50 per cent. But consols, too, had added the virtue of stability to that of improvement. Except in years of crisis consols never fell below 90 during the reign of Queen Victoria; and even in 1848, when thrones were crumbling, the mean price of the year fell but 5 points. Ninety when she ascended the throne, they reached their maximum with her in the year of Diamond Jubilee. What wonder that our parents thought consols a good investment!

Thus there grew up during the nineteenth century a large, powerful, and greatly respected class of persons, well-to-do individually and very wealthy in the aggregate, who owned neither buildings, nor land, nor businesses, nor precious metals, but titles to an annual income in legal-tender money. In particular, that peculiar creation and pride of the nineteenth century, the savings of the middle class, had been mainly thus embarked. Custom and favourable experience had acquired for such investments an unimpeachable reputation for security.

Before the war these medium fortunes had already begun to suffer some loss (as compared with the summit of their prosperity in the middle nineties) from the rise in prices and also in the rate of interest. But the monetary events which have accompanied and have followed the war have taken from them about one-half of their real value in England, seven-eighths in France, eleven-twelfths in Italy, and virtually the whole in Germany and in the succession states of Austria-Hungary and Russia.

Thus the effect of the war, and of the monetary policy which has accompanied and followed it, has been to take away a large part of the real value of the possessions of the investing class. The loss has been so rapid and so intermixed in the time of its occurrence with other worse losses that its full measure is not yet separately apprehended. But it has effected, nevertheless, a far-reaching change in the relative position of different classes. Throughout the Continent the pre-war savings of the middle class, so far as they were invested in bonds, mortgages, or bank deposits, have been largely or entirely wiped out. Nor can it be doubted that this experience must modify social psychology towards the practice of saving and investment. What was deemed most secure has proved least so. He who neither spent nor 'speculated,' who made 'proper provision for his family,' who sang hymns to security and observed most straitly the morals of the edified and the respectable injunctions of the worldly-wise—he, indeed, who gave fewest pledges to Fortune has yet suffered her heaviest visitations.

What moral for our present purpose should we draw from this? Chiefly, I think, that it is not safe or fair to combine the social organisation developed during the ninteeenth century (and still retained) with a *laissez-faire* policy towards the value of money. It is not true that our former arrangements have worked well. If we are to continue to draw the voluntary savings of the community into 'investments', we must make it a prime object of deliberate State policy that the standard of value, in terms of which they are expressed, should be kept stable; adjusting in other ways (calculated to touch all forms of wealth equally and not concentrated on the relatively helpless 'investors') the redistribution of the national wealth, if, in course of time, the laws of inheritance and the rate of accumulation have drained too great a proportion of the income of the active classes into the spending control of the inactive.

II *The Business Class*

It has long been recognised, by the business world and by economists alike, that a period of rising prices acts as a stimulus to enterprise and is beneficial to business men.

In the first place there is the advantage which is the counterpart of the loss to the investing class which we have just examined.

When the value of money falls, it is evident that those persons who have engaged to pay fixed sums of money yearly out of the profits of active business must benefit, since their fixed money outgoings will bear a smaller proportion than formerly to their money turnover. This benefit persists not only during the transitional period of change, but also, so far as old loans are concerned, when prices have settled down at their new and higher level. For example, the farmers throughout Europe, who had raised by mortgage the funds to purchase the land they farmed, now find themselves almost freed from the burden at the expense of the mortgagees.

But during the period of change, while prices are rising month by month, the business man has a further and greater source of windfall. Whether he is a merchant or a manufacturer, he will generally buy before he sells, and on at least a part of his stock he will run the risk of price changes. If, therefore, month after month his stock appreciates on his hands, he is always selling at a better price than he expected and securing a windfall profit upon which he had not calculated. In such a period the business of trade becomes unduly easy. Any one who can borrow money and is not exceptionally unlucky must make a profit, which he may have done little to deserve. Thus, when prices are rising, the business man who borrows money is able to repay the lender with what, in terms of real value, not only represents no interest, but is even less than the capital originally advanced.

But if the depreciation of money is a source of gain to the business man, it is also the occasion of opprobrium. To the consumer the business man's exceptional profits appear as the cause (instead of the consequence) of the hated rise of prices. Amidst the rapid fluctuations of his fortunes he himself loses his conservative instincts, and begins to think more of the large gains of the moment than of the lesser, but permanent, profits of normal business. The welfare of his enterprise in the relatively distant future weighs less with him than before, and thoughts are excited of a quick fortune and clearing out. His excessive gains have come to him unsought and without fault or design on his part, but once acquired he does not lightly surrender them, and will struggle to retain his booty. With such impulses and so placed, the business man is himself not free from a suppressed uneasiness. In his heart he loses his former self-confidence in his relation to society, in his utility and necessity in the economic scheme. He fears the future of his business and his class, and the less secure he feels his fortune to be the tighter he clings to it. The business man, the prop of society and the builder of the future, to whose activities and rewards there had been accorded, not long ago, an almost religious sanction, he of all men and classes most respectable, praiseworthy, and necessary, with whom interference was not only disastrous but almost impious, was now to suffer sidelong glances, to feel himself suspected and attacked, the victim of unjust and injurious laws—to become, and know himself half guilty, a profiteer.

No man of spirit will consent to remain poor if he believes his betters to have gained their goods by lucky gambling. To convert the business man into the profiteer is to strike a blow at capitalism, because it destroys the psychological equilibrium which permits the perpetuance of unequal rewards. The economic doctrine of normal profits, vaguely apprehended by every one, is a necessary condition for the justification of capitalism. The business man is only tolerable so long as his gains can be held to bear some relation to what, roughly and in some sense, his activities have contributed to society.

This, then, is the second disturbance to the existing economic order for which the depreciation of money is responsible. If the fall in the value of money discourages investment, it also discredits enterprise.

Not that the business man was allowed, even during the period of boom, to retain the whole of his exceptional profits. A host of popular remedies vainly attempted to cure the evils of the day; which remedies themselves—subsidies, price and rent fixing, profiteer hunting, and excess profits duties—eventually became not the least part of the evils.

In due course came the depression, with falling prices, which operate on those who hold stocks in a manner exactly opposite to rising prices. Excessive losses, bearing no relation to the efficiency of the business, took the place of windfall gains; and the effort of every one to hold as small stocks as possible brought industry to a standstill, just as previously their efforts to accumulate stocks had over-stimulated it. Unemployment succeeded profiteering as the problem of the hour.

III *The Earner*

It has been a commonplace of economic textbooks that wages tend to lag behind prices, with the result that the real earnings of the wage earner are diminished during a period of rising prices. This has often been true in the past, and may be true even now of certain classes of labour which are ill-placed or ill-organised for improving their position. But in Great Britain, at any rate, and in the United States also, some important sections of labour were able to take advantage of the situation not only to obtain money wages equivalent in purchasing power to what they had before, but to secure a real improvement, to combine this with a diminution in their hours of work (and, so far, of the work done), and to accomplish this (in the case of Great Britain) at a time when the total wealth of the community as a whole had suffered a decrease. This reversal of the usual course has not been due to an accident and is traceable to definite causes.

The organisation of certain classes of labour—railwaymen, miners, dockers, and others—for the purpose of securing wage increases is better than it was. Life in the army, perhaps for the first time in the history of wars, raised in many respects the conventional standard of requirements—the soldier was better clothed, better shod, and often better fed than the labourer, and his wife, adding in wartime a separation allowance to new opportunities to earn, had also enlarged her ideas.

But these influences, while they would have supplied the motive, might have lacked the means to the result if it had not been for another factor—the windfalls of the profiteer. The fact that the business man had been gaining, and gaining notoriously, considerable windfall profits in excess of the normal profits of trade, laid him open to pressure, not only from his employees but from public opinion generally; and enabled him to meet this pressure without financial difficulty. In fact, it was worth his while to pay ransom, and to share with his workmen the good fortune of the day.

Thus the working classes improved their *relative* position in the years following the war, as against all other classes except that of the 'profiteers'. In some important cases they improved their absolute position—that is to say, account being taken of shorter hours, increased money wages, and higher prices, some sections of the working classes secured for themselves a higher real remuneration for each unit of effort or work done. But we cannot estimate the *stability* of this state of affairs, as contrasted with its desirability, unless we know the source from which the increased reward of the working classes was drawn. Was it due to a permanent modification of the economic factors which determine the distribution of the national product between different classes? Or was it due to some temporary and exhaustible influence connected with inflation and with the resulting disturbance in the standard of value?

The period of depression has exacted its penalty from the working classes more in the form of unemployment than by a lowering of real wages, and state assistance to the unemployed has greatly moderated even this penalty. Money wages have followed prices downwards. But the depression of 1921-2 did not reverse or even greatly diminish the relative advantage gained by the working classes over the middle class during the previous years. In 1923 British wage rates stood at an appreciably higher level above the pre-war rates than did the cost of living, if allowance is made for the shorter hours worked.

B CHANGES IN THE VALUE OF MONEY,
AS AFFECTING PRODUCTION

If, for any reason right or wrong, the business world *expects* that prices will fall, the processes of production tend to be inhibited; and if it expects that prices will rise, they tend to be over-stimulated. A fluctuation in the measuring-rod of value does not alter in the least the wealth of the world, the needs of the world, or the productive capacity of the world. It ought not, therefore, to affect the character or the volume of what is produced. A movement of *relative* prices, that is to say of the comparative prices of different commodities, *ought* to influence the character of production, because it is an indication that various commodities are not being produced in the exactly right proportions. But this is not true of a change, as such, in the *general* price level.

The fact that the expectation of changes in the *general* price level affects the processes of production, is deeply rooted in the peculiarities of the existing economic organisation of society. We have already seen that a change in the general level of prices, that is to say a change in the measuring-rod, which fixes the obligation of the borrowers of money (who make the decisions which set production in motion) to the lenders (who are inactive once they have lent their money), effects a redistribution of real wealth between the two groups. Furthermore, the active group can, if they foresee such a change, alter their action in advance in such a way as to minimise their losses to the other group or to increase their gains from it, if and when the expected change in the value of money occurs. If they expect a fall, it may pay them, as a group, to damp production down, although such enforced idleness impoverishes society as a whole. If they expect a rise, it may pay them to increase their borrowings and to swell production beyond the point where the real return is just sufficient to recompense society as a whole for the effort made. Sometimes, of course, a change in the measuring-rod, especially

72

if it is unforeseen, may benefit one group at the expense of the other disproportionately to any influence it exerts on the volume of production; but the tendency, in so far as the active group anticipate a change, will be as I have described it. This is simply to say that the intensity of production is largely governed in existing conditions by the anticipated real profit of the entrepreneur. Yet this criterion is the right one for the community as a whole only when the delicate adjustment of interests is not upset by fluctuations in the standard of value.

There is also a considerable risk directly arising out of instability in the value of money. During the lengthy process of production the business world is incurring outgoings in terms of *money*—paying out in money for wages and other expenses of production—in the expectation of recouping this outlay by disposing of the product for *money* at a later date. That is to say, the business world as a whole must always be in a position where it stands to gain by a rise of price and to lose by a fall of price. Whether it likes it or not, the technique of production under a régime of money-contract forces the business world always to carry a big speculative position; and if it is reluctant to carry this position, the productive process must be slackened. The argument is not affected by the fact that there is some degree of specialisation of function within the business world, in so far as the professional speculator comes to the assistance of the producer proper by taking over from him a part of his risk.

Now it follows from this, not merely that the *actual occurrence* of price changes profits some classes and injures others (which has been the theme of the first section of this chapter), but that a *general fear* of falling prices may inhibit the productive process altogether. For if prices are expected to fall, not enough risk-takers can be found who are willing to carry a speculative 'bull' position, and this means that entrepreneurs will be reluctant to embark on lengthy productive processes involving a money outlay long in advance of money recoupment—whence unemployment. The *fact* of falling prices injures entrepreneurs;

73

consequently the *fear* of falling prices causes them to protect themselves by curtailing their operations; yet it is upon the aggregate of their individual estimations of the risk, and their willingness to run the risk, that the activity of production and of employment mainly depends.

There is a further aggravation of the case, in that an expectation about the course of prices tends, if it is widely held, to be cumulative in its results up to a certain point. If prices are expected to rise and the business world acts on this expectation, that very fact causes them to rise for a time and, by verifying the expectation, reinforces it; and similarly, if it expects them to fall. Thus a comparatively weak initial impetus may be adequate to produce a considerable fluctuation.

The best way to cure this mortal disease of individualism must be to provide that there shall never exist any confident expectation either that prices generally are going to fall or that they are going to rise; and also that there shall be no serious risk that a movement, if it does occur, will be a big one. If, unexpectedly and accidentally, a moderate movement were to occur, wealth, though it might be redistributed, would not be diminished thereby.

To procure this result by removing all possible influences towards an initial movement would seem to be a hopeless enterprise. The remedy would lie, rather, in so controlling the standard of value that whenever something occurred which, left to itself, would create an expectation of a change in the general level of prices, the controlling authority should take steps to counteract this expectation by setting in motion some factor of a contrary tendency. Even if such a policy were not wholly successful, either in counteracting expectations or in avoiding actual movements, it would be an improvement on the policy of sitting quietly by whilst a standard of value, governed by chance causes and deliberately removed from central control, produces expectations which paralyse or intoxicate the government of production.

We see, therefore, that rising prices and falling prices each have their characteristic disadvantage. The inflation which causes the former means injustice to individuals and to classes—particularly to rentiers; and is therefore unfavourable to saving. The deflation which causes falling prices means impoverishment to labour and to enterprise by leading entrepreneurs to restrict production, in their endeavour to avoid loss to themselves; and is therefore disastrous to employment. The counterparts are, of course, also true—namely that deflation means injustice to borrowers, and that inflation leads to the over-stimulation of industrial activity. But these results are not so marked as those emphasised above, because borrowers are in a better position to protect themselves from the worst effects of deflation than lenders are to protect themselves from those of inflation, and because labour is in a better position to protect itself from over-exertion in good times than from under-employment in bad times.

Thus inflation is unjust and deflation is inexpedient. Of the two perhaps deflation is, if we rule out exaggerated inflations such as that of Germany, the worse; because it is worse, in an impoverished world, to provoke unemployment than to disappoint the rentier. But it is not necessary that we should weigh one evil against the other. It is easier to agree that both are evils to be shunned. The individualistic capitalism of today, precisely because it entrusts saving to the individual investor and production to the individual employer, *presumes* a stable measuring-rod of value, and cannot be efficient—perhaps cannot survive—without one.

For these grave causes we must free ourselves from the deep distrust which exists against allowing the regulation of the standard of value to be the subject of *deliberate decision*. We can no longer afford to leave it in the category of which the distinguishing characteristics are possessed in different degrees by the weather, the birth-rate, and the Constitution—matters which are settled by natural causes, or are the resultant of the separate action of many individuals acting independently, or require a revolution to change them.

3   THE FRENCH FRANC

First published in the *Nation and Athenaeum*, 9 January 1926, with the title
'The French Franc: An Open Letter to the French Minister of Finance
(whoever he is or may be)'. This essay was republished in France as part
of a collection entitled *Réflexions sur le franc et sur quelques autres sujets*
(1928).

I   AN OPEN LETTER TO THE FRENCH MINISTER OF
FINANCE (WHOEVER HE IS OR MAY BE)
(January 1926)

Monsieur—When I read in my daily paper the daily projects
of yourself and your predecessors to draft new budgets and to
fund old debts, I get the impression that Paris discusses very
little what seems to me in London to be the technical analysis
of your problem. May I, therefore, divert your attention for a
moment from your Sisyphean task of rolling budgets up Parliament Hill back to certain fundamental calculations?

I have written about the French franc many times in recent
years, and I do not find that I have changed my mind. More
than two years ago I wrote: 'The level of the franc is going to
be settled in the long run, not by speculation or the balance
of trade, or even the outcome of the Ruhr adventure, but by the
proportion of his earned income which the French taxpayer
will permit to be taken from him to pay the claims of the French
rentier.' I still think that this is the root idea from which your
plans ought to develop.

Now it is obvious that there are two methods of attaining the
desired equilibrium. You can increase the burdens on the taxpayer, or you can diminish the claims of the rentier. If you choose
the first alternative, taxation will absorb nearly a quarter of the
national income of France. Is this feasible? If it is ever safe to
speak about the political atmosphere of another country, I should
judge from recent indications that the French public will

76

certainly refuse to submit to the imposition of a burden of additional taxation sufficient to satisfy the claims of the rentier at their present level. And even if such taxation were politically possible, it would probably break down administratively. The pressing task of the French Treasury is not to devise additional taxes, but to construct an administrative machine capable of collecting those which exist. If, therefore, I were in your place, I should not, as a politician, give another minute's thought to new taxes, but would concentrate, so far as concerned the fiscal part of my office, on consolidating and administering the taxes already voted.

Since this by itself is not enough, your next business—provided you accept my conclusion as to the mind of the French public —is to consider coolly how best to reduce the claims of the rentier. Three methods offer themselves: first, a general capital levy; second, a forced reduction of the rate of interest on the public debt; third, a rise of prices which would reduce the real value of the rentier's money claims. Unquestionably, the first is preferable on grounds of virtue, justice, and theory. For Britain in a similar fix I should advocate it. But I think it so probable that such a project would be defeated in France today by the same political and administrative difficulties which stand in the way of further taxation, that I should not lose my time on it. The second method is attractive, if only because it offers no administrative difficulties. I believe that some authorities in France have favoured it. Nevertheless, I should decline this expedient also, if I were in your place, because, unlike a general capital levy or a depreciation of money, this species of discrimination is truly named repudiation, and repudiation of the national debt is a departure from financial virtue so extreme and so dangerous as not to be undertaken but in the last emergency.

We are left, therefore, by a process of the exclusion of alternatives, with one exit only—a rise of internal prices; which leads us away from the fiscal field to the price level, the foreign exchanges, the gold in the Bank of France, the volume of foreign investment, and the balance of trade. Here I must invite your particular attention to an interesting paradox.

Successive finance ministers have, in fact, done their utmost to find an escape through the exit I indicate. They have inflated magnificently, and they have brought down the gold value of the franc by progressive stages with only temporary setbacks. What more could they have done?

I will tell you. The great army of your predecessors have failed, in spite of all their efforts, to depreciate adequately *the internal purchasing power* of the franc. Your present difficulties are due, not to the inflation of the notes or to the fall of the exchange (for these events are tending all the time to help you out of your troubles), but to the failure of these factors to diminish proportionately the internal purchasing power of the rentier's money claims.

The following figures present the essence of your problem. In December 1925 the gold value of the franc on the foreign exchanges was 19 per cent of its pre-war parity; world gold prices were about 158 per cent of their pre-war level; therefore on the pre-war basis a note circulation and a franc price level amounting to 830 per cent (for $158 \div 19 = 8 \cdot 3$) of their pre-war figures would be justified. Now the note circulation, being about 1,000 per cent of its pre-war figure, roughly corresponds to the level of the foreign exchange—though, allowing for increased territory and the loss of gold and silver coin from the circulation, it is probably still too low in relation to the exchange, rather than too high, on a pre-war comparison.

When we come to the internal franc price level, on the other hand, we find an entirely different story. Imported raw materials have inevitably risen to their international parity. But the classes of goods such as food and other articles entering into the cost-of-living index number, which are dominated by home production, are far below their equilibrium value. Wholesale food prices in November 1925 were 490 per cent of pre-war, retail prices in Paris (thirteen items) were 433 per cent, and in the third quarter of 1925 the cost-of-living index for Paris stood at 401 per cent. These figures may understate the real rise of prices, but it certainly seems that French domestic costs are not above five times their pre-war figure. This means that the prices of purely home produce, converted at the present rate of exchange, are not much more than *half* world prices, and are actually below their pre-war level in terms of gold. Thus the inflation of the currency has produced its full effect on the exchanges, and consequently on the prices of imported commodities, but has largely failed to do so on the prices of home-produce.

Now the burden of the rentier on the taxpayer is measured by the internal purchasing power of the francs which have to be taken from the latter to be handed to the former. *Thus if internal prices had risen as fast as the exchange has fallen, the real burden of the national debt service would be reduced by at least a third.* I suggest to you, therefore, that, whilst the solution of your fiscal difficulties can come about in no other way than by a rise in the internal price level, it is not so clear that this need be accompanied either by further inflation or by a further fall in the exchange.

It is for you to decide in your own mind at what level of internal prices you can hope to balance your budget. Your next step must be to bring about this rise in as orderly and scientific a way as you are able. Looking from outside, it appears to me that an internal price level between eight and nine times pre-war might be high enough. In this case there is no justification for any considerable further inflation or fall in the franc exchange. All you have to do is to stabilise the note circulation and the franc exchange at near their present level and to allow time for internal prices to rise correspondingly.

What are the explanations of the present low level of franc prices? I think that they are: (1) the time element—internal prices move slowly, but will move as they should in time; (2) the hoarding of bank notes on an even greater scale than formerly, leading to a sluggish circulation of the available currency; (3) excessive foreign investment by Frenchmen, due to lack of confidence, which drives the exchange down below the figure appropriate to the trading position; and (4) the legal restrictions on rents, etc.

These influences should be remediable as regards (1) by the mere lapse of time, and as regards (2) and (3) by the restoration of internal confidence. The right strategy, therefore, is to restore confidence and then just wait. And the way to restore confidence is, surely, not to heap up taxes, but to stabilise the franc exchange beyond doubt or criticism near its present level.

How to stabilise the franc exchange? Not so difficult as it is supposed to be. The balance of trade is strongly in favour of France. The present level of internal prices encourages exports and discourages imports. The metallic reserve of the Bank of France is worth (at the present exchange) nearly 40 per cent of the note issue. Nothing is required, I expect, but that the Bank of France should declare that for two years at least it will furnish dollar exchange against francs in unlimited amounts on terms *not worse* than some stated rate between dollars and francs, and that the Bank should be prepared, if necessary, to use its gold for the purpose. The rate selected should probably lie somewhere between 1 dollar for 25 francs and 1 dollar for 30 francs, and it would be safer to choose the latter ratio at first, with just a hope that the former might be achieved in the end.[1] The success of the scheme requires no more than that the Bank's undertaking should be believed. With this background of stability you will be able to borrow enough to carry you through the transitional period without further inflation.

For the rest you can trust time. As the internal price level gradually rises to an equilibrium with the exchange and as the machinery for collecting the taxes is gradually improved, your budget receipts will grow month by month until they balance the expenses. Those taxes which are fixed in francs and are not

[1] [This was a happy guess, since the actual figure adopted two and a half years later was 25·5 francs to the dollar.]

ad valorem should, of course, be raised *pari passu* with the rise in prices.

There are two matters on which the government of France needs to exercise an iron resolve—to fix the franc exchange at a minimum figure even if it costs gold to do so, and to collect the taxes in full. These are the indispensable measures. Heroic efforts to increase the rates of taxation are, at this stage, efforts in a wrong direction, and will not be successful.

What are the arguments against these courses? They are entirely political. A policy which will not be successful unless it raises prices by a heavy percentage will be open to the universal unpopularity of *la vie chére*. A policy of bringing about an equilibrium between internal and external prices must be injurious to the export interests which flourish on their disequilibrium. It may not be sufficient to reply that the first must happen in any case unless the taxpayer will sacrifice himself to the rentier, and that the second must happen some day unless the franc is to fall for ever.

But there are political considerations of some weight to set on the other side. A rise in the prices of agricultural produce will not be unpopular with farmers and peasant producers who have been selling their output much too cheap. Further, the government must make it clear that wage earners and officials are not intended to suffer, and will, if it is wise, pass a law providing for automatic quarterly increases of all wages and salaries throughout the next two years corresponding to every increase in the cost of living.

Well, I offer these reflections for what they are worth. Whether or not they commend themselves to your judgement, I am sure that the following questions are those which you need to ponder:

1. Would a rise in the level of internal prices solve your difficulties?

2. Can you solve your difficulties without a rise of prices?

3. Is it not impossible anyhow to prevent a rise in the long run?

4. If so, will you not be judicious to facilitate an orderly rise and to play for time meanwhile?

5. Whether you choose this course or another, is there any sufficient objection to using the gold in the Bank of France to anchor the franc exchange?

Your obedient servant,

J. M. KEYNES

II THE STABILISATION OF THE FRANC (1928)

First published as an article in the *Nation and Athenaeum*, 30 June 1928, under the same title.

One blames politicians, not for inconsistency, but for obstinacy. They are the interpreters, not the masters, of our fate. It is their job, in short, to register the *fait accompli*. In this spirit we all applaud M. Poincaré for not allowing himself to be hampered by a regard for consistency. After declaring for years that it would be an act of national bankruptcy and shame to devalue the franc, he has fixed it at about one-fifth of its pre-war gold value, and has retorted with threats of resignation against anyone who would hinder him in so good a deed.

The figure finally chosen seems about right. There are high authorities in France who argue that one-sixth of pre-war (150 francs to the £) would be better and safer. But about one-fifth (124·21 francs to the £) has the great advantage of conforming to the rate which has actually existed for some eighteen months. None of the relevant statistics suggests that M. Poincaré has made the mistake of stabilising at a figure which involves deflation. No lower value for the franc (in terms of gold) than that now chosen has ever existed except during the hectic twelve months from December 1925 to November 1926, when internal prices had no time to adjust themselves to the furious fluctuations of the exchanges. Moreover, the budget balances with the burden of the *rentes* on the taxpayer bearable at the present level. I see no sufficient reason, therefore, to choose a lower figure.

Is the value too low? For that is the line of criticism in France itself. There are two chief tests. Is it lower than the figure to which internal prices are adjusted? Does it demand too great a sacrifice from the rentier? The official index numbers, if taken at their face value, suggest that prices are in line with a gold value of the franc nearer to one-quarter (100 francs to the £) than to one-fifth of the pre-war value. But the French index numbers are very crude affairs subject to a wide margin of error, and the two and a half years which has elapsed since the franc was worth more than the figure now fixed, is a fair time to allow for an adjustment of prices upward—a much quicker business than a downward adjustment can be. House rents doubtless must rise, but it is probable that other prices will trend only a little upward if at all, compared with gold prices abroad. As for the rentier, a very drastic capital levy having been brought about *de facto* and the awkward consequences surmounted, it is asking too much to undo gratuitously what is already done. Three other arguments, however, of a practical order are probably those which have convinced M. Poincaré. To choose a higher value for the franc might disturb the equilibrium of the budget which has been so painfully achieved. It would upset the industrialist exporters—who have their means of exerting political influence. And—most tangible of all —it would involve the Bank of France in a loss on the foreign exchange, said to amount to some £300 million, which, as an agent of the government, it has bought up at the present rate. To fix 100 francs to the £, for example, might cost the Bank of France £60 million, of which no mean proportion might accrue to foreigners. This is just the sort of argument which M. Poincaré and every other Frenchman is able to understand.

The deed, therefore, is done. Since it removes an element of uncertainty from the money markets and stock exchanges of the world, and since French importers and manufacturers need hesitate no longer, a good deal of purchasing power, which has been lying idle, may be returned to active employment. M. Poincaré has, therefore, done something—perhaps for the first time in his career—to make the rest of us feel more cheerful.

§The decree of Stabilisation has been accompanied by an unexpected change in the regulations governing the French gold reserves—a change for the worse. Hitherto the maximum of the note issue has been fixed from time to time, but the whole of the Bank of France's gold has been a free reserve. Now the senseless and vicious percentage system has been introduced, by which an amount of gold equal to 35 per cent of the note issue is to be wholly immobilised. But this is not all. The Bank of France is also to hold 35 per cent gold cover against its deposits on current account—the future amount of which it is difficult to calculate because the present figures include the sinking fund account. Since the note issue and the current accounts are at present about 66 milliard francs, this means that nearly £190 million (which is substantially more than the *total* amount of gold now held by the Bank of England and is some 10 per cent of all the monetary gold in the world) will be locked up, and the Bank of France's effective reserve will be such sum—probably substantial —as it may choose to hold in excess of this figure. Apart from its large recent acquisitions, of which the amount is not yet disclosed, the Bank of France now holds about £147 million— so that it is evident how important a sum the new law withdraws. Moreover, there are tentative proposals for putting gold into circulation at a later date, whilst the last vestiges of the pre-war bimetallism disappear. These new regulations confirm the opinion that the Bank of England has shown a grave want of wisdom in locking away so much of its own less ample resources. Standards are being set up, as to the conventional and respectable percentage of a gold cover against notes, which, if they are applied all round, will keep credit tight for years.

Apart, however, from this question of gold cover,§ it is interesting to compare the several fortunes of France and Great

Britain over the post-war period. In Great Britain our authorities have never talked such rubbish as their French colleagues or offended so grossly against all sound principles of finance. But Great Britain has come out of the transitional period with the weight of her war debt aggravated, her obligations to the United States unabated, and deflationary finance still in the ascendant; with the heavy burden of taxes appropriate to the former and a million unemployed as the outcome of the latter. France, on the other hand, has written down her internal war debt by four-fifths, and has persuaded her allies to let her off more than half of her external debt; and now she is avoiding the sacrifices of deflation. Yet she has contrived to do this without the slightest loss of reputation for conservative finance and capitalist principles. The Bank of France emerges much stronger than the Bank of England; and everyone still feels that France is the last stronghold of tenacious saving and the rentier mentality. Assuredly it does not pay to be good.

Perhaps we deserve what we have got. France has abandoned principle and consistency alike, but she has always refused sacrifices which were avoidable and has obeyed in the end the teachings of experience. We in England have not submitted either to the warnings of theory or to the pressure of facts, obstinately obedient to conventions.

4 CAN LLOYD GEORGE DO IT?

Can Lloyd George Do It?—The Pledge Examined was a pamphlet written jointly by Keynes and Hubert Henderson in support of Lloyd George's pledge in the 1929 general election to reduce unemployment by a programme of public spending. Chapter 7, signed by the two authors, appeared as 'The Cost of the Liberal Scheme' in the *Nation and Athenaeum*, 11 May 1929, the day following the pamphlet's publication. Keynes included Chapters 3, 9, 10 and 11 in *Essays in Persuasion*, changing most of the italics of the pamphlet (reproduced here) to ordinary type.

It has not proved possible to apportion the pamphlet between its joint authors. It was written in the heat of the election campaign, probably without time for a draft copy. As the editor-in-chief of the *Nation* and the chairman of its advisory board, Henderson and Keynes were in close sympathy, and both men had taken a major part through the years leading up to the election in framing the Liberal plans. The pamphlet seems to have been, according to Hubert Henderson's widow, Lady Henderson, '...a true work of collaboration about which there was never any question as to who gave the most'.

§PREFACE

As long ago as April 1924 the *Nation and Athenaeum* opened its columns to a discussion, which remained for some months the principal feature of the paper, on the economic position of Great Britain. A number of our leading economists and industrialists contributed to it, including such men as Sir William Beveridge, Professor Bowley, Mr R. H. Brand, Sir Alfred Mond, Lord Weir, the late Lord Montagu of Beaulieu, the late Sir William Acworth. The starting point of this discussion was the opinion which we had formed that Britain's post-war economic difficulties lay somewhat deeper than—as was then the fashionable view—the world impoverishment and disorganisation left behind by the war, and that it was essential to meet post-war unemployment by a positive policy of national development.

It was to Mr Lloyd George that we then turned as the man to open this discussion, because Mr Lloyd George stood out at that time as the one leading public man who shared this opinion, who openly scouted the optimistic assumption that our post-war unemployment would shortly solve itself without anybody doing anything in particular about it, and who accordingly was exposed to the foolish reproach of being a pessimist and a 'defeatist'. The letter which Mr Lloyd George contributed to the *Nation* (on 12 April 1924) has stood the test of time remarkably well, and stands on record to prove how baseless is the charge, now being spread about, that his interest in the policy of national development has been assumed belatedly for electioneering purposes.

The discussion in the *Nation* led to the question being taken up by the committee of the Liberal Summer School, who, in conjunction with Mr Lloyd George, set up the Liberal Industrial Inquiry. This body spent two years exploring the whole subject in the greatest possible detail with the assistance of some of the leading economists and business men in the country. Their results were published at the beginning of 1928 in the famous Yellow Book (*Britain's Industrial Future*). At the end of March 1928, a special convention of the National Liberal Federation was summoned to consider them, when they were adopted by the Party in a series of resolutions.

Britain's Industrial Future remains the fullest statement of the Liberal programme. Recently the Liberal pamphlet *We Can Conquer Unemployment* has been remarkably successful in crystallizing the essence of the matter in a few broad and simple propositions. We are here supplementing this with a further brief contribution, which is specially directed to answering recent criticisms.

Behind Mr Lloyd George's pledge there lies four years of minutely detailed preparation, and, as we have good reason to know, a severe and lengthy process of thought and study.

J.M.K.
H.D.H.

1 May 1929

THE PLEDGE

If the nation entrusts the Liberal Party at the next General Election with the responsibilities of government, we are ready with schemes of work which we can put immediately into operation, work of a kind which is not merely useful in itself but essential to the well-being of the nation. The work put in hand will reduce the terrible figures of the workless in the course of a single year to normal proportions, and will, when completed, enrich the nation and equip it for competing successfully with all its rivals in the business of the world. These plans will not add one penny to national or local taxation.

It will require a great and sustained effort to redeem this pledge, but some of us sitting at this table have succeeded in putting through even greater and more difficult tasks in the interests of the nation.

> Extract from Mr Lloyd George's address
> to Liberal candidates on 1 March 1929

I MR LLOYD GEORGE'S PLEDGE

Mr Lloyd George's pledge to reduce unemployment has been received by the great public with remarkable sympathy and enthusiasm. Some people have a suspicion that it must, surely, be a little exaggerated. But almost everyone, including the other political parties, have a much stronger suspicion that there is probably something in it after all.

Even those, therefore, who have hesitated to accept so grand an optimism, are—many of them—wholeheartedly supporting the Liberal policy. Even if it takes more than a year to get going, even if it costs the taxpayer something, even if it brings employment to no more than 400,000 or 500,000 additional men, what does it matter?—so feel these friendly doubters. It will be a move in the right direction. It will be far better than 'the snoring and roaring policies' of each of the two other parties. No one has put this point of view more clearly than Lord Grey: 'Even if the policy does not succeed in doing all that is hoped of it,' he says, 'even if the pledge turns out to be over-sanguine, even if the policy takes two or three or four years to accomplish all the results we hope for, it will not be by any means a failure; it will still remain the right policy.'

In this pamphlet we propose to examine the various reasons for doubt and hesitation and the criticisms which have been offered in recent weeks; and we shall try to answer the questions which reasonable men are asking. We shall not shirk any of the difficulties, even when it is not easy to express the answer in popular language.

We hope to show that the Liberal policy is not only common sense, but follows, as the appropriate remedy, from a far-reaching analysis of the fundamentals of our position.

Is the pledge too optimistic? Can Lloyd George do it?

No one can safely say beforehand what delays ingenious obstruction can interpose in getting on with business which will require a certain amount of legislation. But provided Mr Lloyd George is able to get going without delay and without obstruction—and that is what the fulfilment of his pledge within his limit of time assumes—our conclusion will be that his optimism is reasonable.

We believe that the cumulative effect of renewed prosperity will surpass expectations. It may well turn out in practice that a smaller programme than that outlined in *We Can Conquer Unemployment* will be sufficient to set the ball rolling, and to shift the whole outlook of the country from depression to prosperity. The patient looks sick. But once he turns the corner, the rapidity of his convalescence may astonish even the doctors who have cured him.

Indeed, the most solid reason for hesitation as to the fulfilment of the pledge within the stated period of time we find, not in the difficulty of finding work to do or in the difficulty of financing it, but in the 'transfer' problem—in the task of shifting men from industries where they are permanently redundant and settling them in their new work.

But this difficulty, if it proves such, is a reason not for delay, for holding back, or for timidity, but for pushing on with redoubled efforts. For the longer we delay, the more difficult will the task become and the harder will it be to employ those who have been forced into long-continued habits of unemployment.

It is useless to try to tackle the 'transfer' problem seriously until the jobs have first been created elsewhere, and employers are crying out for men. That is why the efforts of the present government in this direction have been so futile. It is useless to transfer men until there is something to transfer them to. Employers will have to be not merely acquiescent, but clamorous, before it will be easy to absorb—for example—many of the least efficient miners into new jobs in localities strange to them.

We should predict, therefore, that at a fairly early stage of the execution of the Liberal programme there will be in many industries an apparent shortage of labour. Then, when men are being clamoured for, will be the time to tackle the transfer problem with both hands. The date at which Mr Lloyd George can declare that his task is fulfilled will mainly depend on the rapidity with which this secondary problem can be handled.

To hold off from initiating the first stage—the stage of getting the great national programmes of development moving—out of doubts whether there are things worth doing and whether there is finance with which to do them, is utterly mistaken. This we hope to prove up to the hilt.

Forward, therefore, to the task—with the confidence, the bold optimism, the push and the drive, which tackled more formidable tasks in the war, and delivered the goods up to the scheduled date.

II THE COMMON SENSE OF THE PROBLEM

The Liberal policy is one of plain common sense. The Conservative belief that there is some law of nature which prevents men from being employed, that it is 'rash' to employ men, and that it is financially 'sound' to maintain a tenth of the population in idleness for an indefinite period, is crazily improbable—the sort of thing which no man could believe who had not had his head fuddled with nonsense for years and years.

The objections which are raised are mostly not the objections of experience or of practical men. They are based on highly abstract theories—venerable, academic inventions, half misunderstood by those who are applying them today, and based on assumptions which are contrary to the facts.

When Mr Baldwin discourses on this subject, it not only *is* nonsense that he talks, but it looks like nonsense to any simple-minded person who considers it with a fresh, unprejudiced mind. There is work to do; there are men to do it. Why not bring them together? No, says Mr Baldwin. There are mysterious, unintelligible reasons of high finance and economic theory why this is impossible. It would be most rash. It would probably ruin the country. Abra would rise, cadabra would fall. Your food would cost you more. If everyone were to be employed, it would be just like the war over again. And even if everyone was employed, how can you be perfectly sure that they would still be employed three years hence? If we build houses to cover our heads, construct transport systems to carry our goods, drain our lands, protect our coasts, what will there be left for our children to do? No, cries Mr Baldwin, it would be most unjust. The more work we do now the less there will be left to do hereafter. Unemployment is the lot of man. This generation must take its fair share of it without grousing. For the more the fewer, and the higher the less.

Yet, in truth, Mr Baldwin and his colleagues are not more capable of expounding the true economic science of the matter than they would be of explaining to you the latest propositions of Einstein. They would be much safer on the ground floor of common sense where Mr Lloyd George—fortified, as it happens, by a certain amount of economic science as well—has encamped his battalions.

Our main task, therefore, will be to confirm the reader's instinct that what *seems* sensible *is* sensible, and what *seems* nonsense *is* nonsense. We shall try to show him that the conclusion, that if new forms of employment are offered more men will be employed, is as obvious as it sounds and contains no hidden snags; that to set unemployed men to work on useful tasks does what it appears to do, namely, increases the national wealth; and that the notion, that we shall, for intricate reasons, ruin ourselves financially if we use this means to increase our well-being, is what it looks like—a bogy.

III   THE FACTS OF UNEMPLOYMENT§

Except for a brief recovery in 1924 before the return to the gold standard, one-tenth or more of the working population of this country have been unemployed for eight years—a fact unprecedented in our history. The number of insured persons counted by the Ministry of Labour as out of work has never been less than one million since the initiation of their statistics in 1923. Today (April 1929) 1,140,000 workpeople are unemployed.

This level of unemployment is costing us out of the Unemployment Fund a cash disbursement of about £50 million a year. This does not include poor relief. Since 1921 we have paid out to the unemployed in cash a sum of about £500 million—and have got literally nothing for it. This sum would have built a million houses; it is nearly double the whole of the accumulated savings of the Post Office Savings Bank; it would build a third of all the roads in the country; it far exceeds the total value of all the mines, of every description, which we possess; it would be enough to revolutionise the industrial equipment of the country; or to proceed from what is heavy to what is lighter, it would provide every third family in the country with a motor-car or would furnish a fund enough to allow the whole population to attend cinemas for nothing to the end of time.

But this is not nearly all the waste. There is the far greater loss to the unemployed themselves, represented by the difference between the dole and a full working wage, and by the loss of strength and morale. There is the loss in profits to employers and in taxation to the Chancellor of the Exchequer. There is the incalculable loss of retarding for a decade the economic progress of the whole country.

The Census of Production of 1924 calculated that the average value of the net annual output of a British working man when employed is about £220. On this basis the waste through unemployment since 1921 has mounted up to approximately £2,000 million, a sum which would be nearly sufficient to build all the railways in the country twice over. It would pay off our debt to America twice over. It is more than the total sum that the Allies are asking from Germany for reparations.

It is important to know and appreciate these figures because they put the possible cost of Mr Lloyd George's schemes into its true perspective. He calculates that a development programme of £100 million a year will bring back 500,000 men into employment. *This expenditure is not large in proportion to the waste and loss accruing year by year* through unemployment, as can be seen by comparing it with the figures quoted above. It only represents 5 per cent of the loss already accumulated on account of unemployment since 1921. It is equal to about $2\frac{1}{2}$ per cent of the national income. If the experiment were to be continued at the rate of £100 million per annum for three years, and if the whole of it were to be entirely wasted, the annual interest payable on it hereafter would increase the budget by less than 2 per cent. In short, it is a *very modest programme*. The idea that it represents a desperate risk to cure a moderate evil is the reverse of the truth. It is a negligible risk to cure a monstrous anomaly.

Nothing has been included in the programme which cannot be justified as worth doing for its own sake. Yet even if half of it were to be wasted, *we should still be better off*. Was there ever a stronger case for a little boldness, for taking a risk if there be one?

It may seem very wise to sit back and wag the head. But while we wait, the unused labour of the workless is not piling up to our credit in a bank, ready to be used at some later date. It is running irrevocably to waste; it is irretrievably lost. Every puff of Mr Baldwin's pipe costs us thousands of pounds.

IV §THE LIBERAL PROGRAMME

The Liberal policy of dealing with unemployment by a vigorous policy of national development aims, on the one hand, at providing immediate jobs for a large number of men, and, on the other, at lifting business and industry out of the rut into which they have fallen and setting them again on the high road of progress along which they should then be able to move forward under their own steam.

Such large arrears of national development have been allowed to accumulate, that there is enough work waiting to keep the programme going for a considerable time; more than enough to bridge the period during which men are being transferred from old industries to new and the country's industrial methods are being rationalised. The government themselves take the view that the difficulties facing us are not of a permanent character, but look like covering a two- to five-year period. In particular, the Minister of Labour has pointed out that in the course of the next five years the pressure of new entrants into industry from the growing generation will be falling very materially. Thus it is no argument against the policy that it will be on a larger scale than could be maintained *permanently*.

The full Liberal programme has been set out in *Britain's Industrial Future* and certain parts of it have been developed in greater detail in *We Can Conquer Unemployment*.

These books have demonstrated that there is no lack of things waiting to be done. When an energetic government gets down to the details, there will doubtless be much opportunity for wise selection. It is difficult to say with certainty, in advance, which of the projects are the most urgent, the most practical and the more capable of being put into execution with the least delay. In order to minimise the amount of 'transfer' of labour required, it will be of great importance to select a *well-balanced* programme.

For fuller details we must refer the reader to the publications mentioned above. But a short summary will be in place here.

I *The national transport system*

The biggest part of the programme consists in bringing our roads and railways up to date, and the services best provided by each of them into due correlation with those best provided by the other.

Roads are entirely a state concern, whilst railways are semi-privately owned. The employment which the modernisation of the former can furnish is more definitely calculable from outside than is the case with the latter. For this reason the roads take a foremost place amongst the concrete examples worked out in *We Can Conquer Unemployment*.

This has given rise to the mistaken idea that the Liberal programme is practically confined to building roads, and that railways (and indeed most other forms of development) are left out of account. This is not correct, as can be found by consulting the text of the two publications in which the programme is expounded. For example, in *Britain's Industrial Future*, it has been emphasised that the idea of developing road transport at the cost of railway traffic is fundamentally false.

We are wholly in agreement, therefore, with those who are urging that a foremost place should be accorded, alongside the road programme, to the modernisation of the railways. An immense amount of work might be advantageously done under this heading, on the improvement of yards and terminals, on the electrification of certain lines, and above all, on the replacement of the present system of small wagons by large wagons, such as nearly all foreign railway systems now employ. In this year's budget, the Government have recognised the need for improvements of this character. They have repealed the Railway Passenger Duty on the understanding that the railway companies will devote the capital equivalent of the duty to capital improvements. This is excellent so far as it goes, but it goes only a very little way. The capital sum in question ($£6\frac{1}{2}$ million) is clearly quite insufficient to provide for the big reform of the 20-ton wagon.

The Liberal Yellow Book proposed to facilitate work of this character by means of guaranteed loans on the lines of the Trade Facilities scheme. The same technique might also be used, as has been proposed by the Joint Conference on Industrial Relations, to provide the fresh capital required for approved schemes of amalgamation and reconstruction in the depressed industries.

The scope for useful development work of this character is, we believe, very large. But it is not possible, of course, to say definitely on what scale such work could be pressed forward, because this is a matter which depends on co-operation between the State and other interests. In the case of the railways, for example, the government could encourage, assist, and urge the railway companies on, but it would be for the railway companies to set the work in hand. Clearly, therefore, work of this character does not lend itself to detailed calculations regarding expenditure and employment, such as are given for other projects in *We Can Conquer Unemployment*. But the fact that railway improvement could not form a reliable basis for the pledge implies no disparagement of its desirability or urgency. And in practice we entertain little doubt that it would prove practicable to get work of this character going on a substantial scale.

As regards roads and bridges, it is proposed to spend a capital sum of £145 million over two years. We are satisfied that this is not an excessive sum to sink in road improvements. The replacement cost of our existing road system is probably at least £1,500 million, so that the scale of extension and reconstruction represented by the proposed outlay is the comparatively modest one of 10 per cent. In view of the rapid development and immense potentialities of road transport, there is nothing extravagant in a road improvement programme upon this scale. And since, according to the high authority of men like Sir Henry Maybury and the late Lord Montagu of Beaulieu, we have not been keeping pace in recent years with traffic requirements, there is everything to be said for pressing forward energetically with the work.

In practice, however, we do not believe that it would be necessary, in order to carry out Mr Lloyd George's pledge, to concentrate on roads to the maximum extent which would be feasible if required.

2 *National housing*

For complete details of the Liberal programme under this heading, we refer the reader to the same two publications as before, supplemented by Mr E. D. Simon's book *How to Abolish the Slums*.

The Conservative policy of cutting subsidies must result in such a restriction of building that there will be no hope of getting more than about 100,000 houses built each year (the pre-war number). The Liberal policy is to continue building 200,000 houses a year and to pay the necessary subsidies.

The Conservative policy would be just about sufficient to meet the increase of population and to replace houses which have to be pulled down to meet the needs of industry or for other reasons. It would provide almost no houses to reduce the overcrowding in the slums or to allow for slum clearances; slum conditions would, in spite of whatever can be done by reconditioning, tend to get worse instead of better.

The Liberal policy, on the other hand, would provide in ten years a million houses to meet the needs of the slums alone. These would go a very long way both in the reduction of overcrowding and in clearing out a large proportion of the worst plague spots. At the same time it would provide continuous employment for an additional 150,000 men. During this ten-year period there would be a saving in unemployment benefit amounting to no less than £75 million. The cost of all these benefits would be a burden of about £12 million a year on the national exchequer at the end of ten years, and a further burden of about £6 million a year on the rates.

Moreover the building industry is now one of the industries in which unemployment is most prevalent.

These national transport and housing programmes must be so carried out as to facilitate the now urgent task of rural preservation. The time has come for taking decisive, national action to preserve the downs, moors, lakes, woods, hills and commons of the countryside, and to conserve their beauties and their amenities for future generations. We owe a great deal to private munificence and to such bodies as the National Trust and the Commons and Footpaths Preservation Society. But as the population increases, and as it is spread more evenly over the land, as a result of better roads, motor transport, electrical power supply, and that decentralisation of industry and of population which we hope to promote, the preservation of Britain's open country passes outside the power of private persons or of societies interested in public welfare. It is, therefore, the Liberal policy to take power to schedule as national open spaces such areas as the Surrey Commons, the South Downs, Salisbury Plain, Dartmoor, Exmoor, and parts of the Peak and Lake Districts. The expense would not be great; the benefit to the future would be immeasurable.

3   *Other developments*

Whilst transport and housing are much the biggest individual items, this must not lead us to overlook the innumerable minor projects, collectively of great magnitude, which are waiting to be carried out as the result of the prolonged negative policy of recent times.

For several years past Royal Commissions, departmental committees, government departments, public boards, local authorities, and semi-official bodies have been having their favourite offspring smothered by the Treasury. There are innumerable schemes pigeonholed in government offices, the children of the most active and progressive brains in the country, which only have to be fished out to provide a great quantity of employment widely distributed in kind and locality.

As soon as we have a new atmosphere of *doing things*, instead of one of smothering negation, everybody's brains will get busy, and there will be masses of claimants for attention, the precise character of which it would be impossible to specify beforehand.

Many such projects, however, are outlined in the previously published Liberal publications. Those which come first in order of magnitude are telephone development, electrical development and land drainage, which could, it is estimated, employ 150,000 men and women.

We place great reliance on the multitude of miscellaneous projects, small individually, but impressive in the mass. We have already referred above to the extension of the Trade Facilities Act for the assistance of private enterprise.

The endeavour should clearly be to press forward with development and reconstruction work on the most extended front—railways, docks, harbours, no less than roads, housing, electricity and telephones.

We believe that the Liberal pamphlet underestimates rather than overestimates the amount of work which is waiting to be done, and also the effects upon employment of expenditure on a given scale. The stress that has been laid by critics, since the Liberal pamphlet appeared, on the scope for railway improvement, illustrates how large and various is the work of a development character which is available.

V THE GOVERNMENT'S CASE

Before Mr Lloyd George gave his pledge at the luncheon of the Liberal candidates on 1 March, the favourite line of the opponents of national development was not to attack it directly, but to pooh-pooh and minimise its possibilities. The principle of pressing forward with desirable public works in times of exceptional unemployment was admitted to be sound; but it was argued (or implied) that the government had already been so zealous in acting on this principle that its possibilities were now exhausted. This remarkable proposition has received its latest and most authoritative expression in the final report of the Balfour Committee on Industry and Trade. After stating that the 'arguments are all in favour' of pressing forward as rapidly as possible with 'necessary public work' in times of exceptional unemployment, the Balfour Committee proceeds as follows:

Nevertheless it would be wrong to expect too great results from action of this kind. A large part of the public work which is susceptible of postponement or acceleration is work of special kinds, which could not provide employment in their own trades for any considerable number of unemployed persons. Moreover, the experience of the post-war depression, when considerable inducement was held out by the Government year after year to local authorities and others to expedite necessary work in order to provide immediate employment, shows that in a long-continued depression the possibilities of *bona fide* anticipation become rapidly exhausted. In these circumstances employment so provided may tend to lose its economic character and to become hardly distinguishable from ordinary relief work.

Another way in which, until recently, it was sought to show that there was 'nothing in' the policy of national development was to minimise the amount of employment which a given capital expenditure could provide. Thus Mr Churchill declared as follows in the House of Commons on 8 November last:

Most careful study has been given during the last few months by the public departments to possible relief works...

(The use of the phrase 'relief works', to describe projects of capital expenditure, is characteristic of the ministerial eagerness to confuse the issue.)

On general grounds we are opposed to such a system, especially when directly conducted by the State. It is surprising to see, in the examples which we have lately studied, how meagre are the results in actually relieving the particular problem of unemployment with which we are coping, compared with the outlay in every case.

In this contention, too, the ministers have been able to claim the support of an official inquiry. Thus the Industrial Transference Board, in the scanty and insipid section headed 'Creation of artificial employment', which disfigured their report, wrote as follows:

As instances of the cost involved we may say that it has been estimated that to give 1,350 unskilled men work on trunk road reconstruction for one year would cost one million pounds. On land drainage, for the same sum, about 1,000 unskilled men could be employed for two to three years. These figures make it clear that any attempt by the State to provide for the problem before us by the creation of a substitute employment market, on a scale sufficient to have any effect at all, would be prohibitive in cost.

Such contentions and such figures, when put forward by official committees, with access to official information, are apt to carry great weight with the British public. An intelligent and open-minded man, impressed by the authority of such bodies as the Balfour Committee and the Industrial Transference Board, might not unreasonably have supposed, until a few weeks ago, that it had been conclusively shown that the policy of national development, however right in principle, could only have a negligible influence upon employment. Ministers did their utmost to spread this impression. 'It is all very well to urge us to do things in general; just tell us some of the particular things that you would have us do'—such was for a long time a favourite ministerial retort. For example, in the speech from which we have already quoted, Mr Churchill challenged his critics in the following terms:

The right hon. gentleman said that we had the choice between paying for idleness or paying for work. We could find no difficulty in making that choice if he explained to us what were the methods by which we were able to choose the one instead of the other.

We deal in chapter VI below with the argument that the work provided will be inadequate in quantity and unsuitable in kind. But the novelty of the Liberal answer to this challenge in *We Can Conquer Unemployment* lay in its reducing the matter to concrete terms. It is now impossible for ministers to treat the Liberal policy of national development, originally set forth in the Yellow Book (*Britain's Industrial Future*), and formally adopted by the Party in March 1928, as a mere vague idea.

Accordingly the line of defence has been shifted. It is now maintained, not that there is nothing to be done, but that anything which is done merely diverts employment from other things. We deal with this in detail in chapter IX.

Meanwhile the government has been living up to its principles. The number of houses built under State schemes, which rose to the high figure of 212,000 during the year ending September 1927, fell away, as the result of the cut in the subsidy, to only 101,000 in the following year. The work of road improvement has been so restricted that, according to the late Lord Montagu of Beaulieu, 'hardly a mile of new trunk road has been planned and constructed during the last two years'. In these two facts we have a reason why employment has been so disappointing during what Mr Churchill calls 'the longest lucid interval that I can recall since 1914'.

VI HOW MUCH EMPLOYMENT WILL
THE LIBERAL PLAN PROVIDE?

In examining the Liberal claim, two distinct points arise, namely, (1) the amount of employment which a given expenditure would provide, and (2) the suitability of the employment to those who are now out of work.

On the first point, the calculations of *We Can Conquer Unemployment* have been the subject of a controversy which has resulted in their vindication. It will be convenient, therefore, to take this point first.

1 *The amount of employment for each 1 million*

The Liberal pamphlet claims that each million pounds spent annually on road improvements would employ, directly or indirectly, 5,000 workpeople. The passage in which this claim is made runs as follows:

Expert opinion is that some 80 per cent of total expenditure represents the amounts paid directly or indirectly in wages. This would mean some 5,500 men per £1 million of total expenditure. Of these, from 2,000 to 2,500 would be employed directly, and the remainder in production of materials and their transport. A very safe total figure is 5,000 men per annum for every £1 million.

Now this is nearly four times the figure given by the Industrial Transference Board in the passage which we have already quoted. Their estimate, we may recall, was that 'to give 1,350 unskilled men work on road reconstruction for one year, would cost one million pounds'. It is true that they said 'unskilled men'. It is, indeed, quite easy to account for the discrepancy between the two estimates. They were ignoring (1) the skilled labour employed directly on the roads, and (2) the whole of the indirect employment on making road materials. But the point is that the Industrial Transference Board used this figure of 1,350 as though it gave the full measure of the employment resulting from expenditure on road improvements. They gave no hint that there was any indirect employment to be considered; and proceeded to infer from the figure of 1,350 the conclusion that a development policy could not make a real impression on the unemployment figures.

Fortunately, this matter has now been cleared up. Cabinet ministers were rash enough to assert that the Liberal estimate was a gross exaggeration. On 4 March, a few days after Mr Lloyd

George gave his pledge, Sir Philip Cunliffe-Lister, the President of the Board of Trade, used the following words:

I have inquired of the Ministry of Transport how many men can be employed to make roads out of relief. They tell me that if you spent £1 million it would employ only 2,000 people for one year.

Of course, Sir Philip Cunliffe-Lister too was forgetting indirect employment. After this, questions were put in the House of Commons which resulted in extracting from Colonel Ashley, the Minister of Transport, the following reluctant admission:

If the works were undertaken predominantly in urban areas on the most economical terms, a figure of 2,000 men employed *direct* on the work for a year for each £1 million expended would probably be a reasonable estimate. If the works consisted largely of selected schemes in rural areas, which admitted of a high proportion of manual labour, the figures might be increased to as much as 2,500.

No sufficient data exists to enable a useful estimate to be framed as regards the volume of employment provided away from the actual site of the works, but it is commonly assumed that for every man employed on the actual works, another man would be indirectly employed in producing and transporting materials and in other ways, and this assumption may not be unreasonable.

Thus we now reach an official admission that the Liberal estimate is not in the least fantastic. In putting the direct employment at from 2,000 to 2,500, Colonel Ashley confirms the precise figures given in the Liberal pamphlet, and he admits that it 'may not be unreasonable' to double these figures to allow for indirect employment. In view of previous ministerial assertions, Colonel Ashley is naturally anxious not to admit more than he must, and he puts this allowance for indirect employment decidedly on the low side. We do not believe that the Liberal pamphlet overstates it in describing its estimate of 5,000 men as 'a very safe total figure'. But what Colonel Ashley now admits is sufficient to show that the Liberal pamphlet indicates correctly the order of magnitude of the employment which road-building would provide, and that the impression conveyed by cabinet ministers and by the Industrial Transference Board was quite incorrect.

Generally speaking, we believe that employment for 5,000 men per £1 million of capital development is a safe average figure for the various items in the Liberal programme, taken as a whole.

2 *The importance of indirect employment*

This episode is instructive in several ways. The calculations of *We Can Conquer Unemployment* have been upheld on the one point on which they have been the subject of specific challenge. This helps to confirm the claim made in the pamphlet that these calculations are based throughout on reliable technical advice. It certainly entitles us to accept the similar estimates as to the effect on employment of a given expenditure on housing, telephones, etc. But that is not all. The roads admission shows how extremely careless and slipshod is the reasoning on which the official case against development is founded. The Industrial Transference Board either forgot, or thought it fair to ignore, the whole factor of indirect employment in connection with the building of roads; and it is evident that this factor is similarly ignored in all the more general assertions as to the 'meagre' results of development expenditure. But why should this factor be ignored? There is nothing fanciful or fine-spun about the proposition that the construction of roads entails a demand for road materials, which entails a demand for labour and also for other commodities, which, in their turn, entail a demand for labour. Such reactions are of the very essence of the industrial process. Why, the first step towards a right understanding of the economic world is to realise how far-reaching such reactions are, to appreciate how vast is the range of trades and occupations which contribute to the production of the commonest commodities. That a demand for a suit of clothes implies a demand for cloth; that a demand for cloth implies a demand for yarns and tops, and so for wool;

that the services of farmers, merchants, engineers, miners, transport workers, clerks, are all involved—this is the ABC of economic science. Yet our ministers and our Industrial Transference Boards argue as though the making of a suit of clothes employed none outside the tailors' shops. Such are the elementary fallacies by which our policy has been dominated in recent years.

Generally speaking, the indirect employment which schemes of capital expenditure would entail is far larger than the direct employment. This fact is one of the strongest arguments for pressing forward with such schemes; for it means that the greater part of the employment they would provide would be spread far and wide over the industries of the country. But the fact that the indirect employment would be spread far and wide does not mean that it is in the least doubtful or illusory. On the contrary, it is calculable within fairly precise limits. We are satisfied on this matter that the estimates given in *We Can Conquer Unemployment*, taken as a whole, understate rather than overstate the case.

3 *The cumulative force of trade activity*

But this is not the whole of the story. In addition to the indirect employment with which we have been dealing, a policy of development would promote employment in other ways. The fact that many workpeople who are now unemployed would be receiving wages instead of unemployment pay would mean an increase in effective purchasing power which would give a general stimulus to trade. Moreover, the greater trade activity would make for further trade activity; for the forces of prosperity, like those of trade depression, work with a cumulative effect. When trade is slack there is a tendency to postpone placing orders, a reluctance to lay in stocks, a general hesitation to go forward or take risks. When, on the other hand, the wheels of trade begin to move briskly the opposite set of forces comes into play, a mood favourable to enterprise and capital extensions spreads through the business community, and the expansion of trade gains accordingly a gathering momentum.

It is not possible to measure effects of this character with any sort of precision, and little or no account of them is, therefore, taken in *We Can Conquer Unemployment*. But, in our opinion, these effects are of immense importance. For this reason we believe that the effects on employment of a given capital expenditure would be far larger than the Liberal pamphlet assumes. These considerations have a bearing, it should be observed, on the time factor in Mr Lloyd George's pledge. It is a mistake to suppose that a long interval would elapse after, let us say, the work of road construction had been commenced before the full effect on employment would be produced. In the economic world, 'coming events cast their shadows before', and the knowledge that large schemes of work were being undertaken would give an immediate fillip to the whole trade and industry of the country.

4 The suitability of the employment

One of the commonest objections brought against the policy of development is that the majority of the unemployed are not fitted for the kind of work which would be offered.

This objection is only plausible if the whole factor of indirect employment is ignored. To argue as though it were proposed to put the great mass of the unemployed on outdoor work like road construction is a mere caricature of the Liberal scheme. As Mr Lloyd George has shown, no fewer than forty-seven different industries play their part in the building of roads, and the greater part of the employment which road building would provide would be in these forty-seven industries, and not on the roads themselves. It is irrelevant, therefore, to point out that only a proportion of the unemployed are fitted for heavy labouring work.

It is equally irrelevant to point out that only a small part of the unemployment figures represents workpeople who can be said to be permanently unemployed, and that the majority are either on short time or have been out of work for a short period only, and have reason to hope that they may again obtain employment in their own trades. This fact makes the task simpler and not more difficult. Development expenditure will give a wide and far-reaching stimulus to industry, and will enable many industries to re-absorb the unemployed or short-time surplus which now attaches to them. This will mean fully as genuine a reduction of unemployment as the absorption of people in new occupations.

For example, the development scheme will involve a large demand for iron and steel. To meet this demand it will not be necessary for the iron and steel industry to draw in labour unfamiliar with the trade. There is a sufficient margin of work-people unemployed or on short-time attached to it. But the absorption of this margin will mean a genuine reduction of unemployment. It is untrue, therefore, to say that men unemployed for short periods only are not 'available' for development schemes. Those on short time in the iron and steel industry are certainly available. Moreover, the substitution of full-time for short-time will mean both in reality and statistically, a reduction of unemployment.

The comparative constancy of the aggregate unemployment figures for the past eight years conceals the most significant changes in their distribution among industries. In 1924 there were nearly 1,200,000 men on the books of the colliery companies; in August 1928 there were less than 900,000. The number of miners unemployed was only 26,000 at the former date, and nearly 300,000 at the latter. It has since fallen to 145,000, partly owing to increased work at the mines, but mainly owing to transference to other occupations. In building, on the other hand, unemployment increased from 64,000 in March 1926 to 104,000 in March 1929; in works of construction such as road-making the change in the same period is from 26,000 to 37,000.

The existing unemployment is not of such a character that

a general fillip to trade, concentrated in the first instance on the building and contracting industries, is an inappropriate remedy. The unemployment is somewhat widely spread, and transference is duly proceeding out of the industries where the curtailment of opportunity looks like lasting. It is the general failure of industry as a whole to show absorptive power which is keeping the aggregate of unemployment at so high a figure.

5 *How long will it take?*

The suggestion that it is impossible to reduce unemployment to normal proportions within a year by a sufficiently vigorous policy comes with a peculiar irony from the members of the present government. For, within the last few weeks, they have not hesitated to base their legislation on this very assumption that unemployment will fall to normal in a year. At the end of 1927 the government introduced and passed an Unemployment Insurance Act, based on the recommendations of the Blanesburgh Committee, which contained what is known as 'the thirty contributions rule'. This rule disqualifies from unemployment benefit anyone who has not paid thirty contributions within the past two years—i.e. anyone who has been continuously out of work for a long period. If allowed to operate it would disqualify most of the surplus miners. But the Act provided that this rule should not take effect for eighteen months. The government spokesmen in the House of Commons defended both the clause, and the postponement of its operation, by declaring their belief that unemployment would be reduced to normal proportions before it took effect.

By the beginning of the present year it had become certain that this expectation would not be fulfilled. In March, accordingly, the government introduced an amending Bill, which postponed the operation of 'the thirty contributions' clause for a further year, but only for a further year; and the Minister of Labour repeated, though somewhat more vaguely, his optimistic assurances. It is thus still the formal position of cabinet ministers that unemployment may fall to normal within this period, without any active exertions on their part. In contrast to Lord Grey, they believe in the pledge but not the policy. Why should it be reasonable to assume, as the basis of an Act of Parliament, that unemployment will fall to normal, of itself, but fantastic to claim that a sufficiently vigorous and determined policy might really bring this about?

VII WHAT WILL IT COST?

Mr Lloyd George has given a pledge that the execution of his programme will not mean an addition to taxation. He has added that, of course, this does not mean that it will cost nothing, but that the cost will be less than the money which it will save in other directions *plus* the buoyancy of the revenue attributable to it *plus* economies on such things as armaments.

Perhaps this part of his pledge has attracted the most criticism from the cold-footed. But this must mean that his critics have not tried to work out the sum. We think he could safely have promised that it will cost *much less*.

Let us begin by weighting the scales against him as much as we can. Let us assume (1) that his programme costs £300 million before it is finished; (2) that not a single item in it brings in one penny of return; and (3) that we are thinking of the gain or loss, not to the national income or well-being, but to the budget in the narrowest sense of the term. Let us assume, further, that the necessary loans cost 6% per annum for interest and sinking fund.

On these assumptions, which include the fantastic hypothesis that you can spend £300 million in the course of three years on the best schemes of developing this country which can be thought of, without any of them bringing in a penny of revenue, the cost to the budget will be £18 million a year.

This sum is about 2½ per cent of the existing revenue. If increasing the employed population by 5 per cent were to raise the yield of the present taxes by 1½ per cent, and if expenditure on armaments were to be reduced by 7½ per cent, the bill would be met.

But this is, of course, far beyond what Mr Lloyd George is pledging himself to accomplish. For he is relying on the actual character of his programme to cost much less than £18 million.

In the first place, the road developments will be financed entirely out of 'betterment' and by pledging the existing assigned revenues of the Road Fund; so that they will cost the budget nothing.

In the second place, housing schemes, which are much the most expensive part of the programme, will, though they need a subsidy, bring in in the shape of rents an appreciable return on the money spent. Mr E. D. Simon calculates that the Liberal programme of building 200,000 houses a year, as compared with the Conservative programme of 100,000, and of subsidising them to the extent necessary to get them let to those for whom they are intended, would cost the budget £1,200,000 a year; so that at the end of three years of this programme, the annual charge on the budget would have risen to £3,600,000. His plan would also involve the rates in a charge of £600,000 a year, or £1,800,000 after a three-year programme, making £5,400,000 altogether. On the other hand, this would provide employment for an additional 150,000 men.

In the third place, many of the miscellaneous items in the programme, as, for example, telephones and Trade Facilities loans, will pay for themselves.

To sum up, a Ministry of Unemployment, which had at its disposal, say, £2,500,000 a year to meet the additional recurrent obligations it was incurring, chargeable on the budget, making altogether £7,500,000 (recurrent) for a three-years' programme, would be amply provided for.

On the other side of the balance sheet, the task of improving the budget by £2,500,000 each year, through improved revenue and economies on armaments, is literally a trifle. We should hope that a Liberal government would do much better than that. It represents 0·33 per cent of the revenue and less than 3 per cent of the expenditure on armaments.

But this is not the end of the calculation. We have made no allowance so far for the gain to the Unemployment Fund through the reduction in the numbers of the unemployed. For, strictly speaking, the Unemployment Fund is outside the budget; so that its gains do not directly relieve the budget. Indirectly, nevertheless, they will relieve the budget; since the existing deficit on the Fund will surely fall on the budget sooner or later.

If the unemployed are reduced by 500,000, this will improve the position of the Fund by nearly £25 million a year. Let the reader note the magnitude of this figure relatively to the annual costs of each year's programme which we have estimated above, namely, *ten* times greater. This includes no allowance for the saving to the Poor Law and, therefore, to the rates.

A *quarter* of the *capital* cost of each year's programme will be balanced by the gain to the Unemployment Fund *within that year*.

Probably an *eighth* would be recovered in that, or the subsequent year, through the gain to the revenue corresponding to the increased national income.

Thus, nearly a *half* of the *capital* cost would be recovered *at the time*. Accordingly there would be no appreciable national loss on the programme, even if it cost on the average 5 per cent per annum and only brought in on the average 2½ per cent.

So far our calculations have related to the limited field of the national finances, and not to the national welfare in its totality. If we are allowed to reckon in the benefits to the unemployed themselves and the national advantage, accruing otherwise than in direct cash receipts, from such things as efficient transport and healthy national housing, surely the case is overwhelming.

Take as gloomy a view as you like—the maximum cost and the maximum risk is of the mildest description, disproportionately small to the possible benefits which may ensue.

VIII IS IT SOCIALISM?

Why must the government play a part itself? Why is it not enough to offer facilities and encouragement to private enterprise?

The answer has been given in the Liberal Yellow Book (*Britain's Industrial Future*). A very large part of those economic enterprises which absorb substantial amounts of capital have fallen under the influence or the control of government departments. It has been an inevitable trend which has proceeded uninterruptedly under whatever political party has been in power.

Whether we like it or not, *it is a fact* that the rate of capital development in the transport system, the public utilities and the housing of this country largely depends on the policy of the Treasury and the government of the day.

If they restrict and curtail, nothing is done. If they choose to go to sleep, we drop behind. But if they facilitate and inspire, the equipment of the country moves forward. The choice between a well-equipped, up-to-date, go-ahead and efficient national plant depends on the mood and policy of the government.

Thus it is not a question of choosing between private and public enterprise in these matters. The choice has been already made. In many directions—though not in all—it is a question of the state putting its hand to the job or of its not being done at all.

Roads, afforestation, reclamation and drainage, electrification, slum clearance and town planning, the development of canals, docks and harbours; these are the things which need to absorb large sums of capital today, and in every case the initiative necessarily lies with a public authority.

But there are other equally important items in the Liberal programme where the object is to facilitate private enterprise. The rehabilitation of agriculture; assistance to the railways to modernise their equipment and rolling stock; an extension of the principles of the Trade Facilities Act by which loans are granted to private enterprise; these things are of no less importance than those activities which must be carried out, as well as set going, by public authority.

For the object is not to develop state enterprise as such. The object is to develop and equip the country through the instrumentality of such forms of organisation as already exist and lie ready to our hands.

That the Liberal programme is not of a Socialistic character has been well emphasised by an impartial and strongly anti-Socialist organ, *The Investors' Chronicle and Money Market Review*—the weekly financial newspaper which has the largest circulation in the country amongst middle-class investors. In their issue of 13 April 1929, they write as follows:

ELECTION TACTICS

A high standard of fairness in criticism is hardly to be looked for on political platforms when a General Election campaign is in progress, but it is rather surprising to find *The Times*, in a leading article on 'cures for unemployment', deliberately representing the Liberal scheme as on all-fours with the policy of Socialist-Labour because they both propose 'to find work for the unemployed through the agency of the State'. Surely that is a perfect example of the half-truth made wholly false by its suppressions? For what Socialist-Labour proposed to do is to provide work (or maintenance) for everybody by withdrawing from private enterprise 'the means of production, distribution and exchange', and substituting State control, while all that the Liberal scheme involves is the assistance of the State, in circumstances of emergency, towards prosecuting national undertakings of a kind which cannot be, or are not likely to be by reason of their character, carried through by private enterprise at all. If roads, for example, are not constructed and maintained by public authorities using public funds, who is to make and maintain them? Certainly private enterprise will not tackle the task, for we are long past the days of toll-gates!

IX WILL IT MERELY DIVERT EMPLOYMENT
FROM OTHER ENTERPRISES?§

The objection which is raised more frequently perhaps, than any other, is that money raised by the state for financing productive schemes must diminish *pro tanto* the supply of capital available for ordinary industry. If this is true, a policy of national development will not really increase employment. It will merely substitute employment on State schemes for ordinary employment. Either that, or (so the argument often runs) it must mean inflation. There is, therefore, little or nothing that the government can usefully do. The case is hopeless, and we must just drift along.

This was the contention of the Chancellor of the Exchequer in his budget speech.

'It is the orthodox Treasury dogma, steadfastly held', he told the House of Commons, 'that whatever might be the political or social advantages, very little additional employment and no permanent additional employment, can, in fact, and as a general rule, be created by State borrowing and State expenditure.' Some State expenditure he concluded, is inevitable, and even wise and right for its own sake, *but not as a cure for unemployment*.

In relation to the actual facts of today, this argument is, we believe, quite without foundation.

In the first place, there is nothing in the argument which limits its applicability to State-promoted undertakings. If it is valid at all, it must apply equally to a new works started by Morris, or Courtaulds, to any new business enterprise entailing capital expenditure. If it were announced that some of our leading captains of industry had decided to launch out boldly, and were about to sink capital in new industrial plant to the tune, between them, of £100 millions, we should all expect to see a great improvement in employment. And, of course, we should be right. But, if the argument we are dealing with were sound, we should be wrong. We should have to conclude that these enterprising business men were merely diverting capital from other uses, and that no real gain to employment could result. Indeed, we should be driven to a still more remarkable conclusion. We should have to conclude that it was virtually out of the question to absorb our unemployed work-people by any means whatsoever (other than the unthinkable inflation), and that the obstacle which barred the path was no other than an insufficiency of capital. This, if you please, in Great Britain, who has surplus savings which she is accustomed to lend abroad on the scale of more than a hundred millions a year.

The argument is certainly not derived from common sense. No ordinary man, left to himself, is able to believe that, if there had been no housing schemes in recent years, there would, nevertheless, have been just as much employment. And, accordingly, most ordinary men are easily persuaded by Mr Lloyd George that, if his schemes for employment are adopted, more men will be employed.

But the argument is not only unplausible. It is also untrue. There are three resources which can enable new investment to provide a net addition to the amount of employment.

The first source of supply comes out of the savings which we are now disbursing to pay the unemployed.

The second source of supply comes from the savings which now run to waste through lack of adequate credit.

The third source of supply comes from a reduction in the *net* amount of foreign lending.

Let us consider these in turn, beginning with the first source. Individual saving means that some individuals are *producing* more than they are *consuming*. This surplus may, and should be, used to increase capital equipment. But, unfortunately, this is not the only way in which it can be used. It can also be used to enable other individuals to *consume* more than they *produce*.

This is what happens when there is unemployment. We are using our savings to pay for unemployment, instead of using them to equip the country. The savings which Mr Lloyd George's schemes will employ will be diverted not from financing other capital equipment, but partly from financing unemployment. From the Unemployment Fund alone we are now paying out £50 million a year; and this is not the whole of the cost of supporting the unemployed.

In the second place, the savings of individuals do not necessarily materialise in investments. The amount of investment in capital improvements depends, on the one hand, on the amount of credit created by the Bank of England; and, on the other hand, on the eagerness of entrepreneurs to invest, of whom the government itself—as we have already seen—is nowadays the most important. So far from the total of investment, as determined by these factors, being necessarily equal to the total of saving, dis-equilibrium between the two is at the root of many of our troubles.

When investment runs ahead of saving we have a boom, intense employment, and a tendency to inflation. When investment lags behind, we have a slump and abnormal unemployment, as at present.

It is commonly objected to this that an expansion of credit necessarily means inflation. But not *all* credit-creation means inflation. Inflation only results when we endeavour, as we did in the war and afterwards, to expand our activities still further after everyone is already employed and our savings are being used up to the hilt.

The suggestion that a policy of capital expenditure, if it does not take capital away from ordinary industry, will spell inflation, would be true enough if we were dealing with boom conditions. And it would become true if the policy of capital expenditure were pushed unduly far, so that the demand for savings began to exceed the supply. But we are far, indeed, from such a position at the present time. A large amount of deflationary slack has first to be taken up before there can be the smallest danger of a development policy leading to inflation. To bring up the bogy of inflation as an objection to capital expenditure at the present time is like warning a patient who is wasting away from emaciation of the dangers of excessive corpulence.

The real difficulty hitherto in the way of an easier credit policy by the Bank of England has been the fear that an expansion of credit might lead to a loss of gold which the Bank could not afford.

Now if the Bank were to try to increase the volume of credit at a time when, on account of the depression of home enterprise, no reliance could be placed on the additional credit being absorbed at home at the existing rate of interest, this might quite well be true. Since market rates of interest would fall, a considerable part of the new credit might find its way to *foreign* borrowers, with the result of a drain of gold out of the Bank. Thus it is not safe for the Bank to expand credit unless it is certain beforehand that there are *home* borrowers standing ready to absorb it at the existing rates of interest.

This is the reason why the Liberal plan is exactly suited to the fundamentals of the present position. It provides the necessary condition for an expansion of credit to be safe.

It is, of course, essential that the Bank of England should loyally co-operate with the government's programme of capital development, and do its best to make it a success. For, unfortunately, it would lie within the power of the Bank, provided it were to pursue a deflationary policy aimed at preventing any expansion in bank credit, to defeat the best-laid plans and to ensure that the expenditure financed by the Treasury *was* at the expense of other business enterprise.

Thus we accept Mr McKenna's contention that an expansion of credit is the key to the situation. But if we were simply to increase credit without providing a specific use for it at home, we should be nervous that too much of this extra credit would be lent to foreigners and taken away in gold. We conclude, therefore, that, whilst an increased volume of bank credit is probably a *sine qua non* of increased employment, a programme of home investment which will absorb this increase is a *sine qua non* of the safe expansion of credit.

The third source of the funds required for the Liberal policy will be found by a net reduction of foreign lending.

An important part of our savings is now finding its outlet in foreign issues. Granted that a big policy of national development could not be financed wholly out of the existing expenditure on unemployment and out of the savings which are at present running to waste, granted that, to meet the borrowing demands of the State other borrowers must go without, why should we assume that these other borrowers must be British business men? The technique of the capital market makes it far more probable that they would be some of the overseas governments or municipalities which London at present finances on so large a scale. It is the bond market that would be principally affected by a British government loan.

Now anything which served to diminish the volume of foreign issues would be welcomed by the Bank of England at the present time for its own sake. The exchange position is uncomfortable and precarious; the recent rise in bank rate is proof of that. A diminution of foreign investment would ease the strain on the exchanges. Why, it is only a year or two since the Bank of England, with this end in view, was maintaining a semi-official embargo on foreign issues. The embargo was a crude instrument, suitable only for temporary use, and we do not suggest its renewal. But the need which that embargo was designed to supply still remains, if in a less acute degree. In relation to our less favourable balance of foreign trade, we are investing abroad dangerously much; and we are investing abroad to this dangerous extent partly because there are insufficient outlets for our savings at home.

It follows, therefore, that a policy of capital expenditure, in so far as it might go beyond the mere absorption of deflationary slack, would serve mainly to divert to home development savings which now find their way abroad, and that this would be a welcome result in the interests of the Bank of England.

It has been objected that if we lend less abroad, our exports will fall off. We see no reason to anticipate this. Immediately, as we have said, the reduction in *net* foreign lending will relieve the pressure on the Bank of England's stock of gold. But, ultimately, its main effect will be realised, not in a reduction of exports, but in an increase of imports. For the new schemes will require a certain amount of imported raw materials, whilst those who are now unemployed will consume more imported food when they are once again earning decent wages.

Here, then, is our answer. The savings which Mr Lloyd George's schemes will employ will be diverted, not from financing other capital equipment, but partly from financing unemployment. A further part will come from the savings which now run to waste through lack of adequate credit. Something will be provided by the very prosperity which the new policy will foster. And the balance will be found by a reduction of foreign lending.

The whole of the labour of the unemployed is available to increase the national wealth. It is crazy to believe that we shall ruin ourselves financially by trying to find means for using it and that 'safety first' lies in continuing to maintain men in idleness.

It is precisely *with* our unemployed productive resources that we shall make the new investments.

We are left with a broad, simple, and surely incontestable proposition. Whatever real difficulties there may be in the way of absorbing our unemployed labour in productive work, an inevitable diversion of resources from other forms of employment is not one of them.

§This conclusion is not peculiar to ourselves or to Mr Lloyd George and his advisers. The theoretical question involved is not a new one. The general problem whether capital developments financed by the government are capable of increasing employment has been carefully debated by economists in recent years. The result has been to establish the conclusion of this chapter as sound and orthodox and the Treasury's dogma as fallacious. For example—to quote authorities of diverse gifts and experience—our preceding argument has closely followed Professor Pigou's reasoning in his recent volume *Industrial Fluctuations* (part II, chapter X), where he quotes a statement of the Treasury dogma and expressly declares it to be fallacious; this conclusion is endorsed by Sir Josiah Stamp; and it has been ardently advocated by Mr McKenna (see, in particular, his 1927 address to his shareholders, reprinted in *Post-War Banking Policy*, p. 118) who, speaking as the chairman of the greatest bank in the world, maintains, without hesitation, that an increase in the volume of money investable in business activity is possible without inflationary consequences.

Indeed, we have not been able to discover any recent pronouncement to the contrary, outside the ranks of the Treasury, by an economist of weight or reputation. It is an error to believe that Mr Baldwin and Mr Churchill and Sir Laming Worthington-Evans are talking impeccable economic orthodoxy when they maintain that government borrowing necessarily attracts to itself resources which would otherwise have been employed in private enterprise, and that Mr Lloyd George is offering no better than a specious dodge when he maintains the contrary. Precisely the opposite is true. The theory underlying the Liberal Party's policy is the theory which is supported by the weight of expert opinion.

X THE POLICY OF NEGATION§

Our whole economic policy during recent years has been dominated by the preoccupation of the Treasury with their departmental problem of debt conversion. The less the government borrows, the better, they argue, are the chances of converting the national debt into loans carrying a lower rate of interest. In the interests of conversion, therefore, they have exerted themselves to curtail, as far as they can, all public borrowing, all capital expenditure by the State, no matter how productive and desirable in itself. We doubt if the general public has any idea how powerful, persistent, and far-reaching this influence has been.

To all well-laid schemes of progress and enterprise, they have (whenever they could) barred the door with, No! Now it is quite true that curtailing capital expenditure exerts some tendency towards lower interest rates for government loans. But it is no less true that it makes for increased unemployment and that it leaves the country with a pre-war outfit.

Even from the budget point of view, it is a question whether the game is worth the candle. It is difficult to believe that, if this question were considered squarely on its merits, any intelligent person could return an affirmative answer. The capital market is an international market. All sorts of influences which are outside our control go to determine the gilt-edged rate of interest; and the effect which the British government can exert on it by curtailing or expanding its capital programme is limited. Suppose, which is putting the case extremely high, that the effect might be as much as ¼ per cent. This, applied to the £2,000 million of War Loan, which are ripe for conversion, would represent a difference in the annual debt charge of £5 million annually. Compare this with the expenditure of the Unemployment Fund—over £50 million last year.

Moreover, in the course of (say) ten years it is not unlikely that a situation will arise—as used to happen from time to time before the war—when for world reasons the rate of interest will be abnormally low, much lower than we could possibly hope for by Treasury contrivances in the exceptionally unfavourable environment of abnormally high world rates. This will be the moment for a successful conversion scheme. Even, therefore, if the Treasury could convert today at a saving of

¼ or ½ per cent, it might be extremely improvident to do so. A premature conversion for an inconsiderable saving would be a grave blunder. We must have the patience to wait for the ideal conjuncture of conditions, and then the Chancellor of the Exchequer of the day will be able to pull off something big.

But apart from budgetary advantages and disadvantages, there is a deep-seated confusion of thought in hindering on these grounds the capital development of the country. The rate of interest can fall for either of two opposite reasons. It may fall on account of an abundant supply of savings, i.e. of money available to be spent on investments; or it may fall on account of a deficient supply of investments, i.e. on desirable purposes on which to spend the savings. Now a fall in the rate of interest for the first reason is, obviously, very much in the national interest. But a fall for the second reason, if it follows from a deliberate restriction of outlets for investment, is simply a disastrous method of impoverishing ourselves.

A country is enriched not by the mere negative act of an individual not spending all his income on current consumption. It is enriched by the positive act of using these savings to augment the capital equipment of the country.

It is not the miser who gets rich; but he who lays out his money in fruitful investment.

The object of urging people to save is *in order* to be able to build houses and roads and the like. Therefore a policy of trying to lower the rate of interest by suspending new capital improvements and so stopping up the outlets and purposes of our savings is simply suicidal. No one, perhaps, would uphold such a policy expressed in so many words. But this, in fact, is what the Treasury has been doing for several years. In some cases, the pressure of public opinion or of other government departments or local authorities has been too much for them. But whenever it has been within their power to choke something off, they have done so.

The futility of their policy and the want of sound reasoning behind it have been finally demonstrated by its failure even to secure a fall in the rate of interest. For, as we have seen above, if outlets for investment at home are stopped up, savings flow abroad on a scale disproportionate to our favourable balance of trade, with the result that the Bank of England tends to lose gold. To counteract this position, the bank rate has to be raised.

So in the end we have the worst of all worlds. The country is backward in its equipment, instead of being thoroughly up to date. Business profits are poor, with the result that the yield of the income tax disappoints the Chancellor of the Exchequer and he is unable either to relieve the taxpayer or to push forward with schemes of social reform. Unemployment is rampant. This want of prosperity actually diminishes the rate of saving and thus defeats even the original object of a lower rate of interest. So rates of interest are, after all, high.§ And there is only one little compensation to set against all this— that the Conservative Party will be driven out of office.

XI THE BREATH OF LIFE§

It is not an accident that the Conservative government have landed us in the mess where we find ourselves. It is the natural outcome of their philosophy:

You must not press on with telephones or electricity, because this will raise the rate of interest.

You must not hasten with roads or housing, because this will use up opportunities for employment which we may need in later years.

You must not try to employ everyone, because this will cause inflation.

You must not invest, because how can you know that it will pay?

You must not do anything, because this will only mean that you can't do something else.

Safety first! The policy of maintaining a million unemployed has now been pursued for eight years without disaster. Why risk a change?

We will not promise more than we can perform. We, therefore, promise nothing.

This is what we are being fed with.

They are slogans of depression and decay—the timidities and obstructions and stupidities of a sinking administrative vitality.

Negation, restriction, inactivity—these are the government's watchwords. Under their leadership we have been forced to button up our waistcoats and compress our lungs. Fears and doubts and hypochondriac precautions are keeping us muffled up indoors. But we are not tottering to our graves. We are healthy children. We need the breath of life. There is nothing to be afraid of. On the contrary. The future holds in store for us far more wealth and economic freedom and possibilities of personal life than the past has ever offered.

There is no reason why we should not feel ourselves free to be bold, to be open, to experiment, to take action, to try the possibilities of things. And over against us, standing in the path, there is nothing but a few old gentlemen tightly buttoned-up in their frock coats, who only need to be treated with a little friendly disrespect and bowled over like ninepins.

Quite likely they will enjoy it themselves, when once they have got over the shock.

5 THE GREAT SLUMP OF 1930 (1930)

This essay originally appeared as two articles in the *Nation and Athenaeum*, 20 and 27 December 1930, under the same title.

I

The world has been slow to realise that we are living this year in the shadow of one of the greatest economic catastrophes of modern history. But now that the man in the street has become aware of what is happening, he, not knowing the why and wherefore, is as full today of what may prove excessive fears as, previously, when the trouble was first coming on, he was lacking in what would have been a reasonable anxiety. He begins to doubt the future. Is he now awakening from a pleasant dream to face the darkness of facts? Or dropping off into a nightmare which will pass away?

He need not be doubtful. The other was *not* a dream. This *is* a nightmare, which will pass away with the morning. For the resources of nature and men's devices are just as fertile and productive as they were. The rate of our progress towards solving the material problems of life is not less rapid. We are as capable as before of affording for every one a high standard of life—high, I mean, compared with, say, twenty years ago—and will soon learn to afford a standard higher still. We were not previously deceived. But today we have involved ourselves in a colossal muddle, having blundered in the control of a delicate machine, the working of which we do not understand. The result is that our possibilities of wealth may run to waste for a time—perhaps for a long time.

I doubt whether I can hope to bring what is in my mind into fully effective touch with the mind of the reader. I shall be saying too much for the layman, too little for the expert. For—though no one will believe it—economics is a technical and difficult subject. It is even becoming a science. However, I will do my best—at the cost of leaving out, because it is too complicated, much that is necessary to a complete understanding of contemporary events.

First of all, the extreme violence of the slump is to be noticed. In the three leading industrial countries of the world—the United States, Great Britain, and Germany—10 million workers stand idle. There is scarcely an important industry anywhere earning enough profit to make it expand—which is the test of progress. At the same time, in the countries of primary production the output of mining and of agriculture is selling, in the case of almost every important commodity, at a price which for many or for the majority of producers, does not cover its cost. In 1921, when prices fell as heavily, the fall was from a boom level at which producers were making abnormal profits; and there is no example in modern history of so great and rapid a fall of prices from a normal figure as has occurred in the past year. Hence the magnitude of the catastrophe.

The time which elapses before production ceases and unemployment reaches its maximum is, for several reasons, much longer in the case of the primary products than in the case of manufacture. In most cases the productive units are smaller and less well organised amongst themselves for enforcing a process of orderly contraction; the length of the production period, especially in agriculture, is longer; the costs of a temporary shut-down are greater; men are more often their own employers and so submit more readily to a contraction of the income for which they are willing to work; the social problems of throwing men out of employment are greater in more primitive communities; and the financial problems of a cessation of production of primary output are more serious in countries where such primary output is almost the whole sustenance of the people. Nevertheless we are fast approaching the phase in which the output of primary producers will be restricted almost as much as that of manufacturers; and this will have a further

10-2

adverse reaction on manufacturers, since the primary producers will have no purchasing power wherewith to buy manufactured goods; and so on, in a vicious circle.

In this quandary individual producers base illusory hopes on courses of action which would benefit an individual producer or class of producers so long as they were alone in pursuing them, but which benefit no one if every one pursues them. For example, to restrict the output of a particular primary commodity raises its price, so long as the output of the industries which use this commodity is unrestricted; but if output is restricted all round, then the demand for the primary commodity falls off by just as much as the supply, and no one is further forward. Or again, if a particular producer or a particular country cuts wages, then, so long as others do not follow suit, that producer or that country is able to get more of what trade is going. But if wages are cut all round, the purchasing power of the community as a whole is reduced by the same amount as the reduction of costs; and, again, no one is further forward.

Thus neither the restriction of output nor the reduction of wages serves in itself to restore equilibrium.

Moreover, even if we were to succeed eventually in re-establishing output at the lower level of money wages appropriate to (say) the pre-war level of prices, our troubles would not be at an end. For since 1914 an immense burden of bonded debt, both national and international, has been contracted, which is fixed in terms of money. Thus every fall of prices increases the burden of this debt, because it increases the value of the money in which it is fixed. For example, if we were to settle down to the pre-war level of prices, the British national debt would be nearly 40 per cent greater than it was in 1924 and double what it was in 1920; the Young Plan would weigh on Germany much more heavily than the Dawes Plan, which it was agreed she could not support; the indebtedness to the United States of her associates in the Great War would represent 40–50 per cent more goods and services than at the date when the settlements were made; the obligations of such debtor countries as those of South America and Australia would become insupportable without a reduction of their standard of life for the benefit of their creditors; agriculturists and householders throughout the world, who have borrowed on mortgage, would find themselves the victims of their creditors. In such a situation it must be doubtful whether the necessary adjustments could be made in time to prevent a series of bankruptcies, defaults, and repudiations which would shake the capitalist order to its foundations. Here would be a fertile soil for agitation, seditions, and revolution. It is so already in many quarters of the world. Yet, all the time, the resources of nature and men's devices would be just as fertile and productive as they were. The machine would merely have been jammed as the result of a muddle. But because we have magneto trouble, we need not assume that we shall soon be back in a rumbling wagon and that motoring is over.

II

We have magneto trouble. How, then, can we start up again? Let us trace events backwards:

1. Why are workers and plant unemployed? Because industrialists do not expect to be able to sell without loss what would be produced if they were employed.

2. Why cannot industrialists expect to sell without loss? Because prices have fallen more than costs have fallen—indeed, costs have fallen very little.

3. How can it be that prices have fallen more than costs? For costs are what a business man pays out for the production of his commodity, and prices determine what he gets back when he sells it. It is easy to understand how for an individual business or an individual commodity these can be unequal. But surely for the community as a whole the business men get back the same amount as they pay out, since what the business men pay out in the course of production constitutes the incomes of

129

the public which they pay back to the business men in exchange for the products of the latter? For this is what we understand by the normal circle of production, exchange, and consumption.

4. No! Unfortunately this is not so; and here is the root of the trouble. It is not true that what the business men pay out as costs of production necessarily comes back to them as the sale proceeds of what they produce. It is the characteristic of a boom that their sale proceeds exceed their costs; and it is the characteristic of a slump that their costs exceed their sale proceeds. Moreover, it is a delusion to suppose that they can necessarily restore equilibrium by reducing their total costs, whether it be by restricting their output or cutting rates of remuneration; for the reduction of their outgoings may, by reducing the purchasing power of the earners who are also their customers, diminish their sale proceeds by a nearly equal amount.

5. How, then, can it be that the total costs of production for the world's business as a whole can be unequal to the total sale proceeds? Upon what does the inequality depend? I think that I know the answer. But it is too complicated and unfamiliar for me to expound it here satisfactorily. (Elsewhere I have tried to expound it accurately.)[1] So I must be somewhat perfunctory.

Let us take, first of all, the consumption goods which come on to the market for sale. Upon what do the profits (or losses) of the producers of such goods depend? The total costs of production, which are the same thing as the community's total earnings looked at from another point of view, are divided in a certain proportion between the cost of consumption goods and the cost of capital goods. The incomes of the public, which are again the same thing as the community's total earnings, are also divided in a certain proportion between expenditure on the purchase of consumption goods and savings. Now if the first proportion is larger than the second, producers of consumption goods will *lose* money; for their sale proceeds, which are equal to the expenditure of the public on consumption goods,

---

[1] [In my *Treatise on Money*.]

will be less (as a little thought will show) than what these goods have cost them to produce. If, on the other hand, the second proportion is larger than the first, then the producers of consumption goods will make exceptional *gains*. It follows that the profits of the producers of consumption goods can only be restored, either by the public spending a larger proportion of their incomes on such goods (which means saving less), or by a larger proportion of production taking the form of capital goods (since this means a smaller proportionate output of consumption goods).

But capital goods will not be produced on a larger scale unless the producers of such goods are making a profit. So we come to our second question—upon what do the profits of the producers of capital goods depend? They depend on whether the public prefer to keep their savings liquid in the shape of money or its equivalent or to use them to buy capital goods or the equivalent. If the public are reluctant to buy the latter, then the producers of capital goods will make a loss; consequently less capital goods will be produced; with the result that, for the reasons given above, producers of consumption goods will also make a loss. In other words, *all* classes of producers will tend to make a loss; and general unemployment will ensue. By this time a vicious circle will be set up, and, as the result of a series of actions and reactions, matters will get worse and worse until something happens to turn the tide.

This is an unduly simplified picture of a complicated phenomenon. But I believe that it contains the essential truth. Many variations and fugal embroideries and orchestrations can be superimposed; but this is the tune.

If, then, I am right, the fundamental cause of the trouble is the lack of new enterprise due to an unsatisfactory market for capital investment. Since trade is international, an insufficient output of new capital goods in the world as a whole affects the prices of commodities everywhere and hence the profits of producers in all countries alike.

Why is there an insufficient output of new capital goods in the world as a whole? It is due, in my opinion, to a conjunction of several causes. In the first instance, it was due to the attitude of lenders—for new capital goods are produced to a large extent with borrowed money. Now it is due to the attitude of borrowers, just as much as to that of lenders.

For several reasons lenders were, and are, asking higher terms for loans than new enterprise can afford. First, the fact that enterprise could afford high rates for some time after the war whilst war wastage was being made good, accustomed lenders to expect much higher rates than before the war. Second, the existence of political borrowers to meet treaty obligations, of banking borrowers to support newly restored gold standards, of speculative borrowers to take part in stock exchange booms and, latterly, of distress borrowers to meet the losses which they have incurred through the fall of prices, all of whom were ready if necessary to pay almost any terms, have hitherto enabled lenders to secure from these various classes of borrowers higher rates than it is possible for genuine new enterprise to support. Third, the unsettled state of the world and national investment habits have restricted the countries in which many lenders are prepared to invest on any reasonable terms at all. A large proportion of the globe is, for one reason or another, distrusted by lenders, so that they exact a premium for risk so great as to strangle new enterprise altogether. For the last two years, two out of the three principal creditor nations of the world, namely, France and the United States, have largely withdrawn their resources from the international market for long-term loans.

Meanwhile, the reluctant attitude of lenders has become matched by a hardly less reluctant attitude on the part of borrowers. For the fall of prices has been disastrous to those who have borrowed, and anyone who has postponed new enterprise has gained by his delay. Moreover, the risks that frighten lenders frighten borrowers too. Finally, in the United States, the vast scale on which new capital enterprise has been undertaken in the last five years has somewhat exhausted for the time being—at any rate so long as the atmosphere of business depression continues—the profitable opportunities for yet further enterprise. By the middle of 1929 new capital undertakings were already on an inadequate scale in the world as a whole, outside the United States. The culminating blow has been the collapse of new investment inside the United States, which today is probably 20 to 30 per cent less than it was in 1928. Thus in certain countries the opportunity for new profitable investment is more limited than it was; whilst in others it is more risky.

A wide gulf, therefore, is set between the ideas of lenders and the ideas of borrowers for the purpose of genuine new capital investment; with the result that the savings of the lenders are being used up in financing business losses and distress borrowers, instead of financing new capital works.

At this moment the slump is probably a little overdone for psychological reasons. A modest upward reaction, therefore, may be due at any time. But there cannot be a real recovery, in my judgement, until the ideas of lenders and the ideas of productive borrowers are brought together again; partly by lenders becoming ready to lend on easier terms and over a wider geographical field, partly by borrowers recovering their good spirits and so becoming readier to borrow.

Seldom in modern history has the gap between the two been so wide and so difficult to bridge. Unless we bend our wills and out intelligences, energised by a conviction that this diagnosis is right, to find a solution along these lines, then, if the diagnosis *is* right, the slump may pass over into a depression, accompanied by a sagging price level, which might last for years, with untold damage to the material wealth and to the social stability of every country alike. Only if we seriously seek a solution, will the optimism of my opening sentences be confirmed—at least for the nearer future.

It is beyond the scope of this essay to indicate lines of future policy. But no one can take the first step except the central banking authorities of the chief creditor countries; nor can any one central bank do enough acting in isolation. Resolute action by the Federal Reserve Banks of the United States, the Bank of France, and the Bank of England might do much more than most people, mistaking symptoms or aggravating circumstances for the disease itself, will readily believe. In every way the most effective remedy would be that the central banks of these three great creditor nations should join together in a bold scheme to restore confidence to the international long-term loan market; which would serve to revive enterprise and activity everywhere, and to restore prices and profits, so that in due course the wheels of the world's commerce would go round again. And even if France, hugging the supposed security of gold, prefers to stand aside from the adventure of creating new wealth, I am convinced that Great Britain and the United States, like-minded and acting together, could start the machine again within a reasonable time; if, that is to say, they were energised by a confident conviction as to what was wrong. For it is chiefly the lack of this conviction which today is paralysing the hands of authority on both sides of the Channel and of the Atlantic.

6 ECONOMY (1931)

I SAVING AND SPENDING (January 1931)

Written as a radio talk for a British Broadcasting Corporation series on
unemployment and published in the *Listener*, 14 January 1931, with the
title, 'The Problem of Unemployment—II'. (Keynes's talk was the second
in the series.)

The slump in trade and employment and the business losses
which are being incurred are as bad as the worst which have
ever occurred in the modern history of the world. No country
is exempt. The privation and—what is sometimes worse—the
anxiety which exist today in millions of homes all over the
world is extreme. In the three chief industrial countries of the
world, Great Britain, Germany and the United States, I
estimate that probably 12 million industrial workers stand idle.
But I am not sure that there is not even more human misery
today in the great agricultural countries of the world—Canada,
Australia, and South America, where millions of small farmers
see themselves ruined by the fall in the prices of their products,
so that their receipts after harvest bring them in much less than
the crops have cost them to produce. For the fall in the prices
of the great staple products of the world such as wheat, wool,
sugar, cotton, and indeed most other commodities has been
simply catastrophic. Most of these prices are now below their
pre-war level; yet costs, as we all know, remain far above their
pre-war level. A week or two ago, it is said, wheat in Liverpool
sold at the lowest price recorded since the reign of Charles II
more than 250 years ago. How is it possible for farmers to live
in such conditions? Of course it is impossible.

You might suppose—and some austere individuals do in fact
believe—that cheapness must be an advantage. For what the
producer loses, the consumer gains. But it is not so. For those
of us who work—and we are in the great majority—can only

consume so long as we produce. So that anything which inter-feres with the processes of production necessarily interferes also with those of consumption.

The reason for this is that there are all kinds of obstacles to the costs and prices of everything falling equally. For example, the wages costs of most manufacturers are practically the same as they were. See how the vicious process works out. The prices of wool and wheat fall. Good for the British consumer of wheat and woollen garments—so one might suppose. But the producers of wool and wheat, since they receive too little for their products, cannot make their usual purchases of British goods. Consequently those British consumers who are at the same time workers who make these goods find themselves out of work. What is the use of cheapness when incomes are falling?

When Dr Johnson, visiting the Island of Skye, was told that twenty eggs might be bought for a penny, he said, 'Sir, I don't gather from this that eggs are plenty in your miserable island, but that pence are few.'

Cheapness which is due to increased efficiency and skill in the arts of production is indeed a benefit. But cheapness which means the ruin of the producer is one of the greatest economic disasters which can possibly occur.

It would not be true to say that we are not taking a grave view of the case. Yet I doubt whether we are taking a grave enough view. In the enforced idleness of millions, enough potential wealth is running to waste to work wonders. Many million pounds' worth of goods could be produced each day by the workers and the plants which stand idle—and the workers would be the happier and the better for it. We ought to sit down to mend matters, in the mood of grave determination and the spirit of action at all costs, which we should have in a war. Yet a vast inertia seems to weigh us down. The peculiarity of the position today—to my mind—is that there is something to be said for nearly all the remedies that anyone has proposed, though some, of course, are better than others.

All the rival policies have something to offer. Yet we adopt none of them.

The worst of it is that we have one excellent excuse for doing nothing. To a large extent the cure lies outside our own power. The problem is an international one, and for a country which depends on foreign trade as much as we do there are narrow limits to what we can achieve by ourselves. But this is not the only reason why we are inactive. Nor is it a sufficient reason. For something we can do by ourselves. The other principal reason, in my opinion, is a serious misunderstanding as to what kind of action is useful and what kind is not. There are today many well-wishers of their country who believe that the most useful thing which they and their neighbours can do to mend the situation is to *save* more than usual. If they refrain from spending a larger proportion of their incomes than usual they believe that they will have helped employment. If they are members of town or county councils they believe that their right course at such a time as this is to oppose expenditure on new amenities or new public works.

Now, in certain circumstances all this would be quite right, but in present circumstances, unluckily, it is quite wrong. It is utterly harmful and misguided—the very opposite of the truth. For the object of saving is to release labour for employment on producing capital goods such as houses, factories, roads, machines, and the like. But if there is a large unemployed surplus already available for such purposes, then the effect of saving is merely to add to this surplus and therefore to increase the number of the unemployed. Moreover, when a man is thrown out of work in this or any other way, his diminished spending power causes further unemployment amongst those who would have produced what he can no longer afford to buy. And so the position gets worse and worse in a vicious circle.

The best guess I can make is that whenever you save five shillings, you put a man out of work for a day. Your saving that five shillings adds to unemployment to the extent of one man for one day—and so on in proportion. On the other hand, whenever you buy goods you increase employment—though they must be British, home-produced goods if you are to increase employment in this country. After all, this is only the plainest common sense. For if you buy goods, someone will have to make them. And if you do not buy goods, the shops will not clear their stocks, they will not give repeat orders, and someone will be thrown out of work.

Therefore, O patriotic housewives, sally out tomorrow early into the streets and go to the wonderful sales which are every-where advertised. You will do yourselves good—for never were things so cheap, cheap beyond your dreams. Lay in a stock of household linen, of sheets and blankets to satisfy all your needs. And have the added joy that you are increasing employment, adding to the wealth of the country because you are setting on foot useful activities, bringing a chance and a hope to Lancashire, Yorkshire, and Belfast.

These are only examples. Do whatever is necessary to satisfy the most sensible needs of yourself and your household, make improvements, build.

For what we need now is not to button up our waistcoats tight, but to be in a mood of expansion, of activity—to do things, to buy things, to make things. Surely all this is the most obvious common sense. For take the extreme case. Suppose we were to stop spending our incomes altogether, and were to save the lot. Why, everyone would be out of work. And before long we should have no incomes to spend. No one would be a penny the richer, and the end would be that we should all starve to death—which would surely serve us right for refusing to buy things from one another, for refusing to take in one another's washing, since that is how we all live. The same is true, and even more so, of the work of a local authority. Now is the time for municipalities to be busy and active with all kinds of sensible improvements.

The patient does not need rest. He needs exercise. You cannot set men to work by holding back, by refusing to place orders, by inactivity. On the contrary, activity of one kind or another is the only possible means of making the wheels of economic progress and of the production of wealth go round again.

Nationally, too, I should like to see schemes of greatness and magnificence designed and carried through. I read a few days ago of a proposal to drive a great new road, a broad boulevard, parallel to the Strand, on the south side of the Thames, as a new thoroughfare joining Westminster to the City. That is the right sort of notion. But I should like to see something bigger still. For example, why not pull down the whole of South London from Westminster to Greenwich, and make a good job of it—housing on that convenient area near to their work a much greater population than at present, in far better buildings with all the conveniences of modern life, yet at the same time providing hundreds of acres of squares and avenues, parks and public spaces, having, when it was finished, something magnificent to the eye, yet useful and convenient to human life as a monument to our age. Would that employ men? Why, of course it would! Is it better that the men should stand idle and miserable, drawing the dole? Of course it is not.

These, then, are the chief observations which I want to leave with you now—first of all, to emphasise the extreme gravity of the situation, with about a quarter of our working population standing idle; next, that the trouble is a world-wide one which we cannot cure by ourselves; and, third, that we can all the same do something by ourselves and that something must take the form of activity, of doing things, of spending, of setting great enterprises afoot.

But I also have one final theme to put before you. I fancy that a reason why some people may be a little horrified at my suggestions is the fear that we are much too poor to be able to afford what they consider to be extravagance. They think that we are poor, much poorer than we were and that what we chiefly need is to cut our coat according to our cloth, by which they mean that we must curtail our consumption, reduce our standard of life, work harder and consume less; and that that is the way out of the wood. This view is not, in my judgement, in accordance with the facts. We have plenty of cloth and only lack the courage to cut it into coats. I want, therefore, to give you some cheerful facts to dispose you to take an ampler view of the economic strength of this country.

Let me first of all remind you of the obvious. The great mass of the population is living much better than it ever lived before. We are supporting in idleness, at a higher standard of life than is possible for those who are in work in most other countries, nearly a quarter of our employable population. Yet at the same time the national wealth is increasing year by year. After paying wages which are far higher than, for example, in France or in Germany, after supporting a quarter of our population in idleness, after adding to the country's equipment of houses and roads and electrical plant and so forth on a substantial scale, we still have a surplus available to be lent to foreign countries, which in 1929 was greater than the surplus for such purposes of any other country in the world, even of the United States.

How do we do it? If the pessimists were right who believe that we are terribly inefficient, over-extravagant and getting poorer, obviously it would be impossible. We can only do it because the pessimists are quite wrong. We are not nearly so rich as we might be if we could manage our affairs better and not get them into such a muddle. But we are not inefficient, we are not poor, we are not living on our capital. Quite the contrary. Our labour and our plant are enormously more productive than they used to be. Our national income is going up quite quickly. That is how we do it.

Let me give you a few figures. As compared with so recent a date as 1924, our productive output per head has probably increased by 10 per cent. That is to say, we can produce the same amount of wealth with 10 per cent fewer men employed. As compared with pre-war the increase in output per head is probably as much as 20 per cent. Apart from changes in the value of money, the national income—even so recently as 1929 with a great mass of unemployment (it cannot, of course, be quite so good today)—was probably increasing by as much as £100 million a year; and this has been going on year by year for a good many years. At the same time we have been quietly carrying through almost a revolution in the distribution of incomes in the direction of equality.

Be confident, therefore, that we are suffering from the growing pains of youth, not from the rheumatics of old age. We are failing to make full use of our opportunities, failing to find an outlet for the great increase in our productive powers and our productive energy. Therefore we must not draw in our horns; we must push them out. Activity and boldness and enterprise, both individually and nationally, must be the cure.

II THE ECONOMY REPORT (15 August 1931)

Published as 'Some Consequences of the Economy Report' in the *New Statesman and Nation*, 15 August 1931. A misprint, which Keynes corrected in a letter to the *New Statesman* the following week, has been eliminated.

The report of the Economy Committee can be considered from several points of view. It is an exceedingly valuable document because it is a challenge to us to make up our minds one way or the other on certain vital matters of policy. In particular it invites us to decide whether it is our intention to make the deflation effective by transmitting the reduction of international prices to British salaries and wages; though if this *is* our intention, it would be absurd to pretend that the process can stop with schoolteachers and policemen. The Committee's report goes too far or not far enough. But this is not the question which I wish to discuss here. I would like to confine myself to what has been so far, as it seems to me, a neglected aspect of the report.

The Committee show no evidence of having given a moment's

thought to the possible repercussions of their programme, either on the volume of unemployment or on the receipts of taxation. They recommend a reduction of the purchasing power of British citizens partly by the reduction of incomes and partly by throwing out of work persons now employed. They give no reason for supposing that this reduction of purchasing power will be offset by increases in other directions; for their idea is that the government should take advantage of the economies proposed, not to tax less, but to borrow less. Perhaps at the back of their heads they have some crude idea that there is a fixed loan fund, the whole of which is always lent, so that, if the government borrows less, private enterprise necessarily borrows more. But they could not believe this on reflection, if they were to try to translate it into definite, concrete terms.

Their proposals do not even offer the possible advantages to our trade balance which might ensue on a reduction of industrial wages. For there is nothing in what they propose calculated to reduce the costs of production; indeed, on the contrary, they propose to increase them by raising the employers' insurance contribution.

Let us try, therefore, to write the missing paragraphs of the report and to make some guesses as to the probable consequences of reducing purchasing power in the manner proposed.

Some part of this reduction of purchasing power may be expected to lead to a reduced buying of foreign goods, e.g. if the dole is cut down, the unemployed will have to tighten their belts and eat less imported food. To this extent the situation will be helped. Some part will be economised by saving less; e.g. if teachers' salaries are cut down, teachers will probably save less or even draw on their past savings, to maintain the standard of life to which they have become accustomed. But for the rest British producers will find the receipts reaching them from the expenditure of consumers (policemen, schoolteachers, men on the dole, etc.) reduced by the balance of, say, £70 million. They cannot meet this loss without reducing their own expenditure or discharging some of their men, or both, i.e. they will have to follow the example of the government, and this will again set moving the same series of consequences, and so on.

The net result would necessarily be a substantial increase in the number of unemployed drawing the dole and a decrease in the receipts of taxation as a result of the diminished incomes and profits. Indeed the immediate consequences of the government's reducing its deficit are the exact inverse of the consequences of its financing additional capital works out of loans. One cannot predict with accuracy the exact quantitative consequences of either, but they are broadly the same. Several of the Committee's recommendations, e.g. those relating to roads, to housing, and to afforestation, do indeed expressly imply that the whole theory underlying the principle of public works as a remedy for unemployment is mistaken, and they ask, in effect, for a reversal of the policies based on this principle. Yet they do not trouble to argue the case. I suppose that they are such very plain men that the advantages of not spending money seem obvious to them. They may even be so plain as to be unaware of the existence of the problem which I am now discussing. But they are flying in the face of a considerable weight of opinion. For the main opposition to the public works remedy is based on the practical difficulties of devising a reasonable programme, not on the principle. But a proposal to reverse measures already in force involves a denial of the principle as well as of the feasibility.

I should like, though it is rash, to make, if only for purposes of illustration, a very rough guess as to the magnitudes of the more immediate consequences of the adoption of economies of £100 million, carried out on the lines of the Committee's recommendations. I should expect something like the following:

(1) An increase of 250,000–400,000 in the number of the unemployed;

(2) A decrease of, say, £20 million in the excess of our imports over our exports;

(3) A decrease of £10 million to £15 million in the savings of the general public;

(4) A decrease of £20 million to £30 million in business profits;

(5) A decrease of £10 million to £15 million in the personal expenditure of business men and others, who depend on business profits, as a result of these profits being less;

(6) A decrease of £5 million to £10 million in the aggregate of capital construction and working capital and other investment at home entered upon by private enterprise, as a result of the lower level of business profits, after allowing for any favourable psychological effects on business 'confidence' of the adoption of the Committee's recommendations;

(7) A *net* reduction in the government deficit not exceeding £50 million, as a result of the budget economies of £100 million being partly offset by the diminished yield of taxation and the cost of the increased unemployment.

The actual figures I have used are, of course, guesswork. But $(?)+(3)+(4)-(5)-(6) = (7)$, where (7) is the net reduction in the government deficit, is a necessary truth—as necessary as $2+2 = 4$. There is nothing rational to dispute about except the size of the various items entering into this equation. It might be held by some, for example, that there would be an *increase* under (6), instead of a decrease; and if there were a large increase of this item—which, however, could not, in my judgement, be maintained with good reason—this would make all the difference in the world to the expediency of the policy proposed.

At the present time, all governments have large deficits. For government borrowing of one kind or another is nature's remedy, so to speak, for preventing business losses from being, in so severe a slump as the present one, so great as to bring production altogether to a standstill. It is much better in every way that the borrowing should be for the purpose of financing capital works, if these works are any use at all, than for the purpose of paying doles (or veterans' bonuses). But so long as the slump lasts on the present scale this is the only effective choice which we possess, and government borrowing for the one purpose or the other (or a diminished Sinking Fund, which has the same effect) is practically inevitable. For this is a case, fortunately perhaps, where the weakness of human nature will, we can be sure, come to the rescue of human wrong-headedness.

This is not to say that there are not other ways in which we can help ourselves. I am not concerned here with the possible advantages—for example—of a tariff or of devaluation or of a national treaty for the reduction of all money incomes. I am simply analysing the results to be expected from the recommendations of the Economy Committee adopted as a means of reducing the uncovered deficit of the budget. And I should add, to prevent misunderstanding, that I should prefer some of their recommendations—for they have done their work in detail with ability and fair-mindedness—to most kinds of additional taxation other than a tariff.

My own policy for the budget, so long as the slump lasts, would be to suspend the Sinking Fund, to continue to borrow for the Unemployment Fund, and to impose a revenue tariff. To get us out of the slump we must look to quite other expedients. When the slump is over, when the demands of private enterprise for new capital have recovered to normal and employment is good and the yield of taxation is increasing, then is the time to restore the Sinking Fund and to look critically at the less productive state enterprises.

III THE ECONOMY BILL (19 September 1931)

Published in the *New Statesman and Nation*, 19 September 1931, with the title of 'The Budget'.

The budget and the Economy Bill are replete with folly and injustice. It is a tragedy that the moral energies and enthusiasm of many truly self-sacrificing and well-wishing people should be so misdirected.

The objects of national policy, so as to meet the emergency, should be primarily to improve our balance of trade, and secondarily to equalise the yield of taxation with the normal recurrent expenditure of the budget by methods which would increase, rather than diminish, output, and hence increase the national income and the yield of the revenue, whilst respecting the principles of social justice. The actual policy of the government fails on each of these tests. It will have comparatively little effect on the balance of trade. It will largely increase unemployment and diminish the yield of the revenue. And it outrages the principles of justice to a degree which I should have thought inconceivable.

To begin with the last. The incomes of well-to-do people have been cut by $2\frac{1}{2}$ to $3\frac{1}{2}$ per cent. The schoolteachers are cut 15 per cent,[1] in addition to the extra taxes which they have to pay. It is a monstrous thing to single out this class and discriminate against them, merely because they happen to be employees of the government. It is particularly outrageous, because efforts have been made in recent years to attract into the profession teachers of higher qualifications by holding out to them certain expectations. It is even proposed to take powers to dissolve existing contracts. That the schoolteachers should have been singled out for sacrifice as an offering to the Moloch of finance is a sufficient proof of the state of hysteria and irresponsibility into which cabinet ministers have worked themselves. For it is impossible to represent this cut as one of unavoidable necessity. The money saved is £6 million. At the same time £32 million is going to the Sinking Fund, whilst tea, sugar, and a tariff as sources of revenue are left untapped. The Prime Minister has offered no defence, except that some of his former colleagues, who have since recovered their heads, were temporarily frightened into considering something of the same kind.

The schoolteachers are the most outstanding case of injustice. But the same considerations apply in varying degrees to all the attacks on the standards of government employees. The principle

---

[1] [Afterwards reduced to 10 per cent.]

of discriminating against persons in the service of the State, because they can be reached most easily, is not right. At least it would have been more decent in the circumstances if the phrase 'equality of sacrifice' had not been used.

Moreover, the government's programme is as foolish as it is wrong. Its direct effect on employment must be disastrous. It is safe to predict that it will increase the volume of unemployment by more than the 10 per cent by which the dole is to be cut. It represents a reckless reversal of all the partial attempts which have been made hitherto to mitigate the consequences of the collapse of private investment; and it is a triumph for the so-called 'Treasury view' in its most extreme form. Not only is purchasing power to be curtailed, but road building, housing, and the like are to be retrenched. Local authorities are to follow suit. If the theory which underlies all this is to be accepted, the end will be that no one can be employed, except those happy few who grow their own potatoes, as a result of each of us refusing, for reasons of economy, to buy the services of anyone else. To raid the Road Fund in order to maintain the Sinking Fund is, in present circumstances, a policy of Bedlam.

Finally there is the problem of the balance of trade, which, after all, is the main point so far as concerns the emergency. Broadly speaking, the cost of production is left unchanged. Cutting the schoolteachers' salaries will not help us to recapture the markets of the world. Those wages and the like which are within the government's direct control happen to be just those which it is most useless to cut in the interests of the export trade. We are told that it is a wicked misrepresentation to say that all this is a preliminary to a general assault on wages. Yet it has less than no sense unless it is. But meanwhile the government have noticed that there is just one point where their activities raise the cost of production, namely, the employers' insurance contribution, which is, in effect, a poll tax on employment. So, in order to prove for certain that they are quite mad, the government have decided to *increase* it.

147

There are only two ways in which the government plan can help the balance of trade. Whenever anyone is thrown out of work or otherwise impoverished, he will perforce consume less. Most of this reduced consumption will merely cause business losses and unemployment to other Englishmen. Some part of it, however, perhaps a fifth, will be at the expense of imports; though even this would not help if those Free Traders are right who think that a reduction of imports leads to a corresponding reduction of exports. But it is a wasteful way of setting about the task of reducing imports. The other way is by increasing both the quantity of unemployment and also the pains of being unemployed, since this may slightly increase the chance of wage-reductions being accepted. Economy can have no other purpose or meaning except to release resources. A small proportion of what is thus released will relieve the balance of trade. The rest will be resources of domestic plant and labour, of which we already have a surplus out of use.

Thus the government's scheme, for the sake of which we are asked to swallow so much, is in the main misdirected, and will not assist the solution of our twin problems of unemployment and an adverse balance of trade.

As regards the latter which, unremedied, will at no distant date break the gold standard even if we cut schoolteachers' salaries to nothing, the only remedies now open to us are devaluation, a drastic restriction of imports by direct methods, a severe cut, not less than 30 per cent in my judgement, in wages and salaries, or a decisive change in the international position. An attack on wages would mean a severe industrial struggle which would drive us off gold-parity within a few weeks; so that this is not in practice an alternative to devaluation. Thus there are only three lines of policy to which it is worth the Cabinet's while to direct their minds. The first and mildest is a plan for the restriction of imports. The second is a plan for getting off gold-parity without allowing the slide to go too far. The third §which was proposed in last week's *New Statesman and Nation*§ is a plan for an international conference—one that means business of the most definite kind, quite different from any conference ever held hitherto—for giving the gold-standard countries a last opportunity. All the rest is waste of time. The advantage of the last alternative is that this alone offers any chance, however slight, of an amelioration of the international position, without which we are faced with a disappearance of income from our foreign investments on a scale which neither a tariff nor devaluation could offset.

7 THE CONSEQUENCES TO THE BANKS OF THE COLLAPSE OF MONEY VALUES (AUGUST 1931)

This article made its first appearance in print in Essays in Persuasion. *It was originally written in August 1931 for the American popular monthly magazine* Vanity Fair, *but in October Keynes revised it considerably— as he wrote to the managing editor, 'partly to meet the new situation [the departure of England from the gold standard], partly to meet your criticisms and partly on second thoughts'.* Vanity Fair *published a slightly longer version of the article (the text here given) in January 1932.*

A year ago it was the failure of agriculture, mining, manufactures, and transport to make normal profits, and the unemployment and waste of productive resources ensuing on this, which was the leading feature of the economic situation. Today, in many parts of the world, it is the serious embarrassment of the banks which is the cause of our gravest concern. The shattering German crisis of July 1931, which took the world more by surprise than it should, was in its essence a banking crisis, though precipitated, no doubt, by political events and political fears. That the top-heavy position which ultimately crumbled to the ground should have been built up at all was, in my judgement, a sin against the principles of sound banking. One watched its erection with amazement and terror. But the fact which was primarily responsible for bringing it down was a factor for which the individual bankers were not responsible and which very few people foresaw —namely, the enormous change in the value of gold money and consequently in the burden of indebtedness which debtors, in all countries adhering to the gold standard, had contracted to pay in terms of gold.

§The German crisis was heralded by the Credit Anstalt trouble in Austria. It was brought to a head by the difficulties of the Darmstadter Bank in Berlin. It led to distrust of the

150

London position on account of the heavy advances, out of relation to the liquid resources held against them, which London had made to Berlin. It culminated in Great Britain's suspension of the gold standard. Its final *sequela* as I write these lines is a feverish removal of foreign balances from New York. But all this nervousness, and hysteria and panic, which is making a farce of our currency arrangements and bringing the world's financial machine to a standstill, is only superficially traceable, though it has all happened suddenly, to quite recent events. It has its roots in the slow and steady sapping of the real resources of the banks as a result of the progressive collapse of money values over the past two years. It is to this deep, underlying cause that I wish to direct attention in this article.§

Let us begin at the beginning of the argument. There is a multitude of real assets in the world which constitute our capital wealth—buildings, stocks of commodities, goods in course of manufacture and of transport, and so forth. The nominal owners of these assets, however, have not infrequently borrowed *money* in order to become possessed of them. To a corresponding extent the actual owners of wealth have claims, not on real assets, but on money. A considerable part of this 'financing' takes place through the banking system, which interposes its guarantee between its depositors who lend it money, and its borrowing customers to whom it loans money wherewith to finance the purchase of real assets. The inter-position of this veil of money between the real asset and the wealth owner is a specially marked characteristic of the modern world. Partly as a result of the increasing confidence felt in recent years in the leading banking systems, the practice has grown to formidable dimensions. The bank deposits of all kinds in the United States, for example, stand in round figures at $50,000 million; those of Great Britain at £2,000 million. In addition to this there is the great mass of bonded and mortgage indebtedness held by individuals.

All this is familiar enough in general terms. We are also

familiar with the idea that a change in the value of money can gravely upset the relative positions of those who possess claims to money and those who owe money. For, of course, a fall in prices, which is the same thing as a rise in the value of claims on money, means that real wealth is transferred from the debtor in favour of the creditor, so that a larger proportion of the real asset is represented by the claims of the depositor, and a smaller proportion belongs to the nominal owner of the asset who has borrowed in order to buy it. This, we all know, is one of the reasons why changes in prices are upsetting.

But it is not to this familiar feature of falling prices that I wish to invite attention. It is to a further development which we can ordinarily afford to neglect but which leaps to importance when the change in the value of money is *very large*—when it exceeds a more or less determinate amount.

Modest fluctuations in the value of money, such as those which we have frequently experienced in the past, do not vitally concern the banks which have interposed their guarantee between the depositor and the debtor. For the banks allow beforehand for some measure of fluctuation in the value both of particular assets and of real assets in general, by requiring from the borrower what is conveniently called a 'margin'. That is to say, they will only lend him money up to a certain proportion of the value of the asset which is the 'security' offered by the borrower to the lender. Experience has led to the fixing of conventional percentages for the 'margin' as being reasonably safe in all ordinary circumstances. The amount will, of course, vary in different cases within wide limits. But for marketable assets a 'margin' of 20 per cent to 30 per cent is conventionally considered as adequate, and 'margin' of as much as 50 per cent as highly conservative. Thus provided the amount of the downward change in the money value of assets is well within these conventional figures, the direct interest of the banks is not excessive—they owe money to their depositors on one side of their balance sheet and are owed it on the other, and it is no vital concern of theirs just what the money is worth. But consider what happens when the downward change in the money value of assets within a brief period of time *exceeds* the amount of the conventional 'margin' over a large part of the assets against which money has been borrowed. The horrible possibilities to the banks are immediately obvious. Fortunately, this is a very rare, indeed a unique event. For it had never occurred in the modern history of the world prior to the year 1931. There have been large *upward* movements in the money value of assets in those countries where inflation has proceeded to great lengths. But this, however disastrous in other ways, did nothing to jeopardise the position of the banks; for it increased the amount of their 'margins'. There was a large downward movement in the slump of 1921, but that was from an exceptionally high level of values which had ruled for only a few months or weeks, so that only a small proportion of the banks' loans had been based on such values and these values had not lasted long enough to be trusted. *Never* before has there been such a world-wide collapse over almost the whole field of the money values of real assets as we have experienced in the last two years. And, finally, during the last few months—so recently that the bankers themselves have, as yet, scarcely appreciated it—it has come to exceed in very many cases the amount of the conventional 'margins'. In the language of the market the 'margins' have run off. The exact details of this are not likely to come to the notice of the outsider until some special event—perhaps some almost accidental event—occurs which brings the situation to a dangerous head.[1] For, so long as a bank is in a position to wait quietly for better times and to ignore meanwhile the fact that the security against many of its loans is no longer as good as it was when the loans were first made, nothing appears on the surface and there is no cause for panic. Nevertheless, even at this stage the underlying position is likely to have a very adverse effect on new business. For the banks, being aware that

[1] The preceding sentence appears only in *Essays in Persuasion*—Ed.

many of their advances are in fact 'frozen' and involve a larger latent risk than they would voluntarily carry, become particularly anxious that the remainder of their assets should be as liquid and as free from risk as it is possible to make them. This reacts in all sorts of silent and unobserved ways on new enterprise. For it means that the banks are less willing than they would normally be to finance any project which may involve a lock-up of their resources.

Now, in estimating the quantitative importance of the factor to which I am calling attention, we have to consider what has been happening to the prices of various types of property. There are, first of all, the principal raw materials and foodstuffs of international commerce. These are of great importance to the banks, because the stocks of these commodities, whether in warehouse or in transit or embodied in half-finished or unsold manufactured articles, are very largely financed through the banks. In the last eighteen months the prices of these commodities have fallen *on the average* by about 25 per cent. But this is an average, and banks cannot average the security of one customer with that of another. Many individual commodities of the greatest commercial importance have fallen in price by 40 to 50 per cent or even more.

Next come the ordinary or common shares of the great companies and corporations which are the market leaders in the stock exchanges of the world. In most countries the average fall amounts to 40 to 50 per cent; and this again is an average, which means that individual shares, even amongst those which would have been considered of good quality two years ago, have fallen enormously more. Then there are the bonds and the fixed interest securities. Those of the very highest grade have, indeed, risen slightly or, at the worst, not fallen by more than 5 per cent, which has been of material assistance in some quarters. But many other fixed interest securities which, while not of the highest grade, were and are good securities, have fallen from 10 to 15 per cent; whilst foreign government bonds have, as is well known, suffered prodigious falls. These declines, even where they are more moderate, may be scarcely less serious, because such bonds (though not in Great Britain) are often owned by the banks themselves outright, so that there is no 'margin' to protect them from loss.

The declines in the prices of commodities and of securities have, broadly speaking, affected most countries alike. When we come to the next category of property—and one of great quantitative importance—namely, real estate, the facts are more various as between one country and another. A great element of stability in Great Britain and, I believe, in France also, has been the continued comparative firmness in real estate values—no slump has been experienced in this quarter, with the result that mortgage business is sound and the multitude of loans granted on the security of real estate are unimpaired. But in many other countries the slump has affected this class of property also; and particularly, perhaps, in the United States, where farm values have suffered a great decline, and also city property of modern construction, much of which would not fetch today more than 60 to 70 per cent of its original cost of construction, and not infrequently much less. This is an immense aggravation of the problem, where it has occurred, both because of the very large sums involved and because such property is ordinarily regarded as relatively free from risk. § Thus a situation has been created in the United States, in which the mortgage banks and mortgage and loan associations and other real-estate financing institutions are holding a great mass of 'frozen' mortgages, the margins on which have been consumed by the fall of real estate values. §

Finally, there are the loans and advances which banks have made to their customers for the purposes of their customers' business. These are, in many cases, in the worst condition of all. The security in these cases is primarily the profit, actual and prospective, of the business which is being financed; and in present circumstances for many classes of producers of raw materials, of farmers and of manufacturers, there are no profits and every prospect of insolvencies, if matters do not soon take a turn for the better.

To sum up, there is scarcely any class of property, except real estate, however useful and important to the welfare of the community, the current money value of which has not suffered an enormous and scarcely precedented decline. This has happened in a community which is so organised that a veil of money is, as I have said, interposed over a wide field between the actual asset and the wealth owner. The ostensible proprietor of the actual asset has financed it by borrowing money from the actual owner of wealth. Furthermore, it is largely through the banking system that all this has been arranged. That is to say, the banks have, for a consideration, interposed their guarantee. They stand between the real borrower and the real lender. They have given their guarantee to the real lender; and this guarantee is only good if the money value of the asset belonging to the real borrower is worth the money which has been advanced on it.

It is for this reason that a decline in money values so severe as that which we are now experiencing threatens the solidarity of the whole financial structure. Banks and bankers are by nature blind. They have not seen what was coming. Some of them have even welcomed the fall of prices towards what, in their innocence, they have deemed the just and 'natural' and inevitable level of pre-war, that is to say, to the level of prices to which their minds became accustomed in their formative years. In the United States some of them employ so-called 'economists' who tell us even today that our troubles are due to the fact that the prices of some commodities and some services have not yet fallen enough, regardless of what should be the obvious fact that their cure, if it could be realised, would be a menace to the solvency of their institution. A 'sound' banker, alas! is not one who foresees danger and avoids it, but one who, when he is ruined, is ruined in a conventional and orthodox way along with his fellows, so that no one can really blame him.

But today they are beginning at last to take notice. In many countries bankers are becoming unpleasantly aware of the fact that, when their customers' margins have run off, they are themselves 'on margin'. I believe that, if today a really conservative valuation were made of all doubtful assets, quite a significant proportion of the banks of the world would be found to be insolvent; and with the further progress of deflation this proportion will grow rapidly. Fortunately our own domestic British banks are probably at present—for various reasons— among the strongest. But there is a degree of deflation[1] which no bank can stand. And over a great part of the world, and not least in the United States, the position of the banks, though partly concealed from the public eye, may be in fact the weakest element in the whole situation. It is obvious that the present trend of events cannot go much further without something breaking. If nothing is done, it will be amongst the world's banks that the really critical breakages will occur.

Modern capitalism is faced, in my belief, with the choice between finding some way to increase money values towards their former figure, or seeing widespread insolvencies and defaults and the collapse of a large part of the financial structure; after which we should all start again, not nearly so much poorer as we should expect, and much more cheerful perhaps, but having suffered a period of waste and disturbance and social injustice, and a general rearrangement of private fortunes and the ownership of wealth. Individually many of us would be 'ruined', even though collectively we were much as before. But under the pressure of hardship and excitement, we might have found out better ways of managing our affairs.

The present signs suggest that the bankers of the world are bent on suicide. At every stage they have been unwilling to

[1] [The paragraph has been reproduced as it appears in *Essays in Persuasion*. The sentences given thus far were substituted for the following in the *Vanity Fair* version of the article: President Hoover's plans to render some of the banks' better assets more liquid may help to tide over an immediate emergency. But nothing on earth can put the banks in good shape or save them from ultimate default except a general recovery in prices and money-values. For there is a degree of deflation...—*Ed.*]

adopt a sufficiently drastic remedy. And by now matters have been allowed to go so far that it has become extraordinarily difficult to find any way out. §In Great Britain we have gone some way towards solving our own problem by abandoning the gold standard, but unfortunately we have only made matters worse for countries still adhering to it.§

It is necessarily part of the business of a banker to maintain appearances and to profess a conventional respectability which is more than human. Lifelong practices of this kind make them the most romantic and the least realistic of men. It is so much their stock-in-trade that their position should not be questioned, that they do not even question it themselves until it is too late. Like the honest citizens they are, they feel a proper indignation at the perils of the wicked world in which they live—when the perils mature; but they do not foresee them. A bankers' conspiracy! The idea is absurd! I only wish there were one! So, if they are saved, it will be, I expect, in their own despite.

PART III
THE RETURN TO THE GOLD STANDARD

1 AURI SACRA FAMES (September 1930)

From *A Treatise on Money* (1930), chapter xxxv, 'Problems of International Management—II. The Gold Standard' (vol. ii).

The choice of gold as a standard of value is chiefly based on tradition. In the days before the evolution of representative money it was natural, for reasons which have been many times told, to choose one or more of the metals as the most suitable commodity for holding a store of value or a command of purchasing power.

Some four or five thousand years ago the civilised world settled down to the use of gold, silver, and copper for pounds, shillings, and pence, but with silver in the first place of importance and copper in the second. The Mycenaeans put gold in the first place. Next, under Celtic or Dorian influences, came a brief invasion of iron in place of copper over Europe and the northern shores of the Mediterranean. With the Achaemenid Persian Empire, which maintained a bimetallic standard of gold and silver at a fixed ratio (until Alexander overturned them), the world settled down again to gold, silver, and copper, with silver once more of predominant importance; and there followed silver's long hegemony (except for a certain revival of the influence of gold in Roman Constantinople), chequered by imperfectly successful attempts at gold-and-silver bimetallism, especially in the eighteenth century and the first half of the nineteenth, and only concluded by the final victory of gold during the fifty years before the war.

Dr Freud relates that there are peculiar reasons deep in our subconsciousness why gold in particular should satisfy strong instincts and serve as a symbol. The magical properties, with which Egyptian priestcraft anciently imbued the yellow metal, it has never altogether lost. Yet, whilst gold as a store of value has always had devoted patrons, it is, as the sole standard of purchasing power, almost a parvenu. In 1914 gold had held this position in Great Britain *de jure* over less than a hundred years (though *de facto* for more than two hundred), and in most other countries over less than sixty. For except during rather brief intervals gold has been too scarce to serve the needs of the world's principal medium of currency. Gold is, and always has been, an extraordinarily scarce commodity. A modern liner could convey across the Atlantic in a single voyage all the gold which has been dredged or mined in seven thousand years. At intervals of five hundred or a thousand years a new source of supply has been discovered—the latter half of the nineteenth century was one of these epochs—and a temporary abundance has ensued. But as a rule, generally speaking, there has been not enough.

Of late years the *auri sacra fames* has sought to envelop itself in a garment of respectability as densely respectable as was ever met with, even in the realms of sex or religion. Whether this was first put on as a necessary armour to win the hard-won fight against bimetallism and is still worn, as the gold-advocates allege, because gold is the sole prophylactic against the plague of fiat moneys, or whether it is a furtive Freudian cloak, we need not be curious to inquire. But we may remind the reader of what he well knows—namely, that gold has become part of the apparatus of conservatism and is one of the matters which we cannot expect to see handled without prejudice.

One great change, nevertheless—probably, in the end, a fatal change—has been effected by our generation. During the war individuals threw their little stocks into the national melting-pots. Wars have sometimes served to disperse gold, as when Alexander scattered the temple hoards of Persia or Pizarro those of the Incas. But on this occasion war concentrated gold in the vaults of the central banks; and these banks have not released it. Thus, almost throughout the world, gold has been withdrawn from circulation. It no longer passes from hand to hand, and the touch of the metal has been taken away from men's greedy palms. The little household gods, who dwelt in purses and stockings and tin boxes, have been swallowed by a single golden image in each country, which lives underground and is not seen. Gold is out of sight—gone back again into the soil. But when gods are no longer seen in a yellow panoply walking the earth, we begin to rationalise them; and it is not long before there is nothing left.

Thus the long age of commodity money has at last passed finally away before the age of representative money. Gold has ceased to be a coin, a hoard, a tangible claim to wealth, of which the value cannot slip away so long as the hand of the individual clutches the material stuff. It has become a much more abstract thing—just a standard of value; and it only keeps this nominal status by being handed round from time to time in quite small quantities amongst a group of central banks, on the occasions when one of them has been inflating or deflating its managed representative money in a different degree from what is appropriate to the behaviour of its neighbours. Even the handing round is becoming a little old-fashioned, being the occasion of unnecessary travelling expenses, and the most modern way, called 'earmarking', is to change the ownership without shifting the location. It is not a far step from this to the beginning of arrangements between central banks by which, without ever formally renouncing the rule of gold, the quantity of metal actually buried in their vaults may come to stand, by a modern alchemy, for what they please, and its value for what they choose. Thus gold, originally stationed in heaven with his consort silver, as Sun and Moon, having first doffed his sacred attributes and come to earth as an autocrat, may next descend to the sober status of a constitutional king with a Cabinet of banks; and it may never be necessary to proclaim a republic. But this is not yet—the evolution may be quite otherwise. The friends of gold will have to be extremely wise and moderate if they are to avoid a revolution.

2 ALTERNATIVE AIMS IN MONETARY POLICY (1923)[1]

From *A Tract on Monetary Reform*, chapter IV, 'Alternative Aims in Monetary Policy'.

The instability of money has been compounded, in most countries except the United States, of two elements: the failure of the national currencies to remain stable in terms of what was supposed to be the standard of value, namely gold; and the failure of gold itself to remain stable in terms of purchasing power. Attention has been mainly concentrated (e.g. by the Cunliffe Committee) on the first of these two factors. It is often assumed that the restoration of the gold standard, that is to say, of the convertibility of each national currency at a fixed rate in terms of gold, must be, in any case, our objective; and that the main question of controversy is whether national currencies should be restored to their pre-war gold value or to some lower value nearer to the present facts; in other words, the choice between *deflation* and *devaluation*.

This assumption is hasty. If we glance at the course of prices during the last five years, it is obvious that the United States, which has enjoyed a gold standard throughout, has suffered as severely as many other countries, that in the United Kingdom the instability of gold has been a larger factor than the instability of the exchange, that the same is true even of France, and that in Italy it has been nearly as large. On the other hand, in India, which has suffered violent exchange fluctuations, the standard of value has been more stable than in any other country.

We should not, therefore, by fixing the exchanges get rid of our currency troubles. It is even possible that this step might weaken our control. The problem of stabilisation has several sides, which we must consider one by one:

[1] [I.e. prior to the restoration of the gold standard in Great Britain.]

1. Devaluation *versus* deflation. Do we wish to fix the standard of value, whether or not it be gold, near the existing value? Or do we wish to restore it to the pre-war value?

2. Stability of prices *versus* stability of exchange. Is it more important that the value of a national currency should be stable in terms of purchasing power, or stable in terms of the currency of certain foreign countries?

3. The restoration of a gold standard. In the light of our answers to the first two questions, is a gold standard, however imperfect in theory, the best available method for attaining our ends in practice?

I DEVALUATION VERSUS DEFLATION

The policy of reducing the ratio between the volume of a country's currency and its requirements of purchasing power in the form of money, so as to increase the exchange value of the currency in terms of gold or of commodities, is conveniently called *deflation*.

The alternative policy of stabilising the value of the currency somewhere near its present value, without regard to its pre-war value, is called *devaluation*.

Up to the date of the Genoa Conference of April 1922, these two policies were not clearly distinguished by the public, and the sharp opposition between them has been only gradually appreciated. Even now (October 1923) there is scarcely any European country in which the authorities have made it clear whether their policy is to stabilise the value of their currency or to raise it. Stabilisation at the existing level has been recommended by international conferences; and the actual value of many currencies tends to fall rather than to rise. But, to judge from other indications, the heart's desire of the state banks of Europe, whether they pursue it successfully, as in Czechoslovakia, or unsuccessfully, as in France, is to *raise* the value of their currencies.

The simple arguments against deflation fall under two heads.

In the first place, deflation is not *desirable*, because it effects, what is always harmful, a change in the existing standard of value, and redistributes wealth in a manner injurious, at the same time, to business and to social stability. Deflation, as we have already seen, involves a transference of wealth from the rest of the community to the rentier class and to all holders of titles to money; just as inflation involves the opposite. In particular it involves a transference from all borrowers, that is to say from traders, manufacturers, and farmers, to lenders, from the active to the inactive.

But whilst the oppression of the taxpayer for the enrichment of the rentier is the chief lasting result, there is another, more violent, disturbance during the period of transition. The policy of gradually raising the value of a country's money to (say) 100 per cent above its present value in terms of goods amounts to giving notice to every merchant and every manufacturer, that for some time to come his stock and his raw materials will steadily depreciate on his hands, and to every one who finances his business with borrowed money that he will, sooner or later, lose 100 per cent on his liabilities (since he will have to pay back in terms of commodities twice as much as he has borrowed). Modern business, being carried on largely with borrowed money, must necessarily be brought to a standstill by such a process. It will be to the interest of everyone in business to go out of business for the time being; and of everyone who is contemplating expenditure to postpone his orders so long as he can. The wise man will be he who turns his assets into cash, withdraws from the risks and the exertions of activity, and awaits in country retirement the steady appreciation promised him in the value of his cash. A probable expectation of deflation is bad enough; a certain expectation is disastrous. For the mechanism of the modern business world is even less adapted to fluctuations in the value of money upwards than it is to fluctuations downwards.

In the second place, in many countries, deflation, even were it desirable, is not *possible*; that is to say, deflation in sufficient degree to restore the currency to its pre-war parity. For the burden which it would throw on the taxpayer would be insupportable. This practical impossibility might have rendered the policy innocuous, if it were not that, by standing in the way of the alternative policy, it prolongs the period of uncertainty and severe seasonal fluctuation, and even, in some cases, can be carried into effect sufficiently to cause much interference with business. The fact that the restoration of their currencies to the pre-war parity is still the declared official policy of the French and Italian governments is preventing, in those countries, any rational discussion of currency reform. All those—and in the financial world they are many—who have reasons for wishing to appear 'correct', are compelled to talk foolishly. In Italy, where sound economic views have much influence and which may be nearly ripe for currency reform, Signor Mussolini has threatened to raise the lira to its former value. Fortunately for the Italian taxpayer and Italian business, the lira does not listen even to a dictator and cannot be given castor oil. But such talk can postpone positive reform; though it may be doubted if so good a politician would have propounded such a policy, even in bravado and exuberance, if he had understood that, expressed in other but equivalent words, it was as follows: 'My policy is to halve wages, double the burden of the national debt, and to reduce by 50 per cent the prices which Sicily can get for her exports of oranges and lemons.'

If the restoration of many European currencies to their pre-war parity with gold is neither desirable nor possible, what are the forces or the arguments which have established this undesirable impossibility as the avowed policy of most of them? The following are the most important:

1. *To leave the gold value of a country's currency at the low level to which war has driven it is an injustice to the rentier class and to others whose income is fixed in terms of currency, and*

practically a breach of contract; whilst to restore its value would meet a debt of honour.

The injury done to pre-war holders of fixed interest-bearing stocks is beyond dispute. Real justice, indeed, might require the restoration of the purchasing power, and not merely the gold value, of their money incomes, a measure which no one in fact proposes; whilst nominal justice has not been infringed, since these investments were not in gold bullion but in the legal tender of the realm. Nevertheless, if this class of investors could be dealt with separately, considerations of equity and the expedience of satisfying reasonable expectation would furnish a strong case.

But this is not the actual situation. The vast issues of war loans have swamped the pre-war holdings of fixed interest-bearing stocks, and society has largely adjusted itself to the new situation. To restore the value of pre-war holdings by deflation means enhancing at the same time the value of war and post-war holdings, and thereby raising the total claims of the rentier class not only beyond what they are entitled to, but to an intolerable proportion of the total income of the community. Indeed justice, rightly weighed, comes down on the other side. Much the greater proportion of the money contracts still outstanding were entered into when money was worth more nearly what it is worth now than what it was worth in 1913. Thus, in order to do justice to a minority of creditors, a great injustice would be done to a great majority of debtors.

When, therefore, the depreciation of the currency has lasted long enough for society to adjust itself to the new values, deflation is even worse than inflation. Both are 'unjust' and disappoint reasonable expectation. But whereas inflation, by easing the burden of national debt and stimulating enterprise, has a little to throw into the other side of the balance, deflation has nothing.

2. *The restoration of a currency to its pre-war gold value enhances a country's financial prestige and promotes future confidence.*

Where a country can hope to restore its pre-war parity at an early date, this argument cannot be neglected. This might be said of Great Britain, Holland, Sweden, Switzerland, and (perhaps) Spain, but of no other European country. The argument cannot be extended to those countries which, even if they could raise somewhat the value of their legal-tender money, could not possibly restore it to its old value. It is of the essence of the argument that the *exact* pre-war parity should be recovered. It would not make much difference to the financial prestige of Italy whether she established the lira at 100 to the £ sterling or at 60; and it would be much better for her prestige to establish it definitely at 100 than to let it fluctuate between 60 and 100.

This argument is limited, therefore, to those countries the gold value of whose currencies is within (say) 5 or 10 per cent of their former value. Its force in these cases depends, I think, upon what answer we give to the problem discussed below, namely, whether we intend to pin ourselves in the future, as in the past, to an unqualified gold standard. If we still prefer such a standard to any available alternative, and if future 'confidence' in our currency is to depend not on the stability of its purchasing power but on the fixity of its gold value, then it may be worth our while to stand the racket of deflation to the extent of 5 or 10 per cent. This view is in accordance with that expressed by Ricardo in analogous circumstances a hundred years ago. If, on the other hand, we decide to aim for the future at stability of the price level rather than at a fixed parity with gold, in that case *cadit quaestio*.

3. *If the gold value of a country's currency can be increased, labour will profit by a reduced cost of living, foreign goods will be obtainable cheaper, and foreign debts fixed in terms of gold (e.g. to the United States) will be discharged with less effort.*

This argument, which is pure delusion, exercises quite as much influence as the other two. If the franc is worth more, wages, it is argued, which are paid in francs, will surely buy more, and French imports, which are paid for in francs, will be so much cheaper. No! If francs are worth more they will buy more labour as well as more goods—that is to say, wages will fall; and the French exports, which pay for the imports, will, measured in francs, fall in value just as much as the imports. Nor will it make in the long run any difference whatever in the amount of goods the value of which England will have to transfer to America to pay her dollar debts whether in the end sterling settles down at four dollars to the pound or at its pre-war parity. The burden of this debt depends on the value of gold, in terms of which it is fixed, not on the value of sterling. It is not easy, it seems, for men to apprehend that their money is a mere intermediary, without significance in itself, which flows from one hand to another, is received and is dispensed, and disappears when its work is done from the sum of a nation's wealth.

II STABILITY OF PRICES VERSUS STABILITY OF EXCHANGE

Since, subject to certain qualifications, the rate of exchange of a country's currency with the currency of the rest of the world (assuming for the sake of simplicity that there is only one external currency) depends on the relation between the internal price level and the external price level, it follows that the exchange cannot be stable unless *both* internal *and* external price levels remain stable. If, therefore, the external price level lies outside our control, we must submit either to our own internal price level or to our exchange being pulled about by external influences. If the external price level is unstable, we cannot keep *both* our own price level *and* our exchanges stable. And we are compelled to choose.

In pre-war days, when almost the whole world was on a gold standard, we had all plumped for stability of exchange as against stability of prices, and we were ready to submit to the social consequences of a change of price level for causes quite outside our control, connected, for example, with the discovery of new gold mines in foreign countries or a change of banking policy abroad. But we submitted, partly because we did not dare trust ourselves to a less automatic (though more reasoned) policy, and partly because the price fluctuations experienced were in fact moderate. Nevertheless, there were powerful advocates of the other choice. In particular, the proposals of Professor Irving Fisher for a compensated dollar amounted, unless all countries adopted the same plan, to putting into practice a preference for stability of internal price level over stability of external exchange.

The right choice is not necessarily the same for all countries. It must partly depend on the relative importance of foreign trade in the economic life of the country. Nevertheless, there does seem to be in almost every case a presumption in favour of the stability of prices, if only it can be achieved. Stability of exchange is in the nature of a convenience which adds to the efficiency and prosperity of those who are engaged in foreign trade. Stability of prices, on the other hand, is profoundly important for the avoidance of the various evils described above. Contracts and business expectations, which presume a stable exchange, must be far fewer, even in a trading country such as England, than those which presume a stable level of internal prices. The main argument to the contrary seems to be that exchange stability is an easier aim to attain, since it only requires that the same standard of value should be adopted at home and abroad; whereas an internal standard, so regulated as to maintain stability in an index number of prices, is a difficult scientific innovation, never yet put into practice.

At any rate the unthinking assumption, in favour of the restoration of a fixed exchange as the one thing to aim at, requires more examination than it sometimes receives. Especially is this the case if the prospect that a majority of countries will °adopt the same standard is still remote. When by adopting the gold standard we could achieve stability of exchange with almost the whole world, whilst any other standard would have appeared as a solitary eccentricity, the solid advantages of certainty and convenience supported the conservative preference for gold. Nevertheless, even so, the convenience of traders and the primitive passion for solid metal might not, I think, have been adequate to preserve the dynasty of gold, if it had not been for another, half-accidental circumstance; namely, that for many years past gold had afforded not only a stable exchange but, on the whole, a stable price level also. In fact, the choice between stable exchanges and stable prices had not presented itself as an acute dilemma. And when, prior to the development of the South African mines, we seemed to be faced with a continuously falling price level, the fierceness of the bimetallic controversy testified to the discontent provoked as soon as the existing standard appeared seriously incompatible with the stability of prices.

Indeed, it is doubtful whether the pre-war system for regulating the international flow of gold would have been capable of dealing with such large or sudden divergencies between the price levels of different countries as have occurred lately. The fault of the pre-war régime, under which the rates of exchange between a country and the outside world were fixed, and the internal price level had to adjust itself thereto (i.e. was chiefly governed by external influences), was that it was too slow and insensitive in its mode of operation. The fault of the post-war régime, under which the price level mainly depends on internal influences (i.e. internal currency and credit policy) and the rates of exchange with the outside world have to adjust themselves thereto, is that it is too rapid in its effect and over-sensitive, with the result that it may act violently for merely transitory causes. Nevertheless, when the fluctuations are large and sudden, a quick reaction is necessary for the maintenance of equilibrium; and the necessity for quick reaction has been one of the factors which have rendered the pre-war method inapplicable to post-war conditions, and have made everyone nervous of proclaiming a final fixation of the exchange.

A fluctuating exchange means that relative prices can be knocked about by the most fleeting influences of politics and of sentiment, and by the periodic pressure of seasonal trades. But it also means that this method is a most rapid and powerful corrective of real dis-equilibria in the balance of international payments arising from whatever causes, and a wonderful preventive in the way of countries which are inclined to spend abroad beyond their resources.

Thus when there are violent shocks to the pre-existing equilibrium between the internal and external price levels, the pre-war method is likely to break down in practice, simply because it cannot bring about the readjustment of internal prices *quick enough*. Theoretically, of course, the pre-war method must be able to make itself effective sooner or later, provided the movement of gold is allowed to continue without restriction until the inflation or deflation of prices has taken place to the necessary extent. But in practice there is usually a limit to the rate and to the amount by which the actual currency or the metallic backing for it can be allowed to flow abroad. If the supply of money or credit is reduced faster than social and business arrangements allow prices to fall, intolerable inconveniences result.

III   THE RESTORATION OF A GOLD STANDARD

Our conclusions up to this point are, therefore, that, when stability of the internal price level and stability of the external exchanges are incompatible, the former is generally preferable; and that on occasions when the dilemma is acute the preservation of the former at the expense of the latter is, fortunately perhaps, the line of least resistance.

The restoration of the gold standard (whether at the pre-war parity or at some other rate) certainly will not give us complete stability of internal prices, and can only give us complete stability of the external exchanges if all other countries also restore the gold standard. The advisability of restoring it depends, therefore, on whether on the whole it will give us the best working compromise obtainable between the two ideals.

The advocates of gold, as against a more scientific standard, base their cause on the double contention that in practice gold has provided and will provide a reasonably stable standard of value and that in practice, since governing authorities lack wisdom as often as not, a managed currency will, sooner or later, come to grief. Conservatism and scepticism join arms—as they often do. Perhaps superstition comes in too; for gold still enjoys the prestige of its smell and colour.

The considerable success with which gold maintained its stability of value in the changing world of the nineteenth century was certainly remarkable. After the discoveries of Australia and California it began to depreciate dangerously, and before the exploitation of South Africa it began to appreciate dangerously. Yet in each case it righted itself and retained its reputation.

But the conditions of the future are not those of the past. We have no sufficient ground for expecting the continuance of the special conditions which preserved a sort of balance before the war. For what are the underlying explanations of the good behaviour of gold during the nineteenth century?

In the first place, it happened that progress in the discovery of gold mines roughly kept pace with progress in other directions —a correspondence which was not altogether a matter of chance, because the progress of that period, since it was characterised by the gradual opening up and exploitation of the world's surface, not unnaturally brought to light *pari passu* the remoter deposits of gold. But this stage of history is now almost at an end. A quarter of a century has passed by since the discovery of an important deposit. Material progress is more dependent now on the growth of scientific and technical knowledge, of which the application to gold-mining may be intermittent. Years may elapse without great improvement in the methods of extracting gold; and then the genius of a chemist may realise past dreams and forgotten hoaxes, transmuting base into precious like Subtle, or extracting gold from sea-water as in the Bubble. Gold is liable to be either too dear or too cheap. In either case, it is too much to expect that a succession of accidents will keep the metal steady.

But there was another type of influence which used to aid stability. The value of gold has not depended on the policy or the decisions of a single body of men; and a sufficient proportion of the supply has been able to find its way, without any flooding of the market, into the arts or into the hoards of Asia for its marginal value to be governed by a steady psychological estimation of the metal in relation to other things. This is what is meant by saying that gold has 'intrinsic value' and is free from the dangers of a 'managed' currency. The *independent variety* of the influences determining the value of gold has been in itself a steadying influence. The arbitrary and variable character of the proportion of gold reserves to liabilities maintained by many of the note-issuing banks of the world, so far from introducing an incalculable factor, was an element of stability. For when gold was relatively abundant and flowed towards them, it was absorbed by their allowing their ratio of gold reserves to rise slightly; and when it was relatively scarce, the fact that they had no intention of ever utilising their gold reserves for any practical purpose permitted most of them to view with equanimity a moderate weakening of their proportion. A great part of the flow of South African gold between the end of the Boer War and 1914 was able to find its way into the central gold reserves of European and other countries with the minimum effect on prices.

But the war has effected a great change. Gold itself has become a 'managed' currency. The West, as well as the East, has learnt to hoard gold; but the motives of the United States are not those of India. Now that most countries have abandoned the gold standard, the supply of the metal would, if the chief user of it restricted its holdings to its real needs, prove largely redundant. The United States has not been able to let gold fall to its 'natural' value, because it could not face the resulting depreciation of its standard. It has been driven, therefore, to the costly policy of burying in the vaults of Washington what the miners of the Rand have laboriously brought to the surface. Consequently gold now stands at an 'artificial' value, the future course of which almost entirely depends on the policy of the Federal Reserve Board of the United States. The value of gold is no longer the resultant of the chance gifts of Nature and the judgement of numerous authorities and individuals acting independently. Even if other countries gradually return to a gold basis, the position will not be greatly changed. The tendency to employ some variant of the gold-exchange standard and the probably permanent disappearance of gold from the pockets of the people are likely to mean that the strictly *necessary* gold reserves of the central banks of the gold-standard countries will fall considerably short of the available supplies. The actual value of gold will depend, therefore, on the policy of three or four of the most powerful central banks, whether they act independently or in unison. If, on the other hand, pre-war conventions about the use of gold in reserves and in circulation were to be restored—which is, in my opinion, the much less probable alternative—there might be, as Professor Cassel has predicted, a serious shortage of gold, leading to a progressive appreciation in its value.

Nor must we neglect the possibility of a partial demonetisation of gold by the United States through a closing of its mints to further receipts of gold. The present policy of the United States in accepting unlimited imports of gold can be justified, perhaps, as a temporary measure, intended to preserve tradition and to strengthen confidence through a transitional period. But, looked at as a permanent arrangement, it could hardly be judged otherwise than as a foolish expense. If the Federal Reserve Board intends to maintain the value of the dollar at a level which is irrespective of the inflow or outflow of gold, what object is there in continuing to accept at the mints gold which is not wanted, yet costs a heavy price? If the United States mints were to be closed to gold, everything, except the actual price of the metal, could continue precisely as before.

Confidence in the future stability of the value of gold depends therefore on the United States being foolish enough to go on accepting gold which it does not want, and wise enough, having accepted it, to maintain it at a fixed value. This double event might be realised through the collaboration of a public understanding nothing with a Federal Reserve Board understanding everything. But the position is precarious; and not very attractive to any country which is still in a position to choose what its future standard is to be.

This discussion of the prospects of the stability of gold has partly answered by anticipation the second principal argument in favour of the restoration of an unqualified gold standard, namely that this is the only way of avoiding the dangers of a 'managed' currency.

It is natural, after what we have experienced, that prudent people should desiderate a standard of value which is independent of finance ministers and state banks. The present state of affairs has allowed to the ignorance and frivolity of statesmen an ample opportunity of bringing about ruinous consequences in the economic field. It is felt that the general level of economic and financial education amongst statesmen and bankers is hardly such as to render innovations feasible or safe; that, in fact, a chief object of stabilising the exchanges is to strap down ministers of finance.

These are reasonable grounds of hesitation. But the experience on which they are based is by no means fair to the capacities of statesmen and bankers. The non-metallic standards of which we have experience have been anything rather than scientific experiments coolly carried out. They have been a last resort, involuntarily adopted, as a result of war or inflationary taxation, when the state finances were already broken or the situation out of hand. Naturally in these circumstances such practices have been the accompaniment and the prelude of disaster. But we cannot argue from this to what can be achieved in normal times. I do not see that the regulation of the standard of value is essentially more difficult than many other objects of less social necessity which we attain successfully.

If, indeed, a providence watched over gold, or if Nature had provided us with a stable standard ready-made, I would not, in an attempt after some slight improvement, hand over the management to the possible weakness or ignorance of boards and governments. But this is not the situation. We have no ready-made standard. Experience has shown that in emergencies ministers of finance cannot be strapped down. And—most important of all—in the modern world of paper currency and bank credit there is no escape from a 'managed' currency, whether we wish it or not; convertibility into gold will not alter the fact that the value of gold itself depends on the policy of the central banks.

It is worth while to pause a moment over the last sentence. It differs significantly from the doctrine of gold reserves which we learnt and taught before the war. We used to assume that no central bank would be so extravagant as to keep more gold than it required or so imprudent as to keep less. From time to time gold would flow out into the circulation or for export abroad; experience showed that the quantity required on these occasions bore some rough proportion to the central bank's liabilities; a decidedly higher proportion than this would be fixed on to provide for contingencies and to inspire confidence; and the creation of credit would be regulated largely by reference to the maintenance of this proportion. The Bank of England, for example, would allow itself to be swayed by the tides of gold, permitting the inflowing and outflowing streams to produce their 'natural' consequences unchecked by any ideas as to preventing the effect on prices. Already before the war the system was becoming precarious by reason of its artificiality. The 'proportion' was by the lapse of time losing its relation to the facts and had become largely conventional. Some other figure, greater or less, would have done just as well.[1] The war broke down the convention; for the withdrawal of gold from actual circulation destroyed one of the elements of reality lying behind the convention, and the suspension of convertibility destroyed the other. It would have been absurd to regulate the bank rate by reference to a 'proportion' which had lost all its significance; and in the course of the past ten years a new policy has been evolved. The bank rate is now employed, however incompletely and experimentally, to regulate the expansion and deflation of credit in the interests of business stability and the steadiness of prices. In so far as it is employed to procure stability of the dollar exchange, where this is inconsistent with stability of internal prices, we have a relic of pre-war policy and a compromise between discrepant aims.

Those who advocate the return to a gold standard do not always appreciate along what different lines our actual practice has been drifting. If we restore the gold standard, are we to return also to the pre-war conceptions of bank rate, allowing the tides of gold to play what tricks they like with the internal price level, and abandoning the attempt to moderate the disastrous influence of the credit cycle on the stability of prices and employment? Or are we to continue and develop the experimental innovations of our present policy, ignoring the 'bank ratio' and, if necessary, allowing unmoved a piling up of gold reserves far beyond our requirements or their depletion far below them?

In truth, the gold standard is already a barbarous relic. All of us, from the governor of the Bank of England downwards, are now primarily interested in preserving the stability of business, prices, and employment, and are not likely, when the choice is forced on us, deliberately to sacrifice these to the outworn dogma, which had its value once, of £3 17s 10½d per ounce. Advocates of the ancient standard do not observe how remote it now is from the spirit and the requirements of the age.

[1] See, for what I wrote about this in 1914, *The Economic Journal*, XXIV, 621 [JMK, vol. XI].

A regulated non-metallic standard has slipped in unnoticed. *It exists.* Whilst the economists dozed, the academic dream of a hundred years, doffing its cap and gown, clad in paper rags, has crept into the real world by means of the bad fairies— always so much more potent than the good—the wicked ministers of finance.

For these reasons enlightened advocates of the restoration of gold, such as Mr Hawtrey, do not welcome it as the return of a 'natural' currency, and intend, quite decidedly, that it shall be a 'managed' one. They allow gold back only as a constitutional monarch, shorn of his ancient despotic powers and compelled to accept the advice of a parliament of banks. The adoption of the ideas present in the minds of those who drafted the Genoa Resolutions on Currency is an essential condition of Mr Hawtrey's adherence to gold. He contemplates 'the practice of continuous co-operation among central banks of issue' (Res. 3), and an international convention, based on a gold-exchange standard, and designed 'with a view to preventing undue fluctuations in the purchasing power of gold' (Res. 11).[1] But he is *not* in favour of resuming the gold standard irrespective of 'whether the difficulties in regard to the future purchasing power of gold have been provided against or not'. 'It is not easy', he admits, 'to promote international action, and, should it fail, the wisest course for the time being might be to concentrate on the stabilisation of sterling in terms of commodities, rather than tie the pound to a metal the vagaries of which cannot be foreseen.'[2]

It is natural to ask, in face of advocacy of this kind, why it is necessary to drag in gold at all. Mr Hawtrey lays no stress on the obvious support for his compromise, namely the force of sentiment and tradition, and the preference of Englishmen for shearing a monarch of his powers rather than of his head. But he adduces three other reasons: (1) that gold is required as a liquid reserve for the settlement of international balances of indebtedness; (2) that it enables an experiment to be made

[1] *Monetary Reconstruction,* p. 132.   [2] *Loc. cit.* p. 22.

without cutting adrift from the old system; and (3) that the vested interests of gold producers must be considered. These objects, however, are so largely attained by my own suggestions in the following section that I need not dwell on them here.

On the other hand, I see grave objections to reinstating gold in the pious hope that international co-operation will keep it in order. With the existing distribution of the world's gold the reinstatement of the gold standard means, inevitably, that we surrender the regulation of our price level and the handling of the credit cycle to the Federal Reserve Board of the United States. Even if the most intimate and cordial co-operation is established between the Board and the Bank of England, the preponderance of power will still belong to the former. The Board will be in a position to disregard the Bank. But if the Bank disregard the Board, it will render itself liable to be flooded with, or depleted of, gold, as the case may be. Moreover, we can be confident beforehand that there will be much suspicion amongst Americans (for that is their disposition) of any supposed attempt on the part of the Bank of England to dictate their policy or to influence American discount rates in the interests of Great Britain. We must also be prepared to incur our share of the vain expense of bottling up the world's redundant gold.

It would be rash in present circumstances to surrender our freedom of action to the Federal Reserve Board of the United States. We do not yet possess sufficient experience of its capacity to act in times of stress with courage and independence. The Federal Reserve Board is striving to free itself from the pressure of sectional interests; but we are not yet certain that it will wholly succeed. It is still liable to be overwhelmed by the impetuosity of a cheap money campaign. A suspicion of British influence would, so far from strengthening the Board, greatly weaken its resistance to popular clamour. Nor is it certain, quite apart from weakness or mistakes, that the simultaneous application of the same policy will always be in the interests of both countries. The development of the credit cycle and the state of business may sometimes be widely different on the two sides of the Atlantic.

Therefore, since I regard the stability of prices, credit, and employment as of paramount importance, and since I feel no confidence that an old-fashioned gold standard will even give us the modicum of stability that it used to give, I reject the policy of restoring the gold standard on pre-war lines. At the same time, I doubt the wisdom of attempting a 'managed' gold standard jointly with the United States, on the lines recommended by Mr Hawtrey, because it retains too many of the disadvantages of the old system without its advantages, and because it would make us too dependent on the policy and on the wishes of the Federal Reserve Board.

3 POSITIVE SUGGESTIONS FOR THE FUTURE REGULATION OF MONEY (1923)

From *A Tract on Monetary Reform*, chapter v, 'Positive Suggestions for the Future Regulation of Money'.

A sound constructive scheme must provide:

I. A method for regulating the supply of currency and credit with a view to maintaining, so far as possible, the stability of the internal price level; and

II. A method for regulating the supply of foreign exchange so as to avoid purely temporary fluctuations caused by seasonal or other influences and not due to a lasting disturbance in the relation between the internal and the external price level.

I believe that in Great Britain the ideal system can be most nearly and most easily reached by an adaptation of the actual system which has grown up, half haphazard, since the war.

I. My first requirement in a good constructive scheme can be supplied merely by a development of our existing arrangements on more deliberate and self-conscious lines. Hitherto the Treasury and the Bank of England have looked forward to the stability of the dollar exchange (preferably at the pre-war parity) as their objective. It is not clear whether they intend to stick to this irrespective of fluctuations in the value of the dollar (or of gold); whether, that is to say, they would sacrifice the stability of sterling prices to the stability of the dollar exchange in the event of the two proving to be incompatible. At any rate, my scheme would require that they should adopt the stability of sterling prices as their *primary* objective—though this would not prevent their aiming at exchange stability also as a secondary objective by co-operating with the Federal Reserve Board in a common policy. So long as the Federal

Reserve Board was successful in keeping dollar prices steady the objective of keeping sterling prices steady would be identical with the objective of keeping the dollar–sterling exchange steady. My recommendation does not involve more than a determination that, in the event of the Federal Reserve Board failing to keep dollar prices steady, sterling prices should not, if it could be helped, plunge with them merely for the sake of maintaining a fixed parity of exchange.

If the Bank of England, the Treasury, and the Big Five were to adopt this policy, to what criteria should they look respectively in regulating bank rate, government borrowing, and trade advances? The first question is whether the criterion should be a precise, arithmetical formula or whether it should be sought in a general judgement of the situation based on all the available data. The pioneer of price stability as against exchange stability, Professor Irving Fisher, advocated the former in the shape of his 'compensated dollar', which was to be automatically adjusted by reference to an index number of prices without any play of judgement or discretion. He may have been influenced, however, by the advantage of propounding a method which could be grafted as easily as possible on to the pre-war system of gold reserves and gold ratios. In any case, I doubt the wisdom and the practicability of a system so cut and dried. If we wait until a price movement is actually afoot before applying remedial measures, we may be too late. 'It is not the *past* rise in prices but the *future* rise that has to be counteracted.'[1] It is characteristic of the impetuosity of the credit cycle that price movements tend to be cumulative, each movement promoting, up to a certain point, a further movement in the same direction. Professor Fisher's method may be adapted to deal with long-period trends in the value of gold but not with the, often more injurious, short-period oscillations of the credit cycle. Nevertheless, whilst it would not be advisable to postpone action until it was called for by an actual movement of prices, it would promote confidence,

[1] Hawtrey, *Monetary Reconstruction*, p. 105.

and furnish an objective standard of value, if, an official index number having been compiled of such a character as to register the price of a standard composite commodity, the authorities were to adopt this composite commodity as their standard of value in the sense that they would employ all their resources to prevent a movement of its price by more than a certain percentage in either direction away from the normal, just as before the war they employed all their resources to prevent a movement in the price of gold by more than a certain percentage. The precise composition of the standard composite commodity could be modified from time to time in accordance with changes in the relative economic importance of its various components.

As regards the criteria, other than the actual trend of prices, which should determine the action of the controlling authority, it is beyond the scope of this essay to deal adequately with the diagnosis and analysis of the credit cycle. The more deeply our researches penetrate into this subject, the more accurately shall we understand the right time and method for controlling credit expansion by bank rate or otherwise. But in the meantime we have a considerable and growing body of general experience upon which those in authority can base their judgements. Actual price movements must of course provide the most important datum; but the state of employment, the volume of production, the effective demand for credit as felt by the banks, the rate of interest on investments of various types, the volume of new issues, the flow of cash into circulation, the statistics of foreign trade and the level of the exchanges must be all taken into account. The main point is that the *objective* of the authorities, pursued with such means as are at their command, should be the stability of prices.

II. How can we best combine this primary object with a maximum stability of the exchanges? Can we get the best of both worlds—stability of prices over long periods and stability of exchanges over short periods? It is the great advantage of the gold standard that it overcomes the excessive sensitiveness of the exchanges to temporary influences. Our object must be to secure this advantage, if we can, without committing ourselves to follow big movements in the value of gold itself.

I believe that we can go a long way in this direction if the Bank of England will take over the duty of regulating the price of gold, just as it already regulates the rate of discount. 'Regulate', but not 'peg'. The Bank of England should have a buying and a selling price for gold, just as it did before the war, and this price might remain unchanged for considerable periods, just as bank rate does. But it would not be fixed or 'pegged' once and for all, any more than bank rate is fixed. The Bank's rate for gold would be announced every Thursday morning at the same time as its rate for discounting bills, with a difference between its buying and selling rates corresponding to the pre-war margin between £3 17s 10½d per oz. and £3 17s 9d per oz.; except that, in order to obviate too frequent changes in the rate, the difference might be wider than 1½d per oz.—say, ½ to 1 per cent. A willingness on the part of the Bank both to buy and to sell gold at rates fixed for the time being would keep the dollar–sterling exchange steady within corresponding limits, so that the exchange rate would not move with every breath of wind but only when the Bank had come to a considered judgement that a change was required for the sake of the stability of sterling prices.

If the bank rate and the gold rate in conjunction were leading to an excessive influx or an excessive efflux of gold, the Bank of England would have to decide whether the flow was due to an internal or to an external movement away from stability. To fix our ideas, let us suppose that gold is flowing outwards. If this seemed to be due to a tendency of sterling to depreciate in terms of commodities, the correct remedy would be to raise the bank rate. If, on the other hand, it was due to a tendency of gold to appreciate in terms of commodities, the correct remedy would be to raise the gold rate (i.e. the buying price for gold). If, however, the flow could be explained by seasonal, or other passing influences, then it should be allowed to continue (assuming, of course, that the Bank's gold reserves were equal to any probable calls on them) unchecked, to be redressed later on by the corresponding reaction.

It would effect an improvement in the technique of the system here proposed, without altering its fundamental characteristics, if the Bank of England were to quote a daily price, not only for the purchase and sale of gold for immediate delivery, but also for delivery three months forward. The difference, if any, between the cash and forward quotations might represent either a discount or a premium of the latter on the former, according as the bank desired money rates in London to stand below or above those in New York. The existence of the forward quotation of the Bank of England would afford a firm foundation for a free market in forward exchange, and would facilitate the movement of funds between London and New York for short periods, in much the same way as before the war, whilst at the same time keeping down to a minimum the actual movement of gold bullion backwards and forwards.

The reader will observe that I retain for gold an important role in our system. As an ultimate safeguard and as a reserve for sudden requirements, no superior medium is yet available. But I urge that it is possible to get the benefit of the advantages of gold without irrevocably binding our legal-tender money to follow blindly all the vagaries of gold and future unforeseeable fluctuations in its real purchasing power.

4 THE SPEECHES OF THE BANK CHAIRMEN (1924–1927)

I FEBRUARY 1924

Published as 'The Speeches of the Bank Chairmen' in the *Nation and Athenaeum*, 23 February 1924, and signed 'J.M.K.'. Reginald McKenna was Chancellor of the Exchequer when Keynes was employed at the Treasury in 1915–16, and became a personal friend.

We have an admirable custom in this country by which once a year the overlords of the Big Five desist for a day from the thankless task of persuading their customers to accept loans and, putting on cap and gown, mount the lecturer's rostrum to expound the theory of their practice—a sort of saturnalia, during which we are all ephemerally equal with words for weapons. These occasions are of great general interest. But they are more than this. They have a representative significance; they hold up, as it were, financial fashion plates. What have they found to say this year about monetary policy?

Only one, Mr Walter Leaf, of the Westminster Bank, has refrained himself entirely. Each of the other four has had something to say. They fall into a pair of couples: one of which, Mr Beaumont Pease of Lloyds Bank and Sir Harry Goschen of the National Provincial Bank, feel that there is something improper, or at any rate undesirable, in thinking or speaking about these things at all; and the other of which, Mr Goodenough of Barclays Bank and Mr McKenna of the Midland Bank, so far from deprecating discussion, join in it boldly.

Mr Pease, as I have said, deprecates thinking, or—as he prefers to call it—'the expenditure of mental agility'. He desires 'straightly to face the facts instead of to find a clever way round them', and holds that, in matters arising out of the quantity theory of money, as between brains and character, 'certainly the latter does not come second in order of merit'. In short, the gold standard falls within the sphere of morals or of religion, where free thought is out of place. He goes on to say:

As far as any ordinary joint stock bank is concerned, I do not think it determines its policy consciously on pure monetary grounds. That is to say, its chief concern is to meet the requirements of trade as they arise, regardless of adhesion to any particular theory. Its actions are not the cause of trade movements; they follow after and do not precede them.

I think that this, broadly speaking, is a correct account of the matter, and Mr Pease's emphasis on it is the most valuable part of his speech. It is precisely this automatic element in the reactions of the joint stock banks which makes the policy of the Bank of England about the volume of the banks' balances and the rate of discount so all-important. In conclusion, Mr Pease does not propose to take any particular steps at present towards establishing any particular standard. Nevertheless he is 'hopeful that we may gradually get back to our gold standard, which, in spite of some defects and difficulties, has, as a matter of fact, worked well in the past'.

Sir Harry Goschen goes one better than Mr Pease in a delightful passage which deserves to be quoted in full:

I cannot help thinking that there has been lately far too much irresponsible discussion as to the comparative advantages of inflation and deflation. Discussions of this kind can only breed suspicion in the minds of our neighbours as to whether we shall adopt either of these courses, and, if so, which. I think we had better let matters take their natural course.

Is it more appropriate to smile or to rage at these artless sentiments? Best of all, perhaps, just to leave Sir Harry to take his natural course.

Leaving, then, these impeccable spinsters, we come, in the speeches of Mr Goodenough and Mr McKenna, to rational, even *risqué* conversation. In immediate policy there is a large measure of agreement between them. They agree that monetary policy is capable of determining the level of prices, that our destiny is therefore in our own hands, and that the right course to pursue requires much thought and discussion. Mr Goodenough, however, lays greater stress on the bank rate, and Mr McKenna on the amount of the cash resources in the hands of the banks. They are opposed to any revival at the present time of the Cunliffe Committee's policy of deflation. They both look to internal conditions, and not to the foreign exchanges, as the criterion for expanding or contracting credit; with this difference, however, that Mr McKenna would look chiefly to the level of employment, whilst Mr Goodenough would be more influenced by the stability of internal prices. 'To sum up my views on the currency question,' the latter says, 'I feel that our aim should be to maintain as nearly as possible the existing equilibrium between currency and commodities. . .' Neither of them, however, would be much disturbed by a moderate rise of prices, provided (in the case of Mr McKenna) that the productive resources of the country had not yet reached the limit of their capacity, and (in the case of Mr Goodenough) that the rise was due neither to the speculative withholding of commodities nor to British prices rising relatively to American prices. About our ultimate objective Mr McKenna does not speak; but there is nothing in his speech to suggest that he would not be in favour of pursuing permanently the policy, which he recommends for the present, of 'steering a middle course between inflation and deflation', i.e. of aiming, like Mr Goodenough, at a general stability of prices within certain limits, and of deliberately employing monetary policy to mitigate the evils of the credit cycle: 'Ups and downs in trade we are bound to have, but wise monetary policy can always prevent the cyclical movement from going to extremes. The speculative excesses of an inflationary boom and the cruel impoverishment of a prolonged slump can both be avoided. They are not necessary evils to which we must submit as things without understandable or preventable causes.' Mr Goodenough, on the other hand, whilst desisting from the pursuit of the gold standard for the time being, continues the passage from his speech quoted above—'. . . although always we should keep in mind our ultimate aim, which is a return to a gold standard'. Meanwhile, he puts his hopes on an inflationary movement in America just sufficient to bring sterling back to its former parity with gold, without any disturbance to its present parity with commodities.

§Mr McKenna's speech, in particular, contains so much wise and lucid exposition of the way in which our monetary system works—it is the very best speech which he has made in a notable series—that not all of it can be analysed here, and the interested reader must be referred to the original. But there is one other matter to be mentioned, upon which both he and Mr Goodenough dwell emphatically, namely, the inelasticity imposed on our note issue by the Treasury Minute issued by recommendation of the Cunliffe Committee.

The object of this Minute was to enforce a continuous process of deflation. The policy has been abandoned, but the Minute still stands. Both speakers show some nervousness about this. Mr Goodenough points out that it is possible to get round the Minute to a certain extent merely by transferring gold from the Bank of England Reserve to the Currency Note Account. Nevertheless, 'we have still to consider the steps it would be desirable to take in the not unlikely event of the fiduciary limit to the currency issue being reached. I think it must be admitted that it would be undesirable, in fact impossible, to lay down in advance any hard and fast rule...' If, he finally concludes, the demand for additional notes 'is the reflection of a genuine expansion of trading activity, it may be regarded as a healthy sign, and no undue limitation would be justified'.

Mr McKenna is even more decisive as to some change being required, and he points out clearly the very interesting point that the volume of our currency is now *more* inelastic than before the war, because then it could always be swollen if necessary by the inflow of gold, whereas now there is not any means at all of increasing it, whatever the circumstances.§

What is the net result of these speeches? They strengthen greatly the hands of the currency reformers who believe that the stability of the internal price level and the damping down of the credit cycle are desirable and attainable objects. They are also reassuring, since they show that two of the most influential figures in the City have clearly in mind all the points of immediate practical importance, and can be relied on to use their influence in the right direction. Mr McKenna and Mr Goodenough are both in sympathy with the above aims. Nor would it be fair to say that the spinsters are definitely opposed to these ideas. (There would be just as much impropriety for them, just as much mental agility required, to think one thing as to think another. Their simplicity is quite impartial.) If they could be led gently by the hand beyond their copy-book maxims of 'looking facts firmly in the face' and 'economy and hard work', it might be found that they, too, had no objection to a deliberate attempt to keep prices steady and trade on an even keel, and that, whilst they feel at first the same distaste towards any proposal to 'tamper' with 'the natural course' of prices as they might feel towards an attempt to settle the sex of a child before birth, they are not really prepared to insist on their instinctive preference for having these matters settled by some method of pure chance.

II FEBRUARY 1925

First published as 'The Return Towards Gold' in the *Nation and Athenaeum*, 21 February 1925.

Once more the Bank chairmen have held up for our inspection their financial fashion-plates. The captions vary; but the plates are mostly the same. The first displays marriage with the gold standard as the most desired, the most urgent, the most honourable, the most virtuous, the most prosperous, and the most blessed of all possible states. The other is designed to remind the intending bridegroom that matrimony means heavy burdens from which he is now free; that it is for better, for worse; that it will be for him to honour and obey; that the happy days, when he could have the prices and the bank rate which suited the housekeeping of his bachelor establishment, will be over—though, of course, he will be asked out more when he is married; that Miss G. happens to be an American, so that in future the prices of grapefruit and popcorn are likely to be more important to him than those of eggs and bacon; and, in short, that he had better not be too precipitate. Some of our chairmen were like him who, being asked whether he believed that when he was dead he would enjoy perfect bliss eternally, replied that of course he did, but would rather not discuss such an unpleasant subject.

Like last year there are two distinct issues—the abstract merits of the gold standard, and the date and the mode of our return to it. The first is a question about which, as Mr McKenna justly said, 'we are still in the stage of inquiry rather than of positive opinion, and there is no formulated body of doctrine generally regarded as orthodox'. The supporters of monetary reform, of which I, after further study and reflection, am a more convinced adherent than before, as the most important and significant measure we can take to increase economic welfare, must expound their arguments more fully, more clearly, and more simply, before they can overwhelm the forces of old custom and general ignorance. This is not a battle which can be won or lost in a day. Those who think that it can be finally settled by a sharp hustle back to gold mistake the situation. That will be only the beginning. The issue will be determined, not by the official decisions of the coming year, but by the combined effects of the actual experience of what happens after that and the relative clearness and completeness of the arguments of the opposing parties. Readers of the works, for example, of the great Lord Overstone, will remember how many years it took, and what bitter and disastrous experiences, before the monetary reformers of a hundred years ago established the pre-war policy of bank rate and bank reserves (which, in its day, was a great advance), in the teeth of the opposition of the Bank of England.

The other issue is of practical and immediate importance.

Last year it was a question of whether it was prudent to hasten matters by deliberate deflation; this year it is a question of whether it is prudent to hasten matters by a removal of the embargo against the export of gold. This year, like last year, the bankers, faced with the practical problem, are a little nervous. I think that this nervousness is justified for the following reasons.

In common with many others, I have long held the opinion that monetary conditions in the United States were likely, sooner or later, to bring about a rising price level and an incipient boom; and also that it would be our right policy in such circumstances to employ the usual methods to curb our own price level and to prevent credit conditions here from following in the wake of those in America. The result of this policy, if it was successful, would be a gradual improvement of the sterling exchange; and it would not need a very violent boom in America to justify a rise of the sterling exchange at least as high as the pre-war parity. I have, therefore, maintained for two years past that a return of sterling, sooner or later, towards its pre-war parity would be both a desirable and a probable consequence of a sound monetary policy on the part of the Bank of England coupled with a less sound one on the part of the Federal Reserve Board.

What has actually happened? In the spring of 1923 boom conditions in the United States seemed to be developing; but largely through the action of the Federal Reserve Board, the movement was stopped. Since July 1924, however, there has been a strong and sustained upward movement, which—subject always to the policy of the Federal Reserve Board—is expected to go further. The earlier upward movement of American prices was duly followed by an improvement in sterling exchange; and the relapse by a relapse. Similarly, the movement of American prices during the past six months has been accompanied by the improvement in sterling exchange, which has caught the popular attention. As Mr McKenna pointed out, sterling prices have been a little steadier than dollar prices, and this greater steadiness has involved, as its necessary counterpart, some unsteadiness in the exchange.

The movement of the past six months, however, has been complicated by abnormal factors. The improvement in sterling exchange is more than can be accounted for by our monetary policy. It is true that short-money rates have been maintained at an effective ½ per cent above those in New York, and that British prices have risen somewhat less than American prices. But it is generally agreed that these influences have not been strong enough to account for everything. The Board of Trade returns indicate that there has been a movement of funds on capital account in the past year (and most of it, probably, in the second half of the year) from New York to London of the order of magnitude of £100 million. This is due (in proportions difficult to calculate) to the return of foreign balances previously held in London, to American investment in Europe resulting from the greater confidence engendered by the Dawes Scheme coming on the top of an investment boom in Wall Street, and to speculative purchases of sterling in the expectation of its improving in value relatively to the dollar. This unprecedented movement introduces a precarious element into the situation— we cannot expect that it will continue on the same scale, and it may, at any time, be partly reversed. We require an interval, therefore, to readjust our liabilities either by a recovery of exports relatively to imports or by establishing a rate of interest on permanent loans high enough to check the present (in my judgement excessive) flow of new foreign investment outwards. At present we are in danger of lending long (e.g. to Australia) what we have borrowed short from New York. The strength of our pre-war position lay in the fact that (through the bill market) we had lent large sums short, which we could call in. At the present time this position is partly, though perhaps only temporarily, reversed—which, in itself, is one reason for caution.

What is going to happen next? There are two leading alternatives. It may be that the Federal Reserve Board will come to the conclusion that the incipient boom conditions in the United States are getting dangerous, and will take the position firmly in hand, just as they did two years ago. This, almost certainly, is what the Board ought to do. In this event, the situation would be back again very nearly where it was eighteen months ago, and we should be faced, as we were then, with the alternative of relatively steady sterling prices with the dollar exchange below parity, or of stern deflation in the effort to keep exchange at parity. A premature announcement of the removal of the embargo on the free export of gold would commit us in advance to the latter alternative, the alternative which we deliberately rejected two years ago. This is what the fanatics desire. But with our unemployment figures what they still are, it would not be wise.

The other alternative is that the Federal Reserve Board will allow matters to pursue their present course, in which even we may expect that dollar prices will advance a good deal further. During part of 1924, the Board's open-market policy was decidedly inflationary, and has been largely responsible for the sharp rise of prices already experienced. At the present moment their policy is more cautious; but there is no clear indication that they have any steady or considered policy. It may be that misplaced sympathy with our efforts to raise the sterling exchange will be a factor tending to postpone action on their part; and if they delay much longer, boom conditions may become definitely established. In this event we need have no difficulty in raising sterling to pre-war parity. A firm monetary policy, designed to check a sympathetic rise of sterling prices, ought, without any positive deflation, to do the trick. But it does not follow that the embargo should, therefore, be removed. To link sterling prices to dollar prices at a moment in the credit cycle when the latter were near their peak as the result of a boom which we had not fully shared would ask for trouble.

For when the American boom broke we should bear the full force of the slump. The conditions in which we can link sterling prices to dollar prices without immediate risk to our own welfare will only exist when the mean level of dollar prices appears to be *stabilised* at a somewhat higher level than in recent times.

The removal of the embargo amounts to an announcement that sterling *is* at parity with the dollar and will remain so. I suggest that the right order of procedure is to establish the fact first and to announce it afterwards, rather than to make the announcement first and to chance the fact. Thus the removal of the embargo should be the last stage in the restoration of pre-war conditions, not the first one. The only prudent announcement on the subject would be to the effect that the embargo will not be removed until after sterling has been at parity for some considerable time, and until all the fundamental adjustments consequent upon this have duly taken place. At the same time—if we want to return to parity—steps should be taken to achieve the *fact* by raising bank rate and checking foreign issues. I—without attaching any importance whatever to a return to parity—believe that there is much to be said for these measures in the interests of the stabilisation of our own situation. I do not believe that a somewhat higher bank rate would do any harm, in view of the present tendencies of the price level, to the volume of trade and employment, and that, in any case, the maintenance of our own equilibrium will soon require the support of a higher rate. Several of the bankers declared that they were in favour of removing the embargo, provided this did not involve a risk of raising the bank rate. Unless this was merely a polite way of saying that they were not in favour of removing the embargo, I do not follow their analysis of the present situation.

It would be useless for me to attempt in the space at my disposal to give the reasons for wishing to maintain permanently a managed currency. The most important of them flow from my belief that fluctuations of trade and employment are at the same time the greatest and the most remediable of the economic diseases of modern society, that they are mainly diseases of our credit and banking system, and that it will be easier to apply the remedies if we retain the control of our currency in our own hands. But whilst avoiding these fundamental questions I may mention, in conclusion, one practical argument which is also connected with what I have said above.

A gold standard means, in practice, nothing but to have the same price level and the same money rates (broadly speaking) as the United States. The whole object is to link *rigidly* the City and Wall Street. I beg the Chancellor of the Exchequer and the Governor of the Bank of England and the nameless others who settle our destiny in secret to reflect that this may be a dangerous proceeding.

The United States lives in a vast and unceasing crescendo. Wide fluctuations, which spell unemployment and misery for us, are swamped for them in the general upward movement. A country, the whole of whose economic activities are expanding, year in, year out, by several per cent per annum, cannot avoid, and at the same time can afford, temporary maladjustments. This was our own state during a considerable part of the nineteenth century. Our rate of progress was so great that stability in detail was neither possible nor essential. This is not our state now. Our rate of progress is slow at the best, and faults in our economic structure, which we could afford to overlook whilst we were racing forward and which the United States can still afford to overlook, are now fatal. The slump of 1921 was even more violent in the United States than here, but by the end of 1922 recovery was practically complete. We still, in 1925, drag on with a million unemployed. The United States may suffer industrial and financial tempests in the years to come, and they will scarcely matter to her; but we, if we share them, may almost drown.

And there is a further consideration. Before the war we had

lent great sums to the whole world which we could call in at short notice; our American investments made us the creditors of the United States; we had a surplus available for foreign investment far greater than that of any other country; with no Federal Reserve System, American banking was weak and disorganised. We, in fact, were the predominant partner in the gold standard alliance. But those who think that a return to the gold standard means a return to these conditions are fools and blind. We are now the debtors of the United States. Their foreign investments last year were double ours, and their true net balance available for such investment was probably ten times ours. They hold six times as much gold as we do. The mere *increase* in the deposits of the banks of the Federal Reserve System in the past year has been not far short of half our *total* deposits. A movement of gold or of short credits either way between London and New York, which is only a ripple for them, will be an Atlantic roller for us. A change of fashion on the part of American bankers and investors towards foreign loans, of but little consequence to them, may shake us. If gold and short credits and foreign bonds can flow without restriction or risk of loss backwards and forwards across the Atlantic, fluctuations of given magnitude will produce on us effects altogether disproportionate to the effects on them. It suits the United States that we should return to gold, and they will be ready to oblige us in the early stages. But it would be a mistake to believe that in the long run they will, or ought to, manage their affairs to suit our convenience.

What solid advantages will there be to set against these risks? I do not know. Our bankers speak of 'psychological' advantages. But it will be poor consolation that 'nine people out of ten' expected advantages, if none in fact arrive.

That our bank chairmen should have nothing better to cry than 'Back to 1914', and that they should believe that this represents the best attainable, is not satisfactory. The majority of those who are studying the matter are becoming agreed that

199

faults in our credit system are at least partly responsible for the confusions which result in the paradox of unemployment amidst dearth. The 'Big Five' have vast responsibilities towards the public. But they are so huge, and in some ways, so vulnerable, that there is a great temptation to them to cling to maxims, conventions, and routine; and when their chairmen debate fundamental economic problems, they are most of them on ground with which they are unfamiliar. It is doubtful, never-theless, whether too much conservatism on these matters and too little of the spirit of inquiry will redound, in the long run, to their peace or security. Individualistic capitalism in England has come to the point when it can no longer depend on the momentum of mere expansion; and it must apply itself to the scientific task of improving the structure of its economic machine.

III FEBRUARY 1927[1]

As 'Mr McKenna on Monetary Policy', appeared first in the *Nation and Athenaeum*, 12 February 1927.

The voices of our old friends the bank chairmen herald the approach of spring. They have spoken this year—with the exception of Sir Harry Goschen, who sees 'no reason to be downhearted', and, as in former years, cannot 'remember a time when, throughout the industries of the country, there was such a feeling of expectation and, indeed, optimism'—in some-what chastened tones. Mr Beaumont Pease has done a useful service by publishing some important figures analysing the business of Lloyds Bank, which inaugurate a new policy of giving information instead of withholding it. Mr Walter Leaf made some sound observations on the tendency of business towards amalgamation and, at the same time, of shareholdings towards diffusion, and on the necessity of the state taking some responsibility for guiding this inevitable evolution along the

1 [After the Return to Gold.]

right lines. But none of them except Mr McKenna—and on one point of detail Mr Goodenough—had anything to say about the future of monetary policy. So leaving Sir Harry Goschen to chirrup in the bushes, let us join Mr McKenna in an attempt to dig a few inches below the surface of the soil.

Mr McKenna reminded us of the overwhelming prosperity of the United States as against our own depression during the past five years. He declared that in the 'wide divergence between English and American monetary policy, we have at least a partial explanation of the phenomenon'. He found the measure of this divergence of policy in the expansion and contraction respectively of the bank deposits in the two countries, namely, as follows:

| | (Volume of deposits in 1922 = 100) | |
	United States	Great Britain
1922	100	100
1923	107	94
1924	115	94
1925	127	93
1926	131	93

He explained in some detail what is fundamental, yet too little understood, that the volume of bank deposits in Great Britain does not depend, except within narrow limits, on the depositors or on the Big Five, but on the policy of the Bank of England. And he concluded that we can scarcely expect a materially increased scale of production and employment in this country until the Bank of England revises its policy.

Whilst I do not agree with Mr McKenna in every detail of his argument, I am certain that the broad lines of his diagnosis are correct. He has done a service by his persistent efforts to educate the public and his colleagues to the vital importance of some fundamental principles of monetary policy of which the truth is as certain as the day, but to which the City is blind as night.

Nevertheless, he has on this occasion shirked, in my opinion, half the problem. How far and subject to what conditions is a reversal of the Bank of England's policy consistent with maintaining the gold standard? Is the Bank of England in its new-forged golden fetters as free an agent as Mr McKenna's policy requires? §We cannot answer this without transversing again some country already familiar to readers of the *Nation*.§

What matters is, not some abstraction called the general level of prices, but the relationships between the various price levels which measure the value of our money for different purposes. Prosperity, in so far as it is governed by monetary factors, depends on these various price levels being properly adjusted to one another. Unemployment and trade depression in Great Britain have been due to a rupture of the previous equilibrium between the sterling price level of articles of international commerce and the internal value of sterling for the purposes on which the average Englishman spends his money income. Moreover, in proportion as we are successful in moving towards the new equilibrium of lower sterling prices all round, we increase the burden of the national debt and aggravate the problem of the budget. If the Bank of England and the Treasury were to succeed in reducing the sheltered price level to its former equilibrium with the unsheltered price level, they would *ipso facto* have increased the real burden of the national debt by about £1,000 million as compared with two years ago.

§There are four price levels which between them tell the broad outlines of the story. The wholesale general index of the United States Bureau of Labour is a fair indication of the value of gold in the world's commerce. Our own Board of Trade general index is an alternative indicator of much the same thing. So many of the articles covered by these two index-numbers are the same that they are likely to move on the whole together —so closely indeed, apart from temporary divergencies, that in terms of gold they have both averaged the same figure, namely, 154, over the last thirty months, and have also both begun and ended this period at the same figure, namely, about 149. Thus we may regard these as alternative pointers to the unsheltered value of sterling. We come next to the British cost of living index and the British wages index. These, taken in conjunction with such things as rent, cost of social insurance, railway charges, and the various items on either side of the national budget, which are practically fixed in terms of money, are pointers to the sheltered value of sterling. The difficulties of our export trades, in so far as these are attributable to monetary policy, are measured by the ratio of the sheltered value to the unsheltered value.

The following table gives these four indexes in terms of gold, i.e., those which precede the return to gold are corrected by reference to the gold value of sterling. The fifth column gives the ratio of the sheltered value of sterling to the unsheltered value by taking the average of the first two columns as representing the unsheltered value and the average of the next two as representing the sheltered:

In terms of gold, pre-war = 100.

	U.S. Bureau of Labour wholesale	U.K. Board of Trade wholesale	Cost of living	Wages	Ratio of sheltered price levels to unsheltered
1924					
3rd quarter	149	150	157	163	107
4th quarter	154	160	169	168	107
1925					
1st quarter	161	165	173	177	107
2nd quarter	156	159	173	181	112
3rd quarter	160	156	174	180	112
4th quarter	157	153	176	180	115
1926					
1st quarter	154	147	171	180	117
2nd quarter	152	145	168	180	117
3rd quarter	150	150	172	180	117
4th quarter	148	150	178	180	120

Thus the disparity as measured by the last column, so far from curing itself, has become slowly, but progressively, worse. Sheltered prices in terms of sterling have remained practically stationary for nearly two and a half years. Meanwhile the unsheltered price level has been falling, first as a result of the return to gold, and subsequently as a result of the relapse in world gold prices which, after rising about 8 per cent between the middle of 1924 and the middle of 1925, have since fallen back to their previous level. Thus the position is assuredly no better than it was eighteen months ago. §

Now Mr McKenna seems to assume that the dis-equilibrium which admittedly existed two years ago has since disappeared. 'Today', he tells us, 'such questions have only historic significance.' But the evidence does not support this view. So far from having disappeared, the disparity between the price levels is actually *greater* than it was two years ago.

How, then, have we lived in the meantime? The real ground of the optimism on the lips of the bank chairmen is to be found, I think, in the fact that there has been no strain on our resources which we have not been able to meet. Is this so great a paradox as it appears? Or so comforting?

We have undoubtedly balanced the difference in our account partly by drawing on the large margin of safety which we used to possess, and partly, during the Coal Strike, by increasing our short-loan indebtedness to the rest of the world. Before the war we probably had a favourable balance on international account, apart from capital transactions, of something like £300 million per annum measured in sterling at its present value. The war and the fall in the value of fixed money payments may have reduced this annual surplus to about £225 million; i.e. this is what our surplus would be to-day if our export trades were as flourishing as in 1913. Let us suppose that as the result of our relatively high level of internal prices we have lost £200 million of exports gross, namely, about a quarter of the whole, or (say) £150 million net, i.e. after deducting that part of the lost exports which would have consisted of imported raw material, and that we consequently have unemployed (say) 1 million men who would otherwise, directly or indirectly, have been producing these exports. All these figures are, of course, very rough illustrations of what is reasonably probable, not scientific estimates of statistical facts.

How does our international balance sheet then stand? We still have a surplus of £75 million per annum. Provided, therefore, we do not invest abroad more than this sum, we are in equilibrium. We can continue permanently with our higher level of sheltered prices, with a quarter of our foreign trade lost, and with a million men unemployed, but also with some surplus still left for the City of London to invest abroad and, as the crown of all, the gold standard entirely unthreatened. The gold standard may have reduced the national wealth, as compared with an alternative monetary policy, by £150 million a year. Never mind! 'Our economic reserves of strength', as Mr Leaf puts it, 'are far greater than any of us supposed.' 'We are tougher than we thought', in the words of the Chancellor of the Exchequer. In short, we can afford it!

The special losses of the Coal Strike period are not allowed for in the above. They seem to have amounted to round £100 million, and to have been met by increasing our short-loan indebtedness, partly with the aid of the usual time-lag in the settlement of adverse balances, and partly by a relatively attractive rate of discount drawing foreign balances to London.

In determining the future of our national policy, we have three alternatives before us:

(1) We can seek at all costs to restore the pre-war equilibrium of large exports and large foreign investments. The return to gold has rendered this impossible without an all-round attack on wages, such as the Prime Minister has repudiated, or a considerable rise of external gold prices which we wait for in vain.

(2) We can continue indefinitely in the pseudo-equilibrium described above with trade depressed and a million unemployed. This pseudo-equilibrium has been the result, though probably not the intention, of the Bank of England's policy up to date. I see no convincing reason why it should not be continued for some time yet. Mr Norman [Montagu Norman, Governor of the Bank of England—*Ed.*] may have an awkward period

ahead owing to the delayed results of the Coal Strike. But even if the worst comes, a partial reimposition of the embargo on foreign investments might be enough.

(3) The third course consists in accepting the loss of export trade and a corresponding reduction of foreign investment and in diverting the labour previously employed in the former and the savings previously absorbed in the latter to the task of improving the efficiency of production and the standard of life at home. If the return to gold has the effect in the end of bringing about this result, it may have been a blessing in disguise. For this course has manifold advantages which I must not stop to enumerate at the end of a long article. I believe that a further improvement in the standard of life of the masses is dependent on our taking it.

This brings us back to Mr McKenna. I assume that his object in advocating an expansion of credit is to absorb the unemployed in a general crescendo of home industry and indirectly to help a little the export industries also by the economies of full-scale production. In short, he favours the third course. For he can hardly hope to lower the sheltered price level or to effect an adequate economy in manufacturing costs by expanding credit. As on some previous occasions, Mr McKenna has done less than justice to his own ideas by pretending to greater confidence in the effects of the return to gold than he really has.

Now, within the limitations of the gold standard this is a very difficult policy, and—in view of the £100 million which we may still owe on account of the Coal Strike—possibly a dangerous one. If Mr McKenna were Governor of the Bank of England with a free hand, I believe it to be probable that he could greatly reduce the numbers of the unemployed whilst maintaining gold parity. But can we expect Mr Norman to do so, moving within the limitations of his own mentality?

5 THE ECONOMIC CONSEQUENCES
OF MR CHURCHILL (1925)

The Economic Consequences of Mr Churchill originated as a series of three articles on England's return to the gold standard which appeared in the *Evening Standard*, 22, 23 and 24 July 1925, under the heading 'Unemployment and Monetary Policy'. Keynes expanded these into the pamphlet which was published the same month by the Hogarth Press of Leonard and Virginia Woolf, chapters I, III and V corresponding to the *Evening Standard* articles. In the United States the pamphlet was published as *The Economic Consequences of Sterling Parity*. For *Essays in Persuasion* Keynes condensed the material of the whole pamphlet.

§I WHY UNEMPLOYMENT IS WORSE

World trade and home consumption are both moderately good —running on a level keel, midway between slump and boom. The United States has had a year of abundant prosperity; India and the Dominions are doing fairly well; in France and Italy unemployment is non-existent or negligible; and in Germany during the last six months the numbers receiving the dole have decreased rapidly, by more than half, to 4·5 per cent against our 10 per cent. The aggregate of world production is probably greater than at any time since 1914. Therefore our troubles are not due either to world-wide depression or to reduced consumption at home. And it is obvious what does cause them. It is a question of *relative price* here and abroad. The prices of our exports in the international market are too high. About this there is no difference of opinion.

Why are they too high? The orthodox answer is to blame it on the working man for working too little and getting too much. In some industries and some grades of labour, particularly the unskilled, this is true; and other industries, for example the railways, are over-staffed. But there is no more truth in it than there was a year ago. Moreover, it is not true in those export industries where unemployment is greatest.

On the contrary, the explanation can be found for certain in another direction. For we know as a fact that the value of sterling money abroad has been raised by 10 per cent, whilst its purchasing power over British labour is unchanged. This alteration in the external value of sterling money has been the deliberate act of the government and the Chancellor of the Exchequer, and the present troubles of our export industries are the inevitable and predictable consequence of it.§

The[1] policy of improving the foreign-exchange value of sterling up to its pre-war value in gold from being about 10 per cent below it, means that, whenever we sell anything abroad, either the foreign buyer has to pay 10 per cent *more in his money* or we have to accept 10 per cent *less in our money*. That is to say, we have to reduce our sterling prices, for coal or iron or shipping freights or whatever it may be, by 10 per cent in order to be on a competitive level, unless prices rise elsewhere. Thus the policy of improving the exchange by 10 per cent involves a reduction of 10 per cent in the sterling receipts of our export industries.

Now, if these industries found that their expenses for wages and for transport and for rates and for everything else were falling 10 per cent at the same time, they could afford to cut their prices and would be no worse off than before. But of course, this does not happen. Since they use, and their employees consume, all kinds of articles produced at home, it is impossible for them to cut their prices 10 per cent, unless wages and expenses in home industries generally have fallen 10 per cent. Meanwhile, the weaker export industries are reduced to a bankrupt condition. Failing a fall in the value of gold itself, nothing can retrieve their position except a general fall of all internal prices and wages. Thus Mr Churchill's policy of improving the exchange by 10 per cent was, sooner or later, a policy of reducing everyone's wages by 2s in the £. He who

[1] In the original *Essays in Persuasion*, the section beginning here was entitled 'The Misleading of Mr Churchill'—Ed.

wills the end wills the means. What now faces the Government is the ticklish task of carrying out their own dangerous and unnecessary decision.

§The statistics bear out this reasoning. The following table is, by itself, an adequate explanation of the difficulties of our export industries compared with a year ago:

	United States Cost of living Gold	Great Britain Cost of living		Great Britain Wages	
		Gold	Sterling	Gold	Sterling
		(Pre-war = 100)			
March 1924	156	157	178	155	176
June	154	150	169	157	178
October	157	162	176	164	178
December	158	174	181	172	179
March 1925	158	176	179	177	181
April	158	172	175	178	181
May	158[1]	172	173	180	181
June	158[1]	172	172	181	181
July	158[1]	173	173	180	180

[1] Provisional.

This table shows that a year ago the cost of living and the level of wages in this country, expressed in terms of gold (i.e. reduced from their sterling value in proportion to the depreciation of the sterling exchange), were in conformity with the dollar cost of living in the United States. Since then the sterling exchange has been raised by 10 per cent, whilst there has been no appreciable change in the sterling cost of living and the sterling level of wages in this country compared with the dollar cost of living in the United States. It follows, of necessity, that our money wages and cost of living are now about 10 per cent too high. The government's policy has secured that we receive 10 per cent less sterling for our exports; yet our industrialists have to pay out in wages just as much as before, and their employees have to expend just as much as before to maintain their standard of life.§ The movement away from equilibrium began in October last and has proceeded, step by step, with the improvement of the exchange—brought about first by the anticipation, and then by the fact, of the restoration of gold, and not by an improvement in the intrinsic value of sterling.[1] The President of the Board of Trade has asserted in the House of Commons that the effect of the restoration of the gold standard upon our export trade has been 'all to the good'. The Chancellor of the Exchequer has expressed the opinion that the return to the gold standard is no more responsible for the condition of affairs in the coal industry than is the Gulf Stream. These statements are of the feather-brained order. It is open to ministers to argue that the restoration of gold is worth the sacrifice and that the sacrifice is temporary. They can also say, with truth, that the industries which are feeling the wind most have private troubles of their own. When a *general* cause operates, those which are weak for other reasons are toppled over. But because an epidemic of influenza carries off only those who have weak hearts, it is not permissible to say that the influenza is 'all to the good', or that it has no more to do with the mortality than the Gulf Stream has.

The effect has been the more severe because we were not free from trouble a year ago. Whilst, at that date, sterling wages and sterling cost of living were in conformity with values in the United States, they were already too high compared with those in some European countries. It was also probable that certain of our export industries were over-stocked both with plant and with labour, and that some transference of capital and of men into home industries was desirable and, in the long run, even inevitable. Thus we already had an awkward problem; and one of the arguments against raising the international value of sterling was the fact that it greatly aggravated, instead of mitigating, an existing disparity between internal and

[1] This view was shared by the Treasury Committee on the Currency who reported that the exchange improvement of last autumn and spring could not be maintained if we did not restore the gold standard; in other words, the improvement in the exchange prior to the restoration of gold was due to a speculative anticipation of this event and to a movement of capital, and not to an intrinsic improvement in sterling itself.

external values, and that, by committing us to a period of deflation, it necessarily postponed active measures of capital expansion at home, such as might facilitate the transference of labour into the home trades. British wages, measured in gold, are now 15 per cent higher than they were a year ago. The gold cost of living in England is now so high compared with what it is in Belgium, France, Italy, and Germany that the workers in those countries can accept a gold wage 30 per cent lower than what our workers receive without suffering at all in the amount of their real wages. What wonder that our export trades are in trouble!

Our export industries are suffering because they are the *first* to be asked to accept the 10 per cent reduction. If *every one* was accepting a similar reduction at the same time, the cost of living would fall, so that the lower money wage would represent nearly the same real wage as before. But, in fact, there is no machinery for effecting a simultaneous reduction. Deliberately to raise the value of sterling money in England means, therefore, engaging in a struggle with each separate group in turn, with no prospect that the final result will be fair, and no guarantee that the stronger groups will not gain at the expense of the weaker.

The working classes cannot be expected to understand, better than Cabinet Ministers, what is happening. Those who are attacked first are faced with a depression of their standard of life, because the cost of living will not fall until all the others have been successfully attacked too; and, therefore, they are justified in defending themselves. Nor can the classes, which are first subjected to a reduction of money wages, be guaranteed that this will be compensated later by a corresponding fall in the cost of living, and will not accrue to the benefit of some other class. Therefore they are bound to resist so long as they can; and it must be war, until those who are economically weakest are beaten to the ground.

This state of affairs is not an inevitable consequence of a

decreased capacity to produce wealth. I see no reason why, with good management, real wages need be reduced on the average. It is the consequence of a misguided monetary policy.

II WHAT MISLED MR CHURCHILL[1]

The arguments of chapter 1[2] are not arguments against the gold standard as such. That is a separate discussion which I shall not touch here. They are arguments against having restored gold in conditions which required a substantial re-adjustment of all our money values. If Mr Churchill had restored gold by fixing the parity lower than the pre-war figure, or if he had waited until our money values were adjusted to the pre-war parity, then these particular arguments would have no force. But in doing what he did in the actual circumstances of last spring, he was just asking for trouble. For he was committing himself to force down money wages and all money values, without any idea how it was to be done. Why did he do such a silly thing?

Partly, perhaps, because he has no instinctive judgement to prevent him from making mistakes; partly because, lacking this instinctive judgement, he was deafened by the clamorous voices of conventional finance; and, most of all, because he was gravely misled by his experts.

His experts made, I think, two serious mistakes. In the first place I suspect that they miscalculated the degree of the mal-adjustment of money values, which would result from restoring sterling to its pre-war gold parity, because they attended to index numbers of prices which were irrelevant or inappropriate to the matter in hand. If you want to know whether sterling values are adjusting themselves to an improvement in the exchange, it is useless to consider, for example, the price of raw cotton in Liverpool. This *must* adjust itself to a movement

---

[1] The title for chapter II and the division into chapters at this point did not occur in the original *Essays in Persuasion* version—Ed.

[2] In the original *Essays in Persuasion* version, the words up to here were replaced by the words 'These arguments'—Ed.

of the exchange, because, in the case of an imported raw material, the parity of international values is necessarily maintained almost hour by hour. But it is not sensible to argue from this that the money wages of dockers or of charwomen and the cost of postage or of travelling by train also adjust themselves hour by hour in accordance with the foreign exchanges. Yet this, I fancy, is what the Treasury did. They compared the usual wholesale index numbers here and in America, and—since these are made up to the extent of at least two-thirds from the raw materials of international commerce, the prices of which necessarily adjust themselves to the exchanges—the true disparity of internal prices was watered down to a fraction of its true value. This led them to think that the gap to be bridged was perhaps 2 or 3 per cent, instead of the true figure of 10 or 12 per cent, which was the indication given by the index numbers of the cost of living, of the level of wages, and of the prices of our manufactured exports—which indexes are a much better rough-and-ready guide for this purpose, particularly if they agree with one another, than are the index numbers of wholesale prices.

But I think that Mr Churchill's experts also misunderstood and underrated the technical difficulty of bringing about a general reduction of internal money values. When we raise the value of sterling by 10 per cent, we transfer about £1,000 million into the pockets of the rentiers out of the pockets of the rest of us, and we increase the real burden of the national debt by some £750 million (thus wiping out the benefit of all our laborious contributions to the Sinking Fund since the war). This, which is bad enough, is inevitable. But there would be no other bad consequences, if only there was some way of bringing about a simultaneous reduction of 10 per cent in all other money payments; when the process was complete, we should each of us have nearly the same real income as before. I think that the minds of his advisers still dwelt in the imaginary academic world, peopled by City editors, members of Cunliffe and Currency Committees *et hoc genus omne*, where the necessary adjustments follow 'automatically' from a 'sound' policy by the Bank of England.

The theory is that depression in the export industries, which are admittedly hit first, coupled if necessary with dear money and credit restriction, *diffuse* themselves evenly and fairly rapidly throughout the whole community. But the professors of this theory do not tell us in plain language how the diffusion takes place.

Mr Churchill asked the Treasury Committee on the Currency to advise him on these matters. He declared in his budget speech that their report 'contains a reasoned marshalling of the arguments which have convinced His Majesty's Government'. Their arguments—if their vague and jejune meditations can be called such—are there for anyone to read. What they ought to have said, but did not say, can be expressed as follows:

Money wages, the cost of living, and the prices which we are asking for our exports have not adjusted themselves to the improvement in the exchange, which the expectation of your restoring the gold standard, in accordance with your repeated declarations, has already brought about. They are about 10 per cent too high. If, therefore, you fix the exchange at this gold parity, you must either gamble on a rise in gold prices abroad, which will induce foreigners to pay a higher gold price for our exports, or you are committing yourself to a policy of forcing down money wages and the cost of living to the necessary extent.

We must warn you that this latter policy is not easy. It is certain to involve unemployment and industrial disputes. If, as some people think, real wages were already too high a year ago, that is all the worse, because the amount of the necessary wage reductions in terms of money will be all the greater.

The gamble on a rise in gold prices abroad may quite likely succeed. But it is by no means certain, and you must be prepared for the other contingency. If you think that the advantages of the gold standard are so significant and so urgent that you are prepared to risk great unpopularity and to take stern administrative action in order to secure them, the course of events will probably be as follows.

To begin with, there will be great depression in the export industries. This, in itself, will be helpful, since it will produce an atmosphere favourable to the reduction of wages. The cost of living will fall somewhat. This will be helpful too, because it will give you a good argument in favour of reducing wages. Nevertheless, the cost of living will not fall sufficiently and, consequently, the export industries will not be able to reduce their prices sufficiently, until wages have fallen in the sheltered industries. Now, wages will not fall in the sheltered industries, merely because there is unemployment in the unsheltered industries. Therefore, you will have to see to it that there is unemployment in the sheltered industries also. The way to do this will be by credit restriction. By means of the restriction of credit by the Bank of England, you can deliberately intensify unemployment to any required degree, until wages *do* fall. When the process is complete the cost of living will have fallen too; and we shall then be, with luck, just where we were before we started.

We ought to warn you, though perhaps this is going a little outside our proper sphere, that it will not be safe politically to admit that you are intensifying unemployment deliberately in order to reduce wages. Thus you will have to ascribe what is happening to every conceivable cause except the true one. We estimate that about two years may elapse before it will be safe for you to utter in public one single word of truth. By that time you will either be out of office, or the adjustment, somehow or other, will have been carried through.

III   THE POLICY OF THE BANK OF ENGLAND[1]

The effect of a high exchange is to diminish the sterling prices both of imports and of exports. §The fall in the price of imported food tends to reduce the cost of living. It is surprising, perhaps, that it has not had more influence in this direction. Probably the explanation is to be found partly in the world-wide rise of food prices, partly in a time-lag (in which case we may look forward to some further fall in the cost of living in the near future), and partly in the fact that by the time a commodity, even an imported commodity, reaches the consumer, its cost has been considerably affected by the various home services performed on it. Nevertheless, the table printed in the first chapter shows that some reduction of money wages on this score is, in fact, already justifiable—though not, for that reason,

---

[1] In the original *Essays in Persuasion* version this section was entitled 'The Balance of Trade and the Bank of England'—Ed.

much the easier to accomplish. Since the higher exchange does not help us to *afford* a higher real wage, it only grants this boon to the workers in order that it may be snatched away again as soon as possible. Meanwhile, the apparent cheapness of foreign products causes us to buy more of them. At the same time, the fall in the sterling price of exports reduces the business of the export industries.§

The result is both to encourage imports and to discourage exports, thus turning the balance of trade against us. It is at this stage that the Bank of England becomes interested; for if nothing was done we should have to pay the adverse balance in gold. The Bank of England has applied, accordingly, two effective remedies. The first remedy is to put obstacles in the way of our usual lending abroad by means of an embargo on foreign loans and, recently, on colonial loans also; and the second remedy is to encourage the United States to lend us money by maintaining the unprecedented situation of a bill rate 1 per cent higher in London than in New York.

The efficacy of these two methods for balancing our account is beyond doubt—I believe that they might remain efficacious for a considerable length of time. For we start with a wide margin of strength. Before the war our capacity to lend abroad was, according to the Board of Trade, about £181 million, equivalent to £280 million at the present price level; and even in 1923 the Board of Trade estimated our net surplus at £102 million. Since new foreign investments bring in no immediate return, it follows that we can reduce our exports by £100 million a year, without any risk of insolvency, provided we reduce our foreign investments by the same amount. So far as the maintenance of the gold standard is concerned, it is a matter of indifference whether we have £100 million worth of foreign investment or £100 million worth of unemployment. If those who used to produce exports lose their job, nevertheless, our financial equilibrium remains perfect, and the Governor of the Bank of England runs no risk of losing gold, provided that the loans, which were formerly paid over in the shape of those exports, are curtailed to an equal extent. Moreover, our credit as a borrower is still very good. By paying a sufficiently high rate of interest, we can not only meet any deficit but the governor can borrow, in addition, whatever quantity of gold it may amuse him to publish in his weekly return.

The President of the Board of Trade calculates that, during the year ended last May, it is probable that there was no actual deficit on our trade account, which was about square. If this is correct, there must be a substantial deficit now. In addition, the embargo on foreign investment is only partially successful. It cannot hold back all types of foreign issues and it cannot prevent British investors from purchasing securities direct from New York. It is here, therefore, that the Bank of England's other remedy comes in. By maintaining discount rates in London at a sufficient margin above discount rates in New York, it can induce the New York money market to lend a sufficient sum[1] to the London money market to balance both our trade deficit and the foreign investments which British investors are still buying in spite of the embargo. Besides, when once we have offered high rates of interest to attract funds from the New York short-loan market, we have to continue them, even though we have no need to increase our borrowings, in order to retain what we have already borrowed.

Nevertheless the policy of maintaining money rates in London at a level which will attract and retain loans from New York does not really differ in any important respect from the French policy, which we have so much condemned, of supporting the exchange with the help of loans from Messrs J. P. Morgan. Our policy would only differ from the French policy if the high rate of discount was not only intended to attract American money, but was also part of a policy for restricting credit at home. This is the aspect to which we must now attend.

---

[1] §The Harvard Economic Service estimates that in recent months American banks have advanced to the London money market between \$200 million and \$300 million§.

To pay for unemployment by changing over from being a lending country to being a borrowing country is admittedly a disastrous course, and I do not doubt that the authorities of the Bank of England share this view. They dislike the embargo on foreign issues, and they dislike having to attract short-loan money from New York. They may do these things to gain a breathing space; but, if they are to live up to their own principles, they must use the breathing space to effect what are euphemistically called 'the fundamental adjustments'. With this object in view there is only one step which lies within their power—namely, to restrict credit. This, in the circumstances, is the orthodox policy of the gold party; the adverse trade balance indicates that our prices are too high, and the way to bring them down is by dear money and the restriction of credit. When this medicine has done its work, there will no longer be any need to restrict foreign loans or to borrow abroad.

Now what does this mean in plain language? Our problem is to reduce money wages and, through them, the cost of living, with the idea that, when the circle is complete, real wages will be as high, or nearly as high, as before. By what *modus operandi* does credit restriction attain this result?

In no other way than by the deliberate intensification of unemployment. The object of credit restriction, in such a case, is to withdraw from employers the financial means to employ labour at the existing level of prices and wages. The policy can only attain its end by intensifying unemployment without limit, until the workers are ready to accept the necessary reduction of money wages under the pressure of hard facts.

This is the so-called 'sound' policy, which is demanded as a result of the rash act of pegging sterling at a gold value, which it did not—measured in its purchasing power over British labour—possess as yet. It is a policy, nevertheless, from which any humane or judicious person must shrink. So far as I can judge, the Governor of the Bank of England shrinks from it. But what is he to do, swimming, with his boat burnt, between

218

the devil and the deep sea? At present, it appears, he compromises. He applies the 'sound' policy half-heartedly; he avoids calling things by their right names; and he hopes—this is his best chance—that something will turn up.

The Bank of England works with so much secrecy and so much concealment of important statistics that it is never easy to state with precision what it is doing. The credit restriction already in force has been effected in several ways which are partly interdependent. First, there is the embargo on new issues which probably retards the normal rate of the circulation of money; then in March the bank rate was raised; more recently market rate was worked up nearer to bank rate; lastly —and far the most important of all—the Bank has manœuvred its assets and liabilities in such a way as to reduce the amount of cash available to the clearing banks as a basis for credit. This last is the essential instrument of credit restriction. Failing direct information, the best reflection of the amount of this restriction is to be found in the deposits of the clearing banks. The tendency of these to fall indicates some significant degree of restriction. Owing, however, to seasonal fluctuations and to the artificial character of the end-June returns, it is not yet possible to estimate with accuracy how much restriction has taken place in the last three months. So far as one can judge, the amount of direct restriction is not yet considerable. But no one can say how much more restriction may become necessary if we continue on our present lines.

Nevertheless, even these limited measures are responsible, in my opinion, for an important part of the recent intensification of unemployment. Credit restriction is an incredibly powerful instrument, and even a little of it goes a long way—especially in circumstances where the opposite course is called for. The policy of deliberately intensifying unemployment with a view to forcing wage reductions is already partly in force, and the tragedy of our situation lies in the fact that, from the misguided standpoint which has been officially adopted, this course is theoretically justifiable. No section of labour will readily accept lower wages merely in response to sentimental speeches, however genuine, by Mr Baldwin. We are depending for the reduction of wages on the pressure of unemployment and of strikes and lockouts; and in order to make sure of this result we are deliberately intensifying the unemployment.

The Bank of England is *compelled* to curtail credit by all the rules of the gold standard game. It is acting conscientiously and 'soundly' in doing so. But this does not alter the fact that to keep a tight hold on credit—and no one will deny that the Bank is doing that—necessarily involves intensifying unemployment in the present circumstances of this country. What we need to restore prosperity today is an easy credit policy. We want to encourage business men to enter on new enterprises, not, as we are doing, to discourage them. Deflation does not reduce wages 'automatically'. It reduces them by causing unemployment. The proper object of dear money is to check an incipient boom. Woe to those whose faith leads them to use it to aggravate a depression!

§IV THE CASE OF THE COAL INDUSTRY

I will illustrate my argument by applying it to the case of the coal industry. This industry has been in bad order ever since the war, apart from a temporary spurt whilst the Ruhr was out of action. Its troubles are due, therefore, to other causes besides the return to gold. By dwelling on these Mr Churchill may endeavour to make out a plausible case for the conclusion that the exchange has no more to do with the difficulties of the coal industry than the Gulf Stream has. It is, therefore, a good example to select, because it is *prima facie* unfavourable to my conclusions.

(1) In the *Economist* (27 June 1925), a correspondent writes: 'In Brazil, American coal at time of writing was quoted at $8.85, against 39s ($9.32) for the British product, while the

freight rates from the United States were around $4, and from the United Kingdom $3.76 (15s 9d).'

When this correspondent wrote the exchange was about 4.78. At today's exchange the price of the coal (39s) would be $9.48 and the freight $3.83. At the exchange of last June (4.31) the price of coal would have been $8.40, and of the freight $3.40.

Thus, last June we could quote 45 cents a ton less than American coal; now American coal can be quoted 63 cents less than ours, *merely on account of the improvement of the exchange.* In Canada and throughout South America, the effect of 10 per cent on the exchange makes the difference between our coal being on a competitive level with coal from the United States, or too dear. The same thing is true in Europe, for the effect of the return to gold has been to raise our exchanges by at least 10 per cent in terms of the currencies of France, Belgium, and Germany above what they would be otherwise.[1]

If our collieries lower their prices, as they are compelled to do, so as to be on as good a competitive level with foreign countries as they were a year ago, they have to lower their sterling prices by something like 1s 9d a ton.[2]

Has a price reduction of 1s 9d a ton no more to do with the troubles of the coal industry than the Gulf Stream? In terms of miners' wages this is a large proportion of the total reduction asked for by the mine owners. It is sufficient to turn a net profit of 6d a ton, which was what the coal industry earned in the first quarter of this year, into a loss of 1s 3d a ton.

(2) Apart from pit-props the coal industry consumes very few foreign goods. Moreover, the wages bill makes up a very high proportion of the total costs of raising coal. Thus, more than any other industry, the coal industry has to sell at the foreign value of sterling and to buy at the home value of sterling. A measure which raises the former without raising the latter

[1] The rise in the case of France and Belgium has been more than this.
[2] The Secretary of the Mining Association, giving evidence before the Coal Inquiry, estimated the figure at 1s; but he did not mention what dates he was comparing.

proportionately is, therefore, certain to prove particularly injurious to the coal industry.

(3) Apart from the direct effect on the exports of coal, the same causes which depress the trade in coal operate to depress the trade in the industry which is the biggest user of coal, namely, iron and steel.

(4) One of the worst troubles of the coal industry, peculiar to itself, is that in the present conditions of demand for coal there are far too many coal miners. The urgent need of the industry is to reduce its numbers. Yet, largely as the result of a change in the localisation of the industry (S. Yorkshire prospering at the expense of S. Wales and Northumberland), the industry is actually taking in much new labour. There are several explanations of this state of affairs. But the remedy can only come from the absorption of labour out of this industry into others. The necessary condition of this, however, is that other industries should be booming. It is in this sort of way— by keeping down the expansion of other industries—that credit restriction reacts on coal.

So far, therefore, from the troubles in the coal industry being due to other causes, §I should pick out coal as being above all others a victim of our monetary policy. On the other hand, it is certainly true that the reason why the coal industry presents so dismal a picture to the eye is because it has other troubles which have weakened its power of resistance and have left it no margin of strength with which to support a new misfortune.

In these circumstances the colliery owners propose that the gap should be bridged by a reduction of wages, irrespective of a reduction in the cost of living—that is to say, by a lowering in the standard of life of the miners. They are to make this sacrifice to meet circumstances for which they are in no way responsible and over which they have no control.

It is a grave criticism of our way of managing our economic affairs, that this should seem to anyone to be a reasonable proposal; though it is equally unreasonable that the colliery owner should suffer the loss, except on the principle that it is the capitalist who bears the risk. If miners were free to transfer themselves to other industries, if a collier out of work or under-paid could offer himself as a baker, a bricklayer, or a railway porter at a lower wage than is now current in these industries, it would be another matter. But notoriously they are not so free. Like other victims of economic transition in past times, the miners are to be offered the choice between starvation and submission, the fruits of their submission to accrue to the benefit of other classes. But in view of the disappearance of an effective mobility of labour and of a competitive wage level between different industries, I am not sure that they are not worse placed in some ways than their grandfathers were.

Why should coal miners suffer a lower standard of life than other classes of labour? They may be lazy, good-for-nothing fellows who do not work so hard or so long as they should. But is there any evidence that they are more lazy or more good-for-nothing than other people?

On grounds of social justice no case can be made out for reducing the wages of the miners. They are the victims of the economic juggernaut. They represent in the flesh the 'funda-mental adjustments' engineered by the Treasury and the Bank of England to satisfy the impatience of the City fathers to bridge the 'moderate gap' between $4.40 and $4.86. *They* (and others to follow) are the 'moderate sacrifice' still necessary to ensure the stability of the gold standard. The plight of the coal miners is the first, but not—unless we are very lucky—the last, of the economic consequences of Mr Churchill.

The truth is that we stand midway between two theories of economic society. The one theory maintains that wages should be fixed by reference to what is 'fair' and 'reasonable' as between classes. The other theory—the theory of the economic juggernaut—is that wages should be settled by economic pressure, otherwise called 'hard facts', and that our vast machine should crash along, with regard only to its equilibrium as a whole, and without attention to the chance consequences of the journey to individual groups.

The gold standard, with its dependence on pure chance, its faith in 'automatic adjustments', and its general regardlessness of social detail, is an essential emblem and idol of those who sit in the top tier of the machine. I think that they are immensely rash in their regardlessness, in their vague optimism and comfortable belief that nothing really serious ever happens. Nine times out of ten, nothing really serious does happen—merely a little distress to individuals or to groups. But we run a risk of the tenth time (and are stupid into the bargain), if we continue to apply the principles of an economics, which was worked out on the hypotheses of *laissez-faire* and free competition, to a society which is rapidly abandoning these hypotheses.

V   IS THERE A REMEDY?

The monetary policy, announced in the budget, being the real source of our industrial troubles, it is impossible to recommend any truly satisfactory course except its reversal. Nevertheless, amongst the alternatives still open to this government, some courses are better than others.

One course is to pursue the so-called 'sound' policy vigorously, with the object of bringing about 'the fundamental adjustments' in the orthodox way by further restricting credit and raising the bank rate in the autumn if necessary, thus intensifying unemployment and using every other weapon in our hands to force down money wages, trusting in the belief that when the process is finally complete the cost of living will have fallen also, thus restoring average real wages to their former level. If this policy can be carried through it will be, in a sense, successful, though it will leave much injustice behind it on account of the inequality of the changes it will effect, the stronger groups gaining at the expense of the weaker. For the method of economic pressure, since it bears most hardly on the weaker industries where wages are already relatively low, tends to increase the existing disparities between the wages of different industrial groups.

The question is how far public opinion will allow such a policy to go. It would be politically impossible for the Government to admit that it was deliberately intensifying unemployment, even though the members of the Currency Committee were to supply them with an argument for it. On the other hand, it is possible for deflation to produce its effects without being recognised. Deflation, once started ever so little, is cumulative in its progress. If pessimism becomes generally prevalent in the business world, the slower circulation of money resulting from this can carry deflation a long way further, without the Bank having either to raise the bank rate or to reduce its deposits. And since the public always understands particular causes better than general causes, the depression will be attributed to the industrial disputes which will accompany it, to the Dawes Scheme, to China, to the inevitable consequences of the Great War, to tariffs, to high taxation, to anything in the world except the general monetary policy which has set the whole thing going.

Moreover, this course need not be pursued in a clear-cut way. A furtive restriction of credit by the Bank of England can be coupled with vague cogitations on the part of Mr Baldwin (who has succeeded to the position in our affections formerly occupied by Queen Victoria) as to whether social benevolence does not require him to neutralise the effects of this by a series of illogical subsidies. Queen Baldwin's good heart will enable us to keep our tempers, whilst the serious work goes on behind the scenes. The budgetary position will render it impossible for the subsidies to be big enough to make any real difference. And in the end, unless there is a social upheaval, 'the fundamental adjustments' will duly take place.

Some people may contemplate this forecast with equanimity. I do not. It involves a great loss of social income, whilst it is going on, and will leave behind much social injustice when it is finished. The best, indeed the only, hope lies in the possibility that in this world, where so little can be foreseen, something may turn up—which leads me to my alternative suggestions. Could we not *help* something to turn up?

There are just two features of the situation which are capable of being turned to our advantage. The first is financial—if the value of gold would fall in the outside world, that would render unnecessary any important change in the level of wages here. The second is industrial—if the cost of living would fall *first*, our consciences would be clear in asking labour to accept a lower money wage, since it would then be evident that the reduction was not part of a plot to reduce real wages.

When the return to the gold standard was first announced, many authorities agreed that we were gambling on rising prices in the United States. The rise has not taken place, so far.[1] Moreover, the policy of the Bank of England has been calculated to steady prices in the United States rather than to raise them. The fact that American banks can lend their funds in London at a high rate of interest tends to keep money rates in New York higher than they would be otherwise, and to draw to London, instead of to New York, the oddments of surplus gold in the world markets. Thus our policy has been to relieve New York of the pressure of cheap money and additional gold which would tend otherwise to force their prices upwards. The abnormal difference between money rates in London and New York is preventing the gold standard from working even according to its own principles. According to orthodox doctrine, when prices are too high in A as compared with B, gold flows out from A and into B, thus lowering prices in A and *raising them in B*, so that an upward movement in B's prices meets halfway the downward movement in A's.

At present the policy of the Bank of England prevents this from happening. I suggest, therefore, that they should reverse

[1] In my opinion, we need not yet abandon the hope that it will take place. The tendency of American prices is upwards, rather than downwards, and it only requires a match to set alight the dormant possibilities of inflation in the United States. This possibility is the one real ground for not being too pessimistic.

226

this policy. Let them reduce the bank rate, and cease to restrict credit. If, as a result of this, the 'bad' American money, which is now a menace to the London money market, begins to flow back again, let us pay it off in gold or, if necessary, by using the dollar credits which the Treasury and the Bank of England have arranged in New York. It would be better to pay in gold, because it would be cheaper and because the flow of actual gold would have more effect on the American price level. If we modified the rules, which now render useless three-quarters of our stock of gold,[1] we could see with equanimity a loss of £60 million or £70 million in gold—which would make a great difference to conditions elsewhere. There is no object in paying 4½ per cent interest on floating American balances which can leave us at any moment, in order to use these balances to buy and hold idle and immobilised gold.

Gold could not flow out on this scale, unless at the same time the Bank of England was abandoning the restriction of credit and was replacing the gold by some other asset, e.g. Treasury bills. That is to say, the Bank would have to abandon the attempt to bring about the fundamental adjustments by the methods of economic pressure and the deliberate intensification of unemployment. Therefore, taken by itself, this policy might be open to the criticism that it was staking too much on the expectation of higher prices in America.

To meet this, I suggest that Mr Baldwin should face the facts frankly and sincerely, in collaboration with the trade union leaders, on the following lines.

So long as members of the Cabinet continue to pretend that the present movement to reduce wages has nothing to do with the value of money, it is natural that the working classes should take it as a concerted attack on real wages. If the Chancellor of the Exchequer is right in his view that his monetary policy has had no more to do with the case than the Gulf Stream, then it follows that the present agitations to lower wages are

---

[1] See the Note on our gold reserves at the end of this chapter.

simply a campaign against the standard of life of the working classes. It is only when the government have admitted the truth of the diagnosis set forth in these chapters that they are in a position to invite the collaboration of the trade union leaders on fair and reasonable terms.

As soon as the government admit that the problem is primarily a monetary one, then they can say to labour:

This is not an attack on real wages. We have raised the value of sterling 10 per cent. This means that money wages must fall 10 per cent. But it also means, when the adjustment is complete, that the cost of living will fall about 10 per cent. In this case there will have been no serious fall in real wages. Now there are two alternative ways of bringing about the reduction of money wages. One way is to apply economic pressure and to intensify unemployment by credit restriction, until wages are *forced down*. This is a hateful and disastrous way, because of its unequal effects on the stronger and on the weaker groups, and because of the economic and social waste whilst it is in progress. The other way is to effect a *uniform* reduction of wages by *agreement*, on the understanding that this shall not mean in the long run any fall in average real wages below what they were in the first quarter of this year. The practical difficulty is that money wages and the cost of living are interlocked. The cost of living cannot fall until *after* money wages have fallen. Money wages must fall *first*, in order to allow the cost of living to fall. Can we not agree, therefore, to have a uniform initial reduction of money wages throughout the whole range of employment, including government and municipal employment, of (say) 5 per cent, which reduction shall not hold good unless after an interval it has been compensated by a fall in the cost of living?

If Mr Baldwin were to make this proposal, the trade union leaders would probably ask him at once what he intended to do about money payments other than wages—rents, profits, and interest. As regards rents and profits he can reply that these are not fixed in terms of money and will therefore fall, when measured in money, step by step with prices. The worst of this reply is that rents and profits, like wages, are sticky and may not fall quick enough to help the transition as much as they should. As regards the interest on bonds, however, and particularly the interest on the national debt, he has no answer at all. For it is of the essence of any policy to lower prices that it benefits the receivers of interest at the expense of the rest of the community; this consequence of deflation is deeply embedded in our system of money contract. On the whole, I do not see how labour's objection can be met except by the rough-and-ready expedient of levying an additional income tax of 1s in the £ on all income other than from employments, which should continue until real wages had recovered to their previous level.[1]

If the proposal to effect a voluntary all-round reduction of wages, whilst sound in principle, is felt to be too difficult to achieve in practice, then, for my part, I should be inclined to stake everything on an attempt to raise prices in the outside world—that is on a reversal of the present policy of the Bank of England. This, I understand from their July *Monthly Review*, is also the recommendation of the high authorities of the Midland Bank.

That there should be grave difficulties in all these suggestions is inevitable. Any plan, such as the government has adopted, for deliberately altering the value of money, must, in modern economic conditions, come up against objections of justice and expediency. They are suggestions to mitigate the harsh consequences of a mistake; but they cannot undo the mistake. They will not commend themselves to those pessimists who believe that it is the level of real wages, and not merely of money wages, which is the proper object of attack. I mention them because our present policy of deliberately intensifying unemployment by keeping a tight hold on credit, just when on other grounds it ought to be relaxed, so as to force adjustments by using the weapon of economic necessity against individuals and against particular industries, is a policy which the country would never permit if it knew what was being done.

---

[1] This will not prevent bondholders from gaining in the long run, if in the long run prices do not rise again. But such profits and losses to bondholders are an inevitable feature of an unstable monetary standard. Since, however, prices generally do rise in the long run, bondholders in the long run are losers, not gainers, from the system.

§A NOTE ON OUR GOLD RESERVES

On 15 July 1925, the Bank of England held nearly £162 million in gold. The active note circulation of bank notes and currency notes amounted to £387 million. Against this note circulation the law provides that £120 million must be held in gold. Thus our free stock of gold, available for export, amounts to £42 million, or about a quarter of the whole. Since we cannot run too near to the legal minimum, the amount actually available in practice is about half this—say £22 million. The £120 million which must be held to satisfy the law is absolutely useless for any other purpose.

A NOTE ON THE INCREASE IN THE VALUE OF
STERLING IN TERMS OF FOREIGN MONEY

Since it is often believed that the restoration of gold only, or chiefly, affects our exchange with the United States, I give the following table of the change in the value of sterling since last June in the principal countries:

*Percentage increase in the value of sterling
(middle of June 1925) since June 1924*

	%		%
Italy	31	Sweden	11
France	27	Brazil	9
Germany	13	Holland	5
Japan	13	China	3
United States	12	Switzerland	2
Czechoslovakia	12	India	−6
Belgium	12	Argentine	−10

The movement in the opposite direction in India and the Argentine, though it increases the buying power of these countries as customers, does not help, in this context, because they are neither of them industrial competitors. The above table shows that the exchange movements of the last year have worsened our competitive position with our chief industrial rivals by 12 per cent or more. Thus the figure of 10 per cent which I have used in the text understates the case. §

6 MITIGATION BY TARIFF[1]

I PROPOSALS FOR A REVENUE TARIFF
(7 MARCH 1931)

'Proposals for a Revenue Tariff' was first published as an article in the *New Statesman and Nation*, 7 March 1931. As the recantation of an avowed free trader, it caused a sensation.

Do you think it a paradox that we can continue to increase our capital wealth by adding both to our foreign investments and to our equipment at home, that we can continue to live (most of us) much as usual or better, and support at the same time a vast body of persons in idleness with a dole greater than the income of a man in full employment in most parts of the world —and yet do all this with one-quarter of our industrial plant closed down and one-quarter of our industrial workers unemployed? It would be not merely a paradox, but an impossibility, if our potential capacity for the creation of wealth were not much greater than it used to be. But this greater capacity does exist. It is to be attributed mainly to three factors—the ever-increasing technical efficiency of our industry (I believe that output per head is 10 per cent greater than it was even so recently as 1924), the greater economic output of women, and the larger proportion of the population which is at the working period of life. The fall in the price of our imports compared with that of our exports also helps. The result is that with three-fourths of our industrial capacity we can now produce as much wealth as we could produce with the whole of it

[1] [For some months before the collapse of the gold standard it had become obvious that this collapse was becoming inevitable unless special steps were taken to mitigate the gravity of our problem. Somewhat in desperation, I made various suggestions, and, amongst them, a proposal for a tariff combined, if possible, with a bounty to exports. Mr Snowden, endowed with more than a normal share of blindness and obstinacy, opposed his negative to all the possible alternatives until at last natural forces took charge and put us out of our misery.]

a few years ago. But how rich we could be if only we could find some way of employing *four*-fourths of our capacity today!

Our trouble is, then, not that we lack the physical means to support a high standard of life, but that we are suffering a breakdown in organisation and in the machinery by which we buy and sell to one another.

There are two reactions to this breakdown. We experience the one or the other according to our temperaments. The one is inspired by a determination to maintain our standards of life by bringing into use our wasted capacity—that is to say, to expand, casting fear and even prudence away. The other, the instinct to contract, is based on the psychology of fear. How reasonable is it to be afraid?

We live in a society organised in such a way that the activity of production depends on the individual business man hoping for a reasonable profit, or at least, to avoid an actual loss. The margin which he requires as his necessary incentive to produce may be a very small proportion of the total value of the product. But take this away from him and the whole process stops. This, unluckily, is just what has happened. The fall of prices relatively to costs, together with the psychological effect of high taxation, has destroyed the necessary incentive to production. This is at the root of our disorganisation. It may be unwise, therefore, to frighten the business man or torment him further. A forward policy is liable to do this. For reasoning by a false analogy from what is prudent for an individual who finds himself in danger of living beyond his means, he is usually, when his nerves are frayed, a supporter, though to his own ultimate disadvantage, of national contraction.

And there is a further reason for nervousness. We are suffering from *international* instability. Notoriously the competitive power of our export trades is diminished by our high standard of life. At the same time the lack of profits in home business inclines the investor to place his money abroad, whilst high taxation exercises a sinister influence in the same direction. Above all,

SPRING RENOVATIONS

Cartoon by David Low by arrangement with the Trustees and the London Evening Standard

233

the reluctance of other creditor countries to lend (which is the root-cause of this slump) places too heavy a financial burden on London. These, again, are apparent arguments against a forward policy; for greater activity at home due to increased employment will increase our excess of imports, and government borrowing may (in their present mood) frighten investors.

Thus the *direct* effect of an expansionist policy must be to cause government borrowing, to throw some burden on the budget, and to increase our excess of imports. In every way, therefore—the opponents of such a policy point out—it will aggravate the want of confidence, the burden of taxation, and the international instability which, they believe, are at the bottom of our present troubles.

At this point the opponents of expansion divide into two groups—those who think that we must not only postpone all ideas of expansion, but must positively contract, by which they mean reduce wages and make large economies in the existing expenditure of the budget, and those who are entirely negative and, like Mr Snowden, dislike the idea of contraction (interpreted in the above sense) almost as much as they dislike the idea of expansion.

The policy of negation, however, is really the most dangerous of all. For, as time goes by, it becomes increasingly doubtful whether we *can* support our standard of life. With 1 million unemployed we certainly can; with 2 million unemployed we probably can; with 3 million unemployed we probably cannot. Thus the negative policy, by allowing unemployment steadily to increase, must lead in the end to an unanswerable demand for a reduction in our standard of life. If we do nothing long enough, there will in the end be nothing else that we can do.

Unemployment, I must repeat, exists because employers have been deprived of profit. The loss of profit may be due to all sorts of causes. But, short of going over to Communism, there is no possible means of curing unemployment except by restoring to employers a proper margin of profit. There are two ways of doing this—by increasing the *demand* for output, which is the expansionist cure, or by decreasing the *cost* of output, which is the contractionist cure. Both of these try to touch the spot. Which of them is to be preferred?

To decrease the cost of output by reducing wages and curtailing budget services may indeed increase foreign demand for our goods (unless, which is quite likely, it encourages a similar policy of contraction abroad), but it will probably diminish the domestic demand. The advantages to employers of a *general* reduction of wages are, therefore, not so great as they look. Each employer sees the advantage to himself of a reduction of the wages which he himself pays, and overlooks both the consequences of the reduction of the incomes of his customers and of the reduction of wages which his competitors will enjoy. Anyway, it would certainly lead to social injustice and violent resistance, since it would greatly benefit some classes of income at the expense of others. For these reasons a policy of contraction sufficiently drastic to do any real good may be quite impracticable.

Yet the objections to the expansionist remedy—the instability of our international position, the state of the budget, and the want of confidence—cannot be thus disposed of. Two years ago there was no need to be frightened. Today it is a different matter. It would not be wise to frighten the penguins and arouse these frigid creatures to flap away from our shores with their golden eggs inside them. A policy of expansion sufficiently drastic to be useful might drive us off the gold standard. Moreover, two years ago the problem was mainly a British problem; today it is mainly international. No domestic cure today can be adequate by itself. An international cure is essential; and I see the best hope of remedying the international slump in the leadership of Great Britain. But if Great Britain is to resume leadership, she must be strong and believed to be strong. It is of paramount importance, therefore, to restore full confidence in London. I do not believe that this is difficult; for the real strength of London is being under-estimated today by foreign opinion, and the position is ripe for a sudden reversal of sentiment. For these reasons I, who opposed our return to the gold standard and can claim, unfortunately, that my Cassandra utterances have been partly fulfilled, believe that our exchange position should be relentlessly defended today, in order, above all, that we may resume the vacant financial leadership of the world, which no one else has the experience or the public spirit to occupy, speaking out of acknowledged strength and not out of weakness.

An advocate of expansion in the interests of domestic employment has cause, therefore, to think twice. I have thought twice, and the following are my conclusions.

I am of the opinion that a policy of expansion, though desirable, is not safe or practicable today, unless it is accompanied by other measures which would neutralise its dangers. Let me remind the reader what these dangers are. There is the burden on the trade balance, the burden on the budget, and the effect on confidence. If the policy of expansion were to justify itself eventually by increasing materially the level of profits and the volume of employment, the net effect on the budget and on confidence would in the end be favourable and perhaps very favourable. But this might not be the initial effect.

What measures are available to neutralise these dangers? A decision to reform the grave abuses of the dole, and a decision to postpone for the present all new charges on the budget for social services in order to conserve its resources to meet schemes for the expansion of employment, are advisable and should be taken. But the main decision which seems to me today to be absolutely forced on any wise Chancellor of the Exchequer, whatever his beliefs about protection, is the introduction of a substantial revenue tariff. It is certain that there is no other measure all the immediate consequences of which will be favourable and appropriate. The tariff which I have in mind would include no discriminating protective taxes, but would cover as wide a field as possible at a flat rate or perhaps two flat rates, each applicable to wide categories of goods. Rebates would be allowed in respect of imported material entering into exports, but raw materials, which make up an important proportion of the value of exports, such as wool and cotton, would be exempt. The amount of revenue to be aimed at should be substantial, not less than £50 million and, if possible, £75 million. Thus, for example, there might be import duties of 15 per cent on all manufactured and semi-manufactured goods without exception, and of 5 per cent on all foodstuffs and certain raw materials, whilst other raw materials would be exempt.[1] I am prepared to maintain that the effect of such duties on the cost of living would be insignificant—no greater than the existing fluctuation between one month and another. Moreover, any conceivable remedy for unemployment will have the effect, and, indeed, will be intended, to raise prices. Equally, the effect on the cost of our exports, after allowing for the rebates which should be calculated on broad and simple lines, would be very small. It should be the declared intention of the free trade parties acquiescing in this decision to remove the duties in the event of world prices recovering to the level of 1929.

Compared with any alternative which is open to us, this measure is unique in that it would at the same time relieve the pressing problems of the budget and restore business confidence. I do not believe that a wise and prudent budget can be framed today without recourse to a revenue tariff. But this is not its only advantage. In so far as it leads to the substitution of home-produced goods for goods previously imported, it will increase employment in this country. At the same time, by relieving the pressure on the balance of trade it will provide a much-needed margin to pay for the additional imports which a policy of expansion will require and to finance loans by London to necessitous debtor countries. In these ways, the buying power which we take away from the rest of the world by restricting

[1] [In a subsequent article I agreed that this precise scale of duties could not be relied on to produce so large a revenue as that suggested above, and that £40 million was a safer estimate.]

certain imports we shall restore to it with the other hand. Some fanatical free traders might allege that the adverse effect of import duties on our exports would neutralise all this; but it would not be true.

Free traders may, consistently with their faith, regard a revenue tariff as our iron ration, which can be used once only in emergency. The emergency has arrived. Under cover of the breathing space and the margin of financial strength thus afforded us, we could frame a policy and a plan, both domestic and international, for marching to the assault against the spirit of contractionism and fear.

If, on the other hand, free traders reject these counsels of expediency, the certain result will be to break the present government and to substitute for it, in the confusion of a crisis of confidence, a Cabinet pledged to a full protectionist programme. §I am not unaccustomed to being in a minority. But on this occasion I believe that 90 per cent of my countrymen will agree with me.§

II ON THE EVE OF GOLD SUSPENSION
(10 SEPTEMBER 1931)

Written for the *Evening Standard*, 10 September 1931, this article appeared under the heading 'We Must Restrict our Imports'.

The moral energies of the nation are being directed into wrong channels, and serious troubles are ahead of us unless we apply our minds with more effect than hitherto to the analysis of the real character of our problems.

The exclusive concentration on the idea of 'economy', national, municipal, and personal—meaning by this the negative act of withholding expenditure which is now stimulating the forces of production into action—may, if under the spur of a sense of supposed duty it is carried far, produce social effects so shocking as to shake the whole system of our national life.

There is scarcely an item in the economy programme of the May Report—whether or not it is advisable on general grounds —which is not certain to increase unemployment, to lower the profits of business, and to diminish the yield of the revenue; so much so that I have calculated that economies of £100 million may quite likely reduce the net budget deficit by not more than £50 million, and we are just hoodwinking ourselves (unless our real object is to *pretend* to balance the budget for the benefit of foreign financiers) if we suppose that we can make the economies under discussion without any repercussions on the number of the unemployed to be supported or on the yield of the existing taxes.

Yet if we carry 'economy' of every kind to its logical conclusion, we shall find that we have balanced the budget at nought on both sides, with all of us flat on our backs starving to death from a refusal, for reasons of economy, to buy one another's services.

The Prime Minister has said that it is like the war over again, and many people believe him. But this is exactly the opposite of the truth. During the war it was useful to refrain from any avoidable expenditure because this would release resources for the insatiable demands of military operations. What are we releasing resources for today? To stand at street corners and draw the dole.

When we already have a great amount of unemployment and un-used resources of every description, economy is only useful from the national point of view *in so far as it it diminishes our consumption of imported goods*. For the rest, its fruits are entirely wasted in unemployment, business losses, and reduced savings. But it is an extraordinarily indirect and wasteful way of reducing imports.

If we throw men out of work and reduce the incomes of government employees so that those directly and indirectly affected cannot afford to buy so much imported food, to this extent the country's financial position is eased. But this is not likely to amount to more than 20 per cent of the total economies enforced. The remaining 80 per cent is wasted, and represents either a mere transference of loss or unemployment due to a refusal of British citizens to purchase one another's services.

What I am saying is absolutely certain, yet I doubt if one in a million of those who are crying out for economy have the slightest idea of the real consequences of what they demand.

This is not to deny that there is a budget problem. Quite the contrary. The point is that the state of the budget is mainly a symptom and a consequence of other causes, that economy is in itself liable to aggravate rather than to remove these other causes, and that consequently the budget problem, attacked merely along the lines of economy, is probably insoluble.

What are our troubles fundamentally due to? Very largely to the world depression, immediately to the unbelievable rashness of high finance in the City, and originally to the policy of returning to the gold standard without the slightest appreciation of the nature of the difficulties which this involved. To say that our problem is a budget problem is like saying that the German problem is a budget problem, forgetting all about reparations.

Now as regards the world depression, there is at the moment absolutely nothing that we can do, for we have now lost the power of international initiative which we seemed to be regaining last May. The results of unsound international banking by the City are also, for the time being, irreparable. The choice left to us was whether or not to adhere to the present gold parity of the exchanges.

This was decided in the affirmative for reasons which I understand but with which I do not agree. The decision was taken in a spirit of hysteria and without a calm consideration of the alternative before us. Ministers have given forecasts of what might have been expected if we had taken a different course which could not survive ten minutes' rational discussion.

I believe that we shall come to regret this decision, just as we already regret most of the critical decisions taken during the last ten years by the persons who form the present Cabinet.

But that is not the point at this moment. The decision to maintain the gold standard at all costs has been taken. The point is that the Cabinet and the public seem to have no clear idea as to what has to be done to implement its own decision, apart from the obvious necessity of raising a foreign loan for immediate requirements; which simply has the effect of replacing money which we had previously borrowed in terms of sterling, by money borrowed in terms of francs and dollars. But they cannot suppose that we can depend permanently on foreign loans. The rest of the problem is primarily concerned with improving our current balance of trade on income account. This is what the Cabinet ought to be thinking about.

There are only two possible lines of attack on this. The one (which is the milder measure open to us) consists in direct measures to restrict imports (and, if possible, subsidise exports); the other is a reduction of all money wages within the country. We may have to attempt both in the end, if we refuse to devaluate.

But the immediate question is which to try first. Now the latter course, if it were to be adequate, would involve so drastic a reduction of wages and such appallingly difficult, probably insoluble, problems, both of social justice and practical method, that it would be crazy not to try first the effects of the alternative, and much milder, measure of restricting imports.

It happens that this course also has other important advantages. It will not only relieve the strain on the foreign exchanges. It would also do more than any other single measure to balance the budget; and it is the only form of taxation open to us which will actually increase profits, improve employment, and raise the spirits and the confidence of the business community.

Finally, it is the only measure for which there is (sensibly enough) an overwhelming support from public opinion. It is credibly reported that the late Cabinet were in favour of a tariff in the proportion of three to one. It looks as if the present Cabinet may favour it in the proportion of four to one. The only third alternative Cabinet is unanimously for it. But sacrifice being the order of the day, we have in the spirit of self-immolation conceived the brilliant contrivance of a 'national' government, the basis of which is that every member of it agrees, so long as it lasts, to sacrifice what he himself believes to be the only sound solution for our misfortunes.

For if we rule out devaluation, which I personally now believe to be the right remedy, but which is not yet the policy of any organised party in the state, there are three possible lines of procedure.

The first is to take the risks of brisk home development, as being preferable to enforced idleness.

The second is to organise a general reduction of wages and, in the interests of social justice, of other money incomes as well, so far as this is feasible.

The third is a drastic restriction of imports.

The 'national' government is pledged, if I understand the position rightly, to avoid all three. Their policy is to reduce the standard of life of as many people as are within their reach in the hope that some small portion of the reductions of standard will be at the expense of imports.

Deliberately to prefer this to a direct restriction of imports is to be *non compos mentis*. §Or is it their hope to bring down wages both by worsening the lot of the unemployed and ensuring at the same time that their numbers shall exceed 3 million?

Here, again, if the end is desired, any sane man would prefer more direct and less wasteful measures for attaining it. By now even members of the Cabinet must surely be becoming uneasy about the course which they have set for themselves.§

III AFTER THE SUSPENSION OF GOLD

A letter to the Editor of *The Times*, written from 46 Gordon Square on 28 September 1931, one week after the gold standard was suspended, and published 29 September 1931.

Until recently I was urging on Liberals[1] and others the importance of accepting a general tariff as a means of mitigating the effects of the obvious dis-equilibrium between money costs at home and abroad. But the events of the last week have made a great difference. At the present gold value of sterling British producers are probably in many directions among the cheapest in the world. In these circumstances we cannot continue as if nothing had happened. It is impossible to have a rational discussion about tariffs so long as the currency question is altogether unsolved. For until we know more about the probable future level of sterling in relation to gold and, above all, until we know how many other countries are going to follow our example, it is impossible to say what our competitive position is going to be.

May I urge that the immediate question for attention is not a tariff but the currency question? It is the latter which is urgent and important. It is at present a non-party issue on which none of the political parties has taken up a dogmatic attitude. It is suitable, therefore, for non-party handling. It is most certainly unsuitable for a general election. It offers immense opportunities for leadership by this country. We are probably in a position to carry the whole of the Empire and more than half of the rest of the world with us, and thus rebuild the financial supremacy of London on a firm basis. Meanwhile, proposals for high protection have ceased to be urgent. To throw the country into a turmoil over them to the neglect of this other more urgent and important problem would be a wrong and foolish thing. Let us give our whole attention and our united

---

[1] [Not all my free trade friends proved to be so prejudiced as I had thought. For after a tariff was no longer necessary, many of them were found voting for it.]

energies to devising a sound international currency policy for ourselves and the rest of the world. For it is futile to suppose that we can recover our former prosperity without such a policy, or that tariffs can be any substitute for it. When the currency question has been settled, then we can return to protection and to our other domestic issues with a solid basis to go upon; and that will be the time for a general election.

7 THE END OF THE GOLD STANDARD
(27 September 1931)[1]

Written for the *Sunday Express* and published 27 September 1931, with the heading 'The Future of the World'.

There are few Englishmen who do not rejoice at the breaking of our gold fetters. We feel that we have at last a free hand to do what is sensible. The romantic phase is over, and we can begin to discuss realistically what policy is for the best.

It may seem surprising that a move which had been represented as a disastrous catastrophe should have been received with so much enthusiasm. But the great advantages to British trade and industry of our ceasing artificial efforts to maintain our currency above its real value were quickly realised.

The division of inside opinion was largely on a different point. The difficult question to decide was one of honour. The City of London considered that it was under an obligation of *honour* to make every possible effort to maintain the value of money in terms of which it had accepted large deposits from foreigners, even though the result of this was to place an intolerable strain on British industry. At what point—that was the difficult problem—were we justified in putting our own interests first?

As events have turned out, we have got the relief we needed and, at the same time, the claims of honour have been, in the judgement of the whole world, satisfied to the utmost. For the step was not taken until it was unavoidable. In the course of a few weeks the Bank of England paid out £200 million in gold or its equivalent, which was about half the total claims of foreigners on London, and did this at a time when the sums which London had re-lent abroad were largely frozen. No banker could do more. Out of the ashes the City of London will rise

---

[1] [On 21 September 1931, the gold standard in Great Britain was suspended.]

with undiminished honour. For she has played the game up to the limits of quixotry, even at the risk of driving British trade almost to a standstill.

No wonder, then, that we feel some exuberance at the release, that stock exchange prices soar, and that the dry bones of industry are stirred. For if the sterling exchange is depreciated by, say, 25 per cent, this does as much to restrict our imports as a tariff of that amount; but whereas a tariff could not help our exports, and might hurt them, the depreciation of sterling affords them a bounty of the same 25 per cent by which it aids the home producer against imports.

In many lines of trade the British manufacturer today must be the cheapest producer in the world in terms of gold. We gain these advantages without a cut of wages and without industrial strife. We gain them in a way which is strictly fair to every section of the community, without any serious effects on the cost of living. For less than a quarter of our total consumption is represented by imports; so that sterling would have to depreciate by much more than 25 per cent before I should expect the cost of living to rise by as much as 10 per cent. This would cause serious hardship to no one, for it would only put things back where they were two years ago. Meanwhile there will be a great stimulus to employment.

I make no forecast as to the figure to which sterling may fall in the next few days, except that it will have to fall for a time appreciably below the figure which cool calculators believe to represent the equilibrium. There will then be speculation and profit-taking in favour of sterling to balance speculation and panic selling on the other side. Our authorities made a great mistake in allowing sterling to open so high, because the inevitable gradual fall towards a truer level must sap confidence and produce on the ignorant the impression of a slide which cannot be stayed. Those who were guilty of undue optimism will quite likely succumb to undue pessimism. But the pessimism will be as unfounded as the optimism was. The equilibrium value of sterling is the same as it was a month ago. There are tremendous forces to support sterling when it begins to fall too far. There is no risk, in my judgement, of a catastrophic fall.

These, in brief, are the consequences in Great Britain. How will the rest of the world be influenced? Not in a uniform way. Let us take first the debtor countries to whom Great Britain has in the past lent large sums in sterling, and from whom interest is due in sterling, such as Australia, Argentina, and India. To these countries the depreciation of sterling represents a great concession. A smaller quantity of their goods will be sufficient to meet their sterling liabilities. The interest due to Great Britain from abroad, which is fixed in sterling, amounts to about £100 million a year. In respect of this sum Great Britain now plays the part of a reasonable creditor who moderates his claim in view of so great a change in the situation as the recent catastrophic fall in commodity prices.

When we try to calculate the effect on other manufacturing countries, whose competition we are now in a better position to meet, the effect is more complex. A large part of the world will, I expect, follow Great Britain in reducing the former gold value of their money. There are already signs in many countries that no great effort will be made to maintain the gold parity. In the last few days Canada, Italy, Scandinavia have moved in our direction. India and the Crown Colonies, including the Straits Settlements, have automatically followed sterling. Australia and the whole of South America had already abandoned the effort to maintain exchange parity. I shall be astonished if Germany delays long before following our example. Will Holland deal final ruin to the rubber and sugar industries of the Dutch Indies by keeping them tied to gold? There will be strong motives driving a large part of the world our way. After all, Great Britain's plight, as the result of the deflation of prices, is far less serious than that of most countries.

Now, in so far as this is the case, we and all the countries following our example will gain the benefits of higher prices. But none of us will secure a competitive advantage at the expense of the others. Thus the competitive disadvantage will be concentrated on those few countries which remain on the gold standard. On these will fall the curse of Midas. As a result of their unwillingness to exchange their exports except for gold their export trade will dry up and disappear until they no longer have either a favourable trade balance or foreign deposits to repatriate. This means in the main France and the United States. Their loss of export trade will be an inevitable, a predictable, outcome of their own action. These countries largely for reasons resulting from the war and the war settlements, are owed much money by the rest of the world. They erect tariff barriers which prevent the payment of these sums in goods. They are unwilling to lend it. They have already taken nearly all the available surplus gold in the whole world. There remained, in logic, only one way by which the rest of the world could maintain its solvency and self-respect; namely, to cease purchasing these countries' exports. So long as the gold standard is preserved— which means that the prices of international commodities must be much the same everywhere—this involved a competitive campaign of deflation, each of us trying to get our prices down faster than the others, a campaign which had intensified unemployment and business losses to an unendurable pitch.

But as soon as the gold exchange is ruptured the problem is solved. For the appreciation of French and American money in terms of the money of other countries makes it impossible for French and American exporters to sell their goods. The recent policy of these countries could not, if it was persistently pursued, end in any other way. They have willed the destruction of their own export industries, and only they can take the steps necessary to restore them. The appreciation of their currencies must also embarrass gravely their banking systems. The United States had, in effect, set the rest of us the problem of finding some way to do without her wheat, her copper, her cotton, and her motor-cars. She set the problem and, as it had only one solution, that solution we have been compelled to find.

Yet this is quite the opposite of the note on which I wish to end. The solution to which we have been driven, though it gives immediate relief to us and transfers the strain to others, is in truth a solution unsatisfactory for everyone. The world will never be prosperous without a trade recovery in the United States. Peace and confidence and a harmonious economic equilibrium for all the closely interrelated countries of the globe is the only goal worth aiming at.

I believe that the great events of the last week may open a new chapter in the world's monetary history. I have a hope that they may break down barriers which have seemed impassable. We need now to take intimate and candid conference together as to the better ordering of our affairs for the future. The President of the United States turned in his sleep last June. Great issues deserve his attention. Yet the magic spell of immobility which has been cast over the White House seems still unbroken. Are the solutions offered us always to be too late? Shall we in Great Britain invite three-quarters of the world, including the whole of our Empire, to join with us in evolving a new currency system which shall be stable in terms of commodities? Or would the gold standard countries be interested to learn the terms, which must needs be strict, on which we should be prepared to re-enter the system of a drastically reformed gold standard?

IV POLITICS

1 A SHORT VIEW OF RUSSIA

*Keynes wrote the three articles which were later published as A Short
View of Russia when he and Lydia Lopokova visited Russia in 1925
soon after their marriage. The articles first appeared in the Nation and
Athenaeum, 10, 17 and 25 October 1925, and were reprinted by the Hogarth
Press as one of the series of Hogarth Essays in December of the same year.
Keynes primarily included chapters I and III in Essays in Persuasion.*

§PREFACE

These chapters are the fruit of a brief visit to Russia in September
1925 by one ignorant of the language and of the country, but
not without experience of the people, and in the company of
an interpreter. The occasion was found in the bicentenary
celebrations of the Academy of Sciences, once the Imperial
Academy of Petersburg, now of Leningrad, at which I represented
the University of Cambridge.

They are not based on intimate knowledge or close experience,
and claim no authority as such. They are merely the impressions,
for what they are worth, of an observer, whose prejudices were
not specially calculated to distort his sight, endeavouring to
convey, as best he can, how Russia struck him.

I use not infrequently in what follows the epithet *religious*
as applicable to the disciples of Lenin. Judging from letters
which I received when these chapters were appearing in the
Nation, I believe that Englishmen will see what I mean; but
in Russia there will be few, I gather, who will approve or
understand this use of language. To the Bolshevists themselves
the word will sound as stupid and offensive, mere vulgar abuse
—as though I were to call the Archbishop of Canterbury a
Bolshevist (which, however, he may indeed deserve, if he
seriously pursues the Gospel precepts); for they claim to be
just the opposite. Religion, mysticism, idealism—it is part of
the Leninist's creed that all such matters are trumpery and

trash, whereas they themselves are materialists, realists, of the earth earthy. Have they not, but the other day, ordained that in the libraries of the proletarian clubs 'the section on religion must contain solely anti-religious literature'?

There may be good reasons out of the past why religion should have a nasty taste in Russian mouths. There may be a consistent and intelligible use of language by which High Church mystics are alone religious and those who try to find a better path on earth are irreligious, by which the cries of dancing dervishes are religious and the Sermon on the Mount irreligious, by which Rasputin was religious and Tolstoy irreligious. Let me, therefore, explain in advance that, when I say that Leninism may be inspired with religious fervour, I do not suggest that the commissars are High Church mystics, dancing dervishes, or Rasputins in mufti.

To English readers these explanations are probably not needed. For here we have long recognised that there are two branches of religion—high and low, mystical sleep-walkers and practical idealists. There are two distinct sublimations of materialistic egotism—one in which the ego is merged in the nameless mystic union, another in which it is merged in the pursuit of an ideal life for the whole community of men. The participants of the first may neglect or ignore the second; many followers of the second condemn what seems to them the idle indulgence or self-deceptions of the first. It has been the peculiarity of some great religious leaders that they have belonged to both classes at once. At any rate, when I speak of religion I include both, and not the former only.

Some instances from our latter-day celebrities may illustrate my explanation. Certain of the politicians of France, M. Poincaré for example, followed hard by some of the politicians of the United States, seem to me to be amongst the most irreligious men now in the world; Trotsky, Mr Bernard Shaw, and Mr Baldwin, each in his way, amongst the most religious. I do not forget that Trotsky has written:

To accept the Workers' Revolution in the name of a high ideal means not only to reject it, but to slander it. All the social illusions which mankind has raved about in religion, poetry, morals, or philosophy, served only the purpose of deceiving and blinding the oppressed. The Socialist Revolution tears the cover off 'illusions', off 'elevating', as well as off humiliating deceptions, and washes off in blood reality's make-up. The Revolution is strong to the extent to which it is realistic, rational, strategic, and mathematical. Can it be that the Revolution, the same one which is now before us, the first since the earth began, needs the seasoning of romantic outbursts, as a cat ragout needs hare sauce?

For he has also looked forward to 'a society which will have thrown off the pinching and stultifying worry about one's daily bread...in which the liberated egotism of man—a mighty force!—will be directed wholly towards the understanding, the transformation, and the betterment of the Universe'. Trotsky himself does not confuse the means with the end:

The Revolution itself is not yet the Kingdom of Freedom. On the contrary, it is developing the features of 'necessity' to the greatest degree...Revolutionary literature cannot but be imbued with a spirit of social hatred, which is a creative historic factor in the epoch of proletarian dictatorship. But under Socialism solidarity will be the basis of society. Literature and Art will be tuned to a different key. All the emotions which we revolutionaries, at the present time, feel apprehensive of naming—so much have they been worn thin by hypocrites and vulgarians—such as disinterested friendship, love for one's neighbour, sympathy, will be the mighty ringing chords of Socialist poetry.

One has a feeling that such sentiments would not come with equal sincerity or seriousness or emotional force from the lips, for example, of Signor Mussolini or of President Calvin Coolidge. The Duce may be a rake susceptible of being reformed, and the President a respectable person whose salvation is out of the question. What are they really? I cannot certainly say—these matters, which are often palpable at close quarters, are hard to distinguish at a distance. Before I went to Russia I was in similar doubts about the Communists. What I thought I learnt on the spot and could not have learnt elsewhere, is a partial answer.§

I WHAT IS THE COMMUNIST FAITH?

It is extraordinarily difficult to be fair-minded about Russia. And even with fair-mindedness, how is a true impression to be conveyed of something so unfamiliar, shifting, and contradictory, of which no one in England has a background of knowledge or experience? No English newspaper has a regular correspondent resident in Russia. We rightly attach small credence to what the Soviet authorities say about themselves. Most of our news is from prejudiced labour deputations or from prejudiced *émigrés*. Thus a belt of fog separates us from what goes on in the other world where the Union of Socialist Soviet Republics rules and experiments and evolves a kind of order. Russia is suffering the penalty of years of 'propaganda' which, by taking away credence from words, almost destroys, in the end, the means of communication at a distance.

Leninism is a combination of two things which Europeans have kept for some centuries in different compartments of the soul—religion and business. We are shocked because the religion is new, and contemptuous because the business, being subordinated to the religion instead of the other way round, is highly inefficient.

Like other new religions, Leninism derives its power not from the multitude but from a small minority of enthusiastic converts, whose zeal and intolerance make each one the equal in strength of a hundred indifferentists. Like other new religions, it is led by those who can combine the new spirit, perhaps sincerely, with seeing a good deal more than their followers, politicians with at least an average dose of political cynicism, who can smile as well as frown, volatile experimentalists, released by religion from truth and mercy but not blinded to facts and expediency, and open therefore to the charge (superficial and useless though it is where politicians, lay or ecclesiastical, are concerned) of hypocrisy. Like other new religions, it seems to take the colour and gaiety and freedom out of everyday life and

256

to offer a drab substitute in the square wooden faces of its devotees. Like other new religions, it persecutes without justice or pity those who actively resist it. Like other new religions, it is filled with missionary ardour and œcumenical ambitions. But to say that Leninism is the faith of a persecuting and propagating minority of fanatics led by hypocrites is, after all, to say no more nor less than that it *is* a religion and not merely a party, and Lenin a Mahomet, not a Bismarck. If we want to frighten ourselves in our capitalist easy-chairs, we can picture the Communists of Russia as though the early Christians led by Attila were using the equipment of the Holy Inquisition and the Jesuit missions to enforce the literal economics of the New Testament; but when we want to comfort ourselves in the same chairs, can we hopefully repeat that these economics are fortunately so contrary to human nature that they cannot finance either missionaries or armies and will surely end in defeat?

There are three questions to answer. Is the new religion partly true, or sympathetic to the souls of modern men? Is it on the material side so inefficient as to render it incapable to survive? Will it, in the course of time, with sufficient dilution and added impurity, catch the multitude?

As for the first question, those who are completely satisfied by Christian capitalism or by egotistic capitalism untempered by subterfuge will not hesitate how to answer it; for they either have a religion or need none. But many, in this age without religion, are bound to feel a strong emotional curiosity towards any religion which is really new and not merely a recrudescence of old ones and has proved its motive force; and all the more when the new thing comes out of Russia, the beautiful and foolish youngest son of the European family, with hair on his head, nearer both to the earth and to heaven than his bald brothers in the West—who, having been born two centuries later, has been able to pick up the middle-aged disillusionment of the rest of the family before he has lost the genius of youth or become addicted to comfort and to habits.

I sympathise with those who seek for something good in Soviet Russia.

But when we come to the actual thing, what is one to say? For me, brought up in a free air undarkened by the horrors of religion, with nothing to be afraid of, Red Russia holds too much which is detestable. Comfort and habits let us be ready to forgo, but I am not ready for a creed which does not care how much it destroys the liberty and security of daily life, which uses deliberately the weapons of persecution, destruction, and international strife. How can I admire a policy which finds a characteristic expression in spending millions to suborn spies in every family and group at home, and to stir up trouble abroad? Perhaps this is no worse and has more purpose than the greedy, warlike, and imperialist propensities of other governments; but it must be far better than these to shift me out of my rut. How can I accept a doctrine which sets up as its bible, above and beyond criticism, an obsolete economic textbook which I know to be not only scientifically erroneous but without interest or application for the modern world? How can I adopt a creed which, preferring the mud to the fish, exalts the boorish proletariat above the bourgeois and the intelligentsia who, with whatever faults, are the quality in life and surely carry the seeds of all human advancement? Even if we need a religion, how can we find it in the turbid rubbish of the Red bookshops? It is hard for an educated, decent, intelligent son of western Europe to find his ideals here, unless he has first suffered some strange and horrid process of conversion which has changed all his values.

Yet we shall miss the essence of the new religion if we stop at this point. The Communist may justly reply that all these things belong not to his ultimate faith but to the tactics of revolution. For he believes in two things: the introduction of a new order upon earth, and the *method* of the revolution as the *only* means thereto.[1] The new order must not be judged either

---

[1] In these chapters I use the term 'Communism' to mean the new order, and not, as is the practice in British Labour politics, to mean the revolution as a means thereto.

by the horrors of the revolution or by the privations of the transitionary period. The revolution is to be a supreme example of the means justified by the end. The soldier of the revolution must crucify his own human nature, becoming unscrupulous and ruthless, and suffering himself a life without security or joy—but as the means to his purpose and not its end.

What, then, is the essence of the new religion as a new order upon earth? Looking from outside, I do not clearly know. Sometimes its mouthpieces speak as though it was purely materialistic and technical in just the same sense that modern capitalism is—as though, that is to say, Communism merely claimed to be in the long run a superior technical instrument for obtaining the same materialistic economic benefits as capitalism offers, that in time it will cause the fields to yield more and the forces of nature to be more straitly harnessed. In this case there is no religion after all, nothing but a bluff to facilitate a change to what may or may not be a better economic technique. But I suspect that, in fact, such talk is largely a reaction against the charges of economic inefficiency which we on our side launch, and that at the heart of Russian Communism there is something else of more concern to mankind.

In one respect Communism but follows other famous religions. It exalts the common man and makes him everything. Here there is nothing new. But there is another factor in it which also is not new but which may, nevertheless, in a changed form and a new setting, contribute something to the true religion of the future, if there be any true religion. *Leninism is absolutely, defiantly non-supernatural, and its emotional and ethical essence centres about the individual's and the community's attitude towards the love of money.*

I do not mean that Russian Communism alters, or even seeks to alter, human nature, that it makes Jews less avaricious or Russians less extravagant than they were before. I do not merely mean that it sets up a new ideal. I mean that it tries to construct a framework of society in which pecuniary motives as influencing action shall have a changed relative importance, in which social approbations shall be differently distributed, and where behaviour, which previously was normal and respectable, ceases to be either the one or the other.

In England today a talented and virtuous youth, about to enter the world, will balance the advantages of entering the civil service and of seeking a fortune in business; and public opinion will esteem him not less if he prefers the second. Money-making, as such, on as large a scale as possible, is not less respectable socially, perhaps more so, than a life devoted to the service of the State or of religion, education, learning, or art. But in the Russia of the future it is intended that the career of money-making, as such, will simply not occur to a respectable young man as a possible opening, any more than the career of a gentleman burglar or acquiring skill in forgery and embezzlement. Even the most admirable aspects of the love of money in our existing society, such as thrift and saving, and the attainment of financial security and independence for one's self and one's family, whilst not deemed morally wrong, will be rendered so difficult and impracticable as to be not worth while. Everyone should work for the community—the new creed runs—and, if he does his duty, the community will uphold him.

This system does not mean a complete levelling down of incomes—at least at the present stage. A clever and successful person in Soviet Russia has a bigger income and a better time than other people. The commissar with £5 a week (*plus* sundry free services, a motor-car, a flat, a box at the ballet, etc.) lives well enough, but not *in the least* like a rich man in London. The successful professor or civil servant with £6 or £7 a week (*minus* sundry impositions), has, perhaps, a real income three times those of the proletarian workers and six times those of the poorer peasants. Some peasants are three or four times richer than others. A man who is out of work receives part pay, not full pay. But no one can afford on these incomes, with high

Russian prices and stiff progressive taxes, to save anything worth saving; it is hard enough to live day by day. The progressive taxation and the mode of assessing rents and other charges are such that it is actually disadvantageous to have an acknowledged income exceeding £8 to £10 a week. Nor is there any possibility of large gains except by taking the same sort of risks as attach to bribery and embezzlement elsewhere—not that bribery and embezzlement have disappeared in Russia or are even rare, but anyone whose extravagance or whose instincts drive him to such courses runs serious risk of detection and penalties which include death.

Nor, at the present stage, does the system involve the actual prohibition of buying and selling at a profit. The policy is not to forbid these professions, but to render them precarious and disgraceful. The private trader is a sort of permitted outlaw, without privileges or protection, like the Jew in the Middle Ages—an outlet for those who have overwhelming instincts in this direction, but not a natural or agreeable job for the normal man.

The effect of these social changes has been, I think, to make a real change in the predominant attitude towards money, and will probably make a far greater change when a new generation has grown up which has known nothing else. People in Russia, if only because of their poverty, are very greedy for money— at least as greedy as elsewhere. But money-making and money-accumulating cannot enter into the life-calculations of a rational man who accepts the Soviet rule in the way in which they enter into ours. A society of which this is even partially true is a tremendous innovation.

Now all this may prove utopian, or destructive of true welfare, though, perhaps, not so utopian, pursued in an intense religious spirit, as it would be if it were pursued in a matter-of-fact way. But is it appropriate to assume, as most of us have assumed hitherto, that it is insincere or wicked?

§11   THE ECONOMICS OF SOVIET RUSSIA

We shall not understand Leninism unless we view it as being at the same time a persecuting and missionary religion and an experimental economic technique. What of the second aspect— Is the economic technique so inefficient that it courts disaster?

The economic system of Soviet Russia has undergone and is undergoing such rapid changes that it is impossible to obtain a precise and accurate account of it. The method of trial-and-error is unreservedly employed. No one has ever been more frankly experimentalist than Lenin was in everything which did not touch the central truths of his faith. At first there was much confusion as to what was essential and what not. For example, the doctrine held at the outset that money must be abolished for most purposes is now seen to be erroneous, there being nothing inconsistent with the essence of Communism in continuing to use money as an instrument of distribution and calculation. The government has also come round to the view that it is wiser to combine a policy of limited toleration with intermittent teasing and harrying towards (for example) the old intelligentsia who have stuck to their country, towards private traders, and even towards foreign capitalists, rather than to attempt to crush out these elements altogether—trusting on the one hand to the complete control of the educational machine and the upbringing of the young, and on the other hand to the gradual improvement of the technique of state trading and to the growth of state capital, to dispense with these pagan auxiliaries in course of time. Thus almost all the members of the non-Communist intelligentsia with pre-war educations are now in the service of the government, often in important and responsible posts with relatively high salaries; private trade is again lawful, though precarious and difficult; and foreign capitalists, who grant short-period trade credits against government imports into Russia, can reckon for the present with some certainty, in my opinion, that they will see their money back in due course. The fluctuating pursuits of these expediencies make it difficult to generalise about anything in Soviet Russia. Almost everything one can say about the country is true and false at the same time—which is the reason why friendly and hostile critics can each in good faith produce totally different pictures of the same thing.

A further difficulty in estimating the efficiency of the economic system is caused by the hard material conditions attending its earlier years, which would have tried severely any economic system. The material losses and disorganisation of the Great War were followed by those of a succession of civil wars, by outlawry from the rest of the world, and by several bad harvests. The bad harvests were partly due to bad management as well as to bad luck. Nevertheless the Soviet experimentalists can fairly claim, I think, that at least five years of peace and fair weather must elapse before they can be judged merely by results.

If one is to make any generalisation in present conditions, it must be this—that at a low level of efficiency the system does function and possesses elements of permanence. I estimate the truth about the economic condition of Russia in its present phase to be roughly as follows.

Russia is now a country of about 140 million inhabitants, of whom six-sevenths are rural and agricultural in their life and one-seventh is urban and industrial. The urban and industrial population, which is what the casual visitor sees, is not self-supporting—it lives, that is to say, at a standard of life which is higher than its output justifies. This excess expenditure on the part of the town population is covered by the exploitation of the peasant, which is only practicable because the town population is a numerically small proportion of the whole country. Thus the Communist government is able to pamper (comparatively speaking) the proletarian worker, who is of course its especial care, by exploiting the peasant; whilst the peasant, in spite of this exploitation, desires no change of government, because he has been given his land. In this way a certain equilibrium has been established both in the economic sphere and in the political, which gives the Soviet government a breathing space in which to try its hand at a serious economic reorganisation.

The official method of exploiting the peasants is not so much by taxation—though the land tax is an important item in the budget—as by price policy. The monopoly of import and export trade and the virtual control of industrial output enable the authorities to maintain relative prices at levels highly disadvantageous to the peasant. They buy his wheat from him much below the world price, and they sell to him textile and other manufactured goods appreciably above the world price,[1] the difference providing a fund out of which can be financed their high overhead costs and the general inefficiency of manufacture and distribution. The monopoly of import and export trade, by permitting a divorce between the internal and external price levels, can be operated in such a way as to maintain the parity of foreign exchange in spite of a depreciation in the purchasing power of the money. The real value of the rouble inside Russia is, admittedly, much depreciated compared with its external value as measured by the current exchange.

These devices, though effective for their purpose at present, and perhaps inevitable for a time, involve two disastrous factors of inefficiency. The low value of agricultural products in terms of industrial products is a serious deterrent to the output of the former, which is the real wealth of the country. The fundamental problem of the Soviet government is to get itself into a sufficiently strong financial position to be able to pay the peasant more nearly the real value of his produce—which would surely have the effect of giving him both the means and the incentive to a far higher output. Meanwhile, the pampering of the proletarian workers of the towns, whose real incomes are

[1] The National Commissariat for Inland Trade for Northern Caucasia reported in September that the peasantry were refraining from offering as much corn as they could because of the unfavourable position with regard to manufactured goods. Peasants were declaring that 'grain prices were good but the costs of wearing apparel incredible'. The Commissariat considered that the peasants should obtain about three yards of cloth for a pood (36 lb.) of grain, whereas in fact they receive less than a yard.

something like double those of the peasants, and are said to have reached, allowing for everything, nearly 80 per cent of their pre-war level, renders town life far too attractive in comparison with country life. The stimulus to migration from the country to the town is much greater than is justified by the power of industry, with its impaired equipment and deficiency of working capital, to absorb new workers. Nothing would stop the migration, if it were not for the housing difficulties and the lack of employment now offering in the towns—a peasant arriving at Moscow is notified at the station that he can find neither work nor lodging. But these deterrents are only effective after the towns have become overcrowded and unemployment has reached unheard-of proportions. For two years unemployment has been severe and increasing, and I believe that by now from 20 to 25 per cent of the industrial workers of Russia are unemployed—say 1,500,000 men out of a total of 6,000,000. Some but not all of these men receive from their trade a dole representing about a third of their normal wages, which, even so, is not much inferior to the working income of the poorer peasants, with the result that this vast army of unemployed is a heavy burden on the financial resources of the state establishments. This condition of affairs serves but to enforce a lesson of bourgeois economics as being equally applicable in a Communist state, namely, that it impairs wealth to interfere with the normal levels of relative prices or with the normal levels of relative wages so as to make some occupations unduly attractive as compared with others. But it also teaches that similar evils can arise in totally different conditions from totally different causes; for the Russian problem of relative wages and relative prices out-of-gear is partly the same as ours.

Thus the real income of the Russian peasant is not much more than half what it used to be, whilst the Russian industrial worker suffers overcrowding and unemployment as never before. Nevertheless, there is, beyond doubt, a certain measure of political and economic stability. The Soviet state is *not* so inefficient as to be unable to survive. It has lived through much worse times than the present. It has established an organisation, covering all the activities of economic life, which is inefficient on normal standards, but which has been evolved out of chaos and the void, yet does exist and function. It has set up a standard of life, which is low compared with ours, but which has been evolved out of starvation and death, yet does provide some comforts. Everyone agrees that the improvement in the last year is enormous. This year's harvest is tolerably good. Conditions are manifestly on the up-grade. Some of the grandiose schemes of the new régime are beginning to take actual shape. Leningrad will soon be supplied with power and light from one of the largest and most modern generating stations in the world. The plant-breeding establishments, which are to supply the peasant with better seeds on the latest Mendelian lines, are extensive and well-equipped. §

After a long debate with Zinovieff [President of the Executive of the Communist International—*Ed*], two Communist ironsides who attended him stepped forward to speak to me a last word with the full faith of fanaticism in their eyes. 'We make you a prophecy,' they said. 'Ten years hence the level of life in Russia will be higher than it was before the war, and in the rest of Europe it will be lower than it was before the war.' Having regard to the natural wealth of Russia and to the inefficiency of the old régime, having regard also to the problems of Western Europe and our apparent inability to handle them, can we feel confident that the comrades will not prove right?

III COMMUNISM'S POWER TO SURVIVE

§My third question is not yet answered.§ Can Communism in the course of time, with sufficient dilution and added impurity, catch the multitude?

I cannot answer what only time will show. But I feel confident of one conclusion—that if Communism achieves a certain success, it will achieve it, not as an improved economic technique, but as a religion. The tendency of our conventional criticisms is to make two opposed mistakes. We hate Communism so much, regarded as a religion, that we exaggerate its economic inefficiency; and we are so much impressed by its economic inefficiency that we under-estimate it as a religion.

On the economic side I cannot perceive that Russian Communism has made any contribution to our economic problems of intellectual interest or scientific value. I do not think that it contains, or is likely to contain, any piece of useful economic technique which we could not apply, if we chose, with equal or greater success in a society which retained all the marks, I will not say of nineteenth-century individualistic capitalism, but of British bourgeois ideals. Theoretically at least, I do not believe that there is any economic improvement for which revolution is a necessary instrument. On the other hand, we have everything to lose by the methods of violent change. In Western industrial conditions the tactics of Red revolution would throw the whole population into a pit of poverty and death.

But as a religion what are its forces? Perhaps they are considerable. The exaltation of the common man is a dogma which has caught the multitude before now. *Any* religion and the bond which unites co-religionists have power against the egotistic atomism of the irreligious.

For modern capitalism is absolutely irreligious, without internal union, without much public spirit, often, though not always, a mere congeries of possessors and pursuers. Such a system has to be immensely, not merely moderately, successful to survive. In the nineteenth century it was in a certain sense idealistic; at any rate it was a united and self-confident system. It was not only immensely successful, but held out hopes of a continuing crescendo of prospective successes. Today it is only moderately successful. If irreligious capitalism is ultimately to defeat religious Communism it is not enough that it should be economically more efficient—it must be many times as efficient.

We used to believe that modern capitalism was capable, not merely of maintaining the existing standards of life, but of leading us gradually into an economic paradise where we should be comparatively free from economic cares. Now we doubt whether the business man is leading us to a destination far better than our present place. Regarded as a means he is tolerable; regarded as an end he is not so satisfactory. One begins to wonder whether the material advantages of keeping business and religion in different compartments are sufficient to balance the moral disadvantages. The Protestant and Puritan could separate them comfortably because the first activity pertained to earth and the second to heaven, which was elsewhere. The believer in progress could separate them comfortably because he regarded the first as the means to the establishment of heaven upon earth hereafter. But there is a third state of mind, in which we do not fully believe either in a heaven which is elsewhere or in progress as a sure means towards a heaven upon earth hereafter; and if heaven is not elsewhere and not hereafter, it must be here and now or not at all. If there is no moral objective in economic progress, then it follows that we must not sacrifice, even for a day, moral to material advantage— in other words, that we may no longer keep business and religion in separate compartments of the soul. In so far as a man's thoughts are capable of straying along these paths, he will be ready to search with curiosity for something at the heart of Communism quite different from the picture of its outward parts which our press paints.

At any rate to me it seems clearer every day that the moral problem of our age is concerned with the love of money, with the habitual appeal to the money motive in nine-tenths of the activities of life, with the universal striving after individual economic security as the prime object of endeavour, with the social approbation of money as the measure of constructive success, and with the social appeal to the hoarding instinct as the foundation of the necessary provision for the family and for the future. The decaying religions around us, which have less and less interest for most people unless it be as an agreeable form of magical ceremonial or of social observance, have lost their moral significance just because—unlike some of their earlier versions—they do not touch in the least degree on these essential matters. A revolution in our ways of thinking and feeling about money may become the growing purpose of contemporary embodiments of the ideal. Perhaps, therefore, Russian Communism does represent the first confused stirrings of a great religion.

The visitor to Russia from the outside, who tries without prejudice to catch the atmosphere, must alternate, I think, between two moods—oppression and elation. Sir Martin Conway, in his true and sincere volume on *Art Treasures in Soviet Russia*, writes thus of his departure out of the country:

After a very long halt the train moved on about half a mile to the Finnish frontier, where passports, visas, and luggage were again examined much less meticulously. The station was new built, a pleasant place, simple, clean, and convenient, and served with much courtesy. It has a charming refreshment room, where simple but nicely cooked food was supplied in an atmosphere of hospitality.

It seems a churlish thing for me to say, after all the kindness shown to me in Russia, but if I am to tell the whole truth I must here put on record that in this frontier station of Finland I experienced a sense as of the removal of a great weight which had been oppressing me. I cannot explain just how this weight had been felt. I did not experience the imposition of it on entering Russia, but as the days passed it seemed slowly to accumulate. The sense of freedom gradually disappeared. Though everyone was kind one felt the presence of an oppression, not on oneself, but all-pervading. Never have I felt so completely a stranger in a strange land; with successive days what at first was a dim feeling took more definite shape and condensed into an ever-increasingly conscious oppression. I imagine one might have passed through the same experience in the Russia of the Tsars. Americans often praise what they call the 'air of liberty' which they claim as characteristic of their country. They possess it in common with all the English-speaking Dominions. The moral atmosphere of Russia is a very different compound of emotional chemistry.

The part of Finland through which our train now bore us was not different in physical character from the lands across the frontier, but we found ourselves passing 'nice little properties' and the signs of comfort and even prosperity...

The mood of oppression could not be better conveyed. In part, no doubt, it is the fruit of Red revolution—there is much in Russia to make one pray that one's own country may achieve its goal not in that way. In part, perhaps, it is the fruit of some beastliness in the Russian nature—or in the Russian and Jewish natures when, as now, they are allied together. But in part it is one face of the superb earnestness of Red Russia, of the high seriousness, which in its other aspect appears as the spirit of elation. There never was anyone so *serious* as the Russian of the revolution, serious even in his gaiety and abandon of spirit —so serious that sometimes he can forget tomorrow and sometimes he can forget today. Often this seriousness is crude and stupid and boring in the extreme. The average Communist is *discoloured* just as the Methodists of every age have been. The tenseness of the atmosphere is more than one is used to support, and a longing comes for the frivolous ease of London.

Yet the elation, when that is felt, is very great. Here—one feels at moments—in spite of poverty, stupidity, and oppression, is the laboratory of life. Here the chemicals are being mixed in new combinations, and stink and explode. Something —there is just a chance—might come out. And even a chance gives to what is happening in Russia more importance than what is happening (let us say) in the United States of America.

I think that it is partly reasonable to be afraid of Russia, like the gentlemen who write to *The Times*. But if Russia is going to be a force in the outside world, it will not be the result of Mr Zinovieff's money. Russia will never matter seriously to the rest of us, unless it be as a moral force. So, now the deeds are done and there is no going back, I should like to give

Russia her chance; to help and not to hinder. For how much rather, even after allowing for everything, if I were a Russian, would I contribute my quota of activity to Soviet Russia than to Tsarist Russia! I could not subscribe to the new official faith any more than to the old. I should detest the actions of the new tyrants not less than those of the old. But I should feel that my eyes were turned towards, and no longer away from, the possibilities of things; that out of the cruelty and stupidity of Old Russia nothing could ever emerge, but that beneath the cruelty and stupidity of New Russia some speck of the ideal may lie hid.

2 THE END OF LAISSEZ-FAIRE

This essay, which was published as a pamphlet by the Hogarth Press in July 1926, was based on the Sidney Ball Lecture given by Keynes at Oxford in November 1924 and a lecture given by him at the University of Berlin in June 1926. Chapters IV and V were used in *Essays in Persuasion*.

§1

The disposition towards public affairs, which we conveniently sum up as individualism and *laissez-faire*, drew its sustenance from many different rivulets of thought and springs of feeling. For more than a hundred years our philosophers ruled us because, by a miracle, they nearly all agreed or seemed to agree on this one thing. We do not dance even yet to a new tune. But a change is in the air. We hear but indistinctly what were once the clearest and most distinguishable voices which have ever instructed political mankind. The orchestra of diverse instruments, the chorus of articulate sound, is receding at last into the distance.

At the end of the seventeenth century the divine right of monarchs gave place to natural liberty and to the compact, and the divine right of the church to the principle of toleration, and to the view that a church is 'a voluntary society of men', coming together, in a way which is 'absolutely free and spontaneous'.[1] Fifty years later the divine origin and absolute voice of duty gave place to the calculations of utility. In the hands of Locke and Hume these doctrines founded Individualism. The compact presumed rights in the individual; the new ethics, being no more than a scientific study of the consequences of rational self-love, placed the individual at the centre. 'The sole trouble Virtue demands', said Hume, 'is that of just Calculation, and a steady preference of the greater Happiness.'[2] These ideas

[1] Locke, *A Letter Concerning Toleration.*
[2] *An Enquiry Concerning the Principles of Morals*, section LX.

accorded with the practical notions of conservatives and of lawyers. They furnished a satisfactory intellectual foundation to the rights of property and to the liberty of the individual in possession to do what he liked with himself and with his own. This was one of the contributions of the eighteenth century to the air we still breathe.

The purpose of promoting the individual was to depose the monarch and the church; the effect—through the new ethical significance attributed to contract—was to buttress property and prescription. But it was not long before the claims of society raised themselves anew against the individual. Paley and Bentham accepted utilitarian hedonism[1] from the hands of Hume and his predecessors, but enlarged it into social utility. Rousseau took the Social Contract from Locke and drew out of it the General Will. In each case the transition was made by virtue of the new emphasis laid on equality. 'Locke applies his Social Contract to modify the natural equality of mankind, so far as that phrase implies equality of property or even of privilege, in consideration of general security. In Rousseau's version equality is not only the starting-point but the goal.'[2]

Paley and Bentham reached the same destination, but by different routes. Paley avoided an egoistic conclusion to his hedonism by a God from the machine. 'Virtue', he says, 'is the doing good to mankind, in obedience to the will of God, and for the sake of everlasting happiness'—in this way bringing back *I* and *others* to a parity. Bentham reached the same result by pure reason. There is no rational ground, he argued, for preferring the happiness of one individual, even oneself, to that of any other. Hence the greatest happiness of the greatest number is the sole rational object of conduct—taking utility

---

[1] 'I omit', says Archdeacon Paley, 'much usual declamation upon the dignity and capacity of our nature, the superiority of the soul to the body, of the rational to the animal part of our constitution; upon the worthiness, refinement, and delicacy of some satisfactions, and the meanness, grossness, and sensuality of others: because I hold that pleasures differ in nothing but in continuance and intensity' (*Principles of Moral and Political Philosophy*, Bk I, chap. 6).

[2] Leslie Stephen, *English Thought in the Eighteenth Century*, II, 192.

from Hume, but forgetting that sage man's cynical corollary: ''Tis not contrary to reason to prefer the destruction of the whole world to the scratching of my finger. 'Tis not contrary to reason for me to choose my total ruin to prevent the least uneasiness of an Indian, or person totally unknown to me... Reason is and ought only to be the slave of the passions, and can never pretend to any other office than to serve and obey them.'

Rousseau derived equality from the state of nature, Paley from the will of God, Bentham from a mathematical law of indifference. Equality and altruism had thus entered political philosophy, and from Rousseau and Bentham in conjunction sprang both democracy and utilitarian socialism.

This is the second current—sprang from long-dead controversies, and carried on its way by long-exploded sophistries—which still permeates our atmosphere of thought. But it did not drive out the former current. It mixed with it. The early nineteenth century performed the miraculous union. It harmonised the conservative individualism of Locke, Hume, Johnson, and Burke with the socialism and democratic egalitarianism of Rousseau, Paley, Bentham, and Godwin.[1]

Nevertheless, that age would have been hard put to it to achieve this harmony of opposites if it had not been for the *economists*, who sprang into prominence just at the right moment. The idea of a divine harmony between private advantage and the public good is already apparent in Paley. But it was the economists who gave the notion a good scientific basis. Suppose that by the working of natural laws individuals pursuing their own interests with enlightenment in conditions of freedom always tend to promote the general interest at the same time! Our philosophical difficulties are resolved—at least for the

---

[1] Godwin carried *laissez-faire* so far that he thought *all* government an evil, in which Bentham almost agreed with him. The doctrine of equality becomes with him one of extreme individualism, verging on anarchy. 'The universal exercise of private judgement', he says, 'is a doctrine so unspeakably beautiful that the true politician will certainly feel infinite reluctance in admitting the idea of interfering with it' (see Leslie Stephen, *op. cit.* II, 277).

practical man, who can then concentrate his efforts on securing the necessary conditions of freedom. To the philosophical doctrine that government has no right to interfere, and the divine that it has no need to interfere, there is added a scientific proof that its interference is inexpedient. This is the third current of thought, just discoverable in Adam Smith, who was ready in the main to allow the public good to rest on 'the natural effort of every individual to better his own condition', but not fully and self-consciously developed until the nineteenth century begins. The principle of *laissez-faire* had arrived to harmonise individualism and socialism, and to make at one Hume's egoism with the greatest good of the greatest number. The political philosopher could retire in favour of the business man—for the latter could attain the philosopher's *summum bonum* by just pursuing his own private profit.

Yet some other ingredients were needed to complete the pudding. First the corruption and incompetence of eighteenth-century government, many legacies of which survived into the nineteenth. The individualism of the political philosophers pointed to *laissez-faire*. The divine or scientific harmony (as the case might be) between private interest and public advantage pointed to *laissez-faire*. But above all, the ineptitude of public administrators strongly prejudiced the practical man in favour of *laissez-faire*—a sentiment which has by no means disappeared. Almost everything which the State did in the eighteenth century in excess of its minimum functions was, or seemed, injurious or unsuccessful.

On the other hand, material progress between 1750 and 1850 came from individual initiative, and owed almost nothing to the directive influence of organised society as a whole. Thus practical experience reinforced *a priori* reasonings. The philosophers and the economists told us that for sundry deep reasons unfettered private enterprise would promote the greatest good of the whole. What could suit the business man better? And could a practical observer, looking about him, deny that the blessings of improvement which distinguished the age he lived in were traceable to the activities of individuals 'on the make'? Thus the ground was fertile for a doctrine that, whether on divine, natural, or scientific grounds, state action should be narrowly confined and economic life left, unregulated so far as may be, to the skill and good sense of individual citizens actuated by the admirable motive of trying to get on in the world.

By the time that the influence of Paley and his like was waning, the innovations of Darwin were shaking the foundations of belief. Nothing could seem more opposed than the old doctrine and the new—the doctrine which looked on the world as the work of the divine watchmaker and the doctrine which seemed to draw all things out of Chance, Chaos, and Old Time. But at this one point the new ideas bolstered up the old. The economists were teaching that wealth, commerce, and machinery were the children of free competition—that free competition built London. But the Darwinians could go one better than that —free competition had built man. The human eye was no longer the demonstration of design, miraculously contriving all things for the best; it was the supreme achievement of chance, operating under conditions of free competition and *laissez-faire*. The principle of the survival of the fittest could be regarded as a vast generalisation of the Ricardian economics. Socialistic interferences became, in the light of this grander synthesis, not merely inexpedient, but impious, as calculated to retard the onward movement of the mighty process by which we ourselves had risen like Aphrodite out of the primeval slime of ocean.

Therefore I trace the peculiar unity of the everyday political philosophy of the nineteenth century to the success with which it harmonised diversified and warring schools and united all good things to a single end. Hume and Paley, Burke and Rousseau, Godwin and Malthus, Cobbett and Huskisson, Bentham and Coleridge, Darwin and the Bishop of Oxford, were all, it was discovered, preaching practically the same thing

—individualism and *laissez-faire*. This was the Church of England and those her apostles, whilst the company of the economists were there to prove that the least deviation into impiety involved financial ruin.

These reasons and this atmosphere are the explanations, whether we know it or not—and most of us in these degenerate days are largely ignorant in the matter—why we feel such a strong bias in favour of *laissez-faire*, and why state action to regulate the value of money, or the course of investment, or the population, provokes such passionate suspicions in many upright breasts. We have not read these authors; we should consider their arguments preposterous if they were to fall into our hands. Nevertheless we should not, I fancy, think as we do, if Hobbes, Locke, Hume, Rousseau, Paley, Adam Smith, Bentham, and Miss Martineau had not thought and written as they did. A study of the history of opinion is a necessary preliminary to the emancipation of the mind. I do not know which makes a man more conservative—to know nothing but the present, or nothing but the past.

II

I have said that it was the economists who furnished the scientific pretext by which the practical man could solve the contradiction between egoism and socialism which emerged out of the philosophising of the eighteenth century and the decay of revealed religion. But having said this for shortness' sake, I hasten to qualify it. This is what the economists are *supposed* to have said. No such doctrine is really to be found in the writings of the greatest authorities. It is what the popularisers and the vulgarisers said. It is what the Utilitarians, who admitted Hume's egoism and Bentham's egalitarianism at the same time, were *driven* to believe in, if they were to effect a synthesis.[1] The language of the

---

[1] One can sympathise with the view of Coleridge, as summarised by Leslie Stephen, that 'the Utilitarians destroyed every element of cohesion, made Society a struggle of selfish interests, and struck at the very roots of all order, patriotism, poetry, and religion'.

economists lent itself to the *laissez-faire* interpretation. But the popularity of the doctrine must be laid at the door of the political philosophers of the day, whom it happened to suit, rather than of the political economists.

The maxim *laissez-nous faire* is traditionally attributed to the merchant Legendre addressing Colbert some time towards the end of the seventeenth century.[1] But there is no doubt that the first writer to use the phrase, and to use it in clear association with the doctrine, is the Marquis d'Argenson about 1751.[2] The Marquis was the first man to wax passionate on the economic advantages of governments leaving trade alone. To govern better, he said, one must govern less.[3] The true cause of the decline of our manufactures, he declared, is the protection we have given to them.[4] 'Laissez faire, telle devrait être la devise de toute puissance publique, depuis que le monde est civilisé.' 'Detestable principe que celui de ne vouloir grandeur que par l'abaissement de nos voisins! Il n'y a que la méchanceté et la malignité du cœur de satisfaites dans ce principe, et l'intérêt y est opposé. Laissez faire, morbleu! Laissez faire!!'

Here we have the economic doctrine of *laissez-faire*, with its most fervent expression in free trade, fully clothed. The phrases and the idea must have passed current in Paris from that time on. But they were slow to establish themselves in literature; and the tradition associating with them the physiocrats, and particularly de Gournay and Quesnay, finds little support in the writings of this school, though they were, of course, proponents of the essential harmony of social and

---

[1] 'Que faut-il faire pour vous aider?' asked Colbert. 'Nous laisser faire', answered Legendre.

[2] For the history of the phrase, see Oncken, 'Die Maxime Laissez faire et laissez passer', from whom most of the following quotations are taken. The claims of the Marquis d'Argenson were overlooked until Oncken put them forward, partly because the relevant passages published during his lifetime were anonymous (*Journal Œconomique*, 1751), and partly because his works were not published in full (though probably passed privately from hand to hand during his lifetime) until 1858 (*Mémoires et Journal inédit du Marquis d'Argenson*).

[3] 'Pour gouverner mieux, il faudrait gouverner moins.'

[4] 'On ne peut dire autant de nos fabriques: la vraie cause de leur declin, c'est la protection outrée qu'on leur accorde.'

individual interests. The phrase *laissez-faire* is not to be found in the works of Adam Smith, of Ricardo, or of Malthus. Even the idea is not present in a dogmatic form in any of these authors. Adam Smith, of course, was a Free Trader and an opponent of many eighteenth-century restrictions on trade. But his attitude towards the Navigation Acts and the usury laws shows that he was not dogmatic. Even his famous passage about 'the invisible hand' reflects the philosophy which we associate with Paley rather than the economic dogma of *laissez-faire*. As Sidgwick and Cliff Leslie have pointed out, Adam Smith's advocacy of the 'obvious and simple system of natural liberty' is derived from his theistic and optimistic view of the order of the world, as set forth in his *Theory of Moral Sentiments*, rather than from any proposition of political economy proper.[1] The phrase *laissez-faire* was, I think, first brought into popular usage in England by a well-known passage of Dr Franklin's.[2] It is not, indeed, until we come to the later works of Bentham—who was not an economist at all—that we discover the rule of *laissez-faire*, in the shape in which our grandfathers knew it, adopted into the service of the Utilitarian philosophy. For example, in *A Manual of Political Economy*,[3] he writes: 'The general rule is that nothing ought to be done or attempted by government; the motto or watchword of government, on these occasions, ought to be—*Be quiet*...The request which agriculture, manufacturers, and commerce present to governments is as modest and reasonable as that which Diogenes made to Alexander: Stand out of my sunshine.'

From this time on it was the political campaign for free trade, the influence of the so-called Manchester School and of the Benthamite Utilitarians, the utterances of secondary economic authorities, and the education stories of Miss Martineau and Mrs Marcet, that fixed *laissez-faire* in the popular mind as the

[1] Sidgwick, *Principles of Political Economy*, p. 20.
[2] Bentham uses the expression '*laissez-nous faire*' (*Works*, p. 440).
[3] Written in 1793, a chapter published in the *Bibliothèque Britannique* in 1798, and the whole first printed in Bowring's edition of this *Works* (1843).

practical conclusion of orthodox political economy—with this great difference, that the Malthusian view of population having been accepted in the meantime by this same school of thought, the optimistic *laissez-faire* of the last half of the eighteenth century gives place to the pessimistic *laissez-faire* of the first half of the nineteenth century.[1]

In Mrs Marcet's *Conversations on Political Economy* (1817) Caroline stands out as long as she can in favour of controlling the expenditure of the rich. But by page 418 she has to admit defeat:

CAROLINE. The more I learn upon this subject, the more I feel convinced that the interests of nations, as well as those of individuals, so far from being opposed to each other, are in the most perfect unison.

MRS B. Liberal and enlarged views will always lead to similar conclusions, and teach us to cherish sentiments of universal benevolence towards each other; hence the superiority of science over mere practical knowledge.

By 1850 the *Easy Lessons for the Use of Young People*, by Archbishop Whately, which the Society for Promoting Christian Knowledge was distributing wholesale, do not admit even of those doubts which Mrs B. allowed Caroline occasionally to entertain. 'More harm than good is likely to be done', the little book concludes, 'by almost any interference of Government with men's money transactions, whether letting and leasing, or buying and selling of any kind.' *True* liberty is 'that every man should be left free to dispose of his own property, his own time, and strength, and skill, in whatever way he himself may think fit, provided he does no wrong to his neighbours'.

In short, the dogma had got hold of the educational machine; it had become a copybook maxim. The political philosophy, which the seventeenth and eighteenth centuries had forged in order to throw down kings and prelates, had been made milk for babes, and had literally entered the nursery.

[1] Cf. Sidgwick, *op. cit.* p. 22: 'Even those economists, who adhered in the main to Adam Smith's limitations of the sphere of government, enforced these limitations sadly rather than triumphantly; not as admirers of the social order at present resulting from "natural liberty", but as convinced that it is at least preferable to any artificial order that government might be able to substitute for it.'

Finally, in the works of Bastiat we reach the most extravagant and rhapsodical expression of the political economist's religion. In his *Harmonies Économiques*,

> I undertake [he says] to demonstrate the Harmony of those laws of Providence which govern human society. What makes these laws harmonious and not discordant is, that all principles, all motives, all springs of action, all interests, co-operate towards a grand final result...And that result is, the indefinite approximation of all classes towards a level, which is always rising; in other words, the *equalisation* of individuals in the general *amelioration*.

And when, like other priests, he drafts his *Credo*, it runs as follows:

> I believe that He who has arranged the material universe has not withheld His regard from the arrangements of the social world. I believe that He has combined and caused to move in harmony free agents as well as inert molecules...I believe that the invincible social tendency is a constant approximation of men towards a common moral, intellectual, and physical level, with, at the same time, a progressive and indefinite elevation of that level. I believe that all that is necessary to the gradual and peaceful development of humanity is that its tendencies should not be disturbed, nor have the liberty of their movements destroyed.

From the time of John Stuart Mill, economists of authority have been in strong reaction against all such ideas. 'Scarcely a single English economist of repute', as Professor Cannan has expressed it, 'will join in a frontal attack upon Socialism in general,' though, as he also adds, 'nearly every economist, whether of repute or not, is always ready to pick holes in most socialistic proposals'.[1] Economists no longer have any link with the theological or political philosophies out of which the dogma of social harmony was born, and their scientific analysis leads them to no such conclusions.

Cairnes, in the introductory lecture on 'Political Economy and *Laissez-faire*', which he delivered at University College, London, in 1870, was perhaps the first orthodox economist to

[1] *Theories of Production and Distribution*, p. 494.

deliver a frontal attack upon *laissez-faire* in general. 'The maxim of *laissez-faire*', he declared, 'has no scientific basis whatever, but is at best a mere handy rule of practice.'[1] This, for fifty years past, has been the view of all leading economists. Some of the most important work of Alfred Marshall—to take one instance—was directed to the elucidation of the leading cases in which private interest and social interest are *not* harmonious. Nevertheless, the guarded and undogmatic attitude of the best economists has not prevailed against the general opinion that an individualistic *laissez-faire* is both what they ought to teach and what in fact they do teach.

III

Economists, like other scientists, have chosen the hypothesis from which they set out, and which they offer to beginners, because it is the simplest, and not because it is the nearest to the facts. Partly for this reason, but partly, I admit, because they have been biased by the traditions of the subject, they have begun by assuming a state of affairs where the ideal distribution of productive resources can be brought about through individuals acting independently by the method of trial and error in such a way that those individuals who move in the right direction will destroy by competition those who move in the wrong direction. This implies that there must be no mercy or protection for those who embark their capital or their labour in the wrong direction. It is a method of bringing the most successful profit-makers to the top by a ruthless struggle for survival, which selects the most efficient by the

[1] Cairnes well described the 'prevailing notion' in the following passage from the same lecture: 'The prevailing notion is that P.E. undertakes to show that wealth may be most rapidly accumulated and most fairly distributed; that is to say, that human well-being may be most effectually promoted, by the simple process of leaving people to themselves; leaving individuals, that is to say, to follow the promptings of self-interest, unrestrained either by State or by the public opinion, so long as they abstain from force and fraud. This is the doctrine commonly known as *laissez-faire*; and accordingly political economy is, I think, very generally regarded as a sort of scientific rendering of this maxim—a vindication of freedom of individual enterprise and of contract as the one and sufficient solution of all industrial problems.'

bankruptcy of the less efficient. It does not count the cost of the struggle, but looks only to the benefits of the final result which are assumed to be permanent. The object of life being to crop the leaves off the branches up to the greatest possible height, the likeliest way of achieving this end is to leave the giraffes with the longest necks to starve out those whose necks are shorter.

Corresponding to this method of attaining the ideal distribution of the instruments of production between different purposes, there is a similar assumption as to how to attain the ideal distribution of what is available for consumption. In the first place, each individual will discover what amongst the possible objects of consumption *he* wants most by the method of trial and error 'at the margin', and in this way not only will each consumer come to distribute his consumption most advantageously, but each object of consumption will find its way into the mouth of the consumer whose relish for it is greatest compared with that of the others, because that consumer will outbid the rest. Thus, if only we leave the giraffes to themselves, (1) the maximum quantity of leaves will be cropped because the giraffes with the longest necks will, by dint of starving out the others, get nearest to the trees; (2) each giraffe will make for the leaves which he finds most succulent amongst those in reach; and (3) the giraffes whose relish for a given leaf is greatest will crane most to reach it. In this way more and juicier leaves will be swallowed, and each individual leaf will reach the throat which thinks it deserves most effort.

This assumption, however, of conditions where unhindered natural selection leads to progress, is only one of the two provisional assumptions which, taken as literal truth, have become the twin buttresses of *laissez-faire*. The other one is the efficacy, and indeed the necessity, of the opportunity for unlimited private money-making as an *incentive* to maximum effort. Profit accrues, under *laissez-faire*, to the individual who, whether by skill or good fortune, is found with his productive resources in the right place at the right time. A system which allows the skilful or fortunate individual to reap the whole fruits of this conjuncture evidently offers an immense incentive to the practice of the art of being in the right place at the right time. Thus one of the most powerful of human motives, namely, the love of money, is harnessed to the task of distributing economic resources in the way best calculated to increase wealth.

The parallelism between economic *laissez-faire* and Darwinianism, already briefly noted, is now seen, as Herbert Spencer was foremost to recognise, to be very close indeed. Just as Darwin invoked sexual love, acting through sexual selection, as an adjutant to natural selection by competition, to direct evolution along lines which should be desirable as well as effective, so the individualist invokes the love of money, acting through the pursuit of profit, as an adjutant to natural selection, to bring about the production on the greatest possible scale of what is most strongly desired as measured by exchange value.

The beauty and the simplicity of such a theory are so great that it is easy to forget that it follows not from the actual facts, but from an incomplete hypothesis introduced for the sake of simplicity. Apart from other objections to be mentioned later, the conclusion that individuals acting independently for their own advantage will produce the greatest aggregate of wealth, depends on a variety of unreal assumptions to the effect that the processes of production and consumption are in no way organic, that there exists a sufficient foreknowledge of conditions and requirements, and that there are adequate opportunities of obtaining this foreknowledge. For economists generally reserve for a later stage of their argument the complications which arise—(1) when the efficient units of production are large relatively to the units of consumption, (2) when overhead costs or joint costs are present, (3) when internal economies tend to the aggregation of production, (4) when the time required for adjustments is long, (5) when ignorance prevails over knowledge, and (6) when monopolies and combinations interfere with equality in bargaining—they reserve, that is to say, for a later stage their analysis of the actual facts. Moreover, many of those who recognise that the simplified hypothesis does not accurately correspond to fact conclude nevertheless that it does represent what is 'natural' and therefore ideal. They regard the simplified hypothesis as health, and the further complications as disease.

Yet besides this question of fact there are other considerations, familiar enough, which rightly bring into the calculation the cost and character of the competitive struggle itself, and the tendency for wealth to be distributed where it is not appreciated most. If we have the welfare of the giraffes at heart, we must not overlook the sufferings of the shorter necks who are starved out, or the sweet leaves which fall to the ground and are trampled underfoot in the struggle, or the overfeeding of the long-necked ones, or the evil look of anxiety or struggling greediness which overcasts the mild faces of the herd.

But the principles of *laissez-faire* have had other allies besides economic textbooks. It must be admitted that they have been confirmed in the minds of sound thinkers and the reasonable public by the poor quality of the opponent proposals—protectionism on one hand, and Marxian socialism on the other. Yet these doctrines are both characterised, not only or chiefly by their infringing the general presumption in favour of *laissez-faire*, but by mere logical fallacy. Both are examples of poor thinking, of inability to analyse a process and follow it out to its conclusion. The arguments against them, though reinforced by the principle of *laissez-faire*, do not strictly require it. Of the two, protectionism is at least plausible, and the forces making for its popularity are nothing to wonder at. But Marxian socialism must always remain a portent to the historians of opinion—how a doctrine so illogical and so dull can have exercised so powerful and enduring an influence over the minds of men and, through them, the events of history. At any rate, the obvious scientific deficiencies of these two schools greatly contributed to the prestige and authority of nineteenth-century *laissez-faire*.

Nor has the most notable divergence into centralised social action on a great scale—the conduct of the late war—encouraged reformers or dispelled old-fashioned prejudices. There is much to be said, it is true, on both sides. War experience in the organisation of socialised production has left some near observers optimistically anxious to repeat it in peace conditions. War socialism unquestionably achieved a production of wealth on a scale far greater than we ever knew in peace, for though the goods and services delivered were destined for immediate and fruitless extinction, none the less they were wealth. Nevertheless, the dissipation of effort was also prodigious, and the atmosphere of waste and not counting the cost was disgusting to any thrifty or provident spirit.

Finally, individualism and *laissez-faire* could not, in spite of their deep roots in the political and moral philosophies of the late eighteenth and early nineteenth centuries, have secured their lasting hold over the conduct of public affairs, if it had not been for their conformity with the needs and wishes of the business world of the day. They gave full scope to our erstwhile heroes, the great business men. 'At least one-half of the best ability in the Western world', Marshall used to say, 'is engaged in business.' A great part of 'the higher imagination' of the age was thus employed. It was on the activities of these men that our hopes of progress were centred.

Men of this class [Marshall wrote][1] live in constantly shifting visions, fashioned in their own brains, of various routes to their desired end; of the difficulties which Nature will oppose to them on each route, and of the contrivances by which they hope to get the better of her opposition. This imagination gains little credit with the people, because it is not allowed to run riot; its strength is disciplined by a stronger will; and its highest glory is to have attained great ends by means so simple that no one will know, and none but experts will even guess, how a dozen other expedients,

[1] 'The Social Possibilities of Economic Chivalry', *Economic Journal*, XVII (1907), 9.

each suggesting as much brilliancy to the hasty observer, were set aside in favour of it. The imagination of such a man is employed, like that of the master chess-player, in forecasting the obstacles which may be opposed to the successful issue of his far-reaching projects, and constantly rejecting brilliant suggestions because he has pictured to himself the counter-strokes to them. His strong nervous force is at the opposite extreme of human nature from that nervous irresponsibility which conceives hasty Utopian schemes, and which is rather to be compared to the bold facility of a weak player, who will speedily solve the most difficult chess problem by taking on himself to move the black men as well as the white.

This is a fine picture of the great captain of industry, the master-individualist, who serves us in serving himself, just as any other artist does. Yet this one, in his turn, is becoming a tarnished idol. We grow more doubtful whether it is he who will lead us into paradise by the hand.

These many elements have contributed to the current intellectual bias, the mental make-up, the orthodoxy of the day. The compelling force of many of the original reasons has disappeared but, as usual, the vitality of the conclusions outlasts them. To suggest social action for the public good to the City of London is like discussing the *Origin of Species* with a bishop sixty years ago. The first reaction is not intellectual, but moral. An orthodoxy is in question, and the more persuasive the arguments the graver the offence. Nevertheless, venturing into the den of the lethargic monster, at any rate I have traced his claims and pedigree so as to show that he has ruled over us rather by hereditary right than by personal merit.

IV§

Let us clear from the ground the metaphysical or general principles upon which, from time to time, *laissez-faire* has been founded. It is *not* true that individuals possess a prescriptive 'natural liberty' in their economic activities. There is *no* 'compact' conferring perpetual rights on those who Have or on those who Acquire. The world is *not* so governed from above that private and social interest always coincide. It is *not* so managed here below that in practice they coincide. It is *not* a correct deduction from the principles of economics that enlightened self-interest always operates in the public interest. Nor is it true that self-interest generally *is* enlightened; more often individuals acting separately to promote their own ends are too ignorant or too weak to attain even these. Experience does *not* show that individuals, when they make up a social unit, are always less clear-sighted than when they act separately.

We cannot therefore settle on abstract grounds, but must handle on its merits in detail what Burke termed 'one of the finest problems in legislation, namely, to determine what the State ought to take upon itself to direct by the public wisdom, and what it ought to leave, with as little interference as possible, to individual exertion'.[1] We have to discriminate between what Bentham, in his forgotten but useful nomenclature, used to term *Agenda* and *Non-Agenda*, and to do this without Bentham's prior presumption that interference is, at the same time, 'generally needless' and 'generally pernicious'.[2] Perhaps the chief task of economists at this hour is to distinguish afresh the *Agenda* of government from the *Non-Agenda*; and the companion task of politics is to devise forms of government within a democracy which shall be capable of accomplishing the *Agenda*. I will illustrate what I have in mind by two examples.

(1) I believe that in many cases the ideal size for the unit of control and organisation lies somewhere between the individual and the modern State. I suggest, therefore, that progress lies in the growth and the recognition of semi-autonomous bodies within the State—bodies whose criterion of action within their own field is solely the public good as they understand it, and from whose deliberations motives of private advantage are excluded, though some place it may still be necessary to leave, until the ambit of men's altruism grows wider, to the separate

§ [1] Quoted by McCulloch in his *Principles of Political Economy*. §
[2] Bentham's *Manual of Political Economy*, published posthumously, in Bowring's edition (1843).

advantage of particular groups, classes, or faculties—bodies which in the ordinary course of affairs are mainly autonomous within their prescribed limitations, but are subject in the last resort to the sovereignty of the democracy expressed through Parliament.

I propose a return, it may be said, towards medieval conceptions of separate autonomies. But, in England at any rate, corporations are a mode of government which has never ceased to be important and is sympathetic to our institutions. It is easy to give examples, from what already exists, of separate autonomies which have attained or are approaching the mode I designate—the universities, the Bank of England, the Port of London Authority, even perhaps the railway companies. In Germany there are doubtless analogous instances.

But more interesting than these is the trend of joint stock institutions, when they have reached a certain age and size, to approximate to the status of public corporations rather than that of individualistic private enterprise. One of the most interesting and unnoticed developments of recent decades has been the tendency of big enterprise to socialise itself. A point arrives in the growth of a big institution—particularly a big railway or big public utility enterprise, but also a big bank or a big insurance company—at which the owners of the capital, i.e. the shareholders, are almost entirely dissociated from the management, with the result that the direct personal interest of the latter in the making of great profit becomes quite secondary. When this stage is reached, the general stability and reputation of the institution are the more considered by the management than the maximum of profit for the shareholders. The shareholders must be satisfied by conventionally adequate dividends; but once this is secured, the direct interest of the management often consists in avoiding criticism from the public and from the customers of the concern. This is particularly the case if their great size or semi-monopolistic position renders them conspicuous in the public eye and vulnerable to public attack. The extreme instance, perhaps, of this tendency in the case of an institution, theoretically the unrestricted property of private persons, is the Bank of England. It is almost true to say that there is no class of persons in the kingdom of whom the Governor of the Bank of England thinks less when he decides on his policy than of his shareholders. Their rights, in excess of their conventional dividend, have already sunk to the neighbourhood of zero. But the same thing is partly true of many other big institutions. They are, as time goes on, socialising themselves.

Not that this is unmixed gain. The same causes promote conservatism and a waning of enterprise. In fact, we already have in these cases many of the faults as well as the advantages of State Socialism. Nevertheless, we see here, I think, a natural line of evolution. The battle of Socialism against unlimited private profit is being won in detail hour by hour. In these particular fields—it remains acute elsewhere—this is no longer the pressing problem. There is, for instance, no so-called important political question so really unimportant, so irrelevant to the reorganisation of the economic life of Great Britain, as the nationalisation of the railways.

It is true that many big undertakings, particularly public utility enterprises and other business requiring a large fixed capital, still need to be semi-socialised. But we must keep our minds flexible regarding the forms of this semi-socialism. We must take full advantage of the natural tendencies of the day, and we must probably prefer semi-autonomous corporations to organs of the central government for which ministers of State are directly responsible.

I criticise doctrinaire State Socialism, not because it seeks to engage men's altruistic impulses in the service of society, or because it departs from *laissez-faire*, or because it takes away from man's natural liberty to make a million, or because it has courage for bold experiments. All these things I applaud. I criticise it because it misses the significance of what is actually happening; because it is, in fact, little better than a dusty survival of a plan to meet the problems of fifty years ago, based on a misunderstanding of what someone said a hundred years ago. Nineteenth-century State Socialism sprang from Bentham, free competition, etc., and is in some respects a clearer, in some respects a more muddled version of just the same philosophy as underlies nineteenth-century individualism. Both equally laid all their stress on freedom, the one negatively to avoid limitations on existing freedom, the other positively to destroy natural or acquired monopolies. They are different reactions to the same intellectual atmosphere.

(2) I come next to a criterion of *Agenda* which is particularly relevant to what it is urgent and desirable to do in the near future. We must aim at separating those services which are *technically social* from those which are *technically individual*. The most important *Agenda* of the State relate not to those activities which private individuals are already fulfilling, but to those functions which fall outside the sphere of the individual, to those decisions which are made by *no one* if the State does not make them. The important thing for government is not to do things which individuals are doing already, and to do them a little better or a little worse; but to do those things which at present are not done at all.

It is not within the scope of my purpose on this occasion to develop practical policies. I limit myself, therefore, to naming some instances of what I mean from amongst those problems about which I happen to have thought most.

Many of the greatest economic evils of our time are the fruits of risk, uncertainty, and ignorance. It is because particular individuals, fortunate in situation or in abilities, are able to take advantage of uncertainty and ignorance, and also because for the same reason big business is often a lottery, that great inequalities of wealth come about; and these same factors are also the cause of the unemployment of labour, or the disappointment of reasonable business expectations, and of the impairment of efficiency and production. Yet the cure lies outside the operations of individuals; it may even be to the interest of individuals to aggravate the disease. I believe that the cure for these things is partly to be sought in the deliberate control of the currency and of credit by a central institution, and partly in the collection and dissemination on a great scale of data relating to the business situation, including the full publicity, by law if necessary, of all business facts which it is useful to know. These measures would involve society in exercising directive intelligence through some appropriate organ of action over many of the inner intricacies of private business, yet it would leave private initiative and enterprise unhindered. Even if these measures prove insufficient, nevertheless, they will furnish us with better knowledge than we have now for taking the next step.

My second example relates to savings and investment. I believe that some coordinated act of intelligent judgement is required as to the scale on which it is desirable that the community as a whole should save, the scale on which these savings should go abroad in the form of foreign investments, and whether the present organisation of the investment market distributes savings along the most nationally productive channels. I do not think that these matters should be left entirely to the chances of private judgement and private profits, as they are at present.

My third example concerns population. The time has already come when each country needs a considered national policy about what size of population, whether larger or smaller than at present or the same, is most expedient. And having settled this policy, we must take steps to carry it into operation. The time may arrive a little later when the community as a whole must pay attention to the innate quality as well as to the mere numbers of its future members.

VI[1]

These reflections have been directed towards possible improvements in the technique of modern capitalism by the agency of

[1] The chapter number did not appear, of course, in the original edition of *Essays in Persuasion*—Ed.

collective action. There is nothing in them which is seriously incompatible with what seems to me to be the essential characteristic of capitalism, namely the dependence upon an intense appeal to the money-making and money-loving instincts of individuals as the main motive force of the economic machine. Nor must I, so near to my end, stray towards other fields. Nevertheless, I may do well to remind you, in conclusion, that the fiercest contests and the most deeply felt divisions of opinion are likely to be waged in the coming years not round technical questions, where the arguments on either side are mainly economic, but round those which, for want of better words, may be called psychological or, perhaps, moral.

In Europe, or at least in some parts of Europe—but not, I think, in the United States of America—there is a latent reaction, somewhat widespread, against basing society to the extent that we do upon fostering, encouraging, and protecting the money-motives of individuals. A preference for arranging our affairs in such a way as to appeal to the money-motive as little as possible, rather than as much as possible, need not be entirely *a priori*, but may be based on the comparison of experiences. Different persons, according to their choice of profession, find the money-motive playing a large or a small part in their daily lives, and historians can tell us about other phases of social organisation in which this motive has played a much smaller part than it does now. Most religions and most philosophies deprecate, to say the least of it, a way of life mainly influenced by considerations of personal money profit. On the other hand, most men today reject ascetic notions and do not doubt the real advantages of wealth. Moreover, it seems obvious to them that one cannot do without the money-motive, and that, apart from certain admitted abuses, it does its job well. In the result the average man averts his attention from the problem, and has no clear idea what he really thinks and feels about the whole confounded matter.

Confusion of thought and feeling leads to confusion of speech.

Many people, who are really objecting to capitalism as a way of life, argue as though they were objecting to it on the ground of its inefficiency in attaining its own objects. Contrariwise, devotees of capitalism are often unduly conservative, and reject reforms in its technique, which might really strengthen and preserve it, for fear that they may prove to be first steps away from capitalism itself. Nevertheless, a time may be coming when we shall get clearer than at present as to when we are talking about capitalism as an efficient or inefficient technique, and when we are talking about it as desirable or objectionable in itself. For my part I think that capitalism, wisely managed, can probably be made more efficient for attaining economic ends than any alternative system yet in sight, but that in itself it is in many ways extremely objectionable. Our problem is to work out a social organisation which shall be as efficient as possible without offending our notions of a satisfactory way of life.

The next step forward must come, not from political agitation or premature experiments, but from thought. We need by an effort of the mind to elucidate our own feelings. At present our sympathy and our judgement are liable to be on different sides, which is a painful and paralysing state of mind. In the field of action reformers will not be successful until they can steadily pursue a clear and definite object with their intellects and their feelings in tune. There is no party in the world at present which appears to me to be pursuing right aims by right methods. Material poverty provides the incentive to change precisely in situations where there is very little margin for experiments. Material prosperity removes the incentive just when it might be safe to take a chance. Europe lacks the means, America the will, to make a move. We need a new set of convictions which spring naturally from a candid examination of our own inner feelings in relation to the outside facts.

3   AM I A LIBERAL?

'Am I a Liberal?' was first given as an address to the Liberal Summer
School which met at Cambridge in August 1925. It was then published
as two articles in the *Nation and Athenaeum*, 8 and 15 August 1925.

The published version varies only slightly from the typescript of the
original speech, with the exception of one interesting omission in which
Keynes elaborates on the theme of his real objection to the Labour Party.
The paragraphs in question occur after the sentence ending...the *class
war will find me on the side of the educated bourgeoisie'*. In his speech to
the Liberal Summer School Keynes continued:

But this is not the fundamental difficulty. I am ready to
sacrifice my local patriotisms to an important general
purpose. What is the real repulsion which keeps me away
from Labour?

I cannot explain it without beginning to approach my
fundamental position. I believe that in the future, more
than ever, questions about the economic framework of
society will be far and away the most important of political
issues. I believe that the right solution will involve intellectual and scientific elements which must be above the
heads of the vast mass of more or less illiterate voters.
Now, in a democracy, every party alike has to depend on
this mass of ill-understanding voters, and no party will
attain power unless it can win the confidence of these
voters by persuading them in a general way either that it
intends to promote their interests or that it intends to gratify
their passions. Nevertheless there are differences between
the several parties in the degree to which the party machine
is democratised through and through and the preparation
of the party programme democratised in its details. In this
respect the Conservative Party is in much the best position.
The inner ring of the party can almost dictate the details
and the technique of policy. Traditionally the management

of the Liberal Party was also sufficiently autocratic. Recently there have been ill-advised [this word was pencilled through —*Ed.*] movements in the direction of democratising the details of the party programme. This has been a reaction against a weak and divided leadership, for which, in fact, there is no remedy except strong and united leadership. With strong leadership the technique, as distinguished from the main principles, of policy could still be dictated above. The Labour Party, on the other hand, is in a far weaker position. I do not believe that the intellectual elements in the party will ever exercise adequate control...

I

If one is born a political animal, it is most uncomfortable not to belong to a party; cold and lonely and futile it is. If your party is strong, and its programme and its philosophy sympathetic, satisfying the gregarious, practical, and intellectual instincts all at the same time, how very agreeable that must be!—worth a large subscription and all one's spare time—that is, if you are a political animal.

So the political animal who cannot bring himself to utter the contemptible words, 'I am no party man', would almost rather belong to any party than to none. If he cannot find a home by the principle of attraction, he must find one by the principle of repulsion and go to those whom he dislikes least, rather than stay out in the cold.

Now take my own case—where am I landed on this negative test? How could I bring myself to be a Conservative? They offer me neither food nor drink—neither intellectual nor spiritual consolation. I should not be amused or excited or edified. That which is common to the atmosphere, the mentality, the view of life of—well, I will not mention names—promotes neither my self-interest nor the public good. It leads nowhere; it satisfies no ideal; it conforms to no intellectual standard; it is not even safe, or calculated to preserve from spoilers that degree of civilisation which we have already attained.

Ought I, then, to join the Labour Party? Superficially that is more attractive. But looked at closer, there are great difficulties. To begin with, it is a class party, and the class is not my class. If I am going to pursue sectional interests at all, I shall pursue my own. When it comes to the class struggle as such, my local and personal patriotisms, like those of every one else, except certain unpleasant zealous ones, are attached to my own surroundings. I can be influenced by what seems to me to be justice and good sense; but the *class* war will find me on the side of the educated *bourgeoisie*.

But, above all, I do not believe that the intellectual elements in the Labour Party will ever exercise adequate control; too much will always be decided by those who do not know *at all* what they are talking about; and if—which is not unlikely— the control of the party is seized by an autocratic inner ring, this control will be exercised in the interests of the extreme left wing—the section of the Labour Party which I shall designate the party of catastrophe.

On the negative test, I incline to believe that the Liberal Party is still the best instrument of future progress—if only it had strong leadership and the right programme.

But when we come to consider the problem of party positively —by reference to what attracts rather than to what repels—the aspect is dismal in every party alike, whether we put our hopes in measures or in men. And the reason is the same in each case. The historic party questions of the nineteenth century are as dead as last week's mutton; and whilst the questions of the future are looming up, they have not yet become party questions, and they cut across the old party lines.

Civil and religious liberty, the franchise, the Irish question, Dominion self-government, the power of the House of Lords, steeply graduated taxation of incomes and of fortunes, the lavish use of the public revenues for 'social reform', that it to say, social insurance for sickness, unemployment and old age, education, housing and public health—all these causes for which the Liberal Party fought are successfully achieved or are obsolete or are the common ground of all parties alike. What remains? Some will say—the land question. Not I—for I believe that this question, in its traditional form, has now become, by reason of a silent change in the facts, of very slight political importance. I see only two planks of the historic Liberal platform still seaworthy—the drink question and free trade. And of these two free trade survives, as a great and living political issue, by an accident. There were always two arguments for free trade— the *laissez-faire* argument which appealed and still appeals to the Liberal individualists, and the economic argument based on the benefits which flow from each country's employing its resources where it has a comparative advantage. I no longer believe in the political philosophy which the doctrine of free trade adorned. I believe in free trade because, in the long run and in general, it is the only policy which is technically sound and intellectually tight.

But take it at the best, can the Liberal Party sustain itself on the land question, the drink question, and free trade alone, even if it were to reach a united and clear-cut programme on the two former? The *positive* argument for being a Liberal, is at present, very weak. How do the other parties survive the positive test?

The Conservative Party will always have its place as a diehard home. But constructively, it is in just as bad case as the Liberal Party. It is often no more than an accident of temperament or of past associations, and not a real difference of policy or of ideals, which now separates the progressive young Conservative from the average Liberal. The old battle-cries are muffled or silent. The Church, the aristocracy, the landed interests, the rights of property, the glories of empire, the pride of the services, even beer and whisky, will never again be the guiding forces of British politics.

The Conservative Party ought to be concerning itself with evolving a version of individualistic capitalism adapted to the progressive change of circumstances. The difficulty is that the capitalist leaders in the City and in Parliament are incapable of distinguishing novel measures for safeguarding capitalism from what they call Bolshevism. If old-fashioned capitalism was intellectually capable of defending itself, it would not be dislodged for many generations. But, fortunately for Socialists, there is little chance of this.

I believe that the seeds of the intellectual decay of individualist capitalism are to be found in an institution which is not in the least characteristic of itself, but which it took over from the social system of feudalism which preceded it—namely, the hereditary principle. The hereditary principle in the transmission of wealth and the control of business is the reason why the leadership of the capitalist cause is weak and stupid. It is too much dominated by third-generation men. Nothing will cause a social institution to decay with more certainty than its attach-ment to the hereditary principle. It is an illustration of this that by far the oldest of our institutions, the Church, is the one which has always kept itself free from the hereditary taint.

Just as the Conservative Party will always have its diehard wing, so the Labour Party will always be flanked by the Party of Catastrophe—Jacobins, Communists, Bolshevists, whatever you choose to call them. This is the party which hates or despises existing institutions and believes that great good will result merely from overthrowing them—or at least that to overthrow them is the necessary preliminary to any great good. This party can only flourish in an atmosphere of social oppression or as a reaction against the Rule of Die-Hard. In Great Britain it is, in its extreme form, numerically very weak. Nevertheless its philosophy in a diluted form permeates, in my opinion, the whole Labour Party. However moderate its leaders may be at heart, the Labour Party will always depend for electoral success on making some slight appeal to the widespread passions and

jealousies which find their full development in the Party of
Catastrophe. I believe that this secret sympathy with the Policy
of Catastrophe is the worm which gnaws at the seaworthiness
of any constructive vessel which the Labour Party may launch.
The passions of malignity, jealousy, hatred of those who have
wealth and power (even in their own body), ill consort with
ideals to build up a true social republic. Yet it is necessary for
a successful Labour leader to be, or at least to appear, a little
savage. It is not enough that he should love his fellow-men; he
must hate them too.

What then do I want Liberalism to be? On the one side,
Conservatism is a well-defined entity—with a right of diehards,
to give it strength and passion, and a left of what one may call
'the best type' of educated, humane, Conservative free traders,
to lend it moral and intellectual respectability. On the other
side, Labour is also well defined—with a left of catastrophists,
to give it strength and passion, and a right of what one may call
'the best type' of educated, humane, socialistic reformers, to lend it
moral and intellectual respectability. Is there room for any thing
between? Should not each of us here decide whether we consider
ourselves to be 'the best type' of Conservative free traders or
'the best type' of socialistic reformers, and have done with it?

Perhaps that is how we shall end. But I still think that there
is room for a party which shall be disinterested as between
classes, and which shall be free in building the future both from
the influences of diehardism and from those of catastrophism,
which will spoil the constructions of each of the others. Let me
sketch out in the briefest terms what I conceive to be the
philosophy and practice of such a party.

To begin with, it must emancipate itself from the dead wood
of the past. In my opinion there is now no place, except in the
left wing of the Conservative Party, for those whose hearts are
set on old-fashioned individualism and *laissez-faire* in all their
rigour—greatly though these contributed to the success of the
nineteenth century. I say this, not because I think that these

doctrines were wrong in the conditions which gave birth to them (I hope that I should have belonged to this party if I had been born a hundred years earlier), but because they have ceased to be applicable to modern conditions. Our programme must deal not with the historic issues of Liberalism, but with those matters—whether or not they have already become party questions—which are of living interest and urgent importance today. We must take risks of unpopularity and derision. *Then* our meetings will draw crowds and our body be infused with strength.

II

I divide the questions of today into five headings: (1) peace questions; (2) questions of government; (3) sex questions; (4) drug questions; (5) economic questions.

On peace questions let us be pacifist to the utmost. As regards the empire, I do not think that there is any important problem except in India. Elsewhere, so far as problems of government are concerned, the process of friendly disintegration is now almost complete—to the great benefit of all. But as regards pacifism and armaments we are only just at the beginning. I should like to take risks in the interests of peace, just as in the past we have taken risks in the interests of war. But I do not want these risks to assume the form of an undertaking to make war in various hypothetical circumstances. I am against pacts. To pledge the whole of our armed forces to defend disarmed Germany against an attack by France in the plenitude of the latter's military power is foolish; and to assume that we shall take part in every future war in western Europe is unnecessary. But I am in favour of giving a very good example, even at the risk of being weak, in the direction of arbitration and of disarmament.

I turn next to questions of government—a dull but important matter. I believe that in the future the government will have to take on many duties which it has avoided in the past. For these purposes Ministers and Parliament will be unserviceable. Our task must be to decentralise and devolve wherever we can, and in particular to establish semi-independent corporations and organs of administration to which duties of government, new and old, will be entrusted—without, however, impairing the democratic principle or the ultimate sovereignty of Parliament. These questions will be as important and difficult in the future as the franchise and the relations of the two Houses have been in the past.

The questions which I group together as sex questions have not been party questions in the past. But that was because they were never, or seldom, the subject of public discussion. All this is changed now. There are no subjects about which the big general public is more interested; few which are the subject of wider discussion. They are of the utmost social importance; they cannot help but provoke real and sincere differences of opinion. Some of them are deeply involved in the solution of certain economic questions. I cannot doubt that sex questions are about to enter the political arena. The very crude beginnings represented by the suffrage movement were only symptoms of deeper and more important issues below the surface.

Birth control and the use of contraceptives, marriage laws, the treatment of sexual offences and abnormalities, the economic position of women, the economic position of the family—in all these matters the existing state of the law and of orthodoxy is still medieval—altogether out of touch with civilised opinion and civilised practice and with what individuals, educated and uneducated alike, say to one another in private. Let no one deceive himself with the idea that the change of opinion on these matters is one which only affects a small educated class on the crust of the human boiling. Let no one suppose that it is the working women who are going to be shocked by ideas of birth control or of divorce reform. For them these things suggest new liberty, emancipation from the most intolerable of tyrannies. A party which would discuss these things openly and wisely at its meetings would discover a new and living interest in the electorate—because politics would be dealing once more with matters about which everyone wants to know and which deeply affect everyone's own life.

These questions also interlock with economic issues which cannot be evaded. Birth control touches on one side the liberties of women, and on the other side the duty of the State to concern itself with the size of the population just as much as with the size of the army or the amount of the budget. The position of wage-earning women and the project of the family wage affect not only the status of women, the first in the performance of paid work, and the second in the performance of unpaid work, but also raise the whole question whether wages should be fixed by the forces of supply and demand in accordance with the orthodox theories of *laissez-faire*, or whether we should begin to limit the freedom of those forces by reference to what is 'fair' and 'reasonable' having regard to all the circumstances.

Drug questions in this country are practically limited to the drink question; though I should like to include gambling under this head. I expect that the prohibition of alcoholic spirits and of bookmakers would do good. But this would not settle the matter. How far is bored and suffering humanity to be allowed, from time to time, an escape, an excitement, a stimulus, a possibility of change?—that is the important problem. Is it possible to allow reasonable licence, permitted saturnalia, sanctified carnival, in conditions which need ruin neither the health nor the pockets of the roisterers, and will shelter from irresistible temptation the unhappy class who, in America, are called addicts?

I must not stay for an answer, but must hasten to the largest of all political questions, which are also those on which I am most qualified to speak—the economic questions.

An eminent American economist, Professor Commons, who has been one of the first to recognise the nature of the economic transition amidst the early stages of which we are now living, distinguishes three epochs, three economic orders, upon the third of which we are entering.

The first is the era of scarcity ,'whether due to inefficiency or to violence, war, custom, or superstition'. In such a period 'there is the minimum of individual liberty and the maximum of communistic, feudalistic or governmental control through physical coercion'. This was, with brief intervals in exceptional cases, the normal economic state of the world up to (say) the fifteenth or sixteenth century.

Next comes the era of abundance. 'In a period of extreme abundance there is the maximum of individual liberty, the minimum of coercive control through government, and individual bargaining takes the place of rationing.' During the seventeenth and eighteenth centuries we fought our way out of the bondage of scarcity into the free air of abundance, and in the nineteenth century this epoch culminated gloriously in the victories of *laissez-faire* and historic Liberalism. It is not surprising or discreditable that the veterans of the party cast backward glances on that easier age.

But we are now entering on a third era, which Professor Commons calls the period of stabilisation, and truly characterises as 'the actual alternative to Marx's communism'. In this period, he says, 'there is a diminution of individual liberty, enforced in part by governmental sanctions, but mainly by economic sanctions through concerted action, whether secret, semi-open, open, or arbitrational, of associations, corporations, unions, and other collective movements of manufacturers, merchants, labourers, farmers, and bankers'.

The abuses of this epoch in the realms of government are Fascism on the one side and Bolshevism on the other. Socialism offers no middle course, because it also is sprung from the presuppositions of the era of abundance, just as much as *laissez-faire* individualism and the free play of economic forces, before which latter, almost alone amongst men, the City editors, all bloody and blindfolded, still piteously bow down.

The transition from economic anarchy to a régime which deliberately aims at controlling and directing economic forces in the interests of social justice and social stability, will present enormous difficulties both technical and political. I suggest, nevertheless, that the true destiny of New Liberalism is to seek their solution.

It happens that we have before us today, in the position of the coal industry, an object-lesson of the results of the confusion of ideas which now prevails. On the one side the Treasury and the Bank of England are pursuing an orthodox nineteenth-century policy based on the assumption that economic adjustments can and ought to be brought about by the free play of the forces of supply and demand. The Treasury and the Bank of England still believe—or, at any rate, did until a week or two ago—that the things, which would follow on the assumption of free competition and the mobility of capital and labour, actually occur in the economic life of today.

On the other side, not only the facts, but public opinion also, have moved a long distance away in the direction of Professor Commons' epoch of stabilisation. The trade unions are strong enough to interfere with the free play of the forces of supply and demand, and public opinion, albeit with a grumble and with more than a suspicion that the trade unions are growing dangerous, supports the trade unions in their main contention that coal-miners ought not to be the victims of cruel economic forces which *they* never set in motion.

The idea of the old-world party, that you can, for example, alter the value of money and then leave the consequential adjustments to be brought about by the forces of supply and demand, belongs to the days of fifty or a hundred years ago when trade unions were powerless, and when the economic juggernaut was allowed to crash along the highway of progress without obstruction and even with applause.

Half the copybook wisdom of our statesmen is based on assumptions which were at one time true, or partly true, but are now less and less true day by day. We have to invent new wisdom for a new age. And in the meantime we must, if we are to do any good, appear unorthodox, troublesome, dangerous, disobedient to them that begat us.

In the economic field this means, first of all, that we must find new policies and new instruments to adapt and control the working of economic forces, so that they do not intolerably interfere with contemporary ideas as to what is fit and proper in the interests of social stability and social justice.

It is not an accident that the opening stage of this political struggle, which will last long and take many different forms, should centre about monetary policy. For the most violent interferences with stability and with justice, to which the nineteenth century submitted in due satisfaction of the philosophy of abundance, were precisely those which were brought about by changes in the price level. But the consequences of these changes, particularly when the authorities endeavour to impose them on us in a stronger dose than even the nineteenth century ever swallowed, are intolerable to modern ideas and to modern institutions.

We have changed, by insensible degrees, our philosophy of economic life, our notions of what is reasonable and what is tolerable; and we have done this without changing our technique or our copybook maxims. Hence our tears and troubles.

A party programme must be developed in its details, day by day, under the pressure and the stimulus of actual events; it is useless to define it beforehand, except in the most general terms. But if the Liberal Party is to recover its forces, it must have an attitude, a philosophy, a direction. I have endeavoured to indicate my own attitude to politics, and I leave it to others to answer, in the light of what I have said, the question with which I began —Am I a Liberal?

4 LIBERALISM AND LABOUR

This essay originated as a speech given at the Manchester Reform Club, 9 February 1926, at a time when the numbers of the three parties in the House of Commons caused speculation as to a possible combination of Liberals and Labour against the Conservatives. The address was published as an article entitled 'Liberalism and Labour' in the *Nation and Athenaeum*, 20 February 1926.

§A series of articles by the editor of the *Nation* has brought to the forefront of politics during recent weeks the future relations between the Liberal Party and the Labour Party. So far as the leaders are concerned on either side, we are not yet much enlightened. Nevertheless, Mr Lloyd George has produced the impression that, on terms, he would not decline a working arrangement between the two parties. And Mr Snowden that he, also on terms, would welcome it. Lord Oxford—perhaps wisely—has avoided the issue for the present by occupying his speech with perfervid declarations that no conversations have occurred as yet.

Lord Oxford may be right to suppose that there is no hurry. No hurry, that is, to decide. But nothing is more necessary than that those of us who have no responsibility should speak our minds. It is the urgent subject for discussion wherever Liberals are gathered together.§

I do not wish to live under a Conservative government for the next twenty years. I believe that the progressive forces of the country are hopelessly divided between the Liberal Party and the Labour Party. I do not believe that the Liberal Party will win *one-third* of the seats in the House of Commons in any probable or foreseeable circumstances. Unless in course of time the mistakes of the Conservative government produce an economic catastrophe—which is not impossible—I do not believe that the Labour Party will win *one-half* of the seats in the House of Commons. Yet it is not desirable that the Labour Party should depend for their chances of office on the occurrence of a national misfortune; for this will only strengthen the influence of the Party of Catastrophe which is already an important element in their ranks. As things are now, we have nothing to look forward to except a continuance of Conservative governments, not merely until they have made mistakes in the tolerable degree which would have caused a swing of the pendulum in former days, but until their mistakes have mounted up to the height of a disaster. I do not like this choice of alternatives.

That is the practical political problem which confronts all those, in whichever party they are ranged, who want to see progressive principles put into effect, and believe that too long a delay in doing so may find the country confronted with extreme alternatives.

The conventional retort by Labour orators is to call upon Liberals to close down their own party and to come over. Now it is evident that the virtual extinction of the Liberal Party is a practical possibility to be reckoned with. A time may come when anyone in active politics will have only two choices before him and not three. But I believe that it would be bad politics and bad behaviour to promote this end; and that it is good politics and good behaviour to resist it.

Good politics to resist it, because the progressive cause in the constituencies would be weakened, and not strengthened, by the disappearance of the Liberal Party. There are many sections of the country, and many classes of voters, which for many years to come will never vote Labour in numbers, or with enthusiasm, sufficient for victory; but which will readily vote Liberal as soon as the weather changes. Labour leaders who deny this are not looking at the facts of politics with unclouded eyes.

Good behaviour to resist it, because most present-day active Liberals, whilst ready on occasion to vote Labour and to act with Labour, would not feel comfortable or sincere or in place as full members of the Labour Party. Take my own case. I am sure that I am less conservative in my inclinations than the average Labour voter; I fancy that I have played in my mind with the possibilities of greater social changes than come within the present philosophies of, let us say, Mr Sidney Webb, Mr Thomas, or Mr Wheatley. The republic of my imagination lies on the extreme left of celestial space. Yet—all the same—I feel that my true home, so long as they offer a roof and a floor, is still with the Liberals.

Why, though fallen upon such evil days, does the tradition of Liberalism hold so much attraction? The Labour Party contains three elements. There are the *Trade Unionists*, once the oppressed, now the tyrants, whose selfish and sectional pretensions need to be bravely opposed. There are the advocates of the methods of violence and sudden change, by an abuse of language called *Communists*, who are committed by their creed to produce evil that good may come and, since they dare not concoct disaster openly, are forced to play with plot and subterfuge. There are the *Socialists*, who believe that the economic foundations of modern society are evil, yet might be good.

The company and conversation of this third element, whom I have called Socialists, many Liberals today would not find uncongenial. But we cannot march with them until we know along what path, and towards what goal, they mean to move. I do not believe that their historic creed of State Socialism, and its newer gloss of Guild Socialism, now interest them much more than they interest us. These doctrines no longer inspire anyone. Constructive thinkers in the Labour Party, and constructive thinkers in the Liberal Party, are trying to replace them with something better and more serviceable. The notions on both sides are a bit foggy as yet, but there is much sympathy between them, and a similar tendency of ideas. I believe that the two sections will become more and more friends and colleagues in construction as time goes on. But the progressive Liberal has this great advantage. He can work out his policies without having to do lip-service to trade-unionist tyrannies, to the beauties of the class war, or to doctrinaire State Socialism—in none of which he believes.

In the realm of practical politics, two things must happen —both of which are likely. There must be one more general election to disillusion Labour optimists as to the measure of their political strength standing by themselves. But equally on our side there must be a certain change. The Liberal Party is divided between those who, if the choice be forced upon them, would vote Conservative, and those who, in the same circumstances, would vote Labour. Historically, and on grounds of past service, each section has an equal claim to call itself Liberal. Nevertheless, I think that it would be for the health of the party if all those who believe, with Mr Winston Churchill and Sir Alfred Mond, that the coming political struggle is best described as capitalism *versus* socialism and, thinking in these terms, mean to die in the last ditch for capitalism, were to leave us. The brains and character of the Conservative Party have always been recruited from Liberals, and we must not grudge them the excellent material with which, in accordance with our historic mission, we are now preserving them from intellectual starvation. It is much better that the Conservative Party should be run by honest and intelligent ex-Liberals, who have grown too old and tough for us, than by diehards. Possibly the Liberal Party cannot serve the State in any better way than by supplying Conservative governments with Cabinets, and Labour governments with ideas.

At any rate, I sympathise with Labour in rejecting the idea of co-operation with a party which included, until the other day, Mr Churchill and Sir Alfred Mond, and still contains several of the same kidney. But this difficulty is rapidly solving itself. When it is solved, the relations between Liberalism and Labour, at Westminster and in the constituencies will, without any compacts, bargains, or formalities, become much more nearly what some of us would like them to be.

It is right and proper that the Conservative Party should be recruited from the Liberals of the previous generation. But there is no place in the world for a Liberal Party which is merely the home of out-of-date or watery Labour men. The Liberal Party should be not less progressive than Labour, not less open to new ideas, not behindhand in constructing the new world. I do not believe that Liberalism will ever be a great party machine in the way in which Conservatism and Labour are great party machines. But it may play, nevertheless, the predominant part in moulding the future. Great changes will not be carried out except with the active aid of Labour. But they will not be sound or enduring unless they have first satisfied the criticism and precaution of Liberals. A certain coolness of temper, such as Lord Oxford has, seems to me at the same time peculiarly *Liberal* in flavour, and also a much bolder and more desirable and more valuable political possession and endowment than sentimental ardours.

The political problem of mankind is to combine three things: economic efficiency, social justice, and individual liberty. The first needs criticism, precaution, and technical knowledge; the second, an unselfish and enthusiastic spirit, which loves the ordinary man; the third, tolerance, breadth, appreciation of the excellencies of variety and independence, which prefers, above everything, to give unhindered opportunity to the exceptional and to the aspiring. The second ingredient is the best possession of the great party of the proletariat. But the first and third require the qualities of the party which, by its traditions and ancient sympathies, has been the home of economic individualism and social liberty.

V THE FUTURE

1 CLISSOLD

A review of *The World of William Clissold* by H. G. Wells, which appeared in the *Nation and Athenaeum*, 22 January 1927. This essay was republished in France as part of a collection entitled *Réflexions sur le franc et sur quelques autres sujets* (1928).

Mr Wells and his publisher having adopted an ingenious device by which his newest book[1] has been reviewed three times over, perhaps it is too much to write about it again at this late date. But, having read the reviews first and the book afterwards, I am left seriously discontented with what the professional critics have had to say. It is a weakness of modern critics not to distinguish—not to distinguish between one thing and another. Even Mr Wells's choice of form has confused his reviewers. They fail to see what he is after. They reject the good beef which he has offered the British public, because mutton should never be underdone. Or their delicacies are sharpened against his abundance and omnivorous vitality, the broadness and coarseness of the brush with which he sweeps the great canvas which is to catch the attention of hundreds of thousands of readers and sway their minds onward.

Mr Wells here presents, not precisely his own mind as it has developed on the basis of his personal experience and way of life, but—shifting his angle—a point of view based on an experience mainly different from his own, that of a successful, emancipated, semi-scientific, not particularly highbrow, English business man. The result is not primarily a work of art. Ideas, not forms, are its substance. It is a piece of educational writing—propaganda, if you like, an attempt to convey to the very big public attitudes of mind already partly familiar to the very small public.

The book is an *omnium gatherum*. I will select two emergent themes of a quasi-economic character. Apart from these, the

---

[1] *The World of William Clissold* (3 vols.).

main topic is women and some of their possible relationships in the modern world to themselves and to men of the Clissold type. This is treated with great candour, sympathy, and observation. It leaves, and is meant to leave, a bitter taste.

The first of these themes is a violent protest against conservatism, an insistent emphasis on the necessity and rapidity of change, the folly of looking backwards, the danger of inadaptability. Mr Wells produces a curious sensation, nearly similar to that of some of his earlier romances, by contemplating vast stretches of time backwards and forwards which give an impression of slowness (no need to hurry in eternity), yet accelerating the time machine as he reaches present day, so that *now* we travel at an enormous pace and no longer have millions of years to turn round in. The conservative influences in our life are envisaged as dinosaurs whom literal extinction is awaiting just ahead. The contrast comes from the failure of our ideas, our conventions, our prejudices to keep up with the pace of material change. Our environment moves too much faster than we do. The walls of our travelling compartment are bumping our heads. Unless we hustle, the traffic will run us down. Conservatism is no better than suicide. Woe to our dinosaurs!

This is one aspect. We stand still at our peril. Time flies. But there is another aspect of the same thing—and this is where Clissold comes in. What a bore for the modern man, whose mind in his active career moves with the times, to stand still in his observances and way of life! What a bore are the feasts and celebrations with which London crowns success! What a bore to go through the social contortions which have lost significance and conventional pleasures which no longer please! The contrast between the exuberant, constructive activity of a prince of modern commerce and the lack of an appropriate environment for him out of office hours is acute. Moreover, there are wide stretches in the career of money-making which are entirely barren and non-constructive. There is a fine passage in the first volume about the profound, ultimate boredom of

City men. Clissold's father, the company promoter and speculator, falls first into megalomania and then into fraud, because
he is bored. Let us, therefore, mould with both hands the
plastic material of social life into our own contemporary image.

We do not merely belong to a latter-day age—we are ourselves
in the literal sense older than our ancestors were in the years
of our maturity and our power. Mr Wells brings out strongly
a too-much neglected feature of modern life, that we live
much longer than formerly and, what is more important, prolong
our health and vigour into a period of life which was formerly
one of decay, so that the average man can now look forward
to a duration of activity which hitherto only the exceptional
could anticipate. I can add, indeed, a further fact which Mr Wells
overlooks (I think), likely to emphasise this yet further in the
next fifty years as compared with the last fifty years—namely,
that the average age of a rapidly increasing population is much
less than that of a stationary population. For example, in the
stable conditions to which we may hope to approximate in the
course of the next two generations, we shall somewhat rapidly
approach to a position in which, in proportion to population,
elderly people (say, sixty-five years of age and above) will be
nearly 100 per cent, and middle-aged people (say, forty-five
years of age and above), nearly 50 per cent more numerous than
in the recent past. In the nineteenth century effective power
was in the hands of men probably not less than fifteen years
older on the average than in the sixteenth century; and before
the twentieth century is out the average may have risen another
fifteen years, unless effective means are found, other than
obvious physical or mental decay, to make vacancies at the
top. Clissold (in his sixtieth year, be it noted) sees more advantage
and less disadvantage in this state of affairs than I do. Most
men love money and security more, and creation and construction
less, as they get older; and this process begins long before their
intelligent judgement on detail is apparently impaired. Mr Wells's
preference for an adult world over a juvenile sex-ridden world

may be right. But the margin between this and a middle-aged money-ridden world is a narrow one. We are threatened, at the best, with the appalling problem of the able-bodied 'retired', of which Mr Wells himself gives a sufficient example in his desperate account of the regular denizens of the Riviera.

We are living, then, in an unsatisfactory age of immensely rapid transition in which most, but particularly those in the vanguard, find themselves and their environment ill-adapted to one another, and are for this reason far less happy than their less sophisticated forebears were or their yet more sophisticated descendants need be. This diagnosis, applied by Mr Wells to the case of those engaged in the practical life of action, is essentially the same as Mr Edwin Muir's, in his deeply interesting volume of criticism, *Transition*, to the case of those engaged in the life of art and contemplation. Our foremost writers, according to Mr Muir, are *uncomfortable* in the world—they can neither support nor can they oppose anything with a full confidence, with the result that their work is inferior in relation to their talents compared with work produced in happier ages—jejune, incomplete, starved, anaemic, like their own feelings to the universe.

In short, we cannot stay where we are; we are on the move— on the move, not necessarily either to better or to worse, but just to an equilibrium. But why not to the better? Why should not we begin to reap spiritual fruits from our material conquests? If so, whence is to come the motive power of desirable change? This brings us to Mr Wells's second theme.

Mr Wells describes in the first volume of *Clissold* his hero's disillusionment with Socialism. In the third volume he inquires if there is an alternative. From whence are we to draw the forces which are 'to change the laws, customs, rules, and institutions of the world'? 'From what classes and types are the revolutionaries to be drawn? How are they to be brought into co-operation? What are to be their methods?' The Labour Movement is represented as an immense and dangerous force of destruction, led by sentimentalists and pseudo-intellectuals, who have 'feelings in the place of ideas'. A constructive revolution cannot possibly be contrived by these folk. The creative intellect of mankind is not to be found in these quarters but amongst the scientists and the great modern business men. Unless we can harness to the job this type of mind and character and temperament, it can never be put through—for it is a task of immense practical complexity and intellectual difficulty. We must recruit our revolutionaries, therefore, from the Right, not from the Left. We must persuade the type of man whom it now amuses to create a great business, that there lie waiting for him yet bigger things which will amuse him more. This is Clissold's 'open conspiracy'. Clissold's direction is to the Left—far, far to the Left; but he seeks to summon from the Right the creative force and the constructive will which is to carry him there. He describes himself as being temperamentally and fundamentally a Liberal. But political Liberalism must die 'to be born again with firmer features and a clearer will'.

Clissold is expressing a reaction against the socialist party which very many feel, including socialists. The remoulding of the world needs the touch of the creative Brahma. But at present Brahma is serving science and business, not politics or government. The extreme danger of the world is, in Clissold's words, lest, 'before the creative Brahma can get to work, Śiva, in other words the passionate destructiveness of labour awakening to its now needless limitations and privations, may make Brahma's task impossible'. We all feel this, I think. We know that we need urgently to create a *milieu* in which Brahma can get to work before it is too late. Up to a point, therefore, most active and constructive temperaments in every political camp are ready to join the open conspiracy.

What, then, is it that holds them back? It is here, I think, that *Clissold* is in some way deficient and apparently lacking in insight. Why do practical men find it more amusing to make money than to join the open conspiracy? I suggest that it is much the same reason as that which makes them find it more amusing to play bridge on Sundays than to go to church. They lack altogether the kind of motive, the possession of which, if they had it, could be expressed by saying that they had a creed. They have no creed, these potential open conspirators, no creed whatever. That is why, unless they have the luck to be scientists or artists, they fall back on the grand substitute motive, the perfect *ersatz*, the anodyne for those who, in fact, want nothing at all—money. Clissold charges the enthusiasts of labour that they have 'feelings in the place of ideas'. But he does not deny that they have feelings. Has not, perhaps, poor Mr Cook something which Clissold lacks? Clissold and his brother Dickon, the advertising expert, flutter about the world seeking for something to which they can attach their abundant *libido*. But they have not found it. They would so like to be apostles. But they cannot. They remain business men.

I have taken two themes from a book which contains dozens. They are not all treated equally well. Knowing the universities much better than Mr Wells does, I declare that his account contains no more than the element of truth which is proper to a caricature. He underestimates altogether their possibilities —how they may yet become temples of Brahma which even Śiva will respect. But *Clissold*, taken altogether, is a great achievement, a huge and meaty egg from a glorious hen, an abundant out-pouring of an ingenious, truthful, and generous spirit.

Though we talk about pure art as never before, this is not a good age for pure artists; nor is it a good one for classical perfections. Our most pregnant writers today are full of im-perfections; they expose themselves to judgement; they do not look to be immortal. For these reasons, perhaps, we, their contemporaries, do them and the debt we owe them less than justice. What a debt every intelligent being owes to Bernard Shaw! What a debt also to H. G. Wells, whose mind seems to have grown up alongside his readers', so that, in successive phrases, he has delighted us and guided our imaginations from boyhood to maturity.

2 ECONOMIC POSSIBILITIES FOR OUR GRANDCHILDREN

This essay was first presented in 1928 as a talk to several small societies, including the Essay Society of Winchester College and the Political Economy Club at Cambridge. In June 1930 Keynes expanded his notes into a lecture on 'Economic Possibilities for our Grandchildren' which he gave at Madrid. It appeared in literary form in two instalments in the *Nation and Athenaeum*, 11 and 18 October 1930, in the midst of the slump.

I

We are suffering just now from a bad attack of economic pessimism. It is common to hear people say that the epoch of enormous economic progress which characterised the nineteenth century is over; that the rapid improvement in the standard of life is now going to slow down—at any rate in Great Britain; that a decline in prosperity is more likely than an improvement in the decade which lies ahead of us.

I believe that this is a wildly mistaken interpretation of what is happening to us. We are suffering, not from the rheumatics of old age, but from the growing-pains of over-rapid changes, from the painfulness of readjustment between one economic period and another. The increase of technical efficiency has been taking place faster than we can deal with the problem of labour absorption; the improvement in the standard of life has been a little too quick; the banking and monetary system of the world has been preventing the rate of interest from falling as fast as equilibrium requires. And even so, the waste and confusion which ensue relate to not more than $7\frac{1}{2}$ per cent of the national income; we are muddling away one and sixpence in the £, and have only 18s 6d, when we might, if we were more sensible, have £1; yet, nevertheless, the 18s 6d mounts up to as much as the £1 would have been five or six years ago. We forget that in 1929 the physical output of the industry of Great Britain

321

was greater than ever before, and that the net surplus of our foreign balance available for new foreign investment, after paying for all our imports, was greater last year than that of any other country, being indeed 50 per cent greater than the corresponding surplus of the United States. Or again—if it is to be a matter of comparisons—suppose that we were to reduce our wages by a half, repudiate four-fifths of the national debt, and hoard our surplus wealth in barren gold instead of lending it at 6 per cent or more, we should resemble the now much-envied France. But would it be an improvement?

The prevailing world depression, the enormous anomaly of unemployment in a world full of wants, the disastrous mistakes we have made, blind us to what is going on under the surface—to the true interpretation of the trend of things. For I predict that both of the two opposed errors of pessimism which now make so much noise in the world will be proved wrong in our own time—the pessimism of the revolutionaries who think that things are so bad that nothing can save us but violent change, and the pessimism of the reactionaries who consider the balance of our economic and social life so precarious that we must risk no experiments.

My purpose in this essay, however, is not to examine the present or the near future, but to disembarrass myself of short views and take wings into the future. What can we reasonably expect the level of our economic life to be a hundred years hence? What are the economic possibilities for our grandchildren?

From the earliest times of which we have record—back, say to two thousand years before Christ—down to the beginning of the eighteenth century, there was no very great change in the standard of life of the average man living in the civilised centres of the earth. Ups and downs certainly. Visitations of plague, famine, and war. Golden intervals. But no progressive, violent change. Some periods perhaps 50 per cent better than others—at the utmost 100 per cent better—in the four thousand years which ended (say) in A.D. 1700.

This slow rate of progress, or lack of progress, was due to two reasons—to the remarkable absence of important technical improvements and to the failure of capital to accumulate.

The absence of important technical inventions between the prehistoric age and comparatively modern times is truly remarkable. Almost everything which really matters and which the world possessed at the commencement of the modern age was already known to man at the dawn of history. Language, fire, the same domestic animals which we have today, wheat, barley, the vine and the olive, the plough, the wheel, the oar, the sail, leather, linen and cloth, bricks and pots, gold and silver, copper, tin, and lead—and iron was added to the list before 1000 B.C.—banking, statecraft, mathematics, astronomy, and religion. There is no record of when we first possessed these things.

At some epoch before the dawn of history—perhaps even in one of the comfortable intervals before the last ice age—there must have been an era of progress and invention comparable to that in which we live today. But through the greater part of recorded history there was nothing of the kind.

The modern age opened, I think, with the accumulation of capital which began in the sixteenth century. I believe—for reasons with which I must not encumber the present argument—that this was initially due to the rise of prices, and the profits to which that led, which resulted from the treasure of gold and silver which Spain brought from the New World into the Old. From that time until today the power of accumulation by compound interest, which seems to have been sleeping for many generations, was reborn and renewed its strength. And the power of compound interest over two hundred years is such as to stagger the imagination.

Let me give in illustration of this a sum which I have worked out. The value of Great Britain's foreign investments today is estimated at about £4,000 million. This yields us an income at the rate of about 6½ per cent. Half of this we bring home

323

and enjoy; the other half, namely, 3¼ per cent, we leave to accumulate abroad at compound interest. Something of this sort has now been going on for about 250 years.

For I trace the beginnings of British foreign investment to the treasure which Drake stole from Spain in 1580. In that year he returned to England bringing with him the prodigious spoils of the *Golden Hind*. Queen Elizabeth was a considerable shareholder in the syndicate which had financed the expedition. Out of her share she paid off the whole of England's foreign debt, balanced her budget, and found herself with about £40,000 in hand. This she invested in the Levant Company—which prospered. Out of the profits of the Levant Company, the East India Company was founded; and the profits of this great enterprise were the foundation of England's subsequent foreign investment. Now it happens that £40,000 accumulating at 3¼ per cent compound interest approximately corresponds to the actual volume of England's foreign investments at various dates, and would actually amount today to the total of £4,000 million which I have already quoted as being what our foreign investments now are. Thus, every £1 which Drake brought home in 1580 has now become £100,000. Such is the power of compound interest!

From the sixteenth century, with a cumulative crescendo after the eighteenth, the great age of science and technical inventions began, which since the beginning of the nineteenth century has been in full flood—coal, steam, electricity, petrol, steel, rubber, cotton, the chemical industries, automatic machinery and the methods of mass production, wireless, printing, Newton, Darwin, and Einstein, and thousands of other things and men too famous and familiar to catalogue.

What is the result? In spite of an enormous growth in the population of the world, which it has been necessary to equip with houses and machines, the average standard of life in Europe and the United States has been raised, I think, about fourfold. The growth of capital has been on a scale which is far beyond a hundred-fold of what any previous age had known. And from now on we need not expect so great an increase of population.

If capital increases, say, 2 per cent per annum, the capital equipment of the world will have increased by a half in twenty years, and seven and a half times in a hundred years. Think of this in terms of material things—houses, transport, and the like.

At the same time technical improvements in manufacture and transport have been proceeding at a greater rate in the last ten years than ever before in history. In the United States factory output per head was 40 per cent greater in 1925 than in 1919. In Europe we are held back by temporary obstacles, but even so it is safe to say that technical efficiency is increasing by more than 1 per cent per annum compound. There is evidence that the revolutionary technical changes, which have so far chiefly affected industry, may soon be attacking agriculture. We may be on the eve of improvements in the efficiency of food production as great as those which have already taken place in mining, manufacture, and transport. In quite a few years— in our own lifetimes I mean—we may be able to perform all the operations of agriculture, mining, and manufacture with a quarter of the human effort to which we have been accustomed.

For the moment the very rapidity of these changes is hurting us and bringing difficult problems to solve. Those countries are suffering relatively which are not in the vanguard of progress. We are being afflicted with a new disease of which some readers may not yet have heard the name, but of which they will hear a great deal in the years to come—namely, *technological unemployment*. This means unemployment due to our discovery of means of economising the use of labour outrunning the pace at which we can find new uses for labour.

But this is only a temporary phase of maladjustment. All this means in the long run *that mankind is solving its economic problem.* I would predict that the standard of life in progressive countries one hundred years hence will be between four and eight times as high as it is today. There would be nothing surprising in this even in the light of our present knowledge. It would not be foolish to contemplate the possibility of a far greater progress still.

II

Let us, for the sake of argument, suppose that a hundred years hence we are all of us, on the average, eight times better off in the economic sense than we are today. Assuredly there need be nothing here to surprise us.

Now it is true that the needs of human beings may seem to be insatiable. But they fall into two classes—those needs which are absolute in the sense that we feel them whatever the situation of our fellow human beings may be, and those which are relative in the sense that we feel them only if their satisfaction lifts us above, makes us feel superior to, our fellows. Needs of the second class, those which satisfy the desire for superiority, may indeed be insatiable; for the higher the general level, the higher still are they. But this is not so true of the absolute needs— a point may soon be reached, much sooner perhaps than we all of us are aware of, when these needs are satisfied in the sense that we prefer to devote our further energies to non-economic purposes.

Now for my conclusion, which you will find, I think, to become more and more startling to the imagination the longer you think about it.

I draw the conclusion that, assuming no important wars and no important increase in population, the *economic problem* may be solved, or be at least within sight of solution, within a hundred years. This means that the economic problem is not—if we look into the future—*the permanent problem of the human race.*

Why, you may ask, is this so startling? It is startling because —if, instead of looking into the future, we look into the past— we find that the economic problem, the struggle for subsistence, always has been hitherto the primary, most pressing problem of the human race—not only of the human race, but of the whole of the biological kingdom from the beginnings of life in its most primitive forms.

Thus we have been expressly evolved by nature—with all our impulses and deepest instincts—for the purpose of solving the economic problem. If the economic problem is solved, mankind will be deprived of its traditional purpose.

Will this be a benefit? If one believes at all in the real values of life, the prospect at least opens up the possibility of benefit. Yet I think with dread of the readjustment of the habits and instincts of the ordinary man, bred into him for countless generations, which he may be asked to discard within a few decades.

To use the language of today—must we not expect a general 'nervous breakdown'? We already have a little experience of what I mean—a nervous breakdown of the sort which is already common enough in England and the United States amongst the wives of the well-to-do classes, unfortunate women, many of them, who have been deprived by their wealth of their traditional tasks and occupations—who cannot find it sufficiently amusing, when deprived of the spur of economic necessity, to cook and clean and mend, yet are quite unable to find anything more amusing.

To those who sweat for their daily bread leisure is a longed -for sweet—until they get it.

There is the traditional epitaph written for herself by the old charwoman:

> Don't mourn for me, friends, don't weep for me never,
> For I'm going to do nothing for ever and ever.

This was her heaven. Like others who look forward to leisure, she conceived how nice it would be to spend her time listening-in —for there was another couplet which occurred in her poem:

> With psalms and sweet music the heavens'll be ringing,
> But I shall have nothing to do with the singing.

Yet it will only be for those who have to do with the singing
that life will be tolerable—and how few of us can sing!

Thus for the first time since his creation man will be faced
with his real, his permanent problem—how to use his freedom
from pressing economic cares, how to occupy the leisure, which
science and compound interest will have won for him, to live
wisely and agreeably and well.

The strenuous purposeful money-makers may carry all of us
along with them into the lap of economic abundance. But it
will be those peoples, who can keep alive, and cultivate into
a fuller perfection, the art of life itself and do not sell themselves
for the means of life, who will be able to enjoy the abundance
when it comes.

Yet there is no country and no people, I think, who can look
forward to the age of leisure and of abundance without a dread.
For we have been trained too long to strive and not to enjoy.
It is a fearful problem for the ordinary person, with no special
talents, to occupy himself, especially if he no longer has roots
in the soil or in custom or in the beloved conventions of a traditional society. To judge from the behaviour and the achievements
of the wealthy classes today in any quarter of the world, the
outlook is very depressing! For these are, so to speak, our
advance guard—those who are spying out the promised land
for the rest of us and pitching their camp there. For they have
most of them failed disastrously, so it seems to me—those who
have an independent income but no associations or duties or
ties—to solve the problem which has been set them.

I feel sure that with a little more experience we shall use
the new-found bounty of nature quite differently from the way
in which the rich use it today, and will map out for ourselves
a plan of life quite otherwise than theirs.

For many ages to come the old Adam will be so strong in
us that everybody will need to do *some* work if he is to be
contented. We shall do more things for ourselves than is usual
with the rich today, only too glad to have small duties and

tasks and routines. But beyond this, we shall endeavour to spread the bread thin on the butter—to make what work there is still to be done to be as widely shared as possible. Three-hour shifts or a fifteen-hour week may put off the problem for a great while. For three hours a day is quite enough to satisfy the old Adam in most of us!

There are changes in other spheres too which we must expect to come. When the accumulation of wealth is no longer of high social importance, there will be great changes in the code of morals. We shall be able to rid ourselves of many of the pseudo-moral principles which have hag-ridden us for two hundred years, by which we have exalted some of the most distasteful of human qualities into the position of the highest virtues. We shall be able to afford to dare to assess the money-motive at its true value. The love of money as a possession—as distinguished from the love of money as a means to the enjoyments and realities of life—will be recognised for what it is, a somewhat disgusting morbidity, one of those semi-criminal, semi-pathological propensities which one hands over with a shudder to the specialists in mental disease. All kinds of social customs and economic practices, affecting the distribution of wealth and of economic rewards and penalties, which we now maintain at all costs, however distasteful and unjust they may be in themselves, because they are tremendously useful in promoting the accumulation of capital, we shall then be free, at last, to discard.

Of course there will still be many people with intense, unsatisfied purposiveness who will blindly pursue wealth—unless they can find some plausible substitute. But the rest of us will no longer be under any obligation to applaud and encourage them. For we shall inquire more curiously than is safe today into the true character of this 'purposiveness' with which in varying degrees Nature has endowed almost all of us. For purposiveness means that we are more concerned with the remote future results of our actions than with their own quality or their immediate effects on our own environment. The 'purposive' man is always trying to secure a spurious and delusive immortality for his acts by pushing his interest in them forward into time. He does not love his cat, but his cat's kittens; nor, in truth, the kittens, but only the kittens' kittens, and so on forward for ever to the end of catdom. For him jam is not jam unless it is a case of jam tomorrow and never jam today. Thus by pushing his jam always forward into the future, he strives to secure for his act of boiling it an immortality.

Let me remind you of the Professor in *Sylvie and Bruno*:

'Only the tailor, sir, with your little bill,' said a meek voice outside the door.

'Ah, well, I can soon settle *his* business,' the Professor said to the children, 'if you'll just wait a minute. How much is it, this year, my man?' The tailor had come in while he was speaking.

'Well, it's been a-doubling so many years, you see,' the tailor replied, a little gruffly, 'and I think I'd like the money now. It's two thousand pound, it is!'

'Oh, that's nothing!' the Professor carelessly remarked, feeling in his pocket, as if he always carried at least *that* amount about with him. 'But wouldn't you like to wait just another year and make it *four* thousand? Just think how rich you'd be! Why, you might be a *king*, if you liked!'

'I don't know as I'd care about being a king,' the man said thoughtfully. 'But it *dew* sound a powerful sight o' money! Well, I think I'll wait—'

'Of course you will!' said the Professor. 'There's good sense in *you*, I see. Good-day to you, my man!'

'Will you ever have to pay him that four thousand pounds?' Sylvie asked as the door closed on the departing creditor.

'*Never*, my child!' the Professor replied emphatically. 'He'll go on doubling it till he dies. You see, it's *always* worth while waiting another year to get twice as much money!'

Perhaps it is not an accident that the race which did most to bring the promise of immortality into the heart and essence of our religions has also done most for the principle of compound interest and particularly loves this most purposive of human institutions.

I see us free, therefore, to return to some of the most sure and certain principles of religion and traditional virtue—that avarice is a vice, that the exaction of usury is a misdemeanour, and the love of money is detestable, that those walk most truly in the paths of virtue and sane wisdom who take least thought for the morrow. We shall once more value ends above means and prefer the good to the useful. We shall honour those who can teach us how to pluck the hour and the day virtuously and well, the delightful people who are capable of taking direct enjoyment in things, the lilies of the field who toil not, neither do they spin.

But beware! The time for all this is not yet. For at least another hundred years we must pretend to ourselves and to everyone that fair is foul and foul is fair; for foul is useful and fair is not. Avarice and usury and precaution must be our gods for a little longer still. For only they can lead us out of the tunnel of economic necessity into daylight.

I look forward, therefore, in days not so very remote, to the greatest change which has ever occurred in the material environment of life for human beings in the aggregate. But, of course, it will all happen gradually, not as a catastrophe. Indeed, it has already begun. The course of affairs will simply be that there will be ever larger and larger classes and groups of people from whom problems of economic necessity have been practically removed. The critical difference will be realised when this condition has become so general that the nature of one's duty to one's neighbour is changed. For it will remain reasonable to be economically purposive for others after it has ceased to be reasonable for oneself.

The *pace* at which we can reach our destination of economic bliss will be governed by four things—our power to control population, our determination to avoid wars and civil dissensions, our willingness to entrust to science the direction of those matters which are properly the concern of science, and the rate of accumulation as fixed by the margin between our production and our consumption; of which the last will easily look after itself, given the first three.

Meanwhile, there will be no harm in making mild preparations for our destiny, in encouraging, and experimenting in, the arts of life as well as the activities of purpose.

But, chiefly, do not let us overestimate the importance of the economic problem, or sacrifice to its supposed necessities other matters of greater and more permanent significance. It should be a matter for specialists—like dentistry. If economists could manage to get themselves thought of as humble, competent people, on a level with dentists, that would be splendid!

PART VI
LATER ESSAYS

1 THE MEANS TO PROSPERITY

In March 1933 *The Times* published a series of four articles by Keynes entitled 'The Means to Prosperity'. They provoked wide discussion and were quickly republished in the same month in pamphlet form. In the English edition, two new chapters of introduction and conclusion were added; chapters II, III, IV and V remained substantially the same as when they appeared in *The Times* of 13, 14, 15 and 16 March 1933. In the American edition, which is reprinted here, Keynes added material from his article 'The Multiplier' which appeared in the *New Statesman and Nation* of 1 April 1933 and made several other changes. Because of this extended discussion of the multiplier we have chosen the American edition. Variations between the American and British editions, except in cases of individual words such as 'British' before 'government' in the former, are noted in the text. Keynes's original footnotes in these sections appear in square brackets.

I. THE NATURE OF THE PROBLEM

If our poverty were due to famine or earthquake or war—if we lacked material things and the resources to produce them, we could not expect to find the means to prosperity except in hard work, abstinence, and invention. In fact, our predicament is notoriously of another kind. It comes from some failure in the immaterial devices of the mind, in the working of the motives which should lead to the decisions and acts of will, necessary to put in movement the resources and technical means we already have. It is as though two motor-drivers, meeting in the middle of a highway, were unable to pass one another because neither knows the rule of the road. Their own muscles are no use; a motor engineer cannot help them; a better road would not serve. Nothing is required and nothing will avail, except a little[1] clear thinking.

So, too, our problem is not a human problem of muscles and endurance. It is not an engineering problem or an agricultural problem. It is not even a business problem, if we mean by

[1] The words 'a very little' appear in the English edition at this point.

business those calculations and dispositions and organising acts by which individual entrepreneurs can better themselves. Nor is it a banking problem, if we mean by banking those principles and methods of shrewd judgement by which lasting connections are fostered and unfortunate commitments avoided. On the contrary, it is, in the strictest sense, an economic problem or, to express it better, as suggesting a blend of economic theory with the art of statesmanship, a problem of political economy.

I call attention to the nature of the problem, because it points us to the nature of the remedy. It is appropriate to the case that the remedy should be found in something which can fairly be called a *device*. Yet there are many who are suspicious of devices, and instinctively doubt their efficacy. There are still people who believe that the way out can only be found by hard work, endurance, frugality, improved business methods, more cautious banking and, above all, the avoidance of devices. But the lorries of these people will never, I fear, get by. They may stay up all night, engage more sober chauffeurs, install new engines, and widen the road; yet they will never get by, unless they stop to think and work out with the driver opposite a small device by which each moves simultaneously a little to his left.

It is the existing situation which we should find paradoxical. There is nothing paradoxical in the suggestion that some immaterial adjustment—some change, so to speak, 'on paper'—should be capable of working wonders. The paradox is to be found in 250,000 building operatives out of work in Great Britain, when more houses are our greatest material need. It is the man who tells us that there is no means, consistent with sound finance and political wisdom, of getting the one to work at the other, whose judgement we should instinctively doubt. The calculations which we ought to suspect are those of the statesman who, being already burdened with the support of the unemployed, tells us that it would involve him in heavy liabilities, present and to come, which the country cannot afford, if he

UNAPPRECIATED ACROBATICS.

Cartoon by David Low by arrangement with the Trustees and the London Evening Standard

337

were to set the men to build the houses; and the sanity to be questioned is his, who thinks it more economical and better calculated to increase the national wealth to maintain unemployed shipbuilders, than to spend a fraction of what their maintenance is costing him, in setting them to construct one of the greatest works of man.

When, on the contrary, I show, a little elaborately, as in the ensuing chapter, that to create wealth will increase the national income and that a large proportion of any increase in the national income will accrue to an Exchequer, amongst whose largest outgoings is the payment of incomes to those who are unemployed and whose receipts are a proportion of the incomes of those who are occupied, I hope the reader will feel, whether or not he thinks himself competent to criticise the argument in detail, that the answer is just what he would expect—that it agrees with the instinctive promptings of his common sense.

Nor should the argument seem strange that taxation may be so high as to defeat its object, and that, given sufficient time to gather the fruits, a reduction of taxation will run a better chance than an increase of balancing the budget. For to take the opposite view today is to resemble a manufacturer who, running at a loss, decides to raise his price, and when his declining sales increase the loss, wrapping himself in the rectitude of plain arithmetic, decides that prudence requires him to raise the price still more— and who, when at last his account is balanced with nought on both sides, is still found righteously declaring that it would have been the act of a gambler to reduce the price when you were already making a loss.

At any rate, the time seems ripe for reconsidering the possibilities of action. In this belief I here re-examine the advantages of an active policy, beginning with the domestic affairs of Great Britain and proceeding to the opportunities of the World Conference. This Conference may be well timed in spite of its delay. For it will come at a season when bitter experience makes the assembled nations readier to consider a plan. The world is less and less disposed 'to wait for the miracle' —to believe that things will right themselves without action on our part.

II. INTERNAL EXPANSION

The reluctance to support schemes of capital development at home as a means to restore prosperity is generally based on two grounds—the meagreness of the employment created by the expenditure of a given sum, and the strain on national and local budgets of the subsidies which such schemes usually require. These are quantitative questions not easily answered with precision. But I will endeavour to give reasons for the belief that the answers to both of them are much more favourable than is commonly supposed.

It is often said that in Great Britain it costs £500 capital expenditure on public works to give one man employment for a year. This is based on the amount of labour directly employed on the spot. But it is easy to see that the materials used and the transport required also give employment. If we allow for this as we should, the capital expenditure per man-year of additional employment is usually estimated, in the case of building for example, at £200.

But if the new expenditure is additional and not merely in substitution for other expenditure, the increase of employment does not stop there. The additional wages and other incomes paid out are spent on additional purchases, which in turn lead to further employment. If the resources of the country were already fully employed, these additional purchases would be mainly reflected in higher prices and increased imports. But in present circumstances this would be true of only a small proportion of the additional consumption, since the greater part of it could be provided without much change of price by home resources which are at present unemployed. Moreover, in so far as the increased demand for food, resulting from the increased purchasing power of the working classes, served either to raise the prices or to increase the sales of the output of primary producers at home and abroad, we should today positively welcome it. It would be much better to raise the price of farm products by increasing the demand for them than by artificially restricting their supply.

Nor have we yet reached the end. The newly employed who supply the increased purchases of those employed on the new capital works will, in their turn, spend more, thus adding to the employment of others; and so on. Some enthusiasts, perceiving the fact of these repercussions, have greatly exaggerated the total result, and have even supposed that the amount of new employment thus created is only limited by the necessary intervals between the receipt of expenditure of income, in other words by the velocity of circulation of money. Unfortunately it is not quite as good as that. For at each stage there is, so to speak, a certain proportion of leakage. At each stage a certain proportion of the increased income is not passed on in increased employment. Some part will be saved by the recipient; some part raises prices and so diminishes consumption elsewhere, except in so far as producers spend their increased profits; some part will be spent on imports; some part is merely a substitution for expenditure previously made out of the dole or private charity or personal savings; and some part may reach the Exchequer without relieving the taxpayer to an equal extent. Thus in order to sum the net effect on employment of the series of repercussions, it is necessary to make reasonable assumptions as to the proportion lost in each of these ways. I would refer those who are interested in the technique of such summations to an article by Mr R. F. Kahn published in *The Economic Journal*, June 1931.

It is obvious that the appropriate assumptions vary greatly according to circumstances. If there were little or no margin of unemployed resources, then, as I have said above, the increased expenditure would largely waste itself in higher prices and increased imports (which is, indeed, a regular feature of the later stages of a boom in new construction). If the dole was as

great as a man's earnings when in work and was paid for by
borrowing, there would be scarcely any repercussions at all.
On the other hand, now that the dole is paid for by taxes and
not by borrowing (so that a reduction in the dole may be
expected to increase the spending power of the taxpayer), we no
longer have to make so large a deduction on this head.[1] Let me
consider in some detail what the net result is likely to be in
present conditions.

Let us call the gross amount of expenditure, provided out of
additional borrowing, the *primary expenditure* and the employment directly created by this expenditure the *primary employment*. I have estimated above on the authority of others—and no
grounds have been given for questioning the reasonable accuracy
of the estimate as a rough guide to the magnitudes involved—
that £200 of primary expenditure will provide one man-year of
primary employment. It will make no difference to the following
argument whether the object of the borrowing is to finance public
works or private enterprise or to relieve the taxpayer. This
primary expenditure will, in any of these cases, set up a series of
repercussions leading to what it is convenient to call *secondary
employment*. Our problem is to ascertain the total employment,
primary and secondary together, created by a given amount
of additional loan-expenditure, i.e. to ascertain the multiplier
relating the total employment to the primary employment.

[1] At this point the two editions diverge. The English edition continues: 'My own estimate,
taking very conservative figures in the light of present circumstances, makes the multiplier
to be at least 2. It follows that the loan-expenditure per man-year of employment is, not
the figure of £500 with which we begun, but £100. Since, however, I am anxious not
to overstate what will be a sufficiently striking conclusion anyhow, let us take it at
1½, i.e. that two men employed by loan-expenditure lead indirectly to the employment,
not of two further men, which represents my own belief, but of one further man. I do
not think that anyone who goes through the detailed calculation can bring it out at less
than this; which means that additional loan-expenditure of £200 on materials, transport,
and direct employment puts, not one man to work for a year, but—taking account of the
whole series of repercussions—one and a half men. This gives us a figure of £133 as
the amount of additional loan-expenditure required today to stimulate a man-year of
employment. But let us, in order to give ourselves a further margin of safety, base our
argument on the figure of £150. This answers, most conservatively, the first of our
two questions.

Next consider the magnitude of the relief to the budget.' The English edition then
follows the argument from page 346, line 5.

The primary expenditure of an additional £100, provided by borrowing, can be divided into two parts. The first part is the money which, for one reason or another, does not become additional income in the hands of an Englishman (or, if we apply the argument to the United States, of an American). This is mainly made up of (i) the cost of imported materials, (ii) the cost of goods, which are not newly produced but merely transferred, such as land or goods taken out of stocks which are not replenished, (iii) the cost of productive resources of men and plant which are not additionally employed but are merely drawn away from other jobs, (iv) the cost of wages which take the place of income previously provided out of funds borrowed for the dole. The second part, which is the money which does become additional income in the hands of an Englishman, has again to be divided into two portions, according as it is saved or spent (spending in this context including all the direct additional expenditure of the recipient, including expenditure on the production of durable objects).

To obtain the multiplier we simply have to estimate these two proportions, namely, what proportion of typical expenditure becomes someone's income and what proportion of this income is spent. For these two proportions, multiplied together, give us the ratio of the first repercussion to the primary effect, since they give us the ratio of the second flow of expenditure to the initial flow of expenditure. We can then sum the whole series of repercussions, since the second repercussion can be expected to bear the same ratio to the first repercussion, as the first bore to the primary effect; and so on.

The abstract argument can be illustrated as follows. Two years ago, when the dole was being financed in Great Britain out of borrowed money, this fact required a substantial deduction, which is no longer necessary, in calculating the proportion of expenditure which becomes additional income. Two years hence, if employment is much better than it is now, it may be necessary to make a substantial deduction in respect of resources which are merely drawn away from other jobs; for the smaller the pool of unemployed resources, the more likely is this result from increased expenditure. I am not disposed to make much deduction at any time for goods taken out of stock, since stocks are seldom really large and the sight of depletion soon stimulates replenishment. *In existing conditions*, therefore, I should say that a deduction of 30 per cent for expenditure which for one reason or another does not increase incomes, leaving 70 per cent accruing to one person or another as current income, would be a reasonable supposition.

What proportion of this additional income will be disbursed as additional expenditure? In so far as it accrues to the wage-earning classes, one can safely assume that most of it will be spent; in so far as it increases profits and salaries and professional earnings, the proportion saved will be larger. We have to strike a rough average. In present circumstances, for example, we might assume that at least 70 per cent of the increased income will be spent and not more than 30 per cent saved.

On these assumptions the first repercussion will be 49 per cent (since $7 \times 7 = 49$) of the primary effect, or (say) one-half; the second repercussion will be one-half of the first repercussion, i.e. one-quarter of the primary effect, and so on. Thus the multiplier is 2, since, if I may take the reader back to his schooldays, he will remember that $1 + \frac{1}{2} + \frac{1}{4} +$ etc. $= 2$. The amount of time which it takes for current income to be spent will separate each repercussion from the next one. But it will be seen that seven-eights of the total effects come from the primary expenditure and the first two repercussions, so that the time-lags involved are not unduly serious.

It is to be noticed that no additional allowance has to be made for any rise of prices which the increased demand may bring with it. The effect of higher prices will be gradually to diminish the proportion which becomes new income, since it will probably be a symptom that the surplus resources are no longer so adequate in certain directions, with the result that a larger proportion of the new expenditure is merely diverted from other jobs. It is also probable that higher prices will mean higher profits, with the result that, more of the increased income being profit and less of it being wages, more of it will be saved. Thus, as men are gradually brought back into employment and as prices gradually rise, the multiplier will gradually diminish. Moreover, in so far as wages rise it is obvious that the amount of employment corresponding to a given expenditure on wages will also gradually diminish. These modifications, however, would only become relevant as and when our remedy was becoming very successful. A given dose of expenditure at the present stage will, for several reasons, produce a much larger effect on employment than it will be prudent to expect later on when the margin of unused resources is reduced.

To illustrate the range of reasonable estimates for the multiplier, let us consider the effect on it of certain other assumptions. If we were to assume that each of the proportions is 60 per cent, the multiplier works out at about $1\frac{1}{2}$, which might be considered to set a minimum limit to its value, since it would seem very improbable that either proportion can be so low as this today. If, on the contrary, we were to expect that the proportion of the primary expenditure which becomes income and the proportion of the income which is spent are each 80 per cent, the multiplier becomes nearly 3 (as those readers who can still do arithmetic will easily verify). I believe myself that it is chiefly in estimating the proportion of expenditure which becomes additional income that we have to be cautious; and the estimates, which I should feel happiest in making, would be based on some such assumption as that not less than 66 per cent of additional expenditure (whether on new capital works or on additional consumption) would become additional income in the hands of an Englishman, and that not less than 75 per cent of this additional income would be spent; whilst I would more readily increase the latter proportion to 80 than the former proportion to 70. In what follows I will base my estimates on these figures, which also lead to a multiplier of 2. It may interest American readers to consider what assumptions would be most appropriate to present conditions in the United States. Personally I should expect the American multiple to be greater than 2, rather than less.

III. THE RELIEF TO THE BUDGET

On the assumptions which I have endeavoured to justify in the previous chapter, a primary expenditure of £100 will directly increase British incomes by two thirds of this amount, i.e. by £66. But the total increase of incomes, including the secondary effects, will be £66 $(1 + \frac{2}{3} + \frac{4}{9} + \ldots)$, i.e. £200. In order to ascertain the total relief to the budget resulting from the effects thus set up, we have to estimate, first the saving in respect of the cost of unemployment relief, and secondly the increased yield of the revenue from taxes levied on the increased income.

Not the whole of the additional income falls to men previously supported by the dole. Some part goes to profits, some part to the salaried and professional classes, and some part in wages for the increased employment of workers, who were not drawing the dole, either because they were already partly employed or for some other reason.

I consider, however, that it would be fairly safe to assume that two-thirds of the increased income, i.e. £44, will accrue to men previously supported by the dole, which means about one-third of a man-year of increased employment taking the average wage at 50s a week.

Since, on the assumptions which we have adopted, 75 per cent of the increased incomes of £66, caused by the primary expenditure of £100, will be spent, and 66 per cent of this secondary expenditure again serves to increase incomes, and so on, it follows that our primary expenditure of £100 will, sooner or later, bring about two-thirds of a man-year of employment for workers previously supported by the dole. At the same time, as we have seen, the total increase of incomes which it will bring about will be £200. If, however, the reader considers some

345

other set of figures more probable, I have here provided him with an apparatus which will enable him to work out the answer on his own assumptions.

We are now ready to estimate the total relief to the budget. For purposes of broad calculation the average cost of a man on the dole is usually taken at £50 a year.[1] Hence a loan expenditure of £100, by affording two-thirds of a man-year of employment for workers previously supported by the dole, reduces the cost of unemployment relief by £33.[2]

But there is a further benefit to the budget,[3] due to the fact that our loan expenditure of £100 will increase the national income by £200. For the yield of the taxes rises and falls more or less in proportion to the national income. Our budgetary difficulties today are mainly due to the decline in the national income. Now for the nation as a whole, leaving on one side transactions with foreigners, its income is exactly equal to its expenditure (including in expenditure both consumption-expenditure and new capital expenditure, but excluding inter-mediate exchanges from one hand to another); —the two being simply different names for the same thing, my expenditure being your income.[4]

Now on the average about 20 per cent of the national income is paid to the Exchequer in taxes. The exact proportion depends on how the new income is distributed between the higher ranges

[1] [This is a conservative figure for male adult workers. In 1932 the complete average, including juveniles and women, was £48·3 (namely £44·2 as the average annual cost of an unemployed person *plus* £4·1 as the average annual employer's and employee's contributions in respect of an employed person).] [This footnote is not in the English edition—Ed.]

[2] The example here follows the English edition in content, but not expression.

[3] In the English edition, the words 'due...For' do not appear.

[4] The English edition continues the paragraph: 'Thus new capital-expenditure of £3 million, paid for by an additional loan and not by reducing consumption-expenditure or existing capital-expenditure, increases the national income by more than £3 million if we allow for repercussions. The calculation to obtain the appropriate multiplier is much the same as in the case of employment; except that it is somewhat greater, since to obtain the national money-income we do not have to make the same deduction for a rise in prices. However, to be on the safe side, let us, as before, take the multiplier as being 1½. It follows that our capital expenditure of £3 million will increase the national income, subject to taxation, by £4,500,000.'

of income subject to direct taxation, and the lower ranges which are touched by indirect taxes; also the yield of some taxes is not closely correlated with changes in national income. To allow for these doubts, let us take the proportion of the new income accruing to the Exchequer at 10 per cent, i.e. £20 of new revenue from £200 increase of income. There will, it is true, be some time-lag in the collection of this, but we need not trouble about that; though it is a powerful argument in favour of proposals for modifying the rigidity of our annual budget and for making our estimates, on this occasion, cover a longer period than one year. Owing to the time-lag in the effect of increased taxation in reducing the national income our existing budgetary procedure is open to the serious objection that the measures which will balance this budget are calculated to unbalance the next one; and vice versa.

Thus the total benefit to the Exchequer of an additional loan-expenditure of £100 is at least £33 *plus* £20, or £53 altogether, i.e. a little more than a half of the loan-expenditure.[1] We need see nothing paradoxical in this. We have reached a point where a considerable proportion of every further decline in the national income is visited on the Exchequer through the agency of the dole and the decline in the yield of the taxes. It is natural, therefore, that the benefit of measures to increase the national income should largely accrue to the Exchequer.

If we apply this reasoning to the projects for loan-expenditure which are receiving support today in responsible quarters, we see that it is a complete mistake to believe that there is a dilemma between schemes for increasing employment and schemes for balancing the budget—that we must go slowly and cautiously with the former for fear of injuring the latter. Quite the contrary. There is no possibility of balancing the budget except by increasing the national income, which is much the same thing as increasing employment.

[1] The English edition uses a different set of numbers, but operates on the same principle and then continues the sentence 'or two-thirds of it, if we were to take the multiplier as 2'.

Take, for example, the proposal to spend £7 million on the new Cunarder. I say that this will benefit the Exchequer by at least a half of this sum, i.e. by £3,500,000, which vastly exceeds the maximum aid which is being asked from the Exchequer.

Or take the expenditure of £100 million on housing whether for rebuilding slums or under the auspices of a National Housing Board, this would benefit the budget by the vast total of some £50 million—a sum far exceeding any needful subsidy. If the mind of the reader boggles at this and he feels that it must be too good to be true, let him recur carefully to the argument which has led up to it. And if he distrusts his own judgement, let me point out that no serious attempt has yet been made to confound the bases of the argument,[1] where I first offered it *coram publico* in the forum of *The Times*.

Substantially the same argument also applies to a relief of taxation by suspending the Sinking Fund and by returning to the practice of financing by loans those services which can properly be so financed, such as the cost of new roads charged on the Road Fund and that part of the cost of the dole which can be averaged out against the better days for which we must hope. For the increased spending power of the taxpayer will have precisely the same favourable repercussions as increased spending power due to loan-expenditure; and in some ways this method of increasing expenditure is healthier and better spread throughout the community. If the Chancellor of the Exchequer will reduce taxation by £50 million through suspending the Sinking Fund and borrowing in those cases where formerly we thought it reasonable to borrow, the half of what he remits will in fact return to him from the saving on the dole and the higher yield of a given level of taxation—though, as I have pointed out above, it will not necessarily return to him in the same budget.[2]

---

[1] In the English edition, this sentence refers to possible future attempts.

[2] The English edition continues: 'I strongly support, therefore, the suggestion which has been made that the next budget should be divided into two parts, one of which shall include those items of expenditure which it would be proper to treat as loan-expenditure in present circumstances.'

I should add that this particular argument does not apply to a relief of taxation balanced by an equal reduction of government expenditure (by reducing schoolteachers' salaries, for example); for this represents a redistribution, not a net increase, of national spending power. It is applicable to all *additional* expenditure made, not in substitution for other expenditure, but out of savings or out of borrowed money, either by private persons or by public authorities, whether for capital purposes or for consumption made possible by a relief of taxation or in some other way.[1]

If these conclusions cannot be refuted, is it not advisable to act upon them? The contrary policy of endeavouring to balance the budget by impositions, restrictions, and precautions will surely fail, because it must have the effect of diminishing the national spending power, and hence the national income.[2]

The argument applies, of course, both ways equally. Just as the effect of increased primary expenditure on employment, on the national income and on the budget is multiplied in the manner described, so also is the effect of decreased primary expenditure. Indeed, if it were not so it would be difficult to explain the violence of the recession both here and, even more, in the United States. Just as an initial impulse of modest dimensions has been capable of producing such devastating repercussions, so also a moderate impulse in the opposite direction will effect a surprising recovery. There is no magic here, no mystery; but a reliable scientific prediction.

Why should this method of approach appear to so many people to be novel and odd and paradoxical? I can only find

---

[1] The English edition continues: 'It is often pointed out that, when loan-expenditure was on a larger scale as a result of official encouragement, this did not prevent an increase of unemployment. But at that time it was offsetting incompletely an even more rapid deterioration in our foreign balance. The effects of an increase or decrease of £100 million in our loan-expenditure are, broadly speaking, equal to the effects of an increase or decrease of £100 million in our foreign balance. Formerly we had no visible benefit from our loan-expenditure, because it was being offset by a deterioration in our foreign balance. Recently we have had no visible benefit from the improvement in our foreign balance, because it has been offset by the reduction in our loan-expenditure. Today for the first time it is open to us, if we choose, to have both factors favourable at once.'

[2] The remaining paragraphs of this chapter do not appear in the English edition.

the answer in the fact that all our ideas about economics, instilled into us by education and atmosphere and tradition are, whether we are conscious of it or not, soaked with theoretical presuppositions which are only properly applicable to a society which is in equilibrium, with all its productive resources already employed. Many people are trying to solve the problem of unemployment with a theory which is based on the assumption that there is no unemployment. Obviously if the productive resources of the nation were already fully occupied, none of the advantages could be expected which, in present circumstances, I predict from an increase of loan-expenditure. For in that case increased loan-expenditure would merely exhaust itself in raising prices and wages and diverting resources from other jobs. In other words, it would be purely inflationary. But these ideas, perfectly valid in their proper setting, are inapplicable to present circumstances, which can only be handled by the less familiar method which I have endeavoured to explain.

IV. THE RAISING OF PRICES

It is the declared policy of the British government, and also of the representatives of the empire assembled at Ottawa, to raise prices. How are we to do it?

To judge from some utterances of the Chancellor of the Exchequer, he has been attracted to the idea of raising the prices of commodities by restricting their supply. Now, it may well benefit the producers of a particular article to combine to restrict its output. Equally it may benefit a particular country, though at the expense of the rest of the world, to restrict the supply of a commodity which it is in a position to control. It may even, very occasionally, benefit the world as a whole to organise the restriction of output of a particular commodity, the supply of which is seriously out of balance with the supply of other things. But as an all-round remedy restriction is worse than useless. For the community as a whole it reduces demand, by destroying the income of the retrenched producers, just as much as it reduces supply. So far from being a means to diminish unemployment it is, rather, a method of distributing more evenly what unemployment there is, at the cost of somewhat increasing it.

How, then, are we to raise prices? It may help us to think clearly, if I proceed by means of a series of very simple, but fundamental propositions.

(1) For commodities as a whole there can be no possible means of raising their prices except by increasing expenditure upon them more rapidly than their supply comes upon the market.

(2) Expenditure can only be increased if the public spend a larger proportion of the incomes they already have, or if their aggregate spending power is increased in some other way.

(3) There are narrow limits to increasing expenditure out of existing incomes—whether by saving less or by increased personal expenditure of a capital nature. Incomes are so curtailed today and taxation so much increased, that many people are already, in the effort to maintain their standard of life, saving less than sound personal habits require. Anyone who can afford to spend more should be encouraged to do so, particularly if he has opportunities to spend on new capital or semi-capital objects. But it is an evasion of the magnitude of the problem to believe that we can solve it in this way. It follows, therefore, that we must aim at increasing aggregate spending power. If we can achieve this, it will partly serve to raise prices and partly to increase employment.

(4) Putting on one side the special case of people who can earn their incomes by actually producing gold, it is broadly true to say that aggregate spending power within a country can only be raised either (i) by increasing the loan-expenditure of the community; or (ii) by improving the foreign balance so that a larger proportion of current expenditure again becomes income in the hands of home producers. By means of public works the

Labour government in Great Britain—though rather half-heartedly and in adverse attendant circumstances—attempted the first. The National government has successfully attempted the second. We have not yet tried both at once.

(5) But there is a great difference between the two methods, inasmuch as only the first is valid for the world as a whole. The second method merely means that one country is withdrawing employment and spending power from the rest of the world. For when one country improves its foreign balance, it follows that the foreign balance of some other country is diminished. Thus we cannot increase total output in this way or raise world prices, unless, as a by-product, it serves to increase loan-expenditure by strengthening confidence in a financial centre such as Great Britain and so making it a more ready lender both at home and abroad.

Currency depreciation and tariffs were weapons which Great Britain had in hand until recently as a means of self-protection. A moment came when we were compelled to use them, and they have served us well. But competitive currency depreciations and competitive tariffs, and more artificial means of improving an individual country's foreign balance such as exchange restrictions, import prohibitions, and quotas, help no one and injure each, if they are applied all round.

We are left, therefore, with the broad conclusion that there is no effective means of raising world prices except by increasing loan-expenditure throughout the world. It was, indeed, the collapse of expenditure financed out of loans advanced by the United States, for use both at home and abroad, which was the chief agency in starting the slump.

A number of popular remedies are rightly popular because they tend to facilitate loan-expenditure. But there are several stages in the task of increasing loan-expenditure; and, if there is a breakdown at any one of them, we shall fail to attain our object. I must ask the reader, therefore, to be patient with a further attempt at orderly analysis.

(1) The first necessity is that bank credit should be cheap and abundant. This is only possible if each central bank is freed from anxiety by feeling itself to possess adequate reserves of international money. The loss of confidence in bank balances held in leading financial centres as constituting international money for this purpose, has greatly aggravated the shortage of reserves. So has the accumulation of a large proportion of the world's gold in a few central banks. On the other hand, we all welcome an increased output of the gold mines or a reduction in India's sterile hoards, because the quantity of reserve money is thus increased. The devaluation of national currencies in terms of gold is another remedy belonging to this category. Or, again, the abandonment of rigid gold parities may help the case, since a central bank which can, if necessary, relieve a strain by allowing the foreign exchanges to move against it, will be satisfied with a smaller reserve of international money. The abatement of the legal proportion of international money, which a bank must hold against its note issue, might also help on a minor scale.

But this is only the first stage. In the early phase of recovery there is not much loan-expenditure which can be safely financed by short-term bank credit. The role of bank credit is to finance the restoration of working capital after business recovery has definitely set in. In ordinary times we were able to rely on the first stage leading automatically to the subsequent stages. But not in the conditions of today.

(2) The second stage, therefore, must be reached, at which the long-term rate of interest is low for all reasonably sound borrowers. This requires a combination of manoeuvres by the government and the central bank in the shape of open-market operations by the bank, of well-judged conversion schemes by the treasury, and of a restoration of financial confidence by a budget policy approved by public opinion and in other ways. It is at this stage that a certain dilemma exists; since it may be true, for psychological reasons, that a temporary reduction of loan-expenditure plays a necessary part in effecting the transition

353

to a lower long-term rate of interest. Since, however, the whole object of the policy is to promote loan-expenditure, we must obviously be careful not to continue its temporary curtailment a day longer than we need.

A few countries have reached the first stage. But Great Britain alone has reached the second stage. It is a great achievement of the Treasury and the Bank of England to have effected so successfully a transition which France and the United States, for whom the task was, until recently, much easier, have bungled so badly.

(3) But there remains a third stage. For even when we have reached the second stage, it is unlikely that private enterprise will, on its own initiative, undertake new loan-expenditure on a sufficient scale. Business enterprise will not seek to expand until *after* profits have begun to recover. Increased working capital will not be required until *after* output is increasing. Moreover, in modern communities a very large proportion of our *normal* programmes of loan expenditure are undertaken by public and semi-public bodies. The new loan-expenditure which trade and industry require in a year is comparatively small even in good times. Building, transport, and public utilities are responsible at all times for a very large proportion of current loan-expenditure.

Thus the first step has to be taken on the initiative of public authority; and it probably has to be on a large scale and organised with determination, if it is to be sufficient to break the vicious circle and to stem the progressive deterioration, as firm after firm throws up the sponge and ceases to produce at a loss in the seemingly vain hope that perseverance will be rewarded.

Some cynics, who have followed the argument thus far, conclude that nothing except a war can bring a major slump to its conclusion. For hitherto war has been the only object of governmental loan-expenditure on a large scale which governments have considered respectable. In all the issues of peace they are timid, over-cautious, half-hearted, without perseverance

354

or determination, thinking of a loan as a liability and not as a link in the transformation of the community's surplus resources, which will otherwise be wasted, into useful capital assets.

I hope that her government will show that Great Britain can be energetic even in the tasks of peace. It should not be difficult to perceive that 100,000 houses are a national asset and 1 million unemployed men a national liability.

(4) Yet if we are to raise world prices, which is our theme, there is yet a fourth stage. Loan-expenditure must spread its beneficent influence round the world. How to assist that will be the subject of the next chapter.

V. A PROPOSAL FOR THE WORLD
ECONOMIC CONFERENCE

We have reached the conclusion that there is no means of raising world prices except by an increase of loan-expenditure throughout the world. How to achieve this should, I suggest, be the central theme of the World Economic Conference. There are, I think, three, and only three, possible lines along which we can lend assistance.

(1) The first, and perhaps the most obvious, means is that of direct foreign loans, in the style to which we have been accustomed in the past, from the strong financial countries, which have a favourable foreign balance or excessive reserves of gold, to the weaker, debtor countries.

The time may be coming for a return to this traditional policy, as opportunity offers. But it would be chimerical to suppose that such foreign loans can play a large part today in bringing about recovery. Those countries which are best able to make them are least likely to do so. Nor is it reasonable to expect private investors to assume new risks of this kind, when those which they have already assumed are turning out so badly.

(2) The second, and more promising, means is for the stronger financial countries to increase loan-expenditure *at home*,

on the lines recommended in chapter II above. For such expenditure will be twice blessed. In so far as it sets up a stream of expenditure on home-produced goods, the favourable repercussions of the initial loan-expenditure on employment will be multiplied. In so far as it leads to expenditure on imported goods, it will set up similar favourable repercussions abroad, and will strengthen the position of the countries from which we buy, both to make reciprocal purchases and also to augment their own loan-expenditure. It will have set the ball rolling.

It may be better, therefore, to use our available resources to finance the additional imports, to which a bold policy of loan-expenditure at home is likely to lead, than to make foreign loans. This will be just as beneficial to the outside world, and decidedly more healthy than further additions to international indebtedness.

(3) Yet, once again, it seems obvious that we are discussing, so far, remedies of which the quantitative effect is hopelessly disproportionate to the problem of raising world prices. I see no reliable prospect of a sufficient rise in world prices within a reasonable time, except as the result of a substantial, and more or less simultaneous, relief of taxation and increase of loan-expenditure in many different countries. We should attach great importance to the *simultaneity* of the movement towards increased expenditure. For the pressure on its foreign balance, which each country fears as the result of increasing its own loan-expenditure, will cancel out if other countries are pursuing the same policy at the same time. Isolated action may be imprudent. General action has no dangers whatever.

We are now advanced a stage further in our argument. We have reached the point where combined international action is of the essence of policy. We have reached, that is to say, the field and scope of the World Economic Conference. The task of this Conference, as I see it, is to devise some sort of joint action of a kind to allay the anxieties of central banks and to relieve the tension on their reserves, or the fear and expectation of tension. This would enable many more countries to reach the first of the stages which I distinguished in chapter IV—the stage at which bank credit is cheap and abundant. We cannot, by international action, make the horses drink. That is their domestic affair. But we can provide them with water. To revive the parched world by releasing a million rivulets of spending power is the primary task of the World Conference.

For the Conference to occupy itself with pious resolutions concerning the abatement of tariffs, quotas, and exchange restrictions will be a waste of time. In so far as these things are not the expression of deliberate national or imperial policies, they have been adopted reluctantly as a means of self-protection, and are symptoms, not causes, of the tension on the foreign exchanges. It is dear to the heart of conferences to pass pious resolutions deploring symptoms, whilst leaving the disease untouched. It should be the role of the British government to make a reality of this forthcoming Conference by concrete proposals which would go to the root of the disease.

There are certain preliminaries which must be accomplished before positive remedies will have a fair chance. We all agree that the settlement of war debts and of reparations are, first of all, indispensable. For these are of primary importance in creating fear of acute tension on the foreign exchanges. But have we a positive scheme of action wherewith to seize the opportunity which the settlement of these issues would create?

No remedies can be quickly efficacious which do not allay the anxieties of treasuries and central banks throughout the world by supplying them with more adequate reserves of international money. There is a considerable variety of schemes which can be devised with this end in view, having a close family resemblance to one another. After much private discussion and borrowing the ideas of others, I am convinced that the following scheme is the best one. If other variants command more support, that would be a reason for preferring them.

There are certain conditions which any scheme for increasing the reserves of international money should satisfy. In the first place, the additional reserves should be based on gold. For whilst gold is rapidly ceasing to be national money, it is becoming, even more exclusively than before, the international money most commonly held in reserve and used to meet a foreign drain. In the second place, it should not be of an eleemosynary character, but should be available, not only to the exceptionally needy, but to all participating countries in accordance with a general formula. Indeed there are few, if any, countries left today which are so entirely without anxiety that they would not welcome some strengthening of their position. In the third place, there should be an elasticity in the quantity of the additional reserves outstanding, so that they would operate, not as a net permanent addition to the world's monetary supply, but as a balancing factor to be released when prices are abnormally low as at present, and to be withdrawn again if prices were to be rising too much. These conditions can be satisfied as follows:

(i) There should be set up an international authority for the issue of gold-notes, of which the face value would be expressed in terms of the gold content of the U.S. dollar.

(ii) These notes would be issuable up to a maximum of $5,000 million and would be obtainable by the participating countries against an equal face value of the gold-bonds of their governments, up to a maximum quota for each country.

(iii) The proportionate quota of each country would be based on some such formula as the amount of gold which it held in reserve at some recent normal date, e.g. at the end of 1928, provided that no individual quota should exceed $450 million and with power to the governing board to modify the rigidity of this formula where special reasons could be given for not adhering to it strictly. (Some provision, for example, would be required for silver-using countries.) The effect of this formula would be that the quota of each country would add to its reserves an amount approximately equal to the gold which it held in 1928, subject to the above maximum proviso. The detailed allocation for each country is given in an appendix to this chapter.

(iv) Each participating government would undertake to pass legislation providing that these gold-notes would be acceptable as the equivalent of gold, except that they should not enter into the active circulation but would be held only by treasuries, central banks, or in the reserves against domestic note issues.

(v) The governing board of the institution would be elected by the participating governments, who would be free to delegate their powers to their central banks, each having a voting power in proportion to its quota.

(vi) The gold-bonds would carry a rate of interest, nominal or very low in the first instance, which could be changed from time to time by the governing board subject to (viii) below. They would be repayable at any time by the government responsible for them, or on notice given by the governing board subject to (viii) below.

(vii) The interest, after meeting expenses, would be retained in gold as a guarantee fund. In addition, each participating government would guarantee any ultimate loss, arising through a default, in proportion to the amount of its maximum quota.

(viii) The governing board would be directed to use their discretion to modify the volume of the note issue or the rate of interest on the bonds, solely with a view to avoiding, so far as possible, a rise in the gold price level of primary products entering into international trade above some agreed norm between the present level and that of 1928—perhaps the level of 1930.

APPENDIX

Under the formula on p. 358 above for distributing the $5,000 million gold-notes in proportion to the gold held in reserve by each country at the end of 1928 subject to a maximum of $450 million to any one country, the allocation would work out as follows:

359

Seven countries (Great Britain, United States, France, Germany, Spain, Argentine and Japan) would qualify for the maximum $450 million each.

(millions of dollars)

Italy	266	Hungary	35
Holland	175	Czechoslovakia	34
Brazil	149	Roumania	30
Belgium	126	Austria	24
India	124	Colombia	24
Canada	114	Peru	20
Australia	108	Jugoslavia	18
Switzerland	103	Egypt	18
Poland	70	Bulgaria	10
Uruguay	68	Portugal	9
Java	68	Finland	8
Sweden	63	Greece	7
Denmark	46	Chile	7
Norway	39	Latvia	5
South Africa	39	Lithuania	3
New Zealand	35	Esthonia	2

No country would have injustice done to it by this particular choice of date except Chile, whose case might deserve special consideration and, to a lesser extent, Greece and Canada. If we were to take the *highest* figure held at the end of any year from 1925 to 1928, the following would be the only changes in the above total:

	1928	Highest of 1925 to 1928
		(millions of dollars)
Denmark	46	56
Greece	7	10
Holland	175	178
Canada	114	158
Chile	7	34
New Zealand	35	38
Java	68	79
South Africa	39	44

VI. THE INTERNATIONAL NOTE ISSUE AND THE GOLD STANDARD

In the last chapter I have proposed the creation of an international note issue designed to relieve the anxieties of the world's central banks, so as to free their hands to promote loan-expenditure and thus raise prices and restore employment. The necessity of this policy is a consequence of the conclusion, which I reiterate with emphasis, that there is no means of raising world prices except by increasing loan-expenditure. But it is desirable that I should attempt to fill in some further details in this far-reaching proposal.

Its adoption would afford a good opportunity, if sufficient agreement could be obtained, to secure promises that the assistance thus given would be used, in the first instance, to abate certain unsound international practices which have become common under stress of hard circumstances. Exchange restrictions should be abolished. Standstill agreements and the immobilisation of foreign balances should be replaced by definitive schemes for gradual liquidation. Tariffs and quotas imposed to protect the foreign balance, and not in pursuance of permanent national policies, should be removed. The stronger financial centres should reopen their money markets to foreign loans. Defaults on public debts held abroad should be terminated, with the aid of the postponement of sinking funds and some writing down of interest or principal, perhaps based on an index number of prices, where incapacity, even in the new circumstances, is proved to the satisfaction of an independent expert body. For my own part, I should withhold participation in the scheme from any country which was acting in defiance of its international agreements and obligations.

Subject to these external conditions, it would be advisable to leave to each participant an unfettered discretion as to the best means of utilising its quota. For there is great variety in the needs of different countries. Some would discharge pressing foreign obligations; some would restore budgetary equilibrium; some would re-establish commercial credit; some would prepare for conversion schemes; some would organise schemes of national development; and so on. But all uses alike would tend in the desired direction.

There remains, however, one essential condition, upon which I have not yet touched. The notes would be gold-notes, and the participants would agree to accept them as the equivalent of gold. This implies that the national currencies of each participant would stand in some defined relationship to gold. It involves, that is to say, a qualified return to the gold standard.

It may seem odd that I, who have lately described gold as 'a barbarous relic', should be discovered as an advocate of such a policy, at a time when the orthodox authorities of this country are laying down conditions for our return to gold which they must know to be impossible of fulfilment. It may be that, never having loved gold, I am not so subject to disillusion. But, mainly, it is because I believe that gold has received such a gruelling that conditions might now be laid down for its future management, which would not have been acceptable otherwise. At any rate my advocacy is subject to the qualifications which follow.

It would be a necessary condition for the adoption of the proposed international note issue that each participating country should adopt a *de facto* parity between gold and its national currency, with buying and selling points for gold separated by not more than 5 per cent. With the increased supply of gold and its equivalent brought into existence by the new note issue, such a commitment by this country would be, in my judgement, both safe and advisable. The *de facto* parity should be alterable, if necessary, from time to time if circumstances were to require, just like bank rate—though by small degrees one would hope. An unchangeable parity would be unwise until we know much more about the future course of international prices, and the success of the board of the new international authority in influencing it; and it would, moreover, be desirable to maintain permanently some power of gradual adjustment between national and international conditions. In addition, the governing board should have some discretionary power to deal with emergencies and exceptional cases. The margin of 5 per cent between the gold points would be essential, in the light of recent experience, as a deterrent and a protection against the wild movements of liquid funds from one international centre to another, and to allow a reasonable independence of bank rate and credit policy to suit differing national circumstances—though there would be nothing to prevent a central bank from maintaining the gold equivalent of its national money within narrower limits in normal practice.

With these precautionary safeguards there would be much to gain and little to lose from the greater stability of the foreign exchanges which would ensue. There can be no object in exchange fluctuations except to offset undesired changes in the international price level or, occasionally, to make an adjustment, with the minimum of friction, to special national conditions, temporary or permanent; and they should not be allowed to occur for any other reason.

It can be claimed, I think, as a considerable incidental advantage of the plan here set forth, that it would enable the condition to be satisfied which our authorities have laid down for even a qualified return to gold on the part of this country, namely, that there must be a more equal distribution of the world's gold reserves. Indeed I can imagine no other way by which this condition could be satisfied within a reasonable time. For if it means that the Bank of France and the Federal Reserve System of the United States are to share out their gold reserves with the impecunious countries of the world, it is clearly quite remote—today more than ever—from anything which can possibly happen. Equally if it means that these countries are to lend abroad sums so much greater than their foreign balance as to lead to a heavy outward drain of gold, this also is what no reasonable person would expect. Moreover, in the conditions of today, with the employment of foreign balances as reserve money completely at an end, and after the experiences by the world's strongest financial centres of the scale on which balances can seek to move, it is not merely a question of the maldistribution of gold. We need a much greater absolute amount of reserve money to support a given level of world prices than was necessary before the recent shocks to international credit. This may not be a permanent requirement. But it exists today, and it must be satisfied before we can expect that ease of mind and absence of anxiety on the part of central banks which is a condition of their freely encouraging the increased loan-expenditure without which world prices cannot rise. Some such plan, therefore, as that which I have proposed has become an indispensable condition of world recovery. It is useless to do lip-service to the need of raising world prices if we neglect the only measures which can have that result.

The alternative, sometimes suggested, of a simultaneous devaluation of all national currencies in terms of gold, whilst offering some advantages, has the great defect that it would only strengthen the position of those countries which already hold large reserves of gold and are, therefore, relatively strong.

VII. CONCLUSION

I have endeavoured to cover a wide field in a few words. But my theme has been essentially simple, and I am hopeful, therefore, that I have been able to convey it to the reader.

Many proposals now current are substantially similar in intention to the proposals of this pamphlet. Some deal with one part of the field; some with another. We shall have need of more than one, if our action is to be adequate to the problem. After making all due allowances for the factors which will cause a larger number of men to appear in the unemployment returns even in good times, Great Britain has the task of putting at least 1 million men back to work. On the figure of £150 primary expenditure to put one man to work for a year, which I have adopted above as my working hypothesis, we should need an increased loan-expenditure *plus* an increased foreign balance amounting altogether to £150 million[1]. We cannot rely on much

---

[1] The English edition has an additional sentence here: 'If we take the more optimistic figure of £100 per man, which I am myself disposed to favour, the primary expenditure required will be £100 million per annum.'

further assistance towards this total from the foreign balance, until after world recovery has set in. Thus it would be prudent to assume that we have urgent need of the addition of at least £100 million to our annual primary expenditure from increased loan-expenditure at home.

This is a formidable, but not an impossible, figure to attain. At least £50 million might reasonably come from a relief of taxation as a result of suspending the Sinking Fund and borrowing for appropriate purposes; though this would not lead to increased primary expenditure of so much as £50 million. On this basis an additional loan-expenditure of (say) £60 million by private enterprise, assisted and unassisted, local authorities, public boards, and the central government, would be a substantial step towards re-establishing employment.

We are, I think, too much discouraged as to the potentialities of fruitful action along these lines, because the effect of previous efforts has been masked by offsetting influences. It is most important to understand that the effects of loan-expenditure and of the foreign balance are *in pari materia*. Thus it was the rapid decline of the foreign balance by £75 million in 1930 and by £207 million in 1931 as compared with 1929,[1] which defeated the attempt of the Labour government to increase employment by loan-expenditure; the additional loan-expenditure for which they were responsible being on a much smaller scale than this. But, again, the improvement of the foreign balance in 1932 by £74 million as compared with 1931 has brought no increase in employment, because it has been offset by the drastic measures of the National government to reduce loan-expenditure. Heaven knows to what plight a combination of the policy of the Labour government in doing nothing to protect the foreign balance, with the policy of the National government to curtail loan-expenditure might not have brought us! Business losses would have risen to

[1] [These figures are the estimates of the Board of Trade, except that the American debt payment in 1932, which was paid for in gold, has been omitted. I believe myself that in all these years the absolute figures may have been some £25 million better than the Board of Trade allows. But this would not affect the comparative figures given above.]

a figure comparable with those in the United States,[1] bankrupting our railways and bringing the industry of the country virtually to a standstill. On the other hand, Great Britain has the other combination still untried—the policy of protecting the foreign balance and at the same time doing all in our power to stimulate loan-expenditure.

I plead, therefore, for a trial of this untried combination in our domestic policy; and for the World Economic Conference an advocacy by our representatives of an expansion of international reserve money on the general lines proposed above.

For we have reached a critical point. In a sense, it is true that the mists are lifting. We can, at least, see clearly the gulf to which our present path is leading. Few of us doubt that we must, without much more delay, find an effective means to raise world prices; or we must expect the progressive breakdown of the existing structure of contract and instruments of indebtedness, accompanied by the utter discredit of orthodox leadership in finance and government, with what ultimate outcome we cannot predict.

The authorities in power have pronounced in favour of raising world prices. It is, therefore, incumbent upon them to have some positive policy directed to that end. If they have one, we do not know what it is. I have tried to indicate some of the fundamental conditions which their policy must satisfy if it is to be successful, and to suggest the kind of plan which might be capable of realising these conditions.

[1] [I should attribute the extremity of the plight of the United States largely to the combined effect of their having no dole financed out of loans, as there was in this country prior to 1932, and no means of improving the foreign balance such as we employed after September 1931.]

2 HOW TO PAY FOR THE WAR

How to Pay for the War developed from two long articles that Keynes wrote for *The Times*, which appeared 14 and 15 November 1939. These led to a voluminous correspondence and Keynes enlarged his ideas in the form of a small book published in February 1940. The original articles will be found in volume XXII.

How to Pay for the War was produced so hurriedly in the confused conditions of the time that many small errors crept into the text. As far as possible, these have been corrected, primarily from lists of errors in Keynes's Papers. A list of these corrections appears as Appendix V.

Brethren, Friends, Countrymen and Fellow Subjects,

What I intend now to say to you, is, next to your Duty to God, and the Care of your Salvation, of the greatest Concern to your selves, and your Children; your *Bread* and *Cloathing*, and every common Necessary of Life entirely depend upon it. Therefore I do most earnestly exhort you as *Men*, as *Christians*, as *Parents*, and as *Lovers of your Country*, to read this Paper with the utmost Attention, or get it read to you by others; which that you may do at the less Expence, I have ordered the Printer to sell it at the lowest Rate.

It is a great Fault among you, that when a Person writes with no other Intention than *to do you good, you will not be at the Pains to read his Advices:* One Copy of this Paper may serve a Dozen of you, which will be less than a Farthing a-piece. It is your Folly that you have no common or general Interest in your View, not even the Wisest among you, neither do you know or enquire, or care who are your Friends, or who are your Enemies.

(From the Drapier's First Letter—1724)

PREFACE

This is a discussion of how best to reconcile the demands of war and the claims of private consumption.

In three articles published in *The Times* last November I put forward a first draft of proposals under the description of 'Compulsory Savings'. It was not to be expected that a new plan of this character would be received with enthusiasm. But it was

25-2

not rejected either by experts or by the public. No one has suggested anything better. That public opinion was, as yet, not ready for such ideas, was the usual criticism. And this was obviously true. Nevertheless a time must come when the necessities of a war economy are realised; and there is much evidence for the belief that the public are not so behindhand.

Amongst the manifold comments provoked there were some valuable suggestions. In the revised draft here set forth in ampler detail I have taken advantage of these. In the first version I was mainly concerned with questions of financial technique and did not secure the full gain in social justice for which this technique opened the way. In this revision, therefore, I have endeavoured to snatch from the exigency of war positive social improvements. The complete scheme now proposed, including universal family allowances in cash, the accumulation of working-class wealth under working-class control, a cheap ration of necessaries, and a capital levy (or tax) after the war, embodies an advance towards economic equality greater than any which we have made in recent times. There should be no paradox in this. The sacrifices required by war direct more urgent attention than before to sparing them where they can be least afforded.

A plan like this cannot be fairly judged except against an alternative. But so far we have had no hint what alternative is in view. The Chancellor of the Exchequer has recently explained to the House of Commons that he is seeking to prevent a rise of wages by subsidising the cost of living. As an ingredient in a comprehensive plan, this is a wise move; something of the kind is recommended in what follows. As a stop-gap arrangement to gain time it is prudent. But taken by itself it is the opposite of a solution. In making money go further it aggravates the problem of reaching equilibrium between the spending power in people's pockets and what can be released for their consumption.

The Chancellor has expressed agreement with this conclusion. I hope, therefore, that he will look with sympathy on an attempt to work his policy into a consistent whole. I have canvassed these

Cartoon by David Low by arrangement with the Trustees and the London Evening Standard

proposals in many quarters and comment has reached me from all shades of opinion. I confidently believe that, put forward with authority, they would not be unpopular. No one is expecting to get off scot-free. The fault of my plan is that it asks, not too much, but too little; and it may look, a year hence, too feeble a beginning for a heavy task.

Since one cannot rule out the possibility that we shall drift or adopt half-measures, I will venture on a prediction of the result of this. I discuss below the mechanism of inflation; and that, I suppose, is what most people are expecting if we shirk. But except at a slow rate and as the second stage of deterioration, this is not my immediate expectation. There is a passage in the *Golden Bough* where the proneness of primitive man to generalise on the basis of a very few experiences is amusingly illustrated. Men like dogs are only too easily 'conditioned' and always expect that, when the bell rings, they will have the same experience as last time. But the psychology which provoked previous price inflations is not present today. So far from there being a natural tendency to raise prices in response to an unsatisfied demand, manufacturers and retailers are as reluctant to charge higher prices except in response to an actual rise in cost as the public are to pay them. They have no desire to flout public opinion and what appears to be the intention of the authorities. They are doubtful how they stand under the Anti-Profiteering Act. With the Excess Profits Tax they have less inducement than usual to maximise profits. In short, it eases their consciences, saves them trouble, and does not even cost them much, to clear their shelves and leave the next customer unsatisfied rather than raise their prices to the level which would equate supply and demand.

Thus the first stage, I suggest, will be a shortage of supplies rather than a runaway price level. This will be a singularly unfair, inefficient and irritating method of restricting consumption. And if it provokes, as it probably will, more widespread rationing, the waste and inefficiency will be aggravated for reasons, explained below, due to the diversity of men's needs and tastes.

Cartoon by David Low by arrangement with the Trustees and the London Evening Standard

371

The right plan is to restrict spending power to the suitable figure and then allow as much consumer's choice as possible how it shall be spent. Moreover, gradually the pressure of spending power will bring in the tide of inflation, which is nature's remedy and the only genuine alternative.

But a further, and even less satisfactory, consequence is also probable. A shortage of supplies relatively to consumers' spending power will exert an unfavourable pressure on our balance of trade. For it will divert goods from export and give a stimulus to the use for current consumption of imports, and home production too, which might otherwise have been employed for war purposes. Thus we shall be prevented from putting forth our full war effort and we shall run down our foreign reserves faster than is prudent.

A reluctance to face the full magnitude of our task and overcome it is a coward's part. Yet the nation is not in this mood and only asks to be told what is necessary. It is a fool's part too. For victory may depend on our making it evident that we can so organise our economic strength as to maintain indefinitely the excommunication of an unrepentant enemy from the commerce and society of the world.

J. M. KEYNES

King's College, Cambridge
February 1940

I THE CHARACTER OF THE PROBLEM

It is not easy for a free community to organise for war. We are not accustomed to listen to experts or prophets. Our strength lies in an ability to improvise. Yet an open mind to untried ideas is also necessary. No one can say when the end will come. In the war services it is recognised that the best security for an early conclusion is a plan for long endurance. It is ludicrous to proceed on a different assumption in the economic services— which is what we are doing at present. On the economic front we lack—to borrow a phrase of Monsieur Reynaud—not material resources but lucidity and courage.

Courage will be forthcoming if the leaders of opinion in all parties will summon out of the fatigue and confusion of war enough lucidity of mind to understand for themselves and to explain to the public what is required; and then propose a plan conceived in a spirit of social justice, a plan which uses a time of general sacrifice, not as an excuse for postponing desirable reforms, but as an opportunity for moving further than we have moved hitherto towards reducing inequalities.

More lucidity, therefore, is our first need. This is not easy. For all aspects of the economic problem are interconnected. Nothing can be settled in isolation. Every use of our resources is at the expense of an alternative use. And when we have decided how much can be made available for civilian consumption, we have still to settle the thorniest question of all, how to distribute it most wisely.

We shall, I assume, raise our output to the highest figure which our resources and our organisation permit. We shall export all we can spare. We shall import all we can afford, having regard to the shipping tonnage available and the maximum rate at which it is prudent to use up our reserves of foreign assets. From the sum of our own output and our imports we have to take away our exports and the requirements of war. Civilian consumption at home will be equal to what is left. Clearly its amount will depend on our policy in the other respects. It can only be increased if we diminish our war effort, or if we use up our foreign reserves.

It is extraordinarily difficult to secure the right outcome for this resultant of many separate policies. It depends on weighing one advantage against another. There is hardly a conceivable decision within the range of the supply services which does not affect it. Is it better that the War Office should have a large reserve of uniforms in stock or that the cloth should be exported to increase the Treasury's reserve of foreign currency? Is it better to employ our shipyards to build warships or merchantmen? Is it better that a twenty-year-old agricultural worker should be left on the farm or taken into the army? How great an expansion of the army should we contemplate? What reduction in working hours and efficiency is justified in the interests of A.R.P.? One could ask a hundred thousand such questions, and the answer to each would have a significant bearing on the amount left over for civilian consumption.

We can start out either by fixing the standard of life of the civilian and discover what is left over for the service departments and for export; or by adding up the demands of the latter and discover what is left over for the civilians. The actual result will be a compromise between the two methods. At present it is hard to say who, if anyone, settles such matters. In the final outcome there seems to be a larger element of chance than of design. It is a case of pull devil, pull baker—with the devil so far on top.

But it makes no great difference to the problem we are now discussing whether the final result is arrived at wisely or foolishly, by chance or by design. On the assumption that our total output is as large as we know how to organise, a definite residual will be left over which is available for civilian consumption. The amount of this residue will certainly be influenced by the reasonable requirements of the civilian population. If an acute shortage develops in a particular direction, baker's pull will become stronger and devil's weaker; and something will be done to allow a larger release. But unless we are to fall far short of our maximum war effort, we cannot allow the amount of mere money in the pockets of the public to have a significant influence, unjustified by other considerations, on the amount which is released to civilians.

This leads up to our fundamental proposition. There will be a certain definite amount left over for civilian consumption. This amount may be larger or smaller than what perfect wisdom and foresight would provide. The point is that its amount will depend only to a minor extent on the amount of money in the pockets of the public and on their readiness to spend it.

This is a great change from peacetime experience. That is why we find it difficult to face the economic consequences of war. We have been accustomed to a level of production which has been below capacity. In such circumstances, if we have more to spend, more will be produced and there will be more to buy. Not necessarily in the same proportion. Supply for immediate consumption may not increase as much as demand, so that prices will rise to some extent. Nevertheless, when men were working harder and earning more, they have been able to increase their consumption in not much less than the same proportion.

In peacetime, that is to say, the size of the cake depends on the amount of work done. But in wartime the size of the cake is fixed. If we work harder, we can fight better. But we must not consume more.

This is the elementary fact which in a democracy the man in the street must learn to understand if the nation is to act wisely —that the size of the civilian's cake is fixed.

What follows from this?

It means, broadly speaking, that the public as a whole cannot increase its consumption by increasing its money earnings. Yet most of us try to increase our earnings in the belief that we can thus increase our consumption—which is usually true. Indeed, in a sense it is true still. For each individual can increase his share of consumption if he has more money to spend. But, since the size of the cake is now fixed and no longer expansible, he can only do so at the expense of other people.

Thus, what is to the advantage of each of us regarded as a solitary individual is to the disadvantage of each of us regarded as members of a community. If all alike spend more, no one benefits. Here is the ideal opportunity for a common plan and for imposing a rule which everyone must observe. By such a plan, as I hope to show, the wage and salary earner can consume as much as before and in addition have money over in the bank for his future benefit and security, which would belong otherwise to the capitalist class.

375

Without such a plan we shall consume no more than otherwise, but will have spent all our money and have nothing over. For prices will rise just enough for the money we spend to be used up by the increased cost of what there is to buy. If all earnings are raised two shillings in the £ and are spent on buying the same quantity of goods as before, this means that prices also will rise two shillings in the £; and no one will be a loaf of bread or a pint of beer better off than he was before.

Unless the whole cost of the war were to be raised by taxes, which is not practically possible, part of it will be met by borrowing, which is another way of saying that a deferment of money expenditure must be made by someone. This will not be avoided by allowing prices to rise, which merely means that consumers' incomes pass into the hands of the capitalist class. A large part of this gain the latter would have to pay over in higher taxes; part they might themselves consume thus raising prices still higher to the disadvantage of other consumers; and the rest would be borrowed from them, so that they alone, instead of all alike, would be the principal owners of the increased national debt—of the right, that is to say, to spend money after the war.

For this reason a demand on the part of the trade unions for an increase in money rates of wages to compensate for every increase in the cost of living is futile, and greatly to the disadvantage of the working class. Like the dog in the fable, they lose the substance in gaping at the shadow. It is true that the better organised sections might benefit at the expense of other consumers. But except as an effort at group selfishness, as a means of hustling someone else out of the queue, it is a mug's game to play. In their minds and hearts the leaders of the trade unions know this as well as anyone else. They do not want what they ask. But they dare not abate their demands until they know what alternative policy is offered. This is legitimate. No coherent plan has yet been put up to them.

I have been charged with attempting to apply totalitarian

methods to a free community. No criticism could be more misdirected. In a totalitarian state the problem of the distribution of sacrifice does not exist. That is one of its initial advantages for war. It is only in a free community that the task of government is complicated by the claims of social justice. In a slave state production is the only problem. The poor and the old and the infant must take their chance; and no system lends itself better to the provision of special privileges to the governing class.

The aim of these pages is, therefore, to devise a means of adapting the distributive system of a free community to the limitations of war. There are three main objects to hold in view: the provision of an increased reward as an incentive and recognition of increased effort and risk, to which free men unlike slaves are entitled; the maximum freedom of choice to each individual how he will use that part of his income which he is at liberty to spend, a freedom which properly belongs to independent personalities but not to the units of a totalitarian ant-heap; and the mitigation of the necessary sacrifice for those least able to bear it, a use of valuable resources which a ruthless power avoids.

II THE CHARACTER OF THE SOLUTION

Even if there were no increases in the rates of money wages, the total of money earnings will be considerably increased by the greater number of insured men engaged in the services and in civilian employments, by overtime, and by the movement into paid employment of women, boys, retired persons and others who were not previously occupied.

It will be shown in the next chapter, what is fairly obvious to common sense, that in a war like this the amount of goods available for consumption will have to be diminished—and certainly cannot be increased above what it was in peacetime.

It follows that the increased quantity of money available to be spent in the pockets of consumers will meet a quantity of goods which is not increased. Unless we establish iron regulations limiting what is to be sold and establishing maximum prices for every article of consumption, with the result that there is nothing left to buy and the consumer goes home with the money burning his pocket, there are only two alternatives. Some means must be found for withdrawing purchasing power from the market; or prices must rise until the available goods are selling at figures which absorb the increased quantity of expenditure—in other words the method of inflation.

The general character of our solution must be, therefore, that it withdraws from expenditure a proportion of the increased earnings. This is the only way, apart from shortages of goods or higher prices, by which we can secure a balance between money to be spent and goods to be bought.

Voluntarily savings would serve this purpose if they were sufficient. In any case voluntary savings are wholly to the good and limit to that extent the dimensions of our problem. No word should be said to discourage the missionary zeal of those who campaign to increase them or the self-restraint and public spirit of those who make them. Nor is there anything in the plan which follows to make voluntary personal economy useless or unnecessary. I aim at a scheme which will achieve the bare minimum; and by the time it has been qualified by practical concessions nothing is more likely than that it will fall short of the bare minimum, and will not be sufficient by itself. Every further economy in personal consumption beyond what is prescribed will either ease the position of some other consumer or will allow an intensification of our war effort.

But the analysis of the national potential and of the distribution of the national income, which will be given in the next two chapters, shows clearly enough how improbable it is that voluntary savings can be sufficient. Those who allege otherwise are deceiving themselves or are victims of their own propaganda. Moreover, many people would, I think, welcome a prescribed plan which indicates to them their minimum duty; and those who feel moved to do more can rest assured that their effort is not useless. A minimum plan will not close the way to the voluntary self-sacrifice of individuals for the public good and the national purpose, any more than our system of taxation does. The nation will still need urgently the fruits of further personal abstention—always bearing it in mind that some forms of economy are much less valuable than others. But I also reckon it a merit of a prescribed plan that it reduces for the average man the necessity for a continuing perplexity how much to economise and for thinking about such things more than is good. An excessive obsession towards saving may be more useful than lovely; it is not always he who decides to save who makes the real sacrifice; and public necessity may sometimes become an excuse for giving full rein with self-approval to an instinct which is also a vice.

The first provision in our radical plan (chapters V and VI) is, therefore, to determine a proportion of each man's earnings which must be deferred—withdrawn, that is to say, from immediate consumption and only made available as a right to consume after the war is over. If the proportion can be fixed fairly for each income group, this device will have a double advantage. It means that rights to immediate consumption during the war can be allotted with a closer regard to relative sacrifice than under any other plan. It also means that rights to deferred consumption after the war, which is another name for the national debt, will be widely distributed amongst all those who are forgoing immediate consumption, instead of being mainly concentrated, as they were last time, in the hands of the capitalist class.

The second provision is to provide for this deferred consumption without increasing the national debt by a general capital levy after the war.

The third provision is to protect from any reductions in current consumption those whose standard of life offers no sufficient margin. This is effected by an exempt minimum, a sharply progressive scale and a system of family allowances.

The net result of these proposals is, to increase the consumption of young families with less than 75s a week, to leave the *aggregate* consumption of the lower income group having £5 a week or less nearly as high as before the war (whilst at the same time giving them rights, in return for extra work, to deferred consumption after the war), and to reduce the aggregate consumption of the higher income group with more than £5 a week by about a third on the average.

The fourth provision (chapter VIII), rendered possible by the previous provisions but not itself essential to them, is to link further changes in money rates of wages, pensions and other allowances to changes in the cost of a limited range of rationed articles of consumption, an iron ration as it has been called, which the authorities will endeavour to prevent, one way or another, from rising in price.

This scheme, put forward in the light of criticism and after further reflection, is more comprehensive than the plan for deferment of income which I proposed in the columns of *The Times* last November. Nevertheless, this original proposal is the lynchpin of the whole construction, failing which the rest would be impracticable. Without this proposal the cost of family allowances would aggravate the problem of consumption by increasing it in one direction without diminishing it in another; and would merely make the progress of inflation more inevitable. The same is true of an iron ration at a low price. Unless we have first of all withdrawn the excess of purchasing power from the market, the cost of subsidising consumption will lead the Treasury deeper into the financial bog. But if a deferment of earnings is agreed, the whole construction stands solid.

A general plan like this, to which all are required to conform, is like a rule of the road—everyone gains and no one can lose. To regard such a rule as an infringement of liberty is somewhat silly. If the rule of the road is imposed, people will travel as much as before. Under this plan people will consume as much as before. The rule of the road allows people as much choice, as they would have without it, along which roads to travel. This plan would allow people as much choice as before what goods they consume.

A comparison with the rule of the road is a very fair comparison. For the plan is intended to prevent people from getting in one another's way in spending their money.

III OUR OUTPUT CAPACITY AND THE NATIONAL INCOME

In order to calculate the size of the cake which will be left for civilian consumption, we have to estimate:

(1) the maximum current output that we are capable of organising from our resources of men and plant and materials;

(2) how fast we can safely draw on our foreign reserves by importing more than we export;

(3) how much of all this will be used up by our war effort.

The statistics from which to build up these estimates are very inadequate. Every government since the last war has been unscientific and obscurantist, and has regarded the collection of essential facts as a waste of money. There is no one today, inside or outside government offices, who does not mainly depend on the brilliant private efforts of Mr Colin Clark (in his *National Income and Outlay*, supplemented by later articles); but, in the absence of statistics which only a government can collect, he could often do no better than make a brave guess. The basis of what follows is given in more detail in Appendix 1 (p. 429), prepared with the assistance of Mr E. Rothbarth.

The money measure of our output capacity will, of course, vary according to the levels which are reached from time to time by wages and prices. To avoid this complication the following figures are all given in terms of pre-war prices.

In the year ending 31 March 1939, the value of our output, measured at cost, including invisible exports, was about £4,800 million. Of this amount

£3,710 million was the current cost (inclusive of the cost of maintaining plant) of the consumption of the public;

£850 million was the current cost (inclusive of the cost of maintenance) of the services provided by the Government, excluding 'transfer' payments to pensioners and holders of the national debt, etc., since these are merely out of one pocket into another, but including capital expenditure;

£290 million was devoted to increasing our privately owned capital equipment in the shape of buildings, plant and transport.

£4,850 million

This output can be increased (1) by absorbing a considerable proportion of the 12¾ per cent of insured workers who were unemployed in that year, (2) by bringing into employment workers from outside the insured population, including boys, women and retired or unoccupied persons, and (3) by more intensive work and overtime (a lengthening of working hours by half an hour would, for example, yield an increase of about 7½ per cent). On the other hand, there will be a loss of efficiency from withdrawals to the armed forces (whose output should be measured, if it is to tally with the other side of the balance sheet, by the cost of their pay, allowances and keep), from shortage of raw material and shipping, and from A.R.P. On balance an increase in output of 15 to 20 per cent should be practicable when our organisation is working properly. Taking an intermediate figure of just under 17½ per cent, let us assume an increase of £825 million in the value of output measured at pre-war prices. It is important to add that no such rise in output has taken place as yet.

There are two other sources from which government requirements can be met. Included in the cost of public and private consumption there is a figure of £420 million for the cost of making good current depreciation, in addition to about £300 million spent on additions to capital. Some of this output, costing £710 (£420 + £290) million altogether, could be diverted to government purposes. Let us put the contribution from this source at £150 million from depreciation funds and £300 million from normal new investment, making £450 million altogether.

The second and only remaining source is from selling our

gold and foreign investments and borrowing abroad. If we are to
be prepared for a prolonged war, we must be strict with ourselves in limiting the rate at which we expend these resources.
I put the maximum contribution which we can safely take from
this source in a year at £350 million.[1]

Altogether this yields us resources for additional government
requirements and current private consumption of £1,625
(£825 + £450 + £350) million a year.

What relation does this bear to present facts? The Chancellor
of the Exchequer announced in the late autumn of 1939 that the
rate of government expenditure already reached represented an
increase of somewhere in the neighbourhood of £1,500 million a
year. Thus *if* we had already reached the increased rate of output
assumed above, we should have had at that time a small margin
(of £125 million) out of which private consumption could be
increased. But everyone knows that we were, and still are, a long
way from having organised output on this scale. Indeed it is
certain, in my opinion, that the existing rate of government
expenditure leaves no margin for increased private consumption;
and that the maintenance of consumption is already leading to
a reduction in stocks of commodities and of foreign reserves at a
higher rate of depletion than that assumed above—at a higher
rate, that is to say, than is safe.

Moreover, it is certain that our war expenditure has not yet
reached its maximum. Let us assume that in the next year
government expenditure rises by no more than a further
£350 million above the estimated level of last autumn, and that
we are successful in raising our output to the maximum suggested above, which is an optimistic view of the prospects. This
will involve a reduction of £225 million below the pre-war rate
of consumption for the community as a whole. We have, therefore, to withdraw from consumption £825 million of increased
incomes *plus* £225 million of incomes previously spent.

That is a modest statement of the problem. Some would say

[1] Some details in justification of this figure are given in Appendix II (p. 432).

that it is a serious understatement, which allows inadequately for the magnitude of the war effort which will be needed. This may be true. Moreover, unless we mend our ways quickly, it greatly overstates our rate of output. Nevertheless, to establish my present argument it is not necessary to go beyond what is already plain. If a greater decrease in consumption proves necessary, that will reinforce all that I have to say.

Now we can see what the problem is and how it comes about. Even if there are no increases in wage rates or in prices, incomes will rise by an amount equal to what is earned in producing the increased output, namely £825 million a year on the above assumptions. Yet in spite of these increased incomes, those who receive them must consume less than before. Whilst earnings will be increased, consumption must be diminished. That is the conclusion to hammer home. It is beyond dispute. And it is gradually penetrating to the general consciousness. But we have become so accustomed to the problem of unemployment and of excess resources that it requires some elasticity of mind to adapt our behaviour to the problem of full employment and of resources which are no longer adequate to supply our needs. In war we move back from the age of plenty to the age of scarcity.

Moreover, the imminence of the new problem has been obscured from our eyes by the fact that after nearly six months of war there still persists a substantial volume of statistical unemployment. This is due to a failure of organisation, partly unavoidable in so short a space of time, partly avoidable if there was more energy and intelligence in the government. But anyone who argues from this that we are still in the age of plenty makes a mistake. The nature of unemployment today is totally different from what it was a year ago. It is no longer caused by a deficiency of demand. There is no longer a potential surplus supply of the things we want. The transition to full employment is hindered by two obstacles. The first is due to the difficulty of shifting labour to the points where it is wanted. The second—and, for the time being, the chief—obstacle is caused by the difficulties, other than the shortage of labour, in the way of existing demand becoming effective. For example, there may be a demand for cloth on the part both of exporters and of home consumers and there may be less than full employment in the woollen industry, and yet this demand will remain ineffective if the manufacturers cannot—for one reason or another, good or bad—obtain raw wool for the purpose of meeting these demands. Shortages of essential raw materials due to shipping delays and other causes, and artificial shortages due to the inefficient workings of our newly born controls who cannot learn their unaccustomed job all at once, are in many cases a more limiting factor than the shortage of labour. And in other cases there is a shortage of plant.

But I repeat that this does not mean we are still in the age of plenty. It means that the age of scarcity has arrived *before* the whole of the available labour has been absorbed. I am not saying that our output cannot be increased beyond its present level. Surely it can and must be so increased as our organisation improves. But we are already making all we know how. We have to learn *how* to make more; and that takes time.

Our ability, for the time being, to draw on stocks is another factor which is obscuring from our eyes the transition to the age of scarcity. There can be little doubt that during the first months of war our rate of private consumption has exceeded our surplus of production on a scale which cannot be continued indefinitely. Government demand has been greatly increased. There is no reason to suppose that private consumption has been sufficiently diminished. It is by drawing on our stocks of commodities and foreign resources and on our working capital that the deficiency has been met. The task of adjusting private expenditure to the supply which will be available is, therefore, more urgent than appears on the surface. It is not true that we can postpone action until after full employment has been reached.

The magnitude of the problem is now stated. The reader will appreciate that there is unavoidable guesswork and crude approximation in the figures which I have given. If anyone knows better, his criticism will be welcome. But I believe that the *size* of the result is roughly right and that more accurate details would not change the broad outline of the picture.

IV CAN THE RICH PAY FOR THE WAR?

We have shown that, quite apart from war increases in rates of wages, the earnings of the country as a whole should increase by as much as £825 million merely as a result of the increase in output and employment. At the same time private consumption will have to diminish by at least £225 million, taking a moderate estimate. Thus altogether £1,000 million of private incomes must be withdrawn from consumption. This figure has been reached on the basis of pre-war wages and prices. Since significant rises in these have already occurred, all our figures should be somewhat increased in terms of present prices and wages. By the end of January 1940, wholesale prices had risen by 27 per cent, the cost of living (seasonally corrected) by 10 per cent, and wages by perhaps 5 per cent; which means that the aggregates I am using should be increased by nearly 10 per cent to conform to the wage and price levels current at that date.

I have heard it argued that, whilst these figures may be correct, they do not prove that the working class need be asked to make any sacrifice. Admittedly they will work harder. But if so their consumption must be increased proportionately. If the cost of living rises, wage rates, and not merely total earnings, must be increased to the same extent. The whole of the real cost of the war, it is claimed, should be borne by the richer classes. Nay, more. The increased demand for the services of labour due to the war, offers a much-needed opportunity for increasing working-class consumption above what it was previously.

Do the workers really claim that they alone should be war-profiteers, taking advantage of the war to increase their consumption, and that more than the whole of the burden of the war should be borne by others? Or is it only some of their leaders who are claiming this on their behalf? This is a political question to which I am not competent to give an answer. Nor is it necessary that I should do so.

For, from the practical point of view, I doubt if this is one of the alternatives offering. At any rate, it is not something which will come about automatically as a result of having no policy and doing nothing. If we drift without a comprehensive plan, not this but inflation or shop shortages will result. And inflation, as we shall see, will be to the clear advantage of the richer class and will result in this class bearing not more, but less, than their fair share. I shall have to urge more than once before I have finished, that my proposals should be compared, not with some imaginary alternative, but with actual alternatives which are happening, or about to happen, before our eyes.

Let us, however, examine the facts. Once again the figures which I use are no better than rough approximations of the truth. We do not know accurately how the national income is distributed between different income groups, although this is clearly a matter of the first importance. There is some fairly good evidence of the proportions belonging to those with less than £250 a year and to those with more than £2,000 a year; but for the important intermediate groups the information is defective. But whilst many details in the following are probably inaccurate, I do not think that the picture as a whole is misleading. As before, we shall use pre-war prices and wages as our measuring rods; for, if we depart from these, we are on shifting sands.

We will begin with the sum-total of personal incomes before the war,[1] add to this the prospective war increase, and take away the rates and taxes which were already being paid in the pre-war years.

The last row of figures leaves us with the incomes out of which the increased war expenditure has to be met either by additional taxes or by borrowing, after allowing for what can be provided out of existing capital. (The manner in which the income group

---

[1] See Appendix I (p. 431) for the basis of this total.

from £250 to £500 is at present escaping its proper share of taxes is strikingly brought out. They actually paid a much smaller proportion of their pre-war incomes than the lower income-group below £250, namely 7·8 per cent compared with 13·4 per cent.)

Income group[1]	Below £250	£250–£500 (£ million)	Above £500	Total
Pre-war	2,910	640	1,700	5,250
War increase	425	100	300	825
Total war incomes	3,335	740	2,000	6,075
Pre-war rates and taxes	390	50	780	1,220
	£2,945	690	1,220	4,855

The figure which we have taken in chapter III for the increased expenditure of the government is £1,850 million, of which £150 million could be taken out of accruing depreciation not made good at home and £350 million from assets and borrowing abroad before allowing anything for normal saving. This leaves £1,350 million to be raised from additional taxes and from new savings (including normal savings) voluntary or involuntary.

We can rely in present circumstances on at least £400 million of voluntary savings, even if taxation is raised to a high level and if the proposal for deferred income made below is also adopted. Indeed I believe that this figure is considerably below the most probable expectation which might be put as much as £150 million higher; and I am reserving this margin against errors in the opposite direction elsewhere in the calculation. I include in this at least £100 million accruing in the hands of the government in the Unemployment Fund, Health Insurance and Pension Funds, War Risk Funds and the like; which is best regarded as diminishing the net government demands on the public by this amount, since it cannot easily be allocated to the personal savings of any group. In addition fully £300 million are

[1] The groups are to be interpreted to cover those who were in these pre-war, even though war increases may be moving them into higher income groups.

likely to accumulate through building societies, life offices, superannuation funds, the undistributed profits of companies (which alone were estimated at £300 million pre-war) and other institutional channels, even if individuals make no voluntary savings in addition to the other demands made on them. If this sum is allocated somewhat arbitrarily (for exact information is lacking) between the different income groups, we are left with the following:

Income group	Below £250	£250–£500 (£ million)	Above £500	Total
War incomes less pre-war taxes	2,945	690	1,220	4,855
Minimum voluntary savings	50	75	175	300
	£2,895	615	1,045	4,555

out of which £950 million has still to be found for the government. Even allowing for a wide margin of error in this calculation, it shows that if everyone with more than £500 a year had the whole of his income in excess of that sum taken from him in taxes, the yield would not be nearly enough,[1] being £625 million or only two-thirds of the government's requirements.

Yet this suggestion is a wild exaggeration beyond what could be expected from our fiscal system. Indeed taxation on this scale would involve such widespread breaches of existing contracts and commitments that the taxable incomes themselves would be largely reduced. An important part of these incomes is spent on rates and other purposes which do not increase personal consumption, on current resources, the alternative uses of which are much less valuable, and on payments to dependants. It follows that an important contribution must be obtained one way or another from the income group below £500 a year.

Nor is it practicable to put the exemption limit at £250 a year.

[1] There are about 840,000 heads of households with more than £500 a year and their aggregate war incomes, after deducting pre-war taxes and minimum saving, is put above at £1,045 million, which leaves £625 million after deducting £500 per head.

There are about 2,430,000 persons with incomes above this level. If the whole of the excess of their remaining incomes above £250 was taken from them, namely £1,050 million[1] and if this caused no reduction in the incomes by repercussion (which is far from the truth), it would only just exceed the government's requirements. If the cost of the war is to be met by the income group above £250 a year, it would mean taking from them in savings and taxation (new and old) about three-quarters of their total wartime incomes, leaving them with just over a quarter of their incomes for their own consumption.

In the light of these figures it is not sane to suppose that the war can be financed without putting some burden on the increased war incomes of the class with £5 a week or less. For this income group accounts for about 88 per cent of the population, for more than 60 per cent of the total personal incomes of the country after allowing for war increases (due to greater output but allowing nothing for higher wage rates) and deducting pre-war rates and taxes, and for about two-thirds of current consumption. Moreover, the incomes of this group will have been increased on the average by some 15 per cent as a result of the war. Is it seriously expected that those with less than £5 a week will be allowed to increase their average consumption by 15 per cent, while all those with more than £5 a week will be left on the average with only a quarter of their incomes to consume? The only question is, therefore, how large the contribution of this class must be, and how it can be obtained with least sacrifice and most justice.

If we have a deliberate plan, considerations of social justice can be weighed and considered. Without such a plan (as at present) they go by default.

As a basis of discussion I offer in the next two chapters a proposal, capable, I expect, of amendment and improvement in a hundred details, but embodying a principle which will achieve

[1] Total available incomes of this group £1,660 million less about £610 million (in respect of 2,430,000 at £250 each).

more social justice than any other plan. It should be judged by comparison, not with some imaginary alternative or unattainable counsels of perfection, but with what is actually happening before our eyes.

V   A PLAN FOR DEFERRED PAY, FAMILY ALLOWANCES AND A CHEAP RATION

I have now reached a stage in the argument where I have to choose between being too definite or being too vague. If I set forth a concrete proposal in all its particulars, I expose myself to a hundred criticisms on points not essential to the principle of the plan. If I go further in the use of figures for illustration, I am involved more and more in guesswork; and I run the risk of getting the reader bogged in details which may be inaccurate and could certainly be amended without injury to the main fabric. Yet if I restrict myself to generalities, I do not give the reader enough to bite on; and am in fact shirking the issue, since the size, the order of magnitude, of the factors involved is not an irrelevant detail.

I propose to run the risk of giving too many details and estimates rather than too few—relying on the reader's benevolent understanding of my method. But I may help him to distinguish between principles which are essential and details which are illustrative if I begin, in this chapter, with some generalities (though not entirely divorced from figures), leaving to the next one the blueprint.

We have reached the broad conclusion that allowing for the increase in war output and taking credit for the pre-war yield of taxes and for those savings on which we can rely in any case, there remains about £950 million of incomes in private hands which must not be spent but must be diverted to the finance of the war.

I suggest that perhaps as much as one-half of this, namely £500 million, can be raised by taxation. Indeed in a full year and disregarding time-lags in collection the war taxes already imposed in Sir John Simon's emergency budget may provide £400 million towards this. I include in this at least £100 million from Excess Profits Tax even if we avoid any significant degree of inflation. Inflation would, of course, greatly increase the yield of this tax; but the yield should be substantial even without this adventitious aid, partly as a reflection of the higher level of output and partly on account of the distribution of profits between individual businesses being materially different from what it was in the base year. Other fiscal devices, including a sales tax on certain classes of non-necessities, should be capable of finding another £100 million. But it would not be easy for our fiscal machine to raise much more than this with due regard to justice and efficiency, except by a general sales tax, a wages tax or the use of inflation as a tax gatherer.

The idea of bridging the remaining gap of £450 million, in addition to the £400 million for which we have already taken credit, by voluntary savings without any aid from inflation is chimerical. It must be remembered that we have already assumed an annual subscription by the public to government loans of £900 million (£350 million in exchange for foreign assets, £150 million from depreciation funds and £400 million from new savings) less such amount as accrues from investment in government funds, etc., from overseas borrowing and from the proceeds of sales of gold; for the total increased expenditure of the government is not £950 million a year but (on our assumptions) £1,850 million. For reasons we have already given, the additional savings would have to come largely from the income group with £5 a week or less and would require a change in their habits of expenditure for which there is no evidence.

For these same reasons the amount by which the potential expenditure of the lower income groups has to be curtailed will be more or less the same whichever method is adopted. Inflation will be the most burdensome alternative, since this will inevitably bring some advantage to the entrepreneur class, and might cost the worker 20 per cent in terms of the real value of his earnings.

Inflation will also be the most burdensome on the smallest incomes—a defect it shares with a general sales tax. New taxes, such as a sales tax or a wages tax, or old taxes aided by inflation are alike in that they finally deprive the workers of the benefit of their earnings from their heavier burden of labour. They will work harder but, as a group, they will *never* derive any personal benefit from it. That is what will happen, will inevitably happen, if the Treasury and the trade union leaders agree on the one thing where they will find agreement easiest, namely to drift along without a definite policy, following the usual methods and rejecting new ideas.

Is there no better way? We have seen that it is physically impossible for the community as a whole to consume *now* the equivalent of their increased war effort. That is obvious. The war effort is to pay for the war; it cannot also supply increased consumption. Those who make the effort have, therefore, only two alternatives between which to choose. They can forgo the equivalent consumption altogether; or they can *postpone* it.

For each individual it is a great advantage to retain the rights over the fruits of his labour even though he must put off the enjoyment of them. His personal wealth is thus increased. For that is what wealth is—command of the right to postponed consumption.

This suggests to us the way out. A suitable proportion of each man's earnings must take the form of *deferred pay*.

With this general principle established, the practical difficulties of our task begin. If we were to apply the principle in the crudest possible way by deferring, let us say, a level 20 per cent of all income remaining after payment of pre-war taxes, it would still be much better than the alternative of inflation. But public opinion requires, justly perhaps, that a deliberate plan, and particularly that a *new* plan, should not merely be better than doing nothing, but *much* better. A new plan is required to meet objections, which apply equally to the old plan, but which in the case of the latter custom has caused us to forget. The new plan is required to satisfy ideals of social justice much higher than we have been attaining without it.

Let us welcome this demand. If we can make the upsetting of established arrangements, which the exigencies of war finance require, the opportunity to improve the social distribution of incomes, all the better.

With this object in view we can add a second and a third principle to the first principle of deferring a proportion of current earnings. We have suggested that about a half of what is required can be obtained by outright taxes, leaving a half to be supplied by deferment of earnings. Let our second principle provide that the bulk of the new taxes shall fall on the income groups of £250 or more, and that the main part of the contribution of the lower income groups shall take the form, not of forgoing income outright, but of merely deferring it.

The third principle must be directed to the maintenance of adequate minimum standards—better and not worse than have existed hitherto. Thus, whilst the second principle puts heavier burdens on the richer classes, the third principle allows special reliefs to the poorer.

To carry out the third principle requires two distinct proposals. In the scheme which I first put forward in *The Times* I attempted to deal with the problem by proposing a minimum exempt income, this minimum to be increased for a married man in accordance with the size of his family. This proposal was rightly criticised on the ground that the resulting allowance was inadequate. The following scheme goes much further and is, I venture to think, a great improvement.

For some years past the weight of opinion has been growing in favour of family allowances. In time of war it is natural that we should be more concerned than usual with the cost of living; and as soon as there is a threat of a rising cost of living and a demand for higher wages to meet it, the question of family allowances must come to the front. For the burden of the rising cost of living depends very largely on the size of a man's family.

At first sight it is paradoxical to propose in time of war an expensive social reform which we have not thought ourselves able to afford in time of peace. But in truth the need for this reform is so much greater in such times that it may provide the most appropriate occasion for it.

I share the view held by many others that this is so. I recommend, therefore, that a family allowance of 5s per week should be paid in cash for each child up to the age of fifteen. I am estimating the net cost of this at £100 million, the basis for which is explained in Appendix III (p. 436).

Is this provision enough? We have to consider the fairly large class with small incomes which will not be increased by the war, or at any rate not sufficiently to keep pace with the increase in the cost of living. And there is the demand of the trade unions for some security against the risk that the rise in prices will outstrip the level of wages, even if a scheme for deferred pay or the like is agreed to.

To meet this an important section of opinion, which has received the weighty support of Sir Arthur Salter, Mr R. H. Brand and Professor and Mrs Hicks, recommends that a minimum ration of consumption goods be made available at a low fixed price, even though this might involve subsidies. If I were advising the Treasury, I should look with anxiety on such a proposal taken by itself, since it might in certain circumstances place an almost insupportable burden on the Exchequer. But if it were made part of a comprehensive scheme, including the deferment of a proportion of earnings, agreed with the trade unions, I would welcome it.

The minimum ration should not comprise all the articles covered by the cost of living index, but should be restricted to a limited list of necessaries available in time of war. Nor should any absolute undertaking be given as to future prices. It should be agreed, however, that in the event of any rise in the cost of the minimum ration, the trade unions would be free to press for a corresponding increase in wages.

But it should be an absolute condition of such an arrangement that a scheme for deferred pay should be accepted at the same time, and that the trade unions should agree, subject to the above safeguard, not to press for any further increases in money wages on the ground of the cost of living.

Without these conditions the weight of purchasing power available in the hands of consumers would render any attempt at price fixation excessively dangerous. The low prices for the minimum ration would merely release more purchasing power for use in other directions, which would drive up other prices to an excessive disparity with that of the fixed ration. To attempt to fix consumption prices whilst allowing an indefinite increase of purchasing power in the hands of consumers would be an obvious error.

For the trade unions such a scheme as this offers great and evident advantages compared with progressive inflation or with a wages tax. In spite of the demands of war, the workers would have secured the enjoyment, sooner or later, of a consumption fully commensurate with their increased effort; whilst family allowances and the cheap ration would actually improve, even during the war, the economic position of the poorer families. We should have succeeded in making the war an opportunity for a positive social improvement. How great a benefit in comparison with a futile attempt to evade a reasonable share of the burden of a just war, ending in a progressive inflation!

VI DETAILS

I have avoided in the previous chapter precise figures of the proportion of earnings to be deferred and of the minimum standard which should be free from deferment. Those who agree on the principle may differ on the details. It is better, therefore, to separate them so far as is possible. I put forward the following as a basis of discussion. The details are a question of degree and of opinion. If these proposals err, it may be in the direction of making concessions to the income group below £5 a week, greater than it will be easy to maintain—concessions which are, I believe, still possible on the assumption that output is adequately increased and that government expenditure does not exceed the estimate given above, but no longer possible if either of these assumptions fail.

The basis on which the details have been arrived at is the following:

(1) The aggregate real consumption of the group with £5 a week or less should be maintained for as long as possible at or near the pre-war level.

(2) Those who remain in the lower half of this group are likely to have benefited least, or not at all, from the aggregate increase in war incomes, and cannot afford, therefore, to have any important part of their current earnings deferred if they are to maintain their standard of life.

(3) Since some rise in the cost of living relatively to wage rates (though not to total earnings) is inevitable, and since it is impossible under any scheme to avoid individual inequalities of treatment, we should make sure by means of family allowances that the inequality will work out in favour of households with families, so that these will be for certain better off.

(4) Since the increased war incomes of the lower income groups probably represent increased work to a greater extent than in the case of the higher income groups, the contribution of the former should be mainly in the form of deferment of earning and the contribution of the latter mainly in the shape of increased taxation.

(5) The increase in the cost of imports is likely to involve an increase in the cost of living relatively to wages of not less than 5 per cent even with the existence of subsidies.

There remains the question whether we can hope to provide the whole of the £950 million required, or rather £1,050 million including the cost of family allowances, by taxation and the deferment of pay. The proposals, which I put forward in *The Times* and the *Economic Journal*, were a little faint-hearted in this respect and avowedly fell short of what was required. It now seems to me better to start with a scheme which aims at being adequate, even if this is a counsel of perfection. For subsequent concessions are sure to whittle away the yield; so that a scheme which is moderately less than adequate at the start will be seriously inadequate at the finish. Since various concessions recommended in the next chapter are likely to cost at least £50 million, I shall aim, therefore, at a scale of deferment which should yield £600 million gross.

Whether the actual scales proposed below will in fact achieve these objects, it is impossible to forecast with accuracy. They *aim* at carrying out the above principles. If it is shown that they would fail to do so, they can be amended accordingly. Put into figures the distribution of the burden *aimed* at is the following:

Income group	Below £250	Above £250	Total
		(£ million)	
Increased taxes[1]	150	350	500
Deferment of earnings	250	350	600
Loss through relative rise in the cost of living	125	50	175
	525	750	1,275
Less increase in war incomes	425	400	825
	100	350	450
Less family allowances[2]	100	—	100
Decrease in real consumption	Nil	350	350

The loss, estimated above, due to a rise in the cost of living relatively to wages, allows for a cost of living 10 per cent above pre-war only partially offset by a 5 per cent rise in wages. This is, roughly speaking, the present position. The estimate assumes that the higher income group will be somewhat less affected by this factor than the lower.

In terms of pre-war real consumption the final result means, very roughly, that the aggregate consumption of the higher

[1] Including increased yield of pre-war taxes.
[2] For the sake of simplicity, I am assuming that the existing income tax allowances for children already cost on the average 5s per child for the income group above £250, which may or may not be correct. Probably it is an overstatement, since the allowance works out at 3s 9d per child up to about £400 earned income, gradually rising thereafter to 7s 6d.

income group will be reduced by fully a third and the aggregate consumption of the lower income group not at all. But the reader will understand that I am by now in deep statistical water and that there is room for serious errors of detail in figures which I have been bold, perhaps too bold, to give.

This distribution of burden may be open to the criticism that it demands too heavy a relative sacrifice from the higher income group. It certainly uses the opportunity of war finance to effect a considerable redistribution of incomes in the direction of greater equality. Does any responsible leader of the working class believe that rising wage rates vainly pursuing a rising cost of living, or any other alternative, will work out more justly than this or more advantageously to the lower income group?

It should be a strong recommendation of what is here proposed that it offers a special protection to the lowest income-group of £3 a week or less, who are not benefiting from war increases of earnings, and to family men who are least able to forgo any improvement which may come their way.

What is the best formula to reach this result? In my *Times* articles I proposed a formula which had the advantage of showing the combined result to the taxpayer of direct taxes and of deferment of pay. This formula was open to various minor criticisms of detail, which the Inland Revenue would have to meet in an actual scheme. But after much reflection I have not been able to find a better one for expressing the general purpose and result of the plan. I am, therefore, retaining it subject to certain changes made necessary by the redistribution within the lower income group which it is now proposed to make through family allowances, or by a more careful consideration of how it interlocks with the burden of direct taxes. The revised formula is given in Appendix IV (p. 437), and its effects in detail are shown below.

(1) *Children's allowances.* The system of children's allowances under the existing income tax appears highly anomalous when it is examined in detail. For a man with an earned income of £250,

it works out at £7 per annum for the first child and nothing for subsequent children; and it gradually rises with income to a maximum of £18. 15s for every child. For non-income-tax payers there is no general children's allowance, though allowances are paid in a number of special cases. In lieu of the whole of the present system of children's allowances, I propose a flat payment of 5s per week per child or £13 per annum, both for income-tax payers and for the insured population.

(2) *Basic minimum income*. As the basic minimum income which should be allowed free of deferment, I propose 35s a week to unmarried and 45s a week to married men. If different figures are preferred, this can be adjusted by altering the percentage to be taken in excess of the basic minimum.

(3) *Incomes in excess of the basic income*. A percentage of all incomes in excess of the basic minimum to be paid over to the government, partly as direct taxes and partly as deferred pay; the combined percentage to be taken rising steeply as the level of income increases. The formula for making the calculations is given in Appendix IV (p. 437), but the effect of it at various income levels is shown more clearly in the following table. Taking as the standard case the married man with no young children, the percentage of his income to be withheld to cover his deferred pay (and also his income tax and surtax) works out thus:

	per cent
Up to 45s weekly	Nil
At 50s	3¼
55s	6
60s	8¾
80s	15¼
100s	19¼
£300 annually	21
£400	25
£500	27
£700	29
£1,000	35
£2,000	37¼
£5,000	53¼
£10,000	64
£20,000	75
£50,000	80
Over £50,000	85

As will be shown in the next table, the proposed family allowances make the result far more favourable than this for the man with young children in the lower income ranges. With two children he is a substantial gainer on balance at all levels up to 75s a week.

(4) *The division between taxation and deferment.* The appropriate part of a man's income withheld under the above formula will be used to discharge his income tax and surtax if any. The balance will be credited to him as a deposit in the manner to be explained in the next chapter. The final result of all this in different individual cases is shown in the following tables:

	Weekly earnings	Deferment of pay	Existing income tax
Unmarried	35s	Nil	Nil
	45s	3s 6d	Nil
	55s	5s 9d	1s 3d
	75s	9s 9d	4s 3d
	80s	10s 9d	5s
	100s	14s 3d	8s 6d
Married	35s	Nil	Nil
	45s	Nil	Nil
	55s	3s 6d	Nil
	75s	10s 6d	Nil
	80s	12s 3d	Nil
	100s	15s 10½d	3s 4½d

	Weekly earnings	Deferment of pay and income tax	Family allowance	Cash remaining for consumption
Married with two young children	35s	Nil	10s	45s
	45s	Nil	10s	55s
	55s	3s 6d	10s	61s 6d
	75s	10s 6d	10s	74s 6d
	80s	12s 3d	10s	77s 9d
	100s	19s 3d	10s	90s 9d
Married with three young children	35s	Nil	15s	50s
	45s	Nil	15s	60s
	55s	3s 6d	15s	66s 6d
	75s	10s 6d	15s	79s 6d
	80s	12s 3d	15s	82s 9d
	100s	19s 3d	15s	95s 9d

Thus a married man with two young children has actually more left in cash for all rates of earnings up to nearly 75s, and with three children for all rates up to nearly 95s. In addition family men will have substantial deferred pay credited to them besides their cash for immediate consumption being increased.

For a married man[1] with an earned income above £5 a week the result is as follows:

Total income	Income tax and surtax payable	Income deferred	Remaining income
	(£)		
300	15	49	236
400	31	68	301
600	93	76	431
1,000	218	135	647
2,000	562	285	1,153
5,000	2,055	630	2,315
10,000	5,268	1,156	3,576
20,000	13,018	1,896	5,088
100,000	80,768	4,133	15,099

At the higher income ranges the percentage of income deferred to total income falls considerably. But it cannot be considered too low if allowance is made for the enormous sums taken in income tax and surtax at these ranges. For example at £100,000, the income deferred is only 4 per cent of total income, but it is 21½ per cent of the income which is left after payment of these taxes.

(5) *Method of collection.* For the insured population the method of collection would be the same as for social insurance. Each insured worker would hold a deferred pay card which would be stamped by the employer. For income-tax payers the method would be the same as for income tax. For incomes up to £750 a year the whole question of deferred pay can be dealt with when considering income-tax allowances. For surtax payers the

---

[1] He also receives £13 per annum for each young child. An unmarried man pays from £13 to £16 more in income tax and has a little less deferred. There should, perhaps, be an additional allowance for married men in these income ranges.

method would be the same as for surtax. Thus no new machinery either of assessment or of collection will be required—a great advantage for a wartime measure.

In the case of fluctuating earnings, the proportion of deferred pay appropriate to each pay period would be withheld in the first instance. But this could be adjusted to the proportion appropriate to the average earnings at quarterly or any other convenient intervals, since the card would carry on its face all the information required for this purpose.

(6) *The depository for deferred pay*. Considerable choice could be allowed to the individual in what institution his deferred pay should be deposited. He might choose his friendly society, his trade union, or any other body approved for the purposes of health insurance; or, failing such preference, the Post Office Savings Bank. Thus there would be an encouragement to the working-man's own institutions to take charge of his resources for him and, if desired, a considerable degree of discretion could be allowed to such bodies as to the conditions in which these resources could be released to the individual to meet his personal emergencies, as is proposed in the next chapter.

The reader will readily perceive that the same results could be obtained by reducing the exemption limits for income tax and raising the rates of income tax and surtax effective at different levels of income to the percentages of income set out in Appendix IV (p. 437). For those who dislike fancy schemes and prefer to keep to well-understood methods, this is the sound alternative. If it is accompanied by family allowances, I see no fiscal objection to this solution. Socially I prefer the more novel proposal, which retains a stronger incentive to effort, gives less sense of sacrifice and indeed requires less, and spreads through the community the advantages of security, which saved resources afford far more widely than before.

VII   THE RELEASE OF DEFERRED PAY AND
A CAPITAL LEVY

That part of the earnings and other income of the public to be deferred under this plan would be placed to the credit of its owner as a blocked deposit in the friendly society or the approved institution selected by him, as proposed above or, failing such choice, in the Post Office Savings Bank carrying interest at 2½ per cent compound. If the yield aimed at in the above scheme was reached, the gross amount accumulated in this way would amount to about £600 million a year. In fact the accumulations might come to less than this because there are various concessions which it would be fair to make.

In the first place there are certain definite commitments to save entered into before the war which a man might reasonably be allowed to meet out of his blocked deposit such as instalments due to a building society, premiums due to a life assurance office, hire purchase commitments, and perhaps bank loans. (I have already allowed £50 million as a margin and, if this is insufficient, there is also, I believe, a substantial hidden reserve in my estimate of the voluntary savings to be expected outside the deferment scheme.) It would also be reasonable to release them for the payment of death duties.

In the second place, a man might be allowed to apply his deferred pay to the purchase of new life insurance or an endowment policy. Schemes to encourage this might be prepared by the life offices on lines adapted to the special circumstances.

In the third place, since these deposits are a man's own property intended to increase his sense of security and as a reserve against his family and personal emergencies, he should be allowed to use his deposit in any case approved by his friendly society or, in the case of the Post Office Savings Bank, by a local committee, as for example to meet illness, unemployment, or special family expenses.

In general, however, the deposits are not intended to be used until after the war when they would be released by a series of instalments at dates, not unduly delayed, to be fixed by the government. Meanwhile they should not reckon in calculations arising out of the means test or eligibility for old age pensions or the capital levy to be proposed below or the like.

The appropriate time for the ultimate release of the deposits will have arrived at the onset of the first post-war slump. For then the present position will be exactly reversed. Instead of demand being in excess of supply, we shall have a capacity to produce in excess of the current demand. Thus the system of deferment will be twice blessed; and will do almost as much good hereafter in preventing deflation and unemployment as it does now in preventing inflation and the exhaustion of scarce resources. For it is exceedingly likely that a time will come after the war when we shall be as anxious to increase consumers' demand as we are now to decrease it. It is only sensible to put off private expenditure from the date when it cannot be used to increase consumption to the date when it will bring into employment resources which otherwise would run to waste.

If the deposits are released in these circumstances, the system will be self-liquidating both in terms of real resources and of finance. In terms of real resources it will be self-liquidating because the consumption will be met out of labour and productive capacity which would otherwise run to waste. In terms of finance it will be self-liquidating because it will avoid the necessity of raising other loans to pay for unemployment or for public works and the like as a means of preventing unemployment.

Nevertheless it has been my experience that no part of the scheme has raised more doubts than this supposed difficulty about the ultimate repayment of the blocked deposits. I am surprised at this criticism which seems to me unreasonable. For the national debt will be no greater than if the same results were produced by voluntary savings. Moreover, the discretion reserved to the Treasury for the date of release makes it easier to handle this particular section of the national debt than the rest of the large volume of short-term debt which the war is likely to leave behind it. The argument is, I suppose, that savings deferred in this way are more likely than normal savings to be spent by their owners as soon as they are free to do so. How far this will prove to be true in fact, I am not sure. It may be that the blocked deposits will be instrumental in spreading the habit of small savings more widely, and that a large proportion will be left undrawn as conservatively as the existing savings bank deposits. But I am not relying on this. Indeed, in so far as the deposits are not spent when the time comes for their release the advantages to employment which I have forecast will not mature. I am doing no more than assume that steps can be taken to prevent the deposits from being spent faster than they can be replaced by new loans which would have been required in any case for the relief or the avoidance of unemployment.

If, however, public opinion still feels a difficulty here, it is one that can be met in a manner which has advantages for its own sake. If the war continues for two years or longer, the national debt will reach an unmanageable figure, which will hamper national finance for years to come. In such circumstances a capital levy will be advisable just as (in my opinion) it was at the end of the last war, if it could have been carried out before the post-war slump. There may be a good case, therefore, for linking a capital levy (or tax) to the deferred pay.

I suggest, therefore, that an undertaking should be given that a capital levy will be enforced after the war to bring in an amount sufficient to discharge the liability in respect of deferred pay. I should still argue that it would be better not to synchronise the two. I would not willingly forgo the great advantages of withholding the deferred pay until the onset of serious unemployment, whereas this would be the worst possible time for the capital levy. If the levy is to be paid in a lump sum, it should be discharged at the earliest possible date after the close of the war, especially if temporary boom conditions seem imminent.

But it might be preferable, as facilitating collection and greatly lessening the disturbance, to collect it in a series of instalments over a period. This procedure would have the special merit that it might pave the way administratively for a permanent capital tax which would be a valuable addition to our fiscal machinery and has certain important advantages over income tax. In any case there will be plenty of treasury bills after the war waiting to be cared for, so that there is no technical reason why the capital levy and the release of the blocked deposits need be simultaneous.

It is often argued in labour circles that a capital levy should form part of the immediate programme for the finance of the war. The sound reasons which lie behind this, namely that the war should be an occasion for diminishing rather than for increasing the existing inequalities of wealth, are completely met by the above proposal. At the same time, the great and indeed overwhelming objections to an immediate wartime levy are avoided. I am not thinking mainly of the administrative difficulties, though these might prove insuperable. The main point is that a capital levy now would do little or nothing to solve the immediate problem. A capital levy on a scale worth having could not be met out of the current consumption of the wealthy. They could only pay it by handing over assets to the government, the capital value of which would be of no assistance whatever to the immediate financial task. Nothing is of the least use now which does not diminish consumption out of current income; and for the reasons which I have given in chapter IV no expedient can be adequate which allows the increased purchasing power of the lower income groups to materialise in a corresponding increase in their consumption. There is no avoiding a postponement of expenditure on the part of this group, except by inflation which allows them to spend and deprives them of the fruit of spending. But the proposal here made secures them the *ultimate* enjoyment of their earnings unabated.

When general principles have been established for the management of blocked deposits, there may be other good opportunities for the use of this device. In particular, men on active service might have their economic position made a little more equal to the position of those remaining in civilian employment by being credited with an appropriate blocked deposit proportional to their length of service. A 'veteran's bonus' is a peculiarly fit obligation for discharge by a capital levy on wealth.

The device might also be useful for dealing with excess profits. A counsel of perfection would require that no excess profits should be allowed during the war. This is not advisable in practice because it would deprive those, who would nevertheless remain in control of their businesses, of any incentive towards economy; and the experience of the last war showed that this is liable to lead to great extravagance and waste. It is in the interest of the Treasury that the gross figure of excess profits before deduction of tax should be as large as possible; and this will not be attained if those in charge of business are deprived of all incentive. The existing tax on excess profits is at the rate of 60 per cent which means that, including income tax, 75 per cent already accrues to the Treasury and even a larger percentage in the case of surtax-payers. If the basis of calculation was rendered more equitable so that what legally reckons as excess profits really are so in fact, there would be room for a moderate increase. But it might be a better plan to require the balance of excess profits after deducting E.P.T. and income tax to be held in a blocked deposit.

VIII RATIONING, PRICE CONTROL AND WAGE CONTROL

The mechanism of reaching equilibrium by means of a rising cost of living, which is vainly pursued by a rising level of wages will be described in the next chapter. But it is admitted on all hands that this is the worst possible solution.

It has been argued here that the only way to escape from this is to withdraw from the market, either by taxation or by deferment, an adequate proportion of consumers' purchasing power, so that there is no longer an irresistible force impelling prices upwards. But there are many who believe that there is another alternative open, namely to control the cost of living by a combination of rationing and price fixing, and that, if this was done, wage control would become manageable.

I believe that it is a dangerous delusion to suppose that equilibrium can be reached by those measures alone. Nevertheless, some measure of rationing and price control should play a part in our general scheme and might be a valuable adjunct to our main proposal. It is relevant, therefore, to debate the matter in this place.

There are two central objections to rationing and price control unaccompanied by a withdrawal of consumers' purchasing power. The first objection arises out of the great variety of personal consumption between one man and another. If our needs and tastes were all the same, there would be no real loss in abolishing consumers' choice. In fact there is a great deal of waste, both of resources and of enjoyment, in allotting to each of us identical rations of every consumable object. There are some articles of consumption—bread, sugar, salt, bacon perhaps —where no great harm is done, though even here there are in fact wide differences of personal habit. But as one proceeds through the list—milk, coffee, beer, spirits, butcher's meat, clothing, boots, books, articles of clothing, furniture—the variety of taste and need dominates the scene. It becomes ludicrous to compel everyone to divide his expenditure between the different articles of expenditure in exactly the same way. Moreover, it would never be practicable to cover every conceivable article by a rationing coupon; and if there are certain articles uncontrolled the pressure of purchasing power will tend to divert production in their direction, although they may be what the consumer least wants and what it is least desirable that he should have. Finally, if by a miracle the method was substantially successful, so that consumption was completely controlled and consumers were left with a significant fraction of their incomes which they were unable to spend, we should merely have arrived by an elaborate, roundabout and wasteful method at the same result as if that fraction of their incomes had been deferred from the outset.

If our object is to prevent a certain proportion of consumers' incomes from being spent, the only sensible thing is to start at that end, withholding by deferment or by taxation that proportion which is not to be spent and then allowing a free choice to the consumer how he shall divide what he is allowed to spend between different articles of consumption. A world of trouble and an ocean of waste will be avoided, and the consumer will enjoy far more satisfaction. A recent cartoon by Low, in which Sir John Simon was depicted struggling with a belt unable to decide whether he should constrict 'the pantry or the pocket', conveyed profound comment on this matter. Constriction of the pocket is the alternative which a free community should prefer. The abolition of consumers' choice in favour of universal rationing is a typical product of that onslaught, sometimes called Bolshevism, on differences between one man and another by which existence is enriched.

A well-conceived policy of rationing has quite a different object from this. Its purpose is not to control aggregate consumption but to divert consumption in as fair a way as possible from an article, the supply of which has to be restricted for special reasons. For example, interruption of trade with Denmark and the Baltic necessarily restricts the supply of bacon below normal, and replacement is only possible by purchases in U.S.A. which would compete with more important claims on our dollar resources; or it is impossible to allot enough shipping tonnage to satisfy the current demand for sugar. It is necessary, therefore, to force people to consume less bacon or less sugar and to buy something else instead—quite a different problem from reducing their aggregate expenditure. If the article is not a conventional necessary or one of general consumption, the end is reached most easily by allowing a rise in the price of the article, the consumption of which we wish to restrict, relatively to other articles. But if this article is a necessary, an exceptional rise in the price of which is undesirable, so that the natural method of restriction is ruled out, then there is a sound case for rationing.

There is hardly less objection to price fixing and legal restrictions against price increases, unaccompanied by any restriction on the volume of purchasing power. For this policy has the effect of positively increasing the pressure of consumption and of facilitating the conversion of money income into the use and depletion of valuable resources. If the quantity of resources which the authorities are prepared to release for civilian consumption is strictly limited, price-fixing practices are likely to end in shortages in the shops and queues of unsatisfied purchasers.

It is, however, undoubtedly the fact that price fixing and propaganda against price raising are much more *à la mode* today than old-fashioned inflation. The political advantages of this policy are obvious. The objection to it is that, unlike old-fashioned inflation, it does nothing to bring about equilibrium, indeed on the contrary. My belief is that, if in the next six months no adequate steps are taken to curtail consumers' purchasing power, the consequences are much more likely to be seen in the shape of shortages in the shops than in a runaway price level. There is a strong feeling both amongst the public and amongst producers and retailers against rising prices. The mentality which used to result formerly in rapid price inflation is replaced today by a different conception both of private advantage and of public spirit. I believe, therefore, that a typical price inflation is much further off than some people are thinking. I welcome this new attitude. For it means that we have a longer time in which to implement a policy of genuine equilibrium before irremediable damage is done. Nevertheless it is no genuine solution. Shop shortages and queues lead to great injustices of distribution, to an abominable waste of time and to a needless fraying of the public temper. It is the alternative which both Russia and Germany have long preferred to old-fashioned inflation, and it is, as I have said, *à la mode*. But it is for us to find the third alternative, which is the genuine solution, preserving both the general interest and the free choice of the individual consumer.

I have not attempted to deal directly with the problem of wages. It is wiser, I expect, to deal with it indirectly. If the necessary proportion of consumers' purchasing power is not withdrawn from the market, a significant rise in prices cannot be avoided, even though there is no runaway inflation. An attempt on the part of the government to keep down the price level of a range of articles in general consumption will require, sooner or later, subsidies on a scale which would impair still further the equilibrium of the budget. (The Chancellor of the Exchequer stated recently that the tentative moves in this direction already made are costing the Treasury £1 million a week.) And a significant rise in the cost of living is certain to be followed by a more or less successful agitation for higher wages.

If, on the other hand, the problem is tackled indirectly by withdrawing purchasing power, there will be no reason why the vicious process should be started by prices being forced up at the demand end. There might be certain subsidies in part compensation for price increases due to the higher cost of imports and some rise of wages for grades of labour which already had a special claim for an improvement. But the main reason for the development of an acute wages problem would have been removed, and we could safely leave the sequel to the common sense and public spirit of trade unionists as to what is or is not reasonable in time of war.

Nevertheless, if a scheme for deferment of pay is adopted, this would make practicable a further measure which might considerably ease the wages problem. For with an adequate proportion of consumers' purchasing power withdrawn, the risk and expense of a deliberate policy to keep down the prices of a limited range of necessities might be no longer prohibitive. I suggest, therefore (contingently on the adoption of a scheme for deferment of pay), that a limited range of essentials, considerably narrower than the list covered by the Ministry of Labour index number for the cost of living, should be drawn up and that the government (without giving any specific pledge) should do their best to prevent any rise in an index number based on the cost of these articles; and that on their side the trade unions (also without giving any specific pledge) should agree that they will not press for any wage increases *on the grounds of the cost of living*, except in so far as the government may be unsuccessful in keeping the above index number from rising. This suggestion is in no way essential to our main proposals, but is a further development which these proposals would facilitate.

IX VOLUNTARY SAVING AND THE MECHANISM OF INFLATION

There exist alternatives to the plan proposed in the previous chapters which are not less drastic and, if they were to be put into operation, not less effective. For example, a retail sales tax of 50 per cent or a wages tax of 20 per cent; or, as I have pointed out above, a heavier income tax, the increased incidence of which was exactly the same as that of the deferment of pay here proposed. The choice between these drastic and equally effective alternatives must be decided on considerations of public psychology, social justice and administrative convenience.

Those, however, who are opposed to a scheme for deferred pay do not, as a rule, oppose it because they prefer one of the drastic alternatives, but because they believe that we can win through by 'normal' methods, that is to say by stiff taxation on existing lines and by voluntary savings stimulated by active propaganda.

Now this policy might mean either of two things. It might mean a repetition *mutatis mutandis* of our policy in the last war, namely a sufficient degree of inflation to raise the yield of taxes and voluntary savings to the required level. The mechanism of this process is the main subject of this chapter.

But it might also mean—and that is what its advocates would claim for it—something much better than this, namely an equilibrium between supply and demand without any aid from an inflation.

The practicability of so happy an outcome is clearly a question of degree. For example, if the increase in the expenditure of the Treasury, compared with the financial year 1938–9, was no more than £1,000 million, or perhaps £1,250 million, we might reasonably expect 'normal' methods to be adequate (supplemented, of course, by drawing on the available capital resources). If, on the other hand, the increase in expenditure is of the order of £1,750 million or more (measured in pre-war prices), it is virtually certain, in the light of the examination of the statistical background which we have made in chapters III and IV, that the normal methods would be inadequate. Between these limits there is room for a difference of opinion. I should be inclined to put the maximum expenditure which we could safely handle by normal methods at an increase of about £1,250 million. And I should be fairly confident that they could not handle an increase of £1,500 million.

We must next emphasise a consideration, commonly overlooked, which is of the first importance. Let us suppose that in the absence of drastic methods we can rely on voluntary savings of (say) £500 million, but that we require £750 million to balance the war budget. We therefore resort to one or other of the 'drastic' methods open to us to find the balance of £250 million. Now the fundamental difficulty, which we have to face and are apt to overlook, is this. As soon as we apply a 'drastic' method we can no longer rely on the same volume of voluntary savings which was available so long as we restricted ourselves to 'normal' methods. For some part of the funds which we extract by our drastic methods are certain to be at the expense of the voluntary savings previously available. To give a simple example, the volume of voluntary savings is not independent of the level of income tax. If income tax is raised, the gross increase in the yield exaggerates the increase in resources from taxes and voluntary savings added together, since the higher tax will not be met entirely by a reduction in consumption but partly at least by a reduction in savings.

Thus, as soon as the rate of expenditure has exceeded the maximum which can be handled by normal methods, our drastic methods must be sufficient to produce a yield greater than this excess, since we can no longer rely on the same yield as before from voluntary sources. For this reason I have put no reliance above on voluntary savings by private individuals as distinct from institutional and contractual saving, though I hope that this may prove unduly pessimistic.

I should mention in passing, what is obvious, that the excellent success of the War Savings campaign gives no useful statistical guide to the prospects of the voluntary method. The terms offered, being attractive compared with the deposit rates of the Post Office Savings Bank and the joint stock banks, naturally attract old savings previously held elsewhere. Moreover, the formation of savings groups is frequently assisted by advances from employers for the purchase of certificates to be paid for gradually by future deductions from earnings. Thus the published totals comprehend both past and future savings, and it is impossible to say what proportion of them is attributable to current savings in the sense of an excess of current income over current expenditure during the period in which the nominal total has been subscribed.

The force of this general argument appears to me to be such as to make it very unlikely that we can achieve our maximum war effort by 'normal' methods of taxation on existing lines supplemented by voluntary saving. The danger of depending on voluntary savings lies in the fact that, if we adopt no drastic method, we are liable to slip insensibly into stimulating voluntary savings by inflation. And that leads us to the main theme of this chapter.

There is no difficulty whatever in paying for the cost of the war out of voluntary savings—provided we put up with the consequences. That is where the danger lies. A government which has control of the banking and currency system can always find the cash to pay for its purchases of home-produced goods. After allowing for the yield of taxation and for the use of foreign reserves to pay for the excess of imports over exports, the balance of the government's expenditure necessarily remains in the hands of the public in the shape of voluntary savings. That is an arithmetical certainty; for the government having taken the goods, out of which a proportion of the income of the public has been earned, there is nothing on which this proportion of income can be spent. If prices go up, the extra receipts swell someone's income, so that there is just as much left over as before. This argument is of such importance and so little understood that it is worth our while to follow it out in detail.

Let us suppose that the value of the output[1] of the country is £5,500 million at pre-war prices, that individual incomes (including transfer payments) come to £6,000 million, that the yield of taxation is £1,400 million, that we supplement our own output by importing £350 million more than we export paid for out of foreign reserves or overseas loans, and that the expenditure of the government, also reckoned at pre-war prices, is £2,750 million, i.e. £2,250 million excluding transfer payments. After deducting £1,400 million which they pay in taxation, individuals are left with £4,600 million which they are free to spend if they choose. But, since the government has already purchased £2,250 million of the output, there is only £3,250 (£5,500 − £2,250) million of goods (valued at pre-war prices) left for the public to buy with their remaining incomes of

[1] I am taking round figures in the neighbourhood of the facts. But I simplify the illustration by ignoring the depletion of capital as a source to meet government expenditure.

416

£4,600 million. Now if the public voluntarily save £1,350 million, that is to say the whole of the difference between their incomes of £4,600 million and the value of the available goods, namely, £3,250 million, at pre-war prices, obviously the problem is solved. There will be just the right amount of goods available to satisfy the demand without any rise of prices.

But if in these circumstances the public do not choose to save so much as £1,350 million, does the system of financing the war by voluntary savings break down? Certainly not. For in the last war we used the voluntary system successfully; yet, since prices rose more steeply than wages, it follows that the readiness of the public to save cannot have been sufficient to satisfy the above conditions. What happens then? How is the paradox explained?

Let us suppose that, instead of saving the necessary £1,350 million, the voluntary savings of the public are, in the first instance, only £700 million, and that they try to spend the rest of their incomes, namely £3,900 million, on goods worth only £3,250 million at pre-war prices. Obviously prices will have to rise 20 per cent which will equate supply and demand; for the goods will then be worth £3,900 (£3,250 + £650) million, which is just equal to the desired expenditure. Moreover, those who have sold for £3,900 million goods which only cost them £3,250 million will have the balance of £650 million left over as extra unspent income, just the amount the government requires.

It soon appears, however, that this only solves the problem momentarily. For we have no reason to expect that the whole of the unspent windfall profits of £650 million will represent permanent savings. A certain time will elapse before this sum reaches those who will be entitled to spend it. But in the next innings, so to speak, it will be added to the total of potentially spendable incomes, so that we shall have incomes of £5,250 million (£4,600 + £650) facing goods which, after allowing for the continuance of the 20 per cent price rise, are only worth £3,900 million. Moreover, it will be impossible for the government to keep down the prices of its own purchases if open market prices have risen 20 per cent. Thus we shall soon find ourselves in much the same position as before with a substantial discrepancy between the amount of money which the public are preparing to spend and the value (at the new price level, 20 per cent higher than before) of the goods available for them to buy. A further rise in prices will be required to provide a temporary respite; and so on.

Fortunately, this is not a complete picture of the second chapter of the story. If it were, the voluntary savings system would *not* have been successful, and we should be faced with a progressive inflation of prices without limit. Yet this is not what happened in the last war. And it is not likely to happen this time, even if we pursue the same policy of depending on voluntary savings.

What, then, is the actual course of events? The initial rise in prices will relate to goods which were produced at the lower pre-war price level, and the resulting profits will belong, as we have seen, to the owners of these goods. That is to say, aggregate incomes will indeed rise by £650 million (apart from the effect of any rise in the price of goods bought by the government), but not everyone's income will rise in the same proportion, if at all. The initial increase of income will mainly belong to a limited class of individuals and of trading and manufacturing companies, whom (without intending any insult, for it is by no fault or intention of theirs) we can call for short 'the profiteers'. Now the profiteers are liable to a very high rate of taxation, both on account of excess profits tax and because many of them will be rich enough to be liable to a high rate of income tax and surtax. Thus the profiteers become, so to speak, tax-collectors for the Treasury. More than half (more than three-quarters in some cases)[1] of the £650 million will become payable as taxes. More-over, it is likely that a considerable proportion of the balance

[1] E.P.T. + income tax is 75 per cent, and E.P.T. + income-tax + surtax on incomes of £5,000 is 83·5 per cent of the increased income.

will be voluntarily saved; not so much because the recipients, being relatively rich, will save more readily, but because the profits will largely belong to companies which will be disinclined, for various reasons, to distribute the bulk of them in higher dividends but will prefer in the circumstances to save them on behalf of their shareholders. Thus, in fact, only a small part of the £650 million (or of this figure augmented by such higher prices as the government may pay for its own purposes) will come on the consumption market in the second innings. Instead of another 20 per cent rise of prices being required to preserve equilibrium, it may be that a rise of 2 or 3 per cent would be sufficient. In this case a modest increase of taxation on the general public will be sufficient to offset the increased consumption of the profiteers, and avoid the necessity (if it were not for what follows in a moment) for any further rise of prices beyond the initial 20 per cent.

Unfortunately this is not yet the complete story; for we have now gone to the other extreme, having slipped in an assumption much less troublesome than the facts. We have assumed that, in spite of the rise of 20 per cent in prices, workers are content with the same money wages as before; so that the profiteers continue to make a profit of £650 million in the second innings and to act as tax-collectors for the Treasury on the same scale as before without the aid of any further rise in prices. But in fact the workers will press for higher wages—with at least partial success. For employers will put up much less resistance than usual to a rise in wages. The scarcity of labour will force them to agree if they are to retain their men; and, since the government is taking away in taxation 75 per cent of their excess profits, it will not cost them much to share their profiteering with their employees and their salaried staff. If, indeed, wages and other money costs were to go up fully in proportion to the cost of living, we should be faced, as before, with an unlimited inflation, proceeding by 20 per cent at each step—the process generally known as the vicious spiral.

But we still have one more card to play. Some costs are fixed by law or by contract, so that the rentier and pensioner class who have fixed money incomes cannot escape the sacrifice. Wage adjustments and the like take time. It takes time, and sometimes a considerable time, before adjustments are made even when the pressure is sufficient to make them inevitable sooner or later. It is these time-lags and other impediments which come to the rescue. Wars do not last for ever. Wages and other costs will chase prices upwards, but nevertheless prices will always (on the above assumptions) keep 20 per cent ahead. However much wages are increased, the act of spending these wages will always push prices this much in advance. If at the end of six months wages and other costs have risen by an average of 10 per cent prices will have risen 32 per cent (120 per cent of 110). If at the end of two years costs have risen 40 per cent, prices will have risen 68 per cent (120 per cent of 140). Thus, after all, the system of voluntary savings will have worked successfully. That is to say, the money will have been raised 'voluntarily' without an unlimited increase of prices. The only condition for its success is that prices should rise relatively to wages to the extent necessary to divert the right amount of working class and other incomes into the hands of the profiteers and thence into the hands of the Treasury, largely in the form of taxes and partly in the form of extra voluntary savings by the profiteers.

The larger the amount of voluntary savings at each stage, the better, of course, it will be for everyone. If the campaign of the National Savings Movement increases the volume of voluntary savings, the necessary rise in prices relatively to wages will be correspondingly smaller. Let us go back to our arithmetical illustration. We started with an excess of spendable incomes, over the available supply of consumption goods valued at pre-war prices, amounting to £1,350 million and we assumed that £700 million of this was voluntarily saved. This left £650 million, or 20 per cent more than the available supply of goods at pre-war prices. But if the National Savings Movement were to be successful in increasing the amount of the voluntary savings by (say) another £100 million, making £800 million altogether instead of £700 million, then the excess of spendable incomes is reduced to £550 million or about 17 per cent above the available supply at pre-war prices. In this case we can reach equilibrium with a rise in prices only 17 per cent (instead of 20 per cent) in excess of the rise in wages and other costs.

Thus an increase in voluntary savings is entirely beneficial. There is nothing to be said against it, except its inadequacy. The question for the individual is whether he would prefer to become £2 richer by deferment of pay, and have no inflation of prices or become £1 richer by voluntary savings, and suffer inflation with its evil social consequences. For the individual (unless he belongs to the profit-making class) the answer is surely obvious. He is certain to gain by the system of deferment. It is like asking him whether he would prefer to have a compulsory rule of the road with few accidents and no traffic congestion, or a voluntary rule with many accidents and much traffic congestion.

For the Treasury and for future taxpayers the answer is not so obvious. A system of deferment of pay—and equally, a system of highly successful voluntary savings—will leave us with a larger national debt, measured in terms of real value, than if we adopt the method of imperfectly successful voluntary savings supplemented by inflation. For inflation is a mighty tax-gatherer. But the Treasury and the tax-payer of the future need only remain in doubt if they expect the price level reached by inflation to continue permanently. For the national debt under the inflationary system is likely to be larger in terms of money than under the system of compulsory savings; so that if prices subsequently fall back, the benefits of inflation will have proved illusory even to the Treasury.

Thus it is quite true that, in the last resort, the amount of saving, necessary to balance the expenditure of the government after allowing for the yield of taxation, can always be obtained by 'voluntary' savings. But whether this is a good name for it is a matter of taste. It is a method of *compulsorily* converting the appropriate part of the earnings of the worker which *he* does not save voluntarily into the voluntary savings (and taxation) of the entrepreneur. 'We shall depend on the voluntary system' is another way of saying 'We shall depend on inflation to the extent that is necessary'. Sir Robert Kindersley in his Savings Campaign could justly argue as follows:

The government needs the money. But this is a free country. Someone, therefore, must save it voluntarily. If you (and your friends) do not do so, the necessary amount will be taken compulsorily from the real value of your earnings through the action of higher prices and handed to the profiteer; and *he* will save it voluntarily (such part as he does not pay in compulsory taxes). In this way we shall avoid any departure, which would be anathema to the city, from the voluntary system.

Ambiguous though this may be, as a defence of the principles of liberty, it would be a sound and convincing argument to the worker in favour of increased saving if it were not for one flaw. An individual cannot by saving more protect himself from the consequences of inflation if others do not follow his example; just as he cannot protect himself from accidents by obeying the rule of the road if others disregard it. We have here the perfect opportunity for social action, where everyone can be protected by making a certain rule of behaviour universal.

This analysis of how inflation works is fundamental. And it is fairly simple. But it is not yet understood by everyone—for the reason, surprising perhaps, that it is comparatively novel. Economists have only got clear about it (although it is a case much simpler than what happens in peace-time when, instead of a fixed maximum output, we have to allow for the effect of fluctuations in employment) in the last quarter of a century; since, that is to say, those now in authority acquired their dogmas. During the last war I was in the Treasury. But I never at that time heard our financial problem discussed along these lines.

It will be interesting, therefore, to throw our minds back and consider, in the light of this analysis, what happened on that occasion.

July	Money wage rates: rough index for the workers mentioned below[1]	Cost of living		Real wage rates according to	
		Labour Gazette index	Modified index[2]	*Labour Gazette*	Modified index
1914	100	100	100	100	100
1915	105–110	125	(120)	84–88	87–92
1916	115–120	145	(135)	79–83	85–89
1917	135–140	180	(160)	75–88	84–88
1918	175–180	205	180	85–88	79–100

Thus, the *Labour Gazette* index of the cost of living rose by 25 points a year and the modified index (compiled in 1918) by 20 points a year, with the truth probably lying between the two; and by the end of the war the value of money was about halved. As against this, money wage rates rose on the average about 10 points a year during the first half of the war and about 30 points a year during the second half. The net result was that the purchasing power of wage rates during the first three years of the war up to July 1917 ranged about 15 per cent less than before the war. The considerable recovery shown in the last year and a half of the war was made possible by the relaxation of financial pressure due to the entry of the United States, but the extent of it is difficult to calculate accurately on account of the statistical deceptions arising out of the change of system and of the diversion of consumption after the introduction of strict rationing and fixed prices.

The above analysis tells us how to interpret these results. The volume of spendable earnings (which increased more

[1] Bricklayers, bricklayers' labourers, compositors, railwaymen, dock labourers, cotton operatives, woollen and worsted operatives, engineering artisans, engineering labourers, shipbuilding platers' time rates, coal-mining, agriculture England and Wales.

[2] The modified index is based on the findings of the Sumner Committee in 1918. The chief differences from the official index arise with respect to clothing, sugar, butter, margarine. The Sumner index allows for substitution when the pre-war qualities were not obtainable on the market. The official index does not.

rapidly than wage rates owing to better employment, overtime, etc.) increased 15 per cent relatively to the supply of consumption goods (rather less than this at first and rather more eventually), as is indicated by the 15 per cent rise in prices relatively to wages. This rise in the cost of living provoked a corresponding rise in wage rates with a time-lag of almost exactly a year and was offset simultaneously by an equal further rise in prices. In each year wages rose almost exactly to the price level of the previous year. Thus the time-lag was just long enough to prevent disaster. If prices have to keep 15 per cent above wages and if wages rise half this amount in the first year and then follow prices with a time-lag of a year, we can get through four years of war by a little less than a doubling of prices. How closely this rule of thumb corresponded with the facts is shown in the following table:

	Theoretical indices		Actual indices[1]	
	Prices	Wage rates	Prices	Wage rates
1914	100	100	100	100
1915	122½	107½	122½	107½
1916	141	122½	140	117½
1917	161	141	170	137½
1918	185½	161	192½	177½

But what a ridiculous system with wages and prices chasing one another upwards in this manner! No one benefited except the profiteer. The seeds of much subsequent trouble were sown. And we ended up with a national debt vastly greater in terms of money than was necessary and very ill distributed through the community. Compare this with a system of deferment of pay. A levy averaging 15 per cent would have allowed the same relationship as before between money wage rates and the cost of living; so that the pressure of the former to chase the latter upwards would have been withdrawn. The real consumption of the working classes would have remained in the aggregate exactly the same as under the inflationary system. If average earnings at the old wage rates were 15 per cent higher than before

[1] Average of the two estimates.

424

on account of fuller employment and overtime (which is approximately what happened in fact), the working-class standard of consumption would have been maintained at the pre-war level without any sacrifice except the harder work accomplished. This harder work would have been recompensed by the workers becoming the owners of a significant proportion of the national debt. For at the end of the war (to take very conservative figures) the money total of the national debt would have been reduced by more than £2,000 million, and of this reduced total more than £500 million would have belonged to wage and salary earners instead of to the profiteers. That is to say, dependence on the method of 'voluntary' savings in the last war put some £2,500 million into the pockets of the entrepreneur class.

In the last war we achieved the miracle of maintaining aggregate working-class consumption at, or near, its pre-war level—the fall in real wage rates being offset by increased employment and hours worked. I am not yet convinced that we may not achieve the same result this time. Until the full economic demands of the war have been disclosed, one cannot tell. But if aggregate earnings at the existing wage rates increase because of overtime and full employment, a rise in basic wage rates sufficient to compensate for higher prices would set our national economy the impossible task of raising consumption *above* the pre-war level. We cannot reward the worker in this way, and an attempt to do so will merely set in motion the inflationary process. But we can reward him by giving him a share in the claims on the future which would belong otherwise to the entrepreneurs.

X THE SYSTEM ADOPTED IN FRANCE

It is worth pointing out that the proposals of this pamphlet are exceedingly mild (and may well prove much milder than we can afford) compared with the measures adopted in either of the other two belligerent countries, enemy and allied.

In Germany there have been rumours of the adoption of a system of deferred pay which would bear a superficial resemblance to the above. But if these reports are correct, this measure would be on the top of other measures already taken which are far more drastic than anything suggested here—a complete fixation of wages, hours and prices, a comprehensive system of rationing supplemented by shop shortages and prohibitions of every kind, and a series of deductions from wages, quite apart from any system of deferred pay, which already add up to a formidable total several times heavier than the scale of deferred pay proposed above for the lower group of incomes. I wish I was in a position to give more exact, quantitative particulars. But I should guess that if we were to enforce in this country a control of general consumption as drastic as that which is already in force in Germany, we should be in a position to increase our war effort by fully 50 per cent and perhaps substantially more. We shall, therefore, reject at our peril initial measures at least on the scale here recommended, or their equivalent.

Since the German system in its entirety is that which it is our object to avoid even as a temporary measure by any means short of jeopardising ultimate victory, it may be more to the point to quote the measures which have been adopted in France. For reasons which are not entirely due to the censorship a veil seems to separate us from what is happening in France almost thicker than that which divides us from the enemy. British public opinion is, I believe, almost completely unaware how far-reaching is the French control over wages and the conditions of labour.

By a series of official decrees culminating in that of 16 November 1939, a complete official control has been established over wages and the conditions of labour, more far-reaching in the munition industries and less so in the others. In the non-munition industries wages must not be changed from their pre-war level by collective agreement or otherwise without the approval of the Minister of Labour. In the munition industries wages are fixed by the Minister of Labour and the Minister of

Munitions (or other service department); employers are prohibited from paying wages in excess of a stipulated maximum (in general the pre-war level); employees may not leave their present employment without permission and may be moved by the authorities at will. Thus any tendency towards a rising wage level has been legally inhibited at the outset.

In addition to this a fund has been established called the National Solidarity Fund out of which will be met any special expenditure in the civilian sphere due to the war, including, I think, any losses arising out of official measures to keep down the cost of living. Into this Fund there will be paid the proceeds of an excess profits tax and a general levy on wages. The levy on wages consists of:

(a) 15 per cent of the wages of workers who are liable to military service, but have been exempted because, as we should express it, they are in a reserved occupation.

(b) The whole of the earnings both of these and of all other workers in respect of their work between 40 and 45 hours a week, and one-third of their earnings in respect of hours worked above 45 a week. (In the numerous cases where the hours of work are now 50 a week or more, this works out at almost another 15 per cent.)

Against this there are rigorous measures to maintain the cost of living at the pre-war level, but, so far, rationing has been avoided. I have no particulars how this is working out in practice or whether it is involving the French Treasury in expensive subsidies in the case of imported or agricultural goods.

This account is imperfect and perhaps inaccurate as an up-to-date statement. I hope that its publication may stimulate a Frenchman into giving us a fuller account of the French home front than I have found readily available at present.

In a talk to the French nation over the wireless at the end of January 1940, M. Daladier commended these stern measures to the civilian population and urged their willing acceptance of them in the following terms:

427

When they left for the frontier, our sons accepted a total transformation of their lives. Those who have stayed behind and do not have to put up with the same sufferings and dangers must also agree to transform their lives. They must sacrifice their personal interests, renounce certain commodities. Above all, they must concentrate all their strength and activity in the service of the French community without which they would be nothing. It would be vain and even criminal to conceal the fact that Germany's material power is one of the most formidable in the world. The issue at stake is not merely the existence of the nation, but our whole conception of life...Today it is to the France behind the lines that I wish to speak. I wish to speak to it with candour and even brutality...It is essential, in a word, that those of the interior succeed in making themselves respected by those at the front through work, renunciation and discipline.

And in conclusion he summed up German propaganda which speaks like Satan, as follows:

It says to the wealthy, 'You are going to lose your money.' It says to the worker, 'This war is the war of the wealthy.' It says to the intellectual and the artist, 'All that you love is threatened by destruction.' It says to him who loves the goods of this world, 'A few months more and you will have to accept painful restriction.' It says to the believer, 'How can your faith accept this massacre?' Finally it says to the adventurer, 'A man like you can make something out of your country's misfortunes.'

It is well to conclude this pamphlet with these eloquent words of the leader of a nation at war—even if it makes the careful humanitarian arguments and apologetically mild proposals of the previous pages sound pitiful and weak.

APPENDICES

I THE NATIONAL INCOME

The discrepancies between various current estimates of national income are more largely due to different ideas of the meaning of this concept than to strictly statistical differences—uncertain though many of the underlying statistical estimates may be. The following note accepts Mr Colin Clark's statistics, but not his concept of gross national income, without attempting to go behind them or to criticise them. The actual figures given are Mr Clark's brought up to date where necessary by Mr Rothbarth for the financial year 1 April 1938–31 March 1939 in terms of the prices of that year.

There are two fundamental concepts which are serviceable for general use. The first is the total current output measured in terms of money cost, already given in the text, namely:

£
million

3,710 current value of private consumption excluding indirect taxation but including the cost of making good current depreciation;

290 current cost of net new investment in buildings, plant, transport and stocks, i.e. current capital outlay in excess of what is required to make good current capital depreciation;

850 current cost of government operations excluding 'transfer' payments to pensioners, holders of national debt, etc., expenditure out of which is already included in the previous items.

4,850

I propose to call this the national output.

The second concept is that of taxable income, namely the aggregate of individual incomes (including charities, private institutions and companies). It differs from the above in that it includes 'transfer' incomes of £500 million and excludes government non-tax income of £50 million from trading profits. It follows that its amount is £5,300 (£4,850 + £500 − £50) million. It can also be broken down into the following constituents:

£ million

Private consumption at market prices (made up of indirect taxes and rates £670 million and current value £3,710 million including current depreciation as above) 4,380

Private saving (made up of £290 million new investment as above and £80 million lent to the government to cover the excess of the cost of government operations over revenue from taxes and trading profits) 370

Direct taxes 550

5,300[1]

It may be useful to add a list of the principal elements out of which these or other concepts of income can be built up.

Government income and outlay (central and local)

£ million

Government income:	Direct taxes	550
	Indirect taxes	460
	Rates	210
	Government trading profits	50
	Loans from the public (net)	80
		1350
Government outlay:	Transfer payments	500
	Government services	850
		1350

The above government outlay does not include government expenditure on investment in new houses, roads, etc. (£50 to £100 million), since this has been already included in the estimate of investment (which, being based on the Census of Production, inevitably includes all such investment whether by government or private agencies). To balance this, the above figure for loans from the public is correspondingly reduced below the actual amount borrowed by the government and represents only that part required to cover the net current deficit exclusive of the above investment expenditure.

[1] The reconciliation between my *Economic Journal* figure of £5,700 million and the above figure is as follows: deduct £380 million for depreciation included twice in Mr Clark's figure (total current depreciation £420 million less £40 million upkeep of roads by the government not included twice), £50 million for government trading profits previously included in private profits, and £30 million due to a revised estimate of the government deficit. The logical difficulties lying behind these figures I am discussing in detail in the March (1940) *Economic Journal* [*JMK*, vol. XXII].

Private income and outlay

	£ million
Private income:	
Wages and profits derived from current output	4,800
Transfer incomes	500
	5,300
Private outlay:	
Consumption at market prices	4,380
Saving	370
Direct taxes	550
	5,300

National output

Private and government consumption apart from making good wastage and depreciation	4,140
Making good wastage and depreciation	420
New investment	290
	4,850
Private wages and profits derived from the above	4,800
Government profits	50
	4,850

Gross investment

Net new investment	290
Making good wastage and depreciation	420
	710

Saving

Net new investment	290
Government deficit	80
	370

Distribution of private incomes

Individuals below £250 a year	2,910
Individuals above £250 a year	2,340
Charities	50
	5,300

Undistributed incomes of companies, etc., are included as part of the incomes of the individuals owning them.

Sources of incomes below £250 per year

	£ million
Wages and salaries	2,390
Incomes of independent workers, employees and unoccupied workers	240
Transfer incomes	280
	2,910

Expenditure of incomes below £250 per year

Value[1] of consumption	2,420
Rates and taxes	390
Saving	100
	2,910

[1] Spread over private consumption and government services, the cost of making good wastage works out at 8½ per cent. This is included in the above value.

Sources of incomes above £250 per year

Salaries and profits	2,170
Transfer incomes	220
	2,390

Expenditure of incomes above £250 per year

Value[1] of consumption	1,290
Rates and taxes	830
Saving	270
	2,390

The sources of the above figures are given in the *Economic Journal*, December 1939, p. 638 [*JMK*, vol. XXII].

II THE EXTENT OF OUR RESOURCES ABROAD

An important source of our war strength, both in itself and especially in comparison with the enemy's, lies in our capacity to finance an adverse balance of trade out of the resources which we had accumulated before the war in the shape of gold and foreign investments.

On 31 March 1939, the gold resources of the Bank of England and the Exchange Equalisation Account amounted to 79,950,000 ounces, worth £671,600,000 at the present value of gold (168s per oz.). Between that date and 1 September there was a substantial reduction to meet withdrawals of foreign balances from London, but the figures for later dates are not being published. The Federal Reserve Board of the United States has, however, published an estimate of the resources of the belligerents on the eve of the war (end of August 1939) according to which British gold holdings had fallen by that date to approximately £500 million. This figure has to be taken in conjunction with a similar estimate of £750 million gold held by France at the end of August and £54 million held by Canada. It takes no account of other Empire gold reserves or of the annual output of newly mined gold within the Empire estimated at £187 million.

This authority estimates British dollar balances at the same date at nearly £150 million. French dollar balances at nearly

[1] See footnote p. 431

£80 million and Canadian dollar balances at nearly £90 million. There is no available estimate of other British balances abroad.

Sir Robert Kindersley has estimated the total nominal capital of British foreign investments at the end of 1938 at nearly £3,700 million, of which, however, only a fraction is easily realisable. About £3,000 million of this total consisted of sterling loans and of shares of companies registered in Great Britain, most of which could not be realised. Nevertheless there is a fair proportion of these holdings which is being repaid each year in ordinary course, say £40 to £50 million annually; and some substantial loans for which repayment could be arranged in existing circumstances (an important Canadian loan already dealt with in this way is a case in point) are included in this total. Perhaps we could put the total figure thus realisable over a period of three years at not less than £250 million.

Holdings in companies registered abroad, estimated by Sir Robert Kindersley at nearly £700 million, can be regarded as much more liquid. The U.S. Federal Reserve Board estimate of British holdings of American readily marketable securities at the outbreak of war is about £185 million, to which can be added in case of necessity a further £225 million of other securities, including direct British-owned property in U.S.A. It is interesting to note that, according to American reports, about 10 per cent of the above marketable securities (i.e. £18 million) was in fact liquidated in the first two months of the war.

Some offset must be allowed against the above for the subsequent withdrawal by foreigners of assets held in Great Britain at the beginning of the war. The existing exchange restrictions are effective against British nationals, but by a strange oversight (unless it is a deliberate decision in the interests of the City as an international banking centre after the war) are not effective against the withdrawal of assets by foreigners. I do not make any important allowance for this, partly because the level of the free exchange (over which such transactions are carried out) does not at present indicate any serious pressure for such withdrawals, and partly because if such pressure were to develop we can scarcely suppose that the post-war interests of the City will be preferred to the immediate task of winning the war. It may be that a large part of apparent foreign balances and other assets, which were still held in London at the outbreak of war, were not free assets strictly speaking, but were necessary to meet various contingent liabilities in sterling or for the purposes of current business.

Indeed, so far from making an important allowance for withdrawals, we can safely reckon, I think, when we are considering the British balance of payments, as distinct from that of the Empire or sterling area, on considerable annual accretions of Empire and other overseas balances left in London. In the last war, even during its darkest days, such increases played an important part and had reached a huge figure by the end of it. I should guess the annual gain from this source at not less than £100 million and it might well be more.

It would not be prudent to add up all the above figures, which are subject to considerable error, in order to reach a final estimate of available foreign resources. Nevertheless, taking everything into account, I suggest that we can put the total of our fairly liquid assets at a figure of the order of £1,000 million at least; and allowing also for the gradual increase in our liabilities to overseas creditors, we can finance for more than three years an adverse balance of payments of the order of £350 million annually.

Our total gold and dollar resources are appreciably greater than in 1914 (cf. table below) in spite of our dollar securities being much less; and immeasurably more liquid, inasmuch as they are now predominantly gold. French holdings of gold and dollar resources are not far short of double what they were in 1914, and Canadian some ten times. Taking Great Britain, France and Canada together, gold and dollar resources are not far short of double what they were in 1914. Germany's similar resources, on the other hand, which in 1914, were nearly half of our own, are today less than one-twenty-fifth of ours and less than one-fiftieth

U.S. Federal Reserve Board estimate
(End of August 1939)

	Central gold reserves	Dollar balances	Securities readily marketable in U.S.A.	Direct and other investments in U.S.A.	Annual gold production (1938)
	(£ million at $4 to the £)				
Great Britain	500	149	184	225	—
France	750	79	46	20	—
Canada	54	89	125	140	41
Other British and French countries	135	—	—	—	146
Total	1,439	317	355	385	187

Comparative gold and dollar resources
(1914 and 1939)

	Total gold and dollar resources		Central gold reserves	Monetary gold outside central reserves	Dollar resources
Year ...	1939	1914	1914	1914	1914[2]
	(Approximate figures in millions of dollars)[1]				
United Kingdom	4,230	3,365	165	600	2,600
France	3,580	2,045	680	965	400
Canada	1,630	115[3]	115	—	?
Total	9,440	5,525	960	1,565	3,000
Germany	160	1,505	330	475	700

of the total Allied resources. Moreover, our liability to Allies, which was our overwhelming financial task in the last war prior to the entry of the United States, is today negligible in comparison. Since all monetary commitments are on a much larger scale now than they were twenty-five years ago and since an evident power to endure indefinitely is essential, utmost economy in the use of foreign resources and utmost effort to add to them by exports are

[1] U.S. *Federal Reserve Bulletin.*
[2] Estimates given in *Review of Economic Statistics*, 1, 230. Much higher estimates were given by Sir G. Paish in 1910 before the U.S. National Monetary Commission. But the above take account of later information and are more reliable.
[3] Gold only.

of the first importance. Nevertheless, I cannot agree that we start, taking everything into account, with inferior financial staying power than in 1914. The ability of the sterling and French area to meet a continuing adverse balance of trade is, taken in the aggregate, enormous; whilst the foreign resources of the enemy are non-existent and already replaced by liabilities.

III THE COST OF FAMILY ALLOWANCES

In round numbers there are 10 million children in the country up to fifteen years of age. Thus the gross cost of a weekly allowance of 5s for every child, i.e. an annual allowance of £13, is £130 million. A more exact estimate is £132 million. There are, however, some important offsets against this as follows:

(1) About £20 million of the above cost is in respect of children of income-tax payers. It has been assumed above as a rough approximation that the existing income-tax allowances already cost as much as the new allowances which will take their place; so that there is no additional cost on this head.

(2) In 1937 there would have been the following saving in respect of existing allowances:

Ordinary pensions	2,500,000
Unemployment benefit	2,750,000
Unemployment assistance	8,500,000
	13,750,000

(3) In 1940 the saving in respect of the children of the unemployed is likely to be less than in 1937. On the other hand, there will be additional wartime savings in respect of payments for evacuated children and separation allowances.

Thus, taking everything into account, a net cost of £100 million should be a safe figure.

If the allowances were to be given only in respect of the second and subsequent children, the cost would be more than halved and could be safely estimated at not above £50 million. An allowance of 3s (in place of 5s) to the second and subsequent children would, therefore, cost less than £30 million, or more exactly £27 million. If the allowances were to be restricted to the third and subsequent children the cost would be more than halved again, amounting (at 5s) to some £20; and a restriction to the fourth and subsequent children again halves it, bringing it down to about £9 million.

IV   THE FORMULA FOR THE AGGREGATE OF DEFERRED PAY AND DIRECT TAXES

The results given in chapter VI above result from the following formula. For incomes up to £750 a year, 35 per cent of the excess of the income over the basic minimum of 35s a week for an unmarried man and 45s for a married man. This is, of course, very far from a flat rate, since the proportionate effect of the fixed allowance is much greater at the lower income ranges, as appears in the table in chapter VI, where the proportion of income withheld is shown to rise under this formula from 3½ per cent at 50s a week to 29 per cent at £700 a year. For the higher income groups the percentage of the excess of income over the basic minimum rises as follows:

	Per cent of excess over basic incomes
£750-£2,000	40
£2,001-£3,000	45
£3,001-£5,000	55
£5,001-£10,000	65
£10,001-£15,000	70
£15,001-£20,000	75
£20,001-£50,000	80
Above £50,000	85

The above does not attempt so elaborate a system of allowances as the income tax, and in particular it makes no distinction between earned and unearned income. As a result of this, some of those who receive special consideration under income tax would have a larger proportion of their earnings deferred than those who do not receive such consideration. It would be easy to tackle those minor anomalies in a fully detailed scheme; but it would only confuse the main issues if I were to attempt to deal with all of them here. It may be that the allowance to married men is insufficient. It might be advisable to grade more finely by introducing a larger number of steps, and there should be a provision to prevent sudden jumps. It would certainly be desirable to include a clause similar to that in the latest Finance Act for mitigation where a man's income has fallen substantially below its pre-war level.

V PRINTING ERRORS IN THE FIRST EDITION
CORRECTED IN THE PRESENT EDITION

Reference in the Present Edition		Reference in the First Edition		
page	line	page	line	
383	30	16	31	For '175' read '225'
383	33	17	1	For '175' read '225'
386	9	20	7	For '175' read '225'
388	4	23	11	For '10' read '13·4'
389	Footnote	24	Footnote	For '1010' read '1045'
389	Footnote	24	Footnote	For '590' read '625'
390	3	25	18	For '1010' read '1050'
390	9	25	27	For 'less' read 'just over'
390	Footnote	25	Footnote	For '1620' read '1660'
398	Footnote	37	Footnote 2	For '3s' read '5s'
402	Table column 4	42	Table column 4	For '310' read '301'
424	Table	72	Table	The column headings should be reversed
431	25	81	28	For '293' read '290'
439	19	83	2	For 'Fund' read 'Account'

ACKNOWLEDGEMENTS

The substance of the plan here proposed was originally published in *The Times* in two articles on 14 and 15 November 1939, followed by a third article replying to criticisms on 28 November and a letter on 1 December. These contributions were supplemented by an article giving the statistical background which appeared in the *Economic Journal*, December 1939, p. 626 [*JMK*, vol. XII].

I have been assisted throughout on the statistical side by Mr E.

Rothbarth of the Statistical Department, Cambridge University, who is responsible, in particular, for the estimated division of total income between the income groups.

The cost of family allowances is based on figures supplied by the Family Endowment Society. Family allowances have been advocated in many quarters, particularly by Mr Amery, Miss Eleanor Rathbone and Mrs Hubback.

The proposal to meet deferred pay out of a post-war capital levy was first made by Professor von Hayek in an article published in the *Spectator* on 24 November 1939.

The proposal for the maintenance of an 'iron ration' at a low price was first made to me by Sir Arthur Salter. It has also been advocated by Mr R. H. Brand in *The Times* and, in more detail, by Professor and Mrs Hicks in the *Manchester Guardian*.

I am indebted to many critics and correspondents besides the above.

INDEX

449